The Diary of Sport

History, Facts & Figures from
Every Day of the Year

Nick Weatherhogg

First published by Pitch Publishing, 2020

Pitch Publishing
A2 Yeoman Gate
Yeoman Way
Worthing
Sussex
BN13 3QZ
www.pitchpublishing.co.uk
info@pitchpublishing.co.uk

A CIP catalogue record is available for this book
from the British Library.

ISBN 978 1 78531 628 9

Typesetting and origination by Pitch Publishing
Printed and bound in India by Replika Press Pvt. Ltd.

Introduction

'Sport has the power to change the world. It has the power to inspire. It has the power to unite people in a way that little else does. It speaks to youth in a language they understand. Sport can create hope where once there was only despair.' Nelson Mandela.

Sport holds a unique place in society, and in individuals. There is very little, as Mandela says, that can unite people in the same way – but very little that divides people quite so strongly. Very little that brings so much joy, and so much pain simultaneously. It can bring both hope and despair, both comedy and tragedy.

The Diary of Sport presents the chaotic beginnings of various sports and the evolution into what we know today. It brings the records, the bizarre events, the sublime performances alongside the absurd. The individuals who make sport so entertaining, both the famous and the infamous. Presented in diary form with something for everyone. Read and enjoy!

Nick Weatherhogg

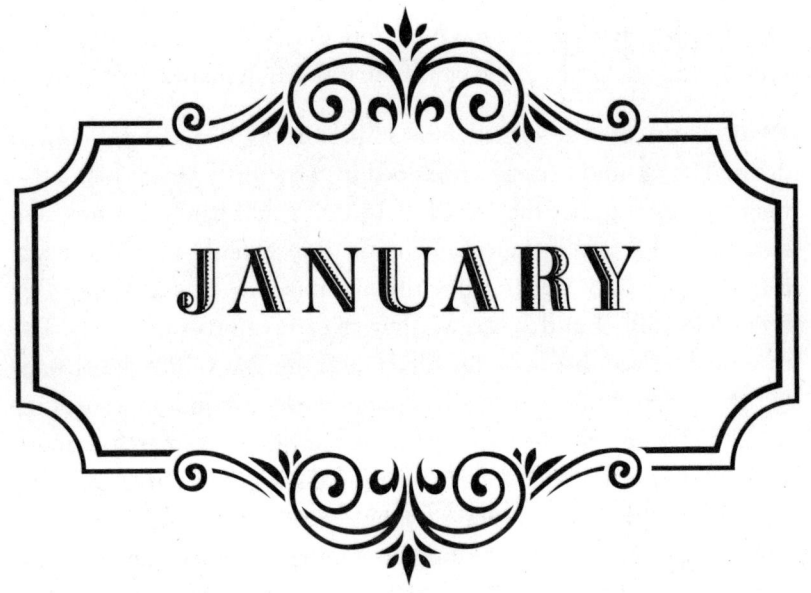

JANUARY

1 January

Any year: The birthday of any thoroughbred horse in the northern hemisphere. Bizarrely it doesn't matter on what date a horse is actually born, its birthday must always be counted as being on 1 January … as long as it is in the northern hemisphere. Any horse from the southern hemisphere has its birthday on 1 August.

1840: Knickerbocker Alleys in New York City, the first indoor bowling team in the world, hosts the world's first bowling match.

1940: Heart of Midlothian beat Hibernian 6-5 in the Edinburgh derby. The ground became enveloped in fog shortly before kick-off – such a dense fog that the crowd of 14,000 could barely see anything … and neither could the commentator Bob Kingsley! He just made it up … for 90 minutes! Ordinarily of course the match would have been called off – but this was wartime so extra efforts were made. The commentary was due to be broadcast, and the War Office didn't want to risk alerting the Germans of bad weather over Edinburgh where they could therefore send the Luftwaffe undetected. So the match went on and Kingsley was ordered not to mention the fog. The only part of the commentary that was accurate was the goals – he couldn't miss any or broadcast ghost goals so he set up a series of runners around each goal to run and tell him when a goal was scored. The fog was so bad by the end that many of the crowd stayed in for at least ten minutes simply because they were unaware the match had ended. Amusingly when Hearts got to their dressing room they realised their left-back John Donaldson was missing – so they sent out a search party. He was found still hugging the wing and calling for the ball, hoping it would appear out of the gloom.

1957: South African cricketer Russell Endean becomes the first international to be dismissed 'handled the ball' after he had scored three runs against England.

1971: During the Martini International golf tournament in Norwich, John Hudson hits a hole-in-one on the 11th hole using a 4-iron. The

12th is considerably longer, so he selects a driver … and gets another hole-in-one! The first (and currently only) time any golfer has achieved aces on successive holes.

2007: Death of Denver Broncos cornerback Darrent Williams at the age of just 24. Williams had been at a New Year's Eve party with teammates. He was killed in a drive-by shooting as he was driving home, hit by a single bullet to the neck. Two teammates in the car were also injured.

2 January

1832: Orchard Lake Curling Club opens – the world's first organised sports club for curling.

1879: On day one of the third Test match ever, Australian fast bowler Frederick 'The Demon' Spofforth achieves the first hat-trick in Test cricket, reducing England to 26/7 in Melbourne.

1902: Heart of Midlothian beat Tottenham Hotspur to claim the 15th Football World Championship. Hearts won the tie 3-1 on aggregate.

1932: The England rugby team are hosting the touring South African side at Twickenham. During the game Springbok full-back Gerry Brand broke a world record by successfully scoring a drop goal from 77.7m (85yds), a record that remains unbroken.

1971: The Old Firm football match takes place at Ibrox Park in Glasgow, the home of Rangers FC. Celtic took the lead in the 90th minute, resulting in Rangers fans immediately heading to the exits. Thousands streamed through stairway 13 and it appears that somebody fell, causing a domino effect with people piling up and falling. As the pile-up worsened, tragically 66 people died with at least 200 injured.

1986: Japanese motorcyclist Yasuo Kaneko rides his Honda XR 500 on the Dakar Rally. As he approached the town of Sète at the end of the first stage he was hit by a civilian car. The driver of the

Peugeot 205 had been drinking, and the 41-year-old Kaneko was killed instantly.

---

3 January

1865: Con Orem and Hugh O'Neill box a competition bout outdoors. This was well before judges' decisions – the boxers continue to fight to a finish, however long it takes. However, the referee did stop this bout – after 193 rounds – simply because it was too dark to continue.

1929: Day five (of seven) of the third Test match between Australia and England, held in Melbourne. Australia finished the day 347/8. Last man out, just a few minutes before close of play, was Don Bradman. Batting at number six, Bradman had scored 112 – his first Test century in only his second Test match.

1939: Akinoumi Setsuo beats Futabayama Sadaji in a sumo bout, bringing to an end Sadaji's winning streak of 69 matches, lasting three years.

1947: Birth of England and British Lions prop forward Fran Cotton. After his retirement Cotton set up one of the best-known sports clothing companies – Cotton Traders.

1969: Birth of Formula One legend Michael Schumacher, widely considered one of the finest Formula One drivers of all time. His name is most associated with Ferrari, for so long the sleeping giant of F1, with whom Schumacher won five consecutive World Championship titles.

1996: Tragedy strikes in Morocco during the Dakar Rally. Laurent Gueguen was driving a support truck for the Citroën team when the truck drove over a Moroccan landmine just off the main track. The truck burst into flames, killing Gueguen. He had two co-drivers with him at the time but they managed to escape the burning vehicle.

4 January

1902: Liverpool entertain Stoke at Anfield in what turns out to be one of the most bizarre matches of all time. Stoke players enjoyed a lunch of fish … and it turned out there was something wrong with it. The first affected was the goalkeeper, who sprinted off the pitch after just eight minutes in search of a toilet (immediately after conceding the first goal). He had a pulse of 148 and did not reappear. By the beginning of the second half Stoke were down to seven players (several of whom weren't feeling great), and the Stoke dressing room apparently resembled 'the cabin of a cross-Channel steamer in bad weather'. Unsurprisingly Liverpool won 7-0.

1967: Holder of the world record for water speed travel, Briton Donald Campbell, dies in an attempt to stretch the record still further. To counteract the possible advantages of wind or current, a water speed record must be the average of two 1km sprints in opposite directions on the same stretch of water. On Coniston Water in the Lake District, Campbell had completed his first leg at an average speed of 297mph (478kmh). On the second leg he was travelling at about 320mph (515kmh) when his boat, the *Bluebird K7*, flipped 15m (50ft) in the air and totally disintegrated on landing on the water again. Campbell was killed instantly.

2002: In the second round of the Mercedes Championship at Kapalua in Hawaii Tiger Woods hits a drive unofficially measured at 455m (1,494ft) on the 18th.

2009: The Argentine stage of the Dakar Rally sees the death of French motorcyclist Pascal Terry in very unfortunate circumstances. Terry ran out of fuel in a deserted part of the rally and sent an emergency signal to organisers for help. However, shortly after he had requested help his brother, another competitor, arrived safely at the stage finishing line – and the name confusion left organisers believing Terry was safe and the search was abandoned. Three days later his absence was discovered and a new search was established. He was found dead about 50m from his motorbike.

It is believed that had the original search continued his life would have been saved.

2016: American Justin Dargahi scores an incredible 26 basketball three-pointers in just one minute. (This was purely a record-breaking attempt, not game play.)

5 January

1869: Kilmarnock FC is formed from a local group of cricketers who are keen to find a competitive sport to play through the winter months. Given the year this was not strictly football as we would recognise it today; it was more a sort of rugby/football hybrid … which explains the name of the ground that still exists today as Rugby Park.

1910: The beginning of the first season of the National Hockey Association, a men's professional ice hockey organisation and the forerunner to the NHL. The league was cancelled almost immediately while a few key points were ironed out, but restarted ten days later and ran for two months. Seven teams played 12 matches each to form a league, with the Montreal Wanderers the inaugural champions.

1950: In awful weather conditions (snow with near zero visibility), a Soviet-built Misunov Li-2 crashes near Koltsovo Airport at Sverdlovsk, resulting in the deaths of all 19 people on board. The plane was carrying the Soviet Air Force ice hockey team VVS Moscow en route to a game against the Chelyabinsk hockey club. All 11 players perished, along with the club doctor and a masseur. Only two members of the Moscow first-team squad survived – Viktor Shuvalov was injured and so did not travel with the team, while winger Vsevolod Bobrov overslept and missed the flight.

1971: Australia host England at Melbourne Cricket Club in the world's first one-day cricket match … and it isn't even planned! England were touring Australia, and were due to play a Test match in Melbourne. However, the first three days were totally washed out, making a Test match unworkable. Rather than just abandoning play altogether the umpires decided to give the crowd something to cheer, and hastily arranged a one-day international with 40 eight-ball overs per side. Australia won the toss and put England in to bat. The match was won by Australia.

2014: Death of legendary footballer Eusébio (birth name Eusébio da Silva Ferreira, aka the Black Panther or the Black Pearl), widely considered one of the greatest footballers of all time. He is most associated with a long and distinguished career with Benfica, for whom he played for 15 years, playing 440 matches in total and scoring 473 times.

6 January

1369: First known record of the ancient sport called Haxey Hood, a game which appears to contain elements of rugby but seems to have very few rules. Four teams in a town or village representing four pubs meet in the town square. The competition is then to simply push a leather tube to their pub – while being tackled, attacked and harried by the opposition. The successful team get to keep the 'ball' to display for a year until the following year's competition.

1681: The first known boxing match takes place between the butcher and the butler of the Duke of Albemarle, which the duke organises to entertain his guests and friends.

1934: Death of renowned football manager Herbert Chapman. Chapman made his name as an innovative and influential manager. He won the FA Cup and two Division One titles with Huddersfield Town in just four years before repeating the success (exactly) at Arsenal. Chapman is also credited with introducing original tactics and modern training methods, as well as promoting European club competitions, numbers on shirts, floodlighting and many other aspects of the game.

1942: Death of Henri de Baillet-Latour, the third president of the International Olympic Committee, and the first one to die in office.

1990: Czechoslovak ice hockey defenceman Luděk Čajka is badly injured during a game when he collides with an opponent and crashes into the board in open play. Čajka was left paralysed and comatose in hospital, where he died 39 days later.

1990: One of the most bizarre horse races ever takes place on a very foggy course in Louisiana. The 23-1 shot Landing Officer, ridden by Sylvester Carmouche, won by 24 lengths. Such an overwhelming victory in such awful conditions demanded an investigation, so the tapes were carefully analysed – showing eight horses entering the final straight and nine crossing the finishing line. The commissioners concluded that Carmouche left the starting line with the others, and simply let them go. He then backed Landing Officer up to a few yards away from the finishing tape and waited for the others to enter the finishing straight, before riding through the tape. Carmouche was banned from racing for ten years.

1994: During the US Figure Skating Championships skater Nancy Kerrigan is savagely attacked by a man with a baton. The injuries put her out of the remainder of the championship. Suspicion fell upon the ex-husband of her rival Tonya Harding, who denied any involvement in the attack. Harding was subsequently found guilty of obstructing the investigation and was then banned from participating in the sport by the US Olympic Committee.

7 January

1936: Tennis champions Howard Kinsley (Wimbledon finalist in 1926) and Helen Moody (winner of 19 Grand Slam titles – four at the French Open, eight at Wimbledon and seven at the US Open) set the world record for a tennis rally (contrived) when they volleyed a ball back and forth 2,001 times. The rally took one hour and 18 minutes, and was stopped deliberately because Kinsley had to go and teach a pre-arranged lesson.

1960: Death of Dorothea Chambers, one of the most successful British women's tennis players of all time. At Wimbledon 1919 she bore the unusual (and unfortunate) distinction of reaching the finals of the women's singles, women's doubles and mixed doubles – losing all three! Chambers was also one of the leading badminton players in the country.

1970: Foundation of South African football team Kaiser Chiefs, south of Johannesburg. The pop group of the same name are actually named after the football club … indirectly. The band members all live in Yorkshire and are massive fans of Leeds United. At the time the band was formed Leeds were captained by the South African Lucas Radebe, who had been signed from the Kaiser Chiefs, so they settled on that!

1973: Administrator Olly Croft founds the British Darts Organisation (BDO), the central organising body for darts tournaments for both professionals and amateurs. The BDO sets the rules and regulations of the game, such as the dimensions of the board, the height of the board and the length of the oche. It also organised the first World Professional Darts Championship in 1978.

1984: Eric Bristow wins the world darts title for the third time in one of the most dominant displays of darts ever witnessed. The victory led to one of the most iconic moments of sports commentating of all time when Sid Waddell said: 'When Alexander of Macedonia was 33, he cried salt tears because there were no more worlds to conquer … Bristow's only 27.'

8 January

1789: Death of Jack Broughton, influential English bare-knuckle boxer. He was the first man to produce a set of rules for boxing, initially for his own amphitheatre but later evolving into the

London Prize Ring Rules, which became the standard for bare-knuckle bouts. Rules included that a round would last as long as both boxers were standing, and would end as soon as one of the fighters went down. Then there would be a 30-second gap between rounds.

1824: Tom Spring becomes the first recognised British boxing champion when he knocks out Jack Langan. In the early days of boxing the outcome was always by submission or knockout as there was no time limit placed on the bout. Spring beat Langan after two and a half hours of fighting.

1962: The future golfing legend Jack Nicklaus makes his first professional performance as a 21-year-old in the Los Angeles Open. He finished 50th (and last) – 21 shots behind the winner Phil Rodgers. He earned the princely sum of $33.33 for his efforts.

1995: Death of Argentine middleweight boxer Carlos Monzón, undisputed world champion for seven years including 14 successful defences of his titles. He fought 99 times in his career, winning 87 of the bouts with 59 knockouts. He died in a car accident while on a weekend furlough from jail, where he was locked up for killing his second wife.

2016: Death of Maria Teresa de Filippis, the first woman ever to compete in Formula One. Driving for Maserati, she competed during the Monaco Grand Prix in May 1958 but failed to qualify. Her first involvement in a GP race was the following month in Belgium when she finished tenth.

9 January

1811: Musselburgh golf course on the outskirts of Edinburgh in Scotland hosts the world's first golf competition for women, over a shortened course. Musselburgh had a long and proud tradition of female golfers – there are clear records of Mary Queen of Scots playing there. To attract women into entering, prizes were offered –

the winner would get a creel (a basket used for carrying fish), with runners-up getting two fine blue silk handkerchiefs from Barcelona.

1942: Joe Louis defends his world heavyweight boxing title for the 20th time, in a fight with Buddy Baer. Despite weighing more than three stone less than his opponent (~20kg) Louis managed to knock Baer out in the first round. The bout was partly organised for a charity relief for the Navy Relief Fund, with a proposed 50 per cent of the gate money going to the fund. Louis donated his entire purse of $47,000 to the fund, leading promoter Mike Jacobs to give the entire gate of $37,000. Baer then gave one sixth of his purse ($4,000). So, having been knocked out in less than three minutes, Baer was the only one to actually make any money from the fight (~$20,000).

1965: Birth of basketball star Muggsy Bogues, the shortest person ever to play in the NBA, standing at just 5ft 3in (1.60m). Despite this he enjoyed a 14-season NBA career before moving over to coaching, leading the Charlotte Sting in the women's league.

1990: Paul Lim becomes the first darts player to complete a nine-dart finish at the World Championship in his round against Jack McKenna. Lim won £52,000 for the achievement, while Phil Taylor received £24,000 for winning the overall competition and becoming world champion.

2007: Death of South African motorbike racer Elmer Symons following an accident in Morocco during the fourth stage of the Dakar Rally. Having previously worked as a mechanic, this was Symons's first attempt as a rider. The emergency services took just eight minutes to get to him, but by then it was already too late.

10 January

1909: The first-ever meeting in one of the most anticipated and hotly contested football derbies in the world. AC Milan beat their neighbours Internazionale 3-2 in the Italian football championship.

1949: Birth of boxer George Foreman. His first major success was winning the gold medal in the 1968 Olympics in the heavyweight division. He turned professional the following year, and won the world heavyweight title from a then undefeated Joe Frazier in 1973. Foreman's first defeat was in the third defence of his title – the famous 'Rumble in the Jungle' with Muhammad Ali in 1974.

1982: The Cincinnati Bengals beat the San Diego Chargers 27-7 in an American Football Championship game. The match has subsequently become known as the Freezer Bowl because it is the coldest AFC match in history. The air temperature on the day was minus 22.8°C (minus 9°F), but with a bitter wind blowing throughout the game the chill factor was recorded as minus 50.6°C (minus 59°F).

2010: In the Africa Cup of Nations group match, Angola are leading Mali 2-0 at half-time. With just 11 minutes to go the score had moved on to 4-0 … and the final score was Angola 4 Mali 4, including two goals scored in injury time.

2011: Lionel Messi of Barcelona and Argentina wins the inaugural FIFA Ballon d'Or, as the best football player in the world, 2010. The Ballon d'Or had been in existence since 1956, when England's Stanley Matthews won the first event, but this was the first which was officially recognised by FIFA, the world's governing body.

2014: Belgian motorbike racer Eric Palante fails to finish the northern Argentine stage of the Dakar Rally so organisers launch a search of the area. His body was found, although there was no indication as to the cause of death.

11 January

1857: Birth of English flat race jockey Fred Archer (aka The Tin Man), who has been described as the 'best all-round jockey that the turf has ever seen'. He was named Champion Jockey at the age of just 17, and then won the title for 13 consecutive seasons – every year until his premature death. He rode 2,748 winners from 8,084 starts, including a then record 246 wins in one season. Tragically he lost his wife in childbirth, and that coupled with suffering from delirium led to him taking his own life at the age of 29.

1892: Death of St Mirren and Scotland international footballer James 'Daddy' Dunlop. Dunlop was playing for St Mirren on New Year's Day when he fell over and cut his knee on some discarded broken glass. The wound became infected, he developed a tetanus infection and died ten days later.

1902: Death of England and Lancashire spin bowler Johnny Briggs, at the age of 39. He was the first bowler to take 100 wickets in Test cricket, and also toured Australia six times, a feat matched only by Colin Cowdrey. Over his first-class career he took 2,221 wickets at an average of just 15.95, taking five wickets in an innings 200 times. Sadly at the age of just 36 he suffered a severe epileptic fit which left him in severe mental distress, meaning that he spent the final three years of his life in an asylum.

1959: On day four of the semi-final of the Quaid-e-Azam Trophy between Bahawalpur and Karachi, Karachi batsman Hanif Mohammad is out to the final ball of the day for a then first-class record score of 499. To make matters worse he was run out looking for his 500th run.

2003: Sunderland earn a goalless draw at home to Blackburn Rovers in the Premier League. It would prove to be their final point of the season as they then lost all of the remaining 15 matches, ending bottom of the league and being relegated. This is the longest consecutive losing stretch in England's top flight.

2004: In the fourth round of the Mercedes Championship at Kapalua in Hawaii, Davis Love III drives a shot measured at 435m (1,428ft) on the 18th – the longest drive ever officially verified.

12 January

1873: Birth of Greek marathon runner Spyridon (aka Spyros) Louis (aka Loues). When the new Olympic Games were announced for Athens there was much local enthusiasm, particularly for the new marathon event. Louis won the first-ever Olympic marathon, and became a national hero.

1944: Birth of 'Smokin' Joe' Frazier, undisputed heavyweight boxing champion of the world from 1970–73. In 1964 he won Olympic gold for heavyweight boxing, and turned professional the following year. In a 16-year career Frazier only lost four times – twice to Muhammad Ali and twice to George Foreman. Frazier died in 2011 of liver cancer.

1964: One of the most remarkable bowling performances ever. Indian slow left-armer Bapu Nadkarni, bowling for India against England on the third day of the Madras Test, bowled 29 overs for just three runs – one single off each of three overs, and 26 maidens.

2001: Death of American racehorse Affirmed, the 11th winner of the United States Triple Crown of Thoroughbred Racing (1978) and Horse of the Year for two consecutive seasons. Racing in the 1970s he won $2.8m.

2017: Death of erstwhile England football manager Graham Taylor. Taylor made a name for himself, after a rather mediocre career as a player, by managing Watford to three promotions in five years to take them from the Fourth Division (now League Two) to the First Division (now the Premier League).

13 January

1889: Death of Staveley footballer William Cropper. Cropper is one of an elite group of sportsmen who played football for Derby

County and cricket for Derbyshire. At the age of just 26 he was playing for Staveley against Grimsby Town when he ruptured his bowel during the match. He died the next day in hospital.

1933: American tennis star Bunny Austin shocks the tennis world when he becomes the first player to appear on centre court at a tournament wearing shorts.

1979: John Spencer compiles the first 147 maximum break in an official competitive match. This should also have been the first live televised maximum … but the camera crew had disappeared for a tea break!

1991: Tragedy strikes in Mali during the Dakar Rally. Charles Cabonne was driving a support truck for the Citroën team during the eighth stage of the rally when he was shot dead by rebels at the side of the road. Organisers cancelled the next two stages and when the race resumed the Malian army accompanied teams passing through the country.

2018: Australian Derek Herron lands a world record basketball shot. He found a safe and secure place near the top of the Maletsunyane Falls in Lesotho, while his friends set up the basket near the bottom, before he successfully threw the basket – a shot of 201.4m (660ft 10in).

14 January

1897: Swiss mountaineer Matthias Zurbriggen is the first person to reach the summit of Aconcagua in the Andes. At 6,962m (22,841ft) it was the highest confirmed climb to date.

1898: On day one of the third Test of England's tour of Australia, home batsman Joe Darling hits the first-ever Test match six. In these early days simply clearing the boundary still only got a four; to get a six a batsman had to hit the ball out of the ground … something Darling managed three times in this innings, the third of which brought up his century.

1954: Possibly the most famous wedding involving a sports star, as baseball player Joe DiMaggio of the New York Yankees marries silver screen icon Marilyn Monroe. Although the marriage was short-lived (274 days to be precise), the two remained very good friends, and DiMaggio never stopped loving her. When Marilyn died DiMaggio had half a dozen long-stemmed roses delivered to her grave twice a week every single week for the rest of his life (nearly 37 years).

1964: Day four of the first Test between India and England in Madras. Indian bowler Bapu Nadkarni bowled a record 131 consecutive dot deliveries (including 21 maidens).

1969: Sir Matt Busby announces that he will be retiring at the end of the season from his role as manager of Manchester United. Busby had been manager of the club since 1945, a reign which began with the rebuilding of Old Trafford after it had been damaged in the Second World War. He then developed the 'Busby Babes', nurturing players such as Bobby Charlton and Duncan Edwards. He was one of the few survivors of the Munich air crash, before leading his team to success in the European Cup just ten years later.

1985: Tennis legend Martina Navratilova becomes only the third player in history to win 100 tennis tournaments (after Chris Evert, who reached the total in 1980, and Jimmy Connors in 1983).

15 January

1910: England beat Wales 11-6 in an international rugby fixture, in the first international game ever played at Twickenham.

1927: The first sports event ever broadcast in the United Kingdom is the Five Nations rugby union international between England and Wales at Twickenham. England won the fixture 11-9 (although under modern scoring allocations it would have been a 13-13 draw).

1967: The first-ever AFL-NFL World Championship game, the challenge which would subsequently become known as the Super Bowl. In the inaugural game the Green Bay Packers (NFL champions) beat their AFL counterparts Kansas City Chiefs by a score of 35-10.

1968: Death of Minnesota North Stars ice hockey centre Willie Masterton. He was hit hard, fell backwards and hit his head on the ice. Like most players of his day he was not wearing a helmet. Masterton started bleeding from his nose, ears and mouth. He was rushed into hospital and died of his injuries.

1998: Fifteen-year-old schoolboy Ian Thorpe becomes the youngest ever male world champion swimmer when he wins the 400m freestyle at the World Championships in Perth. His style and pace rapidly earned him the nickname 'Thorpedo'.

16 January

1902: Birth of Scottish Olympic runner Eric Liddell. In 1924 he refused to run in the 100m heats at the Olympics because they were run on a Sunday and conflicted with his deeply held Christian faith. Instead he ran in the 200m and won the bronze medal, and followed it up with a gold in the 400m. Liddell also represented Scotland in rugby union. After retiring from his athletics career he served as a missionary in China, where he remained until captured by the Japanese in the Second World War. He died in one of the Japanese concentration camps. His story is immortalised in the Oscar-winning movie *Chariots of Fire*.

1935: Birth of American racing driver AJ Foyt, the only man in history (to date) to have won the Indianapolis 500, the Daytona 500, the 24 Hours of Le Mans, and the 24 Hours of Daytona. He holds the USAC (United States Auto Club) record of 159 victories.

1966: The Chicago Bulls are formed and granted the NBA franchise – the third such award for the city of Chicago following the Chicago Stags (who had folded in 1950) and the Chicago Packers (now known as the Washington Wizards). The team started in the NBA that season, just a couple of months after their formation, and became the only NBA team ever to qualify for the play-offs in their inaugural season.

1992: The Professional Darts Corporation (PDC) is formed in the UK when a group of leading players split from the British Darts Organisation (BDO) having become increasingly disillusioned and unhappy with their governance of the sport. The PDC was originally called the World Darts Council (WDC).

2004: Fourteen-year-old Freddy Adu becomes the youngest athlete of all time to sign a professional sport contract in the US when he signs for DC United in the MLS SuperDraft. Three months later he became the youngest ever MLS player when he came on as a substitute against the San Jose Earthquakes.

17 January

1597: The first definite reference to the game of cricket. In a legal dispute in Surrey regarding the ownership and purpose of a small tract of land, coroner John Derrick testified under oath that he had played cricket on the land as a boy. Or, to be more precise, 'from the Free School at Guildford, hee and diverse of his fellows did runne and play at creckett and other plaies'.

1803: The Jockey Club compiles the first set of official rules under which horse races can be conducted, and sanctions racetracks to host meetings under these rules.

1942: Birth of Cassius Marcellus Clay Jr, the future world heavyweight boxing champion of the world who is better known as Muhammad Ali. Clay began boxing when he was 12 and gained his first major success at just 18 when he won Olympic gold in

Muhammad Ali

17 January 1942–3 June 2016

World heavyweight boxing champion. Widely regarded as the greatest
boxer of all time, and one of the greatest sportsmen who ever lived

the light-heavyweight division of the 1960 Rome Olympics. He turned professional later that year.

2014: During the Masters final snooker legend Ronnie O'Sullivan creates another world record when he scores 556 points without reply. In a period of six frames he compiled breaks of 79, 88, 72, 134, 77, 56 and 39 without opponent Ricky Walden potting a single ball.

2015: The beginning of the first World Marathon Challenge. The challenge is running seven full marathons on seven continents in seven days. The first race for this inaugural competition was in Antarctica – and would be followed by Chile, the US, Spain, Morocco, the UAE and Australia. Twelve people competed in the challenge. The first winner was David Gething with a total time for the seven marathons of 25 hours, 36 minutes and three seconds.

18 January

1896: The University of Iowa invite students from the newly formed University of Chicago to play the first-ever college basketball fixture as an experimental game. Chicago beat Iowa 15-12.

1953: The Argentine Grand Prix is the first official Formula One race run in South America. Argentine president Juan Perón was seeking the popularist vote and so allowed free access to the circuit, meaning spectators were literally lining the edge of the track to get a close-up view. On lap 31, one spectator wanted an even closer view, so wandered on to the track. Nino Farina had to swerve to avoid him and lost control of his Ferrari. He ploughed into the crowd, killing 13 spectators.

1961: The £20 maximum wage is abolished, and Fulham immediately boost Johnny 'The Maestro' Haynes's wage to £100 a week in a bid to retain his services.

1967: Death of Goose Tatum, the African American star of multiple sports. Tatum made his name playing baseball in the

Negro League, before joining the Harlem Globetrotters basketball team as the original 'clown prince'.

1975: Death of Mexican jockey Álvaro Pineda in California, from a freak accident. While racing in Arcadia, he was waiting in the starting gates on his horse Austin Mittler when the horse suddenly reared up so far that it toppled backwards, crushing Pineda's head against the steel frame of the gate, killing him instantly. He left a wife and two young children. His younger brother Roberto died in a horse racing accident just three years later.

2014: Manchester City were playing against Cardiff City in the Premier League. City forward Edin Džeko had a shot at goal. Cardiff defender Kevin McNaughton hooked the ball out of the goal. City claimed the ball had crossed the line while Cardiff believed their defender had saved the goal. Referee Neil Swarbrick consulted with his watch and awarded the goal – the first league goal ever awarded by goal line technology.

2015: Batting against the West Indies, South Africa's batsman AB de Villiers shatters two one-day international batting records. He scored his first fifty in just 16 deliveries, and needed just 15 more balls to complete his century in a record 31 deliveries. He went on to score 149 in total in a comfortable victory for South Africa.

19 January

1950: The beginning of the first-ever Ladies Professional Golf Association tour. The opening event was the Tampa Open in Florida and was won by America's Polly Riley by two strokes, with a four-day total of 295. The purse for the event was $3,500, but Ms Riley was not eligible for any prize money because she was an amateur.

1973: The first race of the inaugural World Rally Championship, starting with the Monte Carlo Rally. For the first six years of the WRC only manufacturers were given points; the first drivers' championship was not established until 1979. In the first race the Alpine Renault A110 1800 took five of the first six positions, including all three places on the podium.

1981: On a visit to Los Angeles Muhammad Ali hears of a suicidal man who also happens to be a fan of Ali. He went to see the man, and managed to talk him down from a ninth-storey ledge where he was intending to jump from.

2013: After years of denial Lance Armstrong finally publicly admits to doping offences in all seven of his Tour de France victories. He went further, claiming he could not have possibly won any event without cheating since (he alleged) everyone else was doing it.

2013: Death of legendary baseball player Stan Musial (aka Stan the Man), one of the best and most consistent hitters in baseball history. Musial spent 22 seasons in MLB with the St Louis Cardinals, scoring 475 home runs with a batting average of 0.331. He was World Series champion three times, and the National League (NL) batting champion seven times, as well as being named in the All-Star line-up 24 times including 22 consecutive entries.

20 January

1687: A diary entry by medical student Thomas Kincaid gives the first known description of a golf stroke: 'I found that the only way of playing at the Golve is to stand as you do at fencing with the small sword bending your legs a little and holding the muscles of your legs and back and armes exceeding bent or fixt or stiffe and not at all slackning them in the time you are bringing down the stroak (which you readily doe).'

1987: During a practice match between India and Pakistan at the Brabourne Stadium, one of the Pakistani fielders is injured, and they haven't got a 12th man, so they borrow one! India lent them a young prodigy who was rapidly gaining a reputation as a lad of immense talent – the 13-year-old Sachin Tendulkar. So it is technically correct to say that the Indian batting legend actually played for Pakistan before he played for India.

1994: Death of football manager Sir Matt Busby. He established one of the best youth systems of all time, the so-called 'Busby Babes', and led Manchester United for 25 years, winning 13 trophies.

2007: With Sheffield United losing 2-0 away to Reading their manager decides it is time to go on the offensive, bringing on Northern Ireland international winger Keith Gillespie to replace defender Derek Geary. As Gillespie entered the field he shoved an opponent which was noticed by the referee – who gave him a straight red card. Since the referee had not restarted play from the substitution his red card is officially timed at an unbeatable zero seconds.

2007: Just 15km from the end of the 14th stage of the Dakar Rally, French rider Eric Aubijoux falls off his Yamaha 450WRF and dies immediately. Initially it was thought he had suffered from a heart attack. However, a post-mortem revealed he had died of significant internal bleeding, implying he had been involved in a major accident. Yet his bike was in excellent condition, showing no signs of any accident. The precise cause of Aubijoux's death was never confirmed.

21 January

1927: The first football match ever broadcast on radio in Britain is a 1-1 draw between Arsenal and Sheffield United. To enable listeners to have a clearer vision of exactly what was happening on the pitch one commentator described the play, while a second shouted out grid numbers to let people know where on the pitch the ball was at any time. The numbered grid was published in the *Radio Times*. One of the goalmouths was labelled as grid number one … so a back pass to the goalkeeper to start building up the play all over again was 'back to square one', from where we get the frequently used phrase.

1940: Birth of golfing legend Jack Nicklaus (aka The Golden Bear), considered by many as the greatest golfer of all time. In a professional career lasting a quarter of a century Nicklaus won 18 major championships, being placed in the top three 46 times. Overall he won 73 PGA events, behind only Sam Snead and Tiger Woods. At 26 he became the youngest golfer in history to win the career slam of majors.

1945: Murder of Young Perez, the Jewish Tunisian boxer and erstwhile world flyweight champion. Perez was initially held in the Drancy internment camp in France and was one of 1,000 prisoners moved to Auschwitz in 1943. He was one of just 31 survivors 18 months later from the original 1,000. Perez was then one of those ordered on the infamous death march and was murdered by his captors.

1990: Tennis legend John McEnroe, renowned for his behaviour as much as his play, becomes the first player to be thrown out of the Australian Open. Already with two code violations, McEnroe swore loudly and frequently at the chair umpire Gerry Armstrong, who called a third and final code violation: 'Default Mr McEnroe. Game, set, match.'

2016: Death of alpine skier Bill Johnson. In 1984, at the age of 24, he became the first American to win an Olympic gold medal in the alpine events, competing in Yugoslavia (in Sarajevo, which is now in Bosnia). In 2001, during the US Alpine Championships, a bad crash left him with severe brain damage and comatose for three weeks. He suffered a series of mini-strokes over the next few years until a massive stroke left him confined to care for the remaining years of his life.

22 January

1857: The National Association of Baseball Players is founded in New York.

1862: The first known public competition for ski jumping is held at Trysil in Norway. As well as distance, a panel of judges awarded points for 'elegance and smoothness'.

1880: The initial groundwork towards creating the game of table tennis is made when lawn tennis is adapted to be played on the dining room table using improvised equipment.

1955: Snooker legend Joe Davis makes the first officially ratified 147 maximum snooker break. This was in London, in an exhibition match against Willie Smith.

1959: Death of British racing driver Mike Hawthorn, just three months after he is crowned 1958 Formula One World Champion and announces his retirement. He had also won the Le Mans 24-Hours just four years earlier – the first driver to claim both titles. Ironically he lost his life in a car accident while driving to London. Hawthorn had only recently been told he had just a couple of years to live due to kidney problems.

1973: Birth of Rogério Ceni, the Brazilian goalkeeper. A tremendous stopper, he also gained a reputation as a penalty and free-kick taker, scoring 131 goals – an unprecedented total for a goalkeeper. To put that into context, that is a goalkeeper scoring more goals in his career than the likes of Stanley Matthews, Billy Bremner, Zinedine Zidane or Ryan Giggs.

1995: Anderlecht win 3-2 away to Germinal Ekeren in the Belgian league. All three of Anderlecht's goals were scored by Stan van den Buijs ... the Germinal Ekeren defender who nets a fairly unique hat-trick of own goals.

23 January

1879: The National Archery Association of America is established in Crawfordsville, Indiana.

1939: Death of Austrian footballer Matthias Sindelar (aka the Mozart of Football) at the age of just 35. A poem released shortly after his death implied he took his own life in a suicide pact with his girlfriend, although the official verdict was carbon monoxide poisoning. Voted Austria's greatest ever footballer, he played for his country 43 times, scoring 26 goals.

1976: Australian Rod Laver beats Britain's Mark Cox 6-3 6-4 on the carpet surface to win a tennis tournament in Detroit in the US. The win was Laver's 200th career title (a world record), and would turn out to be his last as he retires shortly afterwards.

1983: At the age of just 26 and already with 11 Grand Slam victories to his credit (five Wimbledon, six French Open), Björn Borg shocks the tennis world by announcing his retirement.

1988: The women's singles final at the Australian Open is the first tennis Grand Slam final to be played indoors under cover after the Open moves to Flinders Park in Melbourne. Just three games had been played before light rain started and the final had to be held up for 83 minutes while the roof was closed. German Steffi Graf beat American Chris Evert 6-1 7-6 in the final.

2017: Liberty Media complete the $8 billion takeover of Formula One, with Bernie Ecclestone losing his position as the supremo of the sport after nearly 40 years in charge (although he remains as chief executive).

24 January

1900: Newcastle Badminton Club, the oldest badminton club in the world, is formed in Newcastle-upon-Tyne.

1907: Glenn Curtiss sets a new speed record for a motorbike on board his 4,000cc Curtiss V-8 during a race at Ormond Beach in Florida. Curtiss was clocked at 136.3mph (219.3kmh).

1958: Birth of East German biathlete Frank Ullrich, gold medal winner in the 1980 Winter Olympics in the sprint event. One of the most successful biathletes of all time, Ullrich also won nine gold medals at world championships between 1978 and 1983, as well as 11 victories in World Cup events.

1974: The first-ever English football league game to be played on a Sunday sees Millwall beat Fulham 1-0 at The Den in Division Two. The game kicked off at 11.30am at the request of the police to try to minimise crowd trouble. The first Sunday kick-off in a top-flight match was a week later when Chelsea entertained Stoke City.

2015: The longest competitive match in squash history takes place between Leo Au of Hong Kong and Canadian Shawn DeLierre in the semi-finals of the Holtrand Gas City Open in Alberta, Canada. World number 33 Au won 11-6 4-11 11-6 7-11 16-14 in two hours and 50 minutes.

25 January

1915: Welsh flyweight boxer Jimmy Wilde is beaten by Tancy Lee of Scotland, which brings to a close Wilde's record-breaking run of 103 bouts without defeat. More than 100 years later this remains the record for professional boxing, and given that modern boxers only fight maybe twice a year, this record is unlikely ever to be beaten.

1924: The beginning of the very first Winter Olympic Games. Chamonix in France was chosen as the host, with the delightful setting for many of the events being at the foot of Mont Blanc as 258 athletes from 16 nations participated in these inaugural Games – Austria, Belgium, Canada, Czechoslovakia, Finland, France, Great Britain, Hungary, Italy, Latvia, Norway, Poland, Sweden, Switzerland, United States and Yugoslavia. The winners of the event were Norway with 17 medals, four of which were gold (out of 16 events). (For comparison the 2018 Winter Olympics in South Korea featured 2,922 athletes from 92 nations, competing over 102 events.)

1995: In a Crystal Palace vs. Manchester United game at Selhurst Park, United striker Eric Cantona is sent off for kicking Palace defender Richard Shaw. As he walked towards the tunnel Cantona leapt into the crowd, initially feet first followed by a series of punches. Cantona was sentenced to 120 hours of community service. He called a press conference to explain his actions, the full transcript of which is as follows: 'When the seagulls follow the trawler, it's because they think sardines will be thrown into the sea. Thank you very much' – at which point he got up and left, leaving behavioural psychologists struggling to explain what on earth that was about.

2001: Australian greyhound Brett Lee wins his race at Angle Park in South Australia, running the 515m in a record 28.88 seconds – with an average racing speed of 62.4kmh (or 38.8mph).

2004: Death of Hungarian international footballer Miki Fehér while playing for Portuguese side Benfica away to Vitória de Guimarães. In injury time at the end of the game he had just been given a yellow card when he suddenly bent over in pain before collapsing backwards on to the pitch. Shortly before midnight news came from the hospital that he had passed away by cardiac arrhythmia.

26 January

1871: The Rugby Football Union is formally founded at a meeting of clubs in the Pall Mall Restaurant in Regent Street, London. The initial reason for the meeting was to standardise the rules since many regions and even individual clubs had their own sets of laws. The 21 clubs that attended this first meeting included Harlequins, Blackheath, Civil Service, Guy's Hospital, King's College, Wellington College and St Paul's School, which are still playing today. Other clubs now defunct, or playing under other names, were the Flamingoes, Gipsies, Wimbledon Hornets, Mohicans, Marlborough Nomads, Addison, Lausanne, Belsize

Park, Ravenscourt Park, West Kent, Law, Clapham Rovers and Queen's House (from Greenwich). One notable absentee from the meeting was Wasps who had been invited but, as recorded at the time, 'In true rugby fashion … turned up at the wrong pub, on the wrong day, at the wrong time and so forfeited their right to be called Founder Members.'

1888: The Lawn Tennis Association is founded as the national governing body of tennis in Great Britain. Seven-time Wimbledon champion William Renshaw was elected as the first president.

1906: American Fred Marriot, driving a Stanley Rocket, is the first person to clear 200kmh on a speed trial. The steam-driven vehicle was timed at 205.44kmh (127.66mph).

1993: The final day of the fourth Test between Australia and the West Indies at Adelaide. Australia had been set a modest total of 186 to win (or 185 to draw). Australia were dismissed for 184 leaving the West Indies with a one-run victory, the narrowest win ever in Test cricket.

2000: Death of American tennis player Don Budge, the first person in history to win a calendar Grand Slam (all four major tournaments in the same year). In both 1937 and 1938 he achieved the hat-trick of singles winner, men's doubles winner and mixed doubles winner at Wimbledon.

2003: The 91st women's Australian Open final witnesses the battle of the sisters as 21-year-old Serena Williams beats her older sister Venus 7-6 3-6 6-4.

27 January

1894: The University of Chicago beats the Chicago YMCA 19-11 in the first-ever college fixture for basketball.

1969: Margaret Court beats Billie Jean King 6-4 6-1 in the women's final of the Australian Open tennis tournament. The seeding for this year's competition was unusually accurate – the unseeded Helen Gourlay reached the quarter-finals along with the players seeded 1 to 7; seeds 1 to 4 made the semi-finals, and the top two seeds contested the final.

1973: When the Barbarians beat the touring New Zealand All Blacks team for the first time they produce what has been frequently called 'The greatest try ever scored', finished by Gareth Edwards. The match was played at Cardiff Arms Park and the Barbarians won 23-11.

1984: During the Millrose Games, an indoor athletics meet in New York City, multi-event champion athlete Carl Lewis wins the long jump in a new indoor world best of 8.79m.

1994: A football match with a great deal at stake turns into one of the most bizarre spectacles ever seen in any sport. Barbados were playing against Grenada in the mini-league format of the Caribbean Cup. If Barbados won by a margin of two or more goals then they would go through to the finals. If not Grenada would progress. Part of the farce that ensued must have been due to the organisers who were experimenting with two new rules. Draws were discouraged to try to make matches more exciting – any match ending level after 90 minutes went into extra time. And extra time would be decided by a golden goal (i.e. the first team to score in extra time, and the match would end to avoid any possibility of an equaliser). The other new rule was that for some reason golden goals would count double. Midway through the first half Barbados were winning 2-0, and were sailing through to the finals. Then with about ten minutes to go Grenada scored – 2-1 to Barbados, advantage Grenada. A quick discussion among the Barbados players concluded that they were unlikely to score again in the short time left. They decided their best bet was to let Grenada score again to take it to 2-2, and then score in extra time to get the double-value goal. When they were playing almost unchallenged Grenada worked out what was going on – and so refused to score. So Barbados decided they would score for them. For the final few minutes the crowd were totally confused by the sight of Barbados desperately trying to score an own goal – with the Grenada players earnestly defending the opposition goal to prevent this happening. In the final minutes Barbados did manage to score to take the tie into extra time – and then managed to get their golden goal to progress 4-2. These experimental rules were never used again.

28 January

1900: The Deutscher Fußball Bund (DFB) is founded in Leipzig as the official national football association of Germany, with 86 member clubs.

1978: Birth of legendary Italian goalkeeper Gigi Buffon, holder of numerous footballing records. In 2016 he went 974 minutes without conceding a goal, including ten consecutive clean sheets. With 176 international caps Buffon is not only the most capped Italian of all time but the most capped European. He attended a record five FIFA World Cup tournaments, although in his first in 1998 he was a non-playing substitute.

2005: The West Indies play Pakistan in a one-day international at the Adelaide Oval as part of the Tri-Nations series with Australia. The West Indies batted first and reached 339/4 with captain Brian Lara scoring 156 off 138 balls, including 12 fours and five sixes. This was Lara's 19th and final ODI century.

2017: Serena Williams beats her sister Venus in the final of the Australian Open – a match and a result that brings several records. It was the first time that the final had been contested by two players over 35, and the first time any player had won the Australian Open seven times. Williams's win was her 23rd Grand Slam singles title, overtaking Steffi Graf's record of 22. Shortly after the event Williams announced she was expecting her first baby, the timing meaning that she would have been a few weeks pregnant when she won the title.

29 January

1924: A military patrol event is staged for the first and only time at a Winter Olympic Games. Military patrol was for a team of four members – one officer, one NCO and two privates. It was over a 25km cross-country skiing course (15km for women), that had to climb from 500m to 1,200m (300m to 700m for women). The officer carried a pistol, but did not participate in the shooting element of the competition. All other members carried rifles, and had to carry a backpack of at least 24kg. Switzerland won the gold medal for this unique event. The event was the forerunner to the modern biathlon, although it would be 36 years before this became an official sport for the Winter Olympics.

1961: In the Italian league Internazionale (aka Inter Milan) thrash Catania at the San Siro. And they didn't even need to try too hard, since Catania did most of the work for them. After Egidio Morbello had opened the scoring for Inter, Catania then scored a remarkable four own goals.

1994: Thomas 'The Hitman' Hearns beats Dan Ward in the first round on a technical knockout to win the NABF cruiserweight title in Nevada. The win means that Hearns has now won international titles in an unprecedented six different weight categories, having previously won the USBA welterweight title (1980), the WBC light-middleweight title (1982), the NABF middleweight crown (1986), the NABF and WBO super-middleweight belt (1988), and the WBA light-heavyweight title (1991).

1996: Magic Johnson re-signs for LA Lakers five years after his retirement following the announcement that he has contracted HIV. He played his first game in five years the following day against the Golden State Warriors, coming off the bench. He would only play 32 games in this post-retirement season before retiring for the third and final time.

2003: Daniela Iraschko-Stolz of Austria becomes the first woman ever to jump 200m on skis when she clears exactly 210m (656 feet) on Kulm in Bad Mittendorf in Austria.

30 January

1929: Birth of South African Test spin bowler Hugh Tayfield. Playing for South Africa against Australia when still only 20, he was brought on to bowl when Australia were 31/0 and he took 7-23 to help reduce them to 75 all out. In a 1956/57 Test series against England Tayfield ended his spell in the first innings with 119 dot balls, and started the second with another 18. This sequence of 137 consecutive Test match deliveries without conceding a run remains a record.

1948: The beginning of the V Olympic Winter Games – the first for 12 years due to the Second World War. The Games were held in St Moritz in Switzerland, with 670 athletes from 28 nations contesting 22 events. St Moritz was chosen since she maintained her neutrality during the war and therefore would present no obvious hostility to any country competing. The financial drain of the war proved a problem to many competing countries who turned up ill-equipped for the Games. The Norwegian team, for example, had to borrow skis from the US team in order to compete.

1957: Spain beat the Netherlands 5-1 in a friendly international played in Madrid. Three of the goals are scored by Alfredo Di Stéfano ... his first goals for Spain, and his first international hat-trick, but not his first international goals! Ten years earlier he had played six matches for Argentina, scoring six times. He had also played four games for Colombia, but had failed to score for them.

1964: Lidiya Skoblikova from the Soviet Union wins the 500m speed skating final at the Innsbruck Winter Olympic Games. The following day she repeated her success in the 1,500m event. The day after that she won gold in the 1,000m. And then finally on the next day she won the 3,000m to complete the clean sweep of speed skating medals, a feat never achieved before.

1995: Birth of Venezuelan baseball pitcher Victor Rodriguez, the youngest Seattle Mariners pitcher ever to throw a no-hitter. At the age of just 20 he returned to his homeland for a holiday and was struck by a boat while he was swimming. He was rushed to hospital for surgery where he stayed for six weeks before eventually succumbing to the injuries sustained.

2011: Japan's Sumie Inagaki takes the women's world record in completing the 24-hour run. At an indoor event in Espoo in Finland, Inagaki completed 240.6km (149.5 miles).

31 January

1874: Major Walter Wingfield, the father of modern tennis, produces the rules for playing tennis on grass courts, and patents several items of tennis equipment.

1944: Jewish Hungarian footballer and football manager Árpád Weisz is murdered by the Nazis in an Auschwitz concentration camp, a victim of the Holocaust.

1953: Death of Swiss bobsledder Felix Endrich, gold medallist at the 1948 St Moritz Winter Olympics in the two-man event. In the 1953 world championship he and his partner won gold in the two-man bob. He was also a member of the Swiss four-man team. The sled he was driving cleared a wall and smashed into a tree, breaking his neck. He was rushed to hospital, but was dead on arrival.

1991: The Kaiser Chiefs and Orlando Pirates meet in a friendly football match in the Oppenheimer Stadium in Orkney, South Africa. The stadium had a capacity of 23,000, but to try to increase revenue about 30,000 fans were let in with no segregation between fans of the two teams. The referee allowed a rather controversial goal by the Chiefs which led to hostility from the Pirates fans and eventually a full-blown fight. Forty-two fans lost their lives and hundreds more were injured.

2013: The transfer that never was. Nigerian striker Peter Odemwingie was clearly growing increasingly unhappy at West Bromwich Albion, even to the point of criticising the club publicly. It was no secret that he was keen to move, and so it came as little surprise to see him rushing down to London to sign for Queens Park Rangers … little surprise to anyone, that is, except QPR manager Harry Redknapp who stated he had never shown any interest in signing him and didn't particularly want him. Given Odemwingie's friction with West Brom the proposed move had generated a flurry of media interest, and the cameras gathered at Loftus Road to see Odemwingie stranded in the car park before getting back into his car and returning to the Midlands in disgrace.

FEBRUARY

1 February

1878: Birth of Hungarian polymath Alfréd Hajós, an architect by trade and yet one of the most remarkable sportsmen of his day. At the 1896 Athens Olympic Games he took the gold medal in both the 100m and the 200m swimming. He was also Hungarian champion for the 100m sprint, 400m hurdles and discus. He played centre-forward for the Hungarian football team, and later on worked as their coach and also as a referee. In the 1924 Paris Olympics, which famously included competitions for arts endeavours, Hajós won the silver medal for town planning.

1969: International debut for Welsh rugby full-back JPR Williams. Williams holds the unique record of remaining unbeaten against England in ten matches. In the days of amateur status, further success was limited at times by his obligations in his work as an orthopaedic surgeon.

1981: Sport is clearly about winning and losing, but it should also be about honesty, integrity and a conduct which is beyond reproach. In the third final of the World Cup series New Zealand needed seven runs off the last ball to win. Australian captain Greg Chappell called to his brother Trevor to bowl the final delivery underarm, so the ball rolled up to Brian McKechnie along the ground. The lack of sportsmanship almost caused a diplomatic incident between the two countries, and led to a worldwide ban on underarm bowling in first-class cricket.

1986: Wales entertain Scotland in a rugby union match at Cardiff Arms Park, a fixture in the Five Nations Championship. Wales were leading 16-15 when they were given a penalty just outside their own 10m line. Everyone was waiting for the kick to the corner, but full-back Paul Thorburn, playing only his fifth match for Wales, said he fancied it. The 23-year-old calmly slotted the penalty from a record distance of 64m (~70yards).

2012: Seventy-four people are killed and more than 500 injured in a riot at the Port Said Stadium in Egypt following a Premier League match between Al-Masry and Al-Ahly. After winning the game 3-1 the fans of Al-Masry viciously attacked the opposition fans with swords, knives, clubs, bottles and even fireworks. Seventy-three people, including nine police officers, faced charges including unsociable behaviour, aggression, intimidation, manslaughter, causing death and murder. Ten of the defendants were sentenced to death. As a result of the riot the Egyptian government shut down the domestic league across the whole of Egypt for two years.

2 February

1876: Foundation of the National League of Professional Baseball Clubs – the third governing body for baseball, following the National Association of Base Ball Players (1869–71) and the Association of Professional Base Ball Players (1871–76).

1925: Death of Dutch athlete Jaap Eden, winner of the world championships in two different and unrelated sports. He won the gold medal for the World Allround Championship for speed skating in 1893, 1895 and 1896. He also won gold in the World Cycling Championships in 1894 (for the 10km race), and in 1895 (for the sprint).

1987: Death of Brazilian football goalkeeper Castilho. He was colour-blind, and particularly enjoyed playing with a yellow football which he saw as red, a colour he believed was lucky. After he injured a finger for the fifth time the medics told him he would need two to three months on the sidelines to recover – but instead he insisted the finger was amputated. He was playing again within two weeks. Tragically at the age of 59 he took his own life.

2002: The first-ever game in the women's rugby inaugural Six Nations Championship is contested in Bègles, as France beat Spain 24-0. The other opening fixtures were played the following day, with Wales beating Ireland 13-5 and England beating Scotland 35-8.

2004: Roger Federer becomes men's singles tennis number one ATP player for the first time, replacing Andy Roddick at the top. He stays at the top spot until August 2008 – a record 237 consecutive weeks – before he is replaced by Rafael Nadal.

2011: Australian Jack Bobridge sets a new cycling world record in the 4,000m individual pursuit at the Australian Championships in Sydney with a time of four minutes and 10.534 seconds.

3 February

1876: Baseball player and manager Albert Spalding establishes his own company producing sporting goods, A.G. Spalding. They were the first company manufacturing official balls for baseball, tennis, golf, football and basketball. Spalding was the first player who wore a baseball glove. He also wrote the first official set of rules for baseball – stating in it that only Spalding balls should be used for playing the game!

1956: Having already won the gold medal for the giant slalom five days earlier, and following that with the slalom gold two days later, Austrian Toni Sailer becomes the first skier to complete the clean sweep of the three alpine events when he wins the downhill event at the Winter Olympics in Italy.

1989: Death of American golfer Glenna Vare, who dominates women's golf for several years between the wars. By the time she was 20 she had won the first of her six US Championships. At the age of 21 she lost a play-off in the US women's amateur semi-final to an outrageous fluke – her opponent's ball cannoned off hers and into the hole. However, that was to be her only defeat of the year, winning 59 of the 60 tournaments she had entered, a record untouched by any golfer since.

1990: Cathy Freeman becomes the first Australian indigenous person to win an athletics gold medal when she runs as part of the Australian 4x100m relay team at the Commonwealth Games in New Zealand at the age of just 16.

1996: The final of the 20th Africa Cup of Nations. The tournament had been extended to 16 nations for the first time, and was hosted by South Africa. The hosts and Tunisia got through to the final, with South Africa winning 2-0 in front of 80,000 fans in Johannesburg.

2008: The New York Giants beat the New England Patriots 17-14 to win Super Bowl LXII. This was the first Super Bowl appearance for experienced punter Jeff Feagles after 20 years in the professional game. Feagles retired just a couple of years later with the remarkable record of never having missed a single game in 22 seasons.

4 February

1861: The Atlantics beat the Charter Oak Club 36-27 in a baseball game in South Brooklyn, New York. The game was certainly unusual – it was played on Litchfield Pond which was frozen for the winter – so all the players played on ice skates.

1932: The start of the III Olympic Winter Games, held in Lake Placid in New York. In the voting to stage the Games Lake Placid's main competition came from California who built the world's biggest ski jump in anticipation of winning the bid, only to see their chance taken away. The Games were opened by the future president Franklin D. Roosevelt, who was governor of New York at the time.

1950: The start of the fourth edition of what is now called the Commonwealth Games – but in the early years is known as the British Empire Games. The fourth Empire Games were originally scheduled to take place in Montreal in Canada in 1942, but these were cancelled due to the Second World War, and Auckland in New Zealand won the right to host these Games.

1956: In the final round of matches the Soviet Union beat Canada 2-0 to claim the gold medal in the ice hockey tournament for the Winter Olympics. For one of their players, Vsevolod Bobrov, it marked a unique double. Just four years earlier he had been a member of the Soviet team in the football tournament in the Summer Olympics, scoring five goals in their three matches including a hat-trick against Yugoslavia.

1967: The birth of rallycross, which actually begins as an invitation event for rally drivers, originally designed as a television spectacle at Lydden Circuit in Kent. The success of the event led to a series of races, which eventually led to a brand-new sport!

1990: Briton Donald Ritchie breaks the world record for the 100-mile run, completing the distance overnight at the indoor circuit at Milton Keynes in a time of 12.56.13.

2022: The scheduled starting date for the Beijing Winter Olympic Games in the People's Republic of China. These will be the first Winter Olympics ever held in China, and Beijing will famously become the first city ever to have held both a Summer Olympics and a Winter Olympics.

5 February

1936: Sunderland goalkeeper Jimmy Thorpe collapses into a coma during a game against Chelsea. He never came out of the coma, dying a couple of days later. His death was the catalyst for changing the rules such that players would no longer be able to challenge a goalkeeper for the ball once he had it in his arms.

1985: Birth of Cristiano Ronaldo (real full name Cristiano Ronaldo dos Santos Aveiro), widely regarded as one of the finest footballers of all time. Born and raised on the island of Madeira, he was diagnosed with a racing heart as a teenager, which required an operation before he could begin his professional career.

1992: Birth of Brazilian international footballer Neymar (birth name Neymar da Silva Santos Júnior). Neymar made his professional debut at 17, playing for Brazilian side Santos. He moved to Paris Saint-Germain, becoming the first player ever to cost £200 million (actual fee paid €222 million).

2017: The New England Patriots beat the Atlanta Falcons 34-28 to win Super Bowl LI in Houston, Texas. This was the Patriots' tenth victory – a Super Bowl record. Quarterback Tom Brady became the first player to win five bowls with the same club. (He also played in their three Super Bowl defeats.)

6 February

1958: Manchester United beat Red Star Belgrade in Yugoslavia to claim their place in the European Cup semi-finals. They returned to West Germany to get their flight back to Manchester. In icy cold conditions their plane had two aborted attempts to take off. The pilot made a third attempt, by which time the snow was falling heavily. The plane skidded on snow, ploughed through a fence and into a house with the left wing being ripped off. Twenty people on the flight died at the scene, and another three died later of their injuries. United fatalities were Geoff Bent, Roger Byrne, Eddie Colman, Mark Jones, David Pegg, Tommy Taylor and Billy Whelan. Duncan Edwards survived the crash but died 15 days later in hospital. The club's secretary, trainer and chief coach also perished, along with eight journalists. Survivors included Johnny Berry and Jackie Blanchflower, both of whom never played football again despite the fact Blanchflower was just 24 at the time. Other Manchester United personnel who survived the crash were Bobby Charlton, Bill Foulkes, Harry Gregg, Kenny Morgans, Albert Scanlon, Dennis Viollet, Ray Wood and legendary manager Matt Busby.

1964: American Scott Allen becomes the youngest ever Olympic medal winner in figure skating at Innsbruck, just two days short of his 15th birthday. Allen was awarded the bronze medal for his routine.

1967: Muhammad Ali, holder of the WBC, lineal and *The Ring* heavyweight boxing titles, fights the WBA heavyweight champion, American Ernie Terrell. Ali won on a unanimous decision to claim all available titles and became the undisputed heavyweight champion of the world.

1993: Death of trailblazing tennis star Arthur Ashe – the first black player to play for the US in the Davis Cup, and the only black player to date who has won Wimbledon, the US Open and the Australian Open. Shortly after retiring in 1980 Ashe needed heart bypass surgery, and tragically contracted HIV from infected blood during the necessary transfusion. He spent the majority of the remainder of his life working on educating people about HIV and AIDS as well as fundraising for research into the conditions.

2017: Death of South African rugby star Joost van der Westhuizen at the age of just 45. He played for the Springboks (mainly as a scrum-half) 89 times, scoring 38 tries, and appeared in three World Cups for his country, collecting a winners' medal in 1995. In 2011 it was announced that van der Westhuizen was suffering from motor neurone disease. With the nature of the illness being degenerative his condition steadily worsened, and he spent the final couple of years in a wheelchair and finding communication very difficult.

7 February

1829: The foundation stone is laid at Aintree for the building of the Grand National racecourse.

1882: Heavyweight boxer John Sullivan (aka The Boston Strong Boy) knocks out Paddy Ryan in the eighth round to become the last bare-knuckle boxing champion of the world. A couple of years later (different dates are given from alternative sources) he became the first world heavyweight champion of gloved boxing.

1976: Geoff Hunt of Australia becomes the first-ever winner of the Professional Squash Association World Open Squash

Championship. Hunt beat Mohibullah Khan of Pakistan in the final. This first world final was held at Wembley, with a prize purse of £10,000.

1999: The fourth and final day of the second Test between India and Pakistan, with India winning by 212 runs. The match was most significant for the bowling performance of Indian Anil Kumble in the second innings, in which he became only the second bowler in history to take all ten wickets in a Test match innings. Kumble came on as first change in the tenth over and then continued without change for 26.3 overs, taking 10-74.

2014: The start of the XXII Winter Olympic Games, the Sochi Olympics in Russia. The Games would break several records, including two that had little to do with sport. The Games achieved a record viewing audience worldwide estimated at 2.1 billion people. The Russian organising committee had budgeted US$12 billion for the overall costs of running the Games; it actually ended up costing a staggering $51 billion.

8 February

1887: The first-ever ski jumping competition in the US takes place in Red Wing, Minnesota. The tournament was won by Mikkel Hemmestvedt with a then record of 37 feet (11.3m). Within three years Hemmestvedt had increased his record to 102 feet (31.1m), and another three years later his brother Torjus extended that to 103 feet (31.4m). The record is now 825 feet (251.5m) – at the time of writing.

1948: The end of the St Moritz Winter Olympic Games in Switzerland sees the first (and to date the only) dead heat in Games history. At the top of the final table, neighbours Norway and Sweden both won four gold medals, three silver and three bronze, and so had to be satisfied with an equal first place. Hosts Switzerland were next with three gold medals, four silver and three bronze.

1981: Death of Jimmy 'Nitro' Morgan, the American bobsledder. Tragically he died taking part in the FIBT World Championships at Cortina d'Ampezzo in Italy. Morgan's death led to the shortening of the Italian circuit.

1983: Irish-bred racehorse Shergar is stolen from the Ballymany Stud in County Kildare, Ireland. The highlight of Shergar's career was winning the 1981 Epsom Derby by a record ten lengths. The theft was carried out by masked gunmen who were never apprehended, and Shergar was never seen again. The motive behind the theft was never fully understood.

1992: The 16th Winter Olympic Games open in Albertville in France, the last Winter Olympics to be held in the same calendar year as the Summer Olympics. Germany won the Olympics with ten gold medals, with the Unified Team (a group of Soviet nations) second with nine.

2002: The opening of the 19th Winter Olympics at Salt Lake City in Utah, the US – 2,400 athletes from 78 nations arrived in the States for the fortnight of competition. Norway won the Games with 13 gold medals.

2015: Belgian rugby team Royal Kituro beat Soignies by a record 356-3, running in 56 tries in the process. The Soignies points were from an ambitious drop goal with one of their players desperately trying to prevent them registering a score of zero. Their problems started when the referee initially failed to show up. By the time he did appear, an hour late, the Soignies bus had already gone with a lot of their players on board assuming the game was cancelled. The 16 players who had stayed decided to give it a go!

9 February

1540: The first definite record of a horse race meeting, which takes place at Roodee Fields in Chester.

1895: YMCA PE director William Morgan in Massachusetts invents a new indoor game that he calls Mintonette which, he claims, is derived from badminton, handball and tennis. Any number of players could play (originally), with a match comprising of nine innings of three serves for each team (if the first serve was a foul, the team were allowed a second attempt). Players could push, palm or punch the ball to each other as many times as they liked, as long as it kept moving and did not touch the ground or any part of the body other than the hands and arms. Given the volleying nature of the game it rapidly became known as volley ball (which, over time, became simply volleyball).

1945: The college basketball game between Columbia and Fordham is used to experiment a proposed new rule for the sport and hence this fixture becomes one of the most significant games in the history of basketball. Although the rule was not enshrined in statutes until 1961, this game was the first one ever to experiment with the three-point line, encouraging more long-distance shooting and making the game more exciting for the fans. Columbia beat Fordham 73-58 using the new scoring system.

1964: The end of the Innsbruck Winter Olympic Games in Austria. The Games were declared a big success, with few people realising the effort that had gone into holding them. Innsbruck was considered an ideal location for the Games with its nearly ever-present snow ... but the timing of the Games happened at one of the very rare periods where snow was sparse. The Austrian Olympic Committee enlisted the help of the Austrian army, and they carved out 20,000 ice bricks from the top of a mountain for use on the luge and bobsled runs. They then carried about 20,000 tonnes of snow to the alpine skiing courses where it was not only laid, but had to be packed down by hand.

1979: Trevor Francis transfers from Birmingham City to Nottingham Forest, becoming the first £1m player in the UK. Brian Clough, Francis's manager at Forest, always insisted the fee was £999,999 since he claimed he did not want the player to bear the burden of a £1m price tag.

2018: Beginning of the XXIII Winter Olympics, in Pyeongchang in South Korea, where 2,922 competitors from 92 nations would compete in 102 events from seven sports – the first time the number of events has exceeded 100 for a winter Games.

10 February

1847: Birth of Albert 'Monkey' Hornby, one of the best and most influential sportsmen of his day. He is one of only two men who have captained England at both rugby union and cricket. He also played competitive football for Blackburn Rovers. He is best remembered as the captain of the 1882 Test cricket team who lost against Australia, after which a bail was burned giving birth to the Ashes.

1872: The first-ever varsity rugby match sees Oxford rugby club beat Cambridge by one goal to nil. A 'goal' in the early days was what would now be called a converted try.

1957: The opening day of the inaugural Africa Cup of Nations, hosted by the newly independent Republic of the Sudan. Only three teams actually took part in the first competition – Egypt, Ethiopia and Sudan. South Africa originally expressed interest, but pulled out as the tournament approached. On the opening day Egypt beat Sudan 2-1 in Khartoum, and Egypt would go on to be crowned the first champions of Africa.

1974: Women are welcomed at the official USA marathon in San Mateo in California for the first time. Men have competed since 1925, but women had to wait almost 50 years before they were welcome in the event.

1989: In a New Jersey courtroom the WWF admits what most people have suspected for a long time – that wrestling is not a sport, but an exhibition. WWF supremo Vince McMahon stated that professional wrestling should be viewed as 'an activity in which participants struggle hand in hand primarily for the purpose of providing entertainment to spectators rather than conducting a bona fide athletic contest'.

1996: IBM computer Deep Blue becomes the first computer to beat a reigning World Chess champion when it beats world number one Gary Kasparov.

2006: The opening of the Turin Winter Olympic Games in Italy. The opening ceremony was significant since it was the final public performance of the legendary tenor Luciano Pavarotti, who was singing his epic 'Nessun Dorma'.

2009: Death of American freestyle motocross racer Jeremy Lusk. He died in competition attempting to land a spectacular backflip when he under-rotated and came off head first causing massive brain damage. Doctors fought hard to save him but he succumbed to his injuries.

11 February

1445: The first-ever Shrove Tuesday pancake race is run at Olney in Buckinghamshire. One of the oldest sporting contests in the world, while there have been occasional off years for various historical reasons, the pancake race at Olney has been run most years since 1445 and is still run today.

1851: The first first-class cricket match is played in Australia when Tasmania play Victoria in Launceston.

1948: West Indian Andy Ganteaume scores 112 in the first innings of his debut Test match against England. He didn't bat in the second innings ... and he was never selected again – leaving Ganteaume with a Test cricket batting average of 112.

1959: Death of motor racing driver Marshall Teague, the first fatality at the Daytona International Speedway circuit, which had only opened a few weeks earlier. Teague was attempting to set a new land speed record and was doing an estimated 140mph when his Sumar Special spun and flipped. Teague was thrown from the car – still strapped to his seat – and died immediately on impact.

1993: Russian sprinter Irina Privalova takes the world 60m sprint record in a time of 6.92 seconds.

2015: Manchester City's James Milner creates a new Premiership record when he covers 13.56km (8.43 miles) during a match against Stoke City. Milner also scored City's second goal in a 4-1 win.

2018: Asante Kotoko from Ghana are drawn at home to the Congolese team CARA Brazzaville in the CAF (Confédération Africaine de Football) Confederation Cup in what turns out to be a rather odd match. During the match Kotoko were awarded three penalties and CARA were awarded one … and all four were missed. The Kotoko penalties were taken by three different players, no one having the courage to try twice. As the game appeared to be petering out to a goalless draw, in time added on the referee awarded Kotoko their fourth penalty. Substitute Yakubu Mohammed became the fifth player to take a penalty, but the first one to score!

12 February

1995: Ronnie O'Sullivan wins the Masters snooker title at the age of 19 years and 69 days, making him the youngest player ever to win the tournament.

2010: Death of Georgian one-man luger Nodar Kumaritash-vili following a training crash while practising for the Canada Winter Olympics. The sport of luge had actually been introduced to Georgia by his grandfather, and several of his relatives had been accomplished athletes. Kumaritashvili was on his final training run when he lost control and hit an unprotected metal support pole travelling at slightly more than 140kmh (about 90mph). Medics were quickly on the scene and he was airlifted to hospital where he died of his injuries.

2013: Esther Vergeer announces her retirement from wheelchair tennis. She had been undefeated in more than ten years, an unbroken winning streak of 470 matches.

2016: Dominican baseball pitcher Jenrry Manuel Mejía, star of the New York Mets, becomes the first player ever to receive a lifetime ban from MLB. Mejía was banned for the first 80 games of the 2015 season after testing positive for performance-enhancing drugs. In July 2015 he failed a second drug test and saw his suspension extended. And then, almost unbelievably, he failed a third test in February 2016 – leading to the lifetime ban.

13 February

1936: Austrian pair Ilse Pausin and Erik Pausin become the youngest ever Winter Olympic figure skating pairs medal winners when they take the silver medal in Bavaria, Germany. Ilse Pausin is 17 years and six days old at the time, while her brother and partner Erik is 15 years and 301 days old.

1968: The final day of competition in the women's luge competition at the Grenoble Winter Olympics in France. The day descended into chaos when three East German competitors were disqualified. As the competition neared its end these three were all in the top four. Since this would not have been expected the organisers decided to investigate, and discovered that the East German team had actually been heating the luge runners prior to each descent.

1988: During an indoor athletic meeting in Vienna, Austria, Heike Drechsler of East Germany sets a new world record for the women's indoor long jump of 7.37m.

1993: And the award for the referee not paying enough attention goes to Les Mottram. Dundee United were already 2-0 up against Partick Thistle, both goals from Paddy Connolly, when they scored their third and Connolly completed his hat-trick, hammering it in from close range. The ball smacked against the stanchion and bounced straight out, where it was caught by Thistle defender Martin Clark. He gave it to his goalkeeper Andy Murdoch to boot it up towards the halfway line ready for the kick-off – but the referee waved play on. Not only had the referee managed to miss the goal, he missed the handball as well! Thankfully it didn't ultimately affect Dundee United, who went on to win 4-0, but it did cost Connolly who did not complete his hat-trick.

2018: The end of the mixed doubles curling events at the XXIII Olympic Winter Games in South Korea – the first time the mixed doubles curling has ever been competed as an Olympic sport.

14 February

1891: The FA Cup tie between Notts County and Stoke is the match which gives the impetus for the invention of the penalty kick. Notts County were leading 1-0 in their quarter-final tie with just seconds remaining when Stoke were awarded a free kick just inches from the goal line after a Notts County player handled on the line. The free kick was, however, so close to the goal line that the goalkeeper simply stood in front of the ball and fell on it as soon as it was kicked.

1905: Middlesbrough become the first football team in the world to spend £1,000 on a player when they purchase Alf Common from local rivals Sunderland in a desperate hope that his goals will help them to avoid relegation from Division One. The first-ever four-figure transfer fee was very controversial – questions were even raised in the House of Commons, with Middlesbrough heavily criticised for paying such an obscene fee. One MP even argued that this was 'a new type of white slave trade, which might one day see transfer fees reaching £2,000'.

1988: The individual ski jumping competition takes place during the Winter Olympics in Calgary in Canada. Michael 'Eddie the Eagle' Edwards represented Great Britain in this 70m jump – the first British ski jump competitor since 1928. Edwards came 58th – out of 58.

1996: Death of the Liverpool Football Club legend Bob Paisley, who served the club for nearly 50 years as a player, physiotherapist, coach and manager. His debut as a player was delayed because of the Second World War, when he served in the British Army. His Liverpool team were so dominant he once quipped 'Mind you, I've been here during the bad times too – one year we came second.' Sadly for the last few years of his life he suffered from Alzheimer's disease.

2013: South African paralympic multiple champion Oscar Pistorius shoots his girlfriend Reeva Steenkamp, who tragically dies as a result. The attack happened after dark and Pistorius shot Steenkamp through the bathroom door. Pistorius has never denied being the shooter, but has consistently claimed that on hearing noises/movement from the bathroom, he assumed they had an intruder and opened fire. A year later Pistorius was in court charged with murder, but after a six-month trial he was found not guilty of murder but guilty of culpable homicide and was given a five-year jail sentence. In June 2016 the conviction was overturned on appeal by the state and Pistorius was convicted of murder, with his sentence extended to 13 years and five months.

15 February

1932: The end of the fifth and final Test in the Test match series between Australia and South Africa sees Australia win by an innings and 72 runs. Australian batsman Don Bradman played in all five Tests, but did not bat in the final Test due to injury. He batted five times in the series, scoring two centuries and two double centuries, with a top score of 299 not out. In the whole series he scored 806 runs, becoming the only batsman in history to average more than 200 in a Test match series (average 201.5).

1932: The third day of the Melbourne Test match between Australia and South Africa. The first day, which was badly affected by the weather, saw Australia post a total of 153. The second day was rained off entirely. In the remainder of the first day, and the start of the third, South Africa were bowled out twice – for 36 and 45 – leaving Australia the winners by more than an innings. Taking into account the rain disruption, this was the shortest Test match ever – the game was actually played for just five hours and 53 minutes.

1932: The United States four-man bobsled team win the gold medal at the Winter Olympic Games. The event was held at Lake Placid. For one member of the US team, Eddie Eagan, this capped a truly unique double. Eagan had won the gold medal in the light heavyweight class of boxing in the 1920 Belgium Olympics. He remains the only person to have won a gold medal at both the Summer Olympics and the Winter Olympics in different events. As well as his success in these Olympic events Eagan also starred for the New York Giants for several years as a wide receiver.

2014: Renaud Lavillenie of France breaks the world pole vault record with a vault of 6.16m (20ft 2.5in) in Donetsk, Ukraine.

2015: American Adam Barta scores a tenpin bowling record, scoring 2,708 pins in one hour, in Ohio, USA. In that time he bowled 291 balls (roughly one bowl every 12 seconds) – so he achieved an average of about 9.5 for every ball, and 163 of his bowls were strikes.

2015: Anders Fannemel of Norway sets a new world record for the ski jump when he clears an astonishing 215.5m (825ft) at a competition in his homeland.

16 February

1871: Maidenhead United play their first football match at their York Road ground, against Marlow – the same ground they are using today nearly 150 years later. It is the oldest senior football ground in the UK which has been continuously used by the same club.

1936: The official start of the IV Olympic Winter Games, hosted by Garmisch-Partenkirchen in Bavaria, Germany. The Games were officially opened by the Führer Adolf Hitler. The Summer Games would also be hosted by Germany. Norway won the Games with seven gold medals, followed by Germany with three golds. These Games also hold the record for the largest and heaviest medals ever awarded – 100mm in diameter, 4mm thick and weighing 324g.

2005: The entire NHL season is officially cancelled – all 1,230 games! The decision was in response to a player strike which had already been in existence for five months. The Champions Cup, which is awarded annually, was engraved with the words '2004–05 Season Not Played'.

2016: In the Argentine Córdoba province, a football match is called off early in tragic circumstances. Forty-eight-year-old referee César Flores had just sent a player off. He was so unimpressed with the decision that, rather than heading to the bench or even the dressing room, he went straight to his car to get his rifle. He returned to the field of play, and shot and killed the referee. Another player was injured in the shooting. The player fled the scene.

17 February

1818: German Baron Karl von Drais patents his early bicycle invention, called the draisine (which he originally called the *laufmaschine*, or. running machine). This was the first commercially successful two-wheeled, steerable, human-propelled machine. On his first reported ride he covered 13km (~8 miles) in less than an hour. While there were several features which are clearly recognisable on a modern bicycle, many were certainly different. For example, there were no pedals and no chain – propulsion was simply by pushing along the ground with the feet and freewheeling.

1916: Birth of Prince Alexander Obolensky of Russia who, despite being a Russian prince, becomes a naturalised Briton and plays for England at rugby union. In 1936 he scored two tries on his international debut as England beat New Zealand for the first time in their history. In 1940 he was commissioned in the RAF and died in a training exercise preparing for front line duty.

1968: The final day of competition in the alpine skiing slalom in the Grenoble Winter Olympics. The slalom was held in really poor visibility which created challenges for all the contestants. Austrian world champion Karl Schranz claimed that one of the course stewards walked in front of him, causing him to stop. He was allowed to run again and posted the fastest time. Then a jury of appeal studied the run and claimed he had missed a gate and so disqualified him. The International Olympic Committee claimed that this was 'The greatest controversy in the history of the Winter Olympics.'

2002: In the inaugural women's Six Nations rugby championship, England thrash Ireland 79-0 in Worcester.

2002: An Olympic first – the second medal ceremony for the same event. In the Salt Lake City Winter Olympics pairs figure skating, Canadian pair Jamie Salé and David Pelletier were the crowd favourites and skated a seemingly flawless performance. However, the judges awarded the gold medal to the Russian pair of Elena Berezhnaya and Anton Sikharulidze, with the Canadians second. The medals were presented on 11 February. After an internal assessment the organisers decided the most diplomatic response was to award both pairs gold medals, and not award a silver – so they held a new medal ceremony so that Salé and Pelletier could receive their gold medals.

2005: Australia host New Zealand in the first international Twenty20 cricket match. Australia ran to a 44-run victory to cap a remarkable hat-trick. In 1866 Australia beat England in the first-ever Test match; in 1971 they beat the same opposition in the first one-day international.

18 February

1899: England thrash Ireland 13-2, with amateur player G.O. Smith scoring four times, including a hat-trick in the space of five minutes. Smith enjoyed a successful career for The Corinthians for whom he scored 132 goals in 137 matches before moving to the Casuals FC (42 goals in 29 games). He also played first-class cricket for both Oxford University and Surrey.

1975: Death of Wilfred Andrews, the first British president of the FIA (Fédération Internationale de l'Automobile). Andrews had been instrumental in the purchase of RAF Silverstone and its conversion into the Silverstone racing circuit.

1978: Gordon Haller, the US Naval officer, becomes the first man to earn the official title of Ironman. The first World Triathlon Corporation Ironman challenge took place in O'ahu, the third largest Hawaiian island. Competitors started with a 2.4-mile swim (3.86km), followed by a 112-mile bicycle ride (180.25km), and then finished with a normal 26.2-mile marathon (42.2km). Haller completed the challenge in 11 hours, 46 minutes and 58 seconds.

1999: Kevin Keegan is named as the new England football manager. Glenn Hoddle had been sacked two weeks earlier for giving an interview in which he suggested that disabled people were being punished for their wrongs in their previous lives.

2001: American NASCAR driver Dale Earnhardt dies following a collision on the final lap of the Daytona 500. Renowned for his aggressive driving style, he was known variously as 'The Intimidator' and 'The Man in Black'. After making contact with Sterling Marlin and Ken Schrader he hit a retaining wall, dying on impact. Earnhardt's death led to major improvements on safety for the drivers, including improved seat belts, the introduction of head and neck restraints, and the installation of safety barriers at oval tracks.

2004: The oldest footballer ever to take part in a World Cup qualifying match is MacDonald Taylor who turns out for the US Virgin Islands against Saint Kitts and Nevis at the age of 46 years and 175 days. The Virgin Islands lost the first-round tie 4-0.

19 February

1928: The third and final day of competition of the men's ice hockey tournament in the St Moritz Winter Olympics. The final four teams played each other in a round-robin tournament. Switzerland came third to claim the bronze, which would turn out to be their only medal of the Olympics – the lowest medal haul of a host nation at any Olympic Games.

1970: Driving in the NASCAR 125-mile race on the Daytona International Speedway circuit, Tab Prince's Dodge Charger Daytona's engine blew causing the car to slide sideways. Bill Seifert, driving just behind him, had no time to take evasive action and ploughed into the side of Prince's car. Prince died within minutes of a broken back and a compressed spinal cord.

1980: English all-rounder Ian Botham becomes the first man in Test match history to score a century and take ten wickets in the same Test match. During the Test against India in Mumbai Botham scored 114 in England's first innings total of 296. In India's first innings he took 6-58, which he followed up with 7-48 in the second innings.

1984: The 26th running of the Daytona 500 sees NASCAR legend (and part-time farmer) Cale Yarborough become the first man in history to complete a lap of the Daytona International Speedway circuit at an average speed exceeding 200mph – he is actually clocked at an average 201.85mph (324.84kmh). Yarborough went on to win the race, the fourth Daytona 500 victory of his career.

1992: Liverpool defender Rob Jones is handed his international debut for England in the 2-0 win over France. This was nearly

42 years after his grandfather Bill Jones made his England debut against Portugal. Bill was also a Liverpool defender.

20 February

1879: Birth of ice hockey cover-point (now called a defenceman) Hod Stuart. On the pitch he revolutionised the role of a defenceman, the first defender to regularly feature on the scoresheet. Off the field he worked on reducing violence in games, and also raising salaries of players. At the age of just 28 he died in a diving accident.

1895: Birth of English racing driver and car designer/engineer Count Louis Zborowski. After a few years successfully driving for Aston Martin the Count decided to start designing and building his own racing cars, the first of which he called Chitty Bang Bang. In 1924 he started driving for Mercedes but died when he lost control of his car at the Italian Grand Prix and hit a tree. He was just 29 years old.

1927: Golfers in the state of South Carolina are arrested for playing golf on a Sunday and hence violating the Sabbath.

1971: Birmingham City beat Bolton Wanderers 4-0, with all four goals coming from Trevor Francis. At the age of just 16 years and 317 days he was the youngest player ever to score a professional hat-trick in the UK.

1992: The official formation of the Premier League is confirmed as a limited company. All 20 teams in the then first division resigned from the Football League *en masse* to set up the new organisation.

2007: American Charlie Engle, Canadian Ray Zahab and Taiwan's Kevin Lin complete a remarkable endurance race. Running more than 50 miles a day for 111 days, the three men became the first runners ever confirmed to have crossed the entire 4,000 miles (6,400km) of the Sahara Desert. The epic journey took the men through six different countries – Senegal, Mauritania, Mali, Niger,

Libya and finally Egypt. They finished by symbolically dunking their hands in the Red Sea.

2016: On the first day of his final Test match New Zealand batsman and former captain Brendon McCullum scores a century off the Australian bowlers in just 54 balls – the fastest ever in a Test match.

21 February

1937: Birth of Ron Clarke, the Australian athlete, writer and mayor of the Gold Coast for nine years. During a long athletics career he set 17 world records, including the 5,000m four times, the 10,000m twice, the 20,000m, the two mile, the three mile, the six mile and the ten mile. Despite his enormous success his biggest regret was never winning an Olympic gold.

1948: A few racing car drivers under the leadership of William France Sr form the new racing organisation, which they call the National Association for Stock Car Auto Racing, or NASCAR for short. It was set up with three divisions – Modified, Roadster and Strictly Stock, but the Roadster subgroup was quickly removed when it didn't prove popular with the new NASCAR fans.

1958: Death of Duncan Edwards, one of the original 'Busby Babes'. With Manchester United he became the youngest player ever to play in Division One, and then the youngest England international since the Second World War. Edwards was involved in the Munich air disaster, which he initially survived, but succumbed to his injuries two weeks later.

1958: Day one of the second Test in Melbourne between Australia and England in the women's Ashes Test series. England won the toss and bowled Australia out for 38. When it was England's turn to bat they were bowled out for only 35, giving Australia a lead of three runs in the first innings. In the second innings Australia managed 202/9 before declaring, setting a target of 206. England took 64 overs in reaching just 76/8. Betty Wilson of Australia scored a century in the second innings, and bowled with match figures of 11-16, becoming the first person (man or woman) to score 100 runs and take ten wickets in the same Test match.

1976: The first-ever winter Paralympic Games are held in Örnsköldsvik in Sweden, 16 years after the first summer Paralympics. The Games witnessed the debut on the world stage of the sport of 'three-track skiing' – with a ski on the one foot/leg, and two further skis on the competitors' crutches.

2005: The briefest Formula One career ever! The Jordan team brought Mexican CART driver Mario Dominguez over for pre-season testing at a damp, foggy Silverstone. Dominguez jumped in the car and drove very slowly round one lap, and was ordered to pit at the end of it. The management had decreed it would be unsafe to fly a medical helicopter – so the cars would have to stop. He hung around, but there was no more racing to be done – so he headed back to Mexico and never reappeared at a Formula One meet again. His career lasted precisely one practice lap.

22 February

1966: Death of Italian bobsledder Sergio Zardini. He died during a competition at Lake Placid in New York when the Canadian four-man sled hit the 'Zig-Zag Curves' and crushed his head against the infrastructure of the track.

1980: It is not very often that the United States enter any sports contest as underdogs, but at the Winter Olympics in New York the US ice hockey team are drawn to play the mighty Soviet Union in a medal-round game in Lake Placid. The US team were all amateur players, and were the youngest team in the tournament. The Soviets were all professionals, the defending champions, and had won the previous four Olympic finals – their last defeat was in 1960. Against all odds the Americans triumphed 4-3. They would go on to beat Finland and claim the gold medal; the Soviets had to settle for silver overall.

1992: Death of Swiss speed skier Nicolas Bochatay during the Winter Olympics. On the morning of the competition Bochatay was warming up on the slopes when he crashed into the snowcart – a large vehicle used for smoothing out the snow during a competition. Bochatay took a small jump over a bump and landed just before the machine, not noticing it despite it having flashing lights and a siren. (The Swiss team denied this, but it was confirmed by several independent witnesses.) The skier hit the vehicle directly and died instantaneously from internal injuries.

2003: Bowling for Pakistan against England in a World Cup cricket match, pace bowler Shoaib Akhtar bowls one delivery at 161.3kmh (100.2mph).

2004: Judd Trump becomes the youngest snooker player ever to score a maximum break in an official competition. Trump scored the 147 at the Potters under-16 tournament at the age of 14 years and 206 days.

23 February

1874: Major Walter Winfield obtains a patent for a game which he calls 'sphairistike'. This was the forerunner for lawn tennis as we know it.

1884: Cardiff rugby club adopt a rather experimental formation against Gloucester, one which is hailed as a great success and adopted throughout the game. The experiment was to have a row of four backs behind the half-backs – two in the middle ('centres') and two out wide ('wings') … and the rugby 'three-quarters' was founded.

1966: Geoff Hurst makes his England debut, just five months before his heroics in the World Cup. A prolific goalscorer for West

Ham United, he found opportunities for international games restricted by the form of Jimmy Greaves. He got his opportunity following an injury to Greaves in the final group match against France, meaning Hurst would start in the quarter-final against Argentina. Hurst scored the winner, and kept his place for the semi-final and the final.

1980: American speed skater Eric Heiden takes the gold medal in the 10,000m event in a new world record time at the Winter Olympics at Lake Placid in New York. Heiden had entered all five speed skating events at the Games, and had already won the 500m, the 5,000m, the 1,000m and the 1,500m, each one in a Games record time.

1998: Death of Indian Test cricketer Raman Lamba. Fielding in the Bangladeshi league, he was asked to come in to forward short leg while spinner Saifullah Khan was bowling. He was asked to wear a helmet but declined, as was his usual pattern. Batsman Mehrab Hossain hit a short-pitched delivery which hit Lamba on the temple. The ball was hit with such ferocity it actually rebounded off Lamba's head and was caught by the wicketkeeper. Lamba collapsed into a coma with an internal haemorrhage. Three days later his ventilator was switched off and he was declared dead.

2000: Death of Sir Stanley Matthews (aka The Wizard of Dribble). Matthews was 85 at the time of his death, having continued to play football competitively at the highest level until he was 50. He was knighted during his final year of playing – the only active footballer ever to receive such an honour. After retirement he remained active, even turning out for the England Veterans XI against the Brazil Veterans XI at the age of 70, but sadly he had to come off with cartilage problems and this turned out to be his last game. Of the cartilage injury he wryly reflected, 'A promising career cut tragically short.'

2004: In the Football League Division Two fixture, AFC Bournemouth are leading Wrexham 3-0 with just six minutes

Sir Stanley Matthews

1 February 1915–23 February 2000

One of England's finest ever footballers – 'The Wizard of Dribble'

to go, so their manager decides to use their third substitute. He brings on striker James Hayter for fellow forward Steve Fletcher. The final score was a 6-0 win to Bournemouth, with all three of the late goals scored by the substitute Hayter. The official timing between his first and third goals was a record two minutes and 21 seconds.

24 February

1905: Death of ice hockey player Alcide Laurin, the first case of a death directly associated with the sport. Laurin was playing for Alexandria in Ontario, Canada, against local rivals Maxville. He was hit on the chin which was followed by a blow to the left temple from his stick. Twenty-four-year-old Laurin died shortly afterwards, still on the ice.

1955: Birth of French Formula One driver Alain Prost, widely considered one of the greatest drivers of all time. He was one of the few drivers to end up in the points on his F1 debut, finishing sixth in the 1980 Argentina Grand Prix driving for McLaren. His 51 race victories was a record at the time, until beaten by Michael Schumacher.

1993: Death of Bobby Moore, best known as the victorious captain of England's World Cup 1966 team. He had been suffering from bowel and liver cancer. Moore was the first of England's winning team to pass away, the second being Alan Ball 14 years later.

2015: Pool B match at the ICC Cricket World Cup between the West Indies and Zimbabwe at Canberra. The West Indies batted first and reached a total of 372/2 off their 50 overs. Bizarrely the only two wickets were on the second ball of the innings, and the last ball of the innings. Dwayne Smith was out for a duck on the second ball; Marlon Samuels remained unbeaten on 133. And Chris Gayle was dismissed on the final delivery for a total of 215. The West Indies then dismissed Zimbabwe for 289.

25 February

1882: Samuel Johnston scores his first goal for Ireland in the football international against Wales at the age of 15 years and 160 days. This was the youngest goalscorer in an international match by anyone from Europe – a record he still holds more than 130 years later. Sadly for him and his teammates his goal could not prevent Ireland being thrashed 7-1.

1994: The finals of the women's figure skating at the Winter Olympics in Norway. Almost unbelievably Nancy Kerrigan won the silver medal, just seven weeks after the vicious attack on her at the US Championships. Tonya Harding, who had been cited as being involved in the attack, was still allowed to skate and finished eighth.

2002: Death of the thoroughbred steeplechaser Lonesome Glory following an accident on his owner's farm. He was named as the Champion Steeplechase Horse on a record five occasions. Lonesome Glory was the first steeplechase horse ever to win in excess of $1m.

2014: Death of Mexican polo player Carlos Gracida following an accident in a polo match at the Everglades Polo Club in Wellington, Florida. His horse was accidently struck on the head by a mallet and reared up, throwing Gracida to the ground. The horse then rolled on top of him. He was rushed to a local medical centre in a critical condition but passed away shortly after arriving.

2018: British boxer Scott Westgarth dies the day after his bout with Dec Spelman in Doncaster. This tragedy was particularly unusual among boxing fatalities in that Westgarth actually won! Spelman knocked Westgarth to the canvas in the tenth (and final) round, but he recovered sufficiently to finish the round, win on points and even give a press conference. He then spoke to doctors and was admitted to hospital for tests, where he passed away the following day.

26 February

1789: Death of Eclipse, possibly the first 'superstar' in the world of thoroughbred racehorses, with a record of 18 wins from 18 races, including 11 King's Plates. After retiring from racing he was put out to stud and appears in the pedigree of the majority of modern successful racers. He was foaled on 1 April 1764 – the day of a solar eclipse – hence the name. One of the fundamental problems of being a race horse in the 18th century was that his entire racing career involved racing just 63 miles … and walking 1,400 miles to race meetings across England. Eclipse could cover 25ft (7.6m) in a single stride.

1839: The first-ever official running of the Grand National at Aintree Racecourse. Races had been run on each of the three previous years but these were generally seen as trials for this race. The race was not known as the Grand National until 1847 – in these early years it was the Grand Liverpool Steeplechase. The race attracted a field of 17 runners. The first-ever winner was Lottery, ridden by Jem Mason. The other significant event in this inaugural race regarded Conrad, ridden by Martin Beecher. Beecher, a former soldier, had been seriously considering retiring but was persuaded to postpone retirement to ride Conrad. Conrad had a good start and led the field until the first major obstacle – the first of two brooks. On the approach Conrad pulled up sharply and Beecher was thrown over his head into the brook. From that day that first obstacle became known as 'Beecher's Brook'.

1918: A devastating fire in the Happy Valley Racecourse in Hong Kong on their 'Derby Day' sees the loss of 614 lives. With horseracing becoming increasingly popular among the locals a temporary grandstand was erected for the Derby Day. Tragically this structure collapsed on to food stalls, many of which had stoves, and the bamboo matting caught fire and rapidly spread. Sadder still, the fire was so intense that the majority of those who lost their lives could not be recognised (and in 1918 there was no 'identification by dental records' or similar).

1977: Birth of Welsh international rugby union winger Shane Williams. He scored his first international try exactly a week before his 23rd birthday, and scored a total of 60 tries in a 12-year career with Wales. He remains Wales's top try scorer, the highest of all time in the northern hemisphere, and the fourth highest overall.

27 February

1874: Lord's Cricket Ground hosts the first game of baseball to be played in the UK.

1900: Munich gymnastic club (aka MTV 1879) caters for a wide array of different sports, including football (which was basically played as a hobby). On this date the club formally decided that those interested in football would not be permitted to join the German Football Association. Immediately following this announcement 11 members of the club quit and founded Fußball-Club Bayern München (aka FC Bayern Munich).

1921: Death of Yorkshire and England bowler Schofield Haigh. In a career spanning 18 seasons Haigh took 2,012 wickets at an average of 15.94 – of all the bowlers who have taken 1,000 or more wickets, this average is second only to Hedley Verity (who also played for Yorkshire and England).

1959: The Los Angeles Rams buy running back Ollie Matson from the Chicago Cardinals in exchange for nine players. Matson had been the third pick overall in the 1952 draft, the same year he won two Olympic medals – a bronze in the 400m race, and a silver in the 4x400m relay.

1977: Sixteen-year-old Diego Maradona (full name: Diego Armando Maradona Franco) makes his full international debut for Argentina against Hungary, coming on as a substitute in Argentina's 5-1 victory.

1994: The end of the XVII Olympic Winter Games, the Lillehammer Winter Olympics in Norway. Sixty-seven countries participated in 61 events, 14 of which were making their Olympic debuts (many were former Soviet republics). Kim Yoon-Mi of South Korea, the 3,000m speed skater, became the Games' youngest ever gold medal winner at 13. Russia won the Games with 11 gold medals.

28 February

1880: England are the first-ever winners of rugby's Calcutta Cup when they beat Scotland by two goals and three tries to one goal.

1942: Birth of Italian goalkeeper Dino Zoff. He also holds the world record for the longest playing time without conceding a goal in international tournaments – 1,142 minutes between 1972 and 1974.

1988: The final day (of two) of the four-man bobsleigh competition in the Calgary Winter Olympics in Canada. But, as can happen in Olympics, the headlines were grabbed by the team coming last rather than the winners. In last place was the Jamaican bobsleigh team, the only time they have competed in such an event.

2014: Indian batsman Bhuvneshwar Kumar becomes only the second batsman in one-day internationals to be out for a diamond duck. Several batsmen have been run out without facing a single delivery, but this was rather odder. A golden duck is a batsman getting out on the first delivery that they face. A diamond duck is a batsman managing to get themselves out without facing any legitimate deliveries … although they have still batted. The first ball Kumar faced from Sri Lankan Ajantha Mendis was signalled wide by the umpire … but he still went for it, and was stumped by the wicketkeeper. So this gave him the diamond duck.

2015: Rugby union winger George North plays for Wales against France. The game marked North's 50th international cap at the age of 22 years and 322 days, the youngest age that this total has ever been achieved at – smashing the previous best by more than a year. (By way of comparison, at the same age Johnny Wilkinson had won 34 caps, Dan Carter had 24, Richie McCaw and Jonah Lomu both had 20, Bryan Habana had 15, Martin Johnson had one and Shane Williams had none!)

29 February

1964: Australian swimmer Dawn Fraser sets a new world record for the 100m freestyle in a time of 58.9 seconds, swimming in the Olympic trials in Sydney.

1992: Birth of Paralympic swimmer Jessica Long, one of the most decorated Olympic medallists of all time. She swam in the S8 and the SB7 classes. In the Athens Games of 2004, while she was still just 12, she won gold medals in the 100m freestyle, the 400m freestyle and the 4x100m freestyle. Through to and including the 2016 Games in Rio, Long had won 13 gold medals, six silver and four bronze, remarkably winning individual medals in all four swimming strokes.

2008: The first day of the Test match between South Africa and Bangladesh in Chittagong sees South Africa winning the toss and deciding to bat first. Openers Neil McKenzie and captain Graeme Smith came out to face the Bangladesh attack – and by the end of the day they were still there, having scored 405 runs. They only added ten more the following day, but their partnership of 415 remains the highest ever for a first wicket pair in Tests – beating the previous best by just two runs. McKenzie finished with 226, six runs fewer than his captain.

MARCH

1 March

1839: Formation of Sussex County Cricket Club – England's oldest county cricket team. Their first first-class match was just three months later against the MCC at Lord's.

1898: Guildford in Surrey hosts the very first Badminton Open tournament.

1913: Formation of the International Lawn Tennis Federation. The groundwork, planning and organisation were done by an American called Duane Williams, but he sadly never saw his labours come to fruition as he had died the previous year as a passenger on board RMS *Titanic*. The word 'Lawn' was dropped from the title in 1977 in recognition of the fact that few tennis tournaments were still played on grass.

1921: Jules Rimet is elected as the third president of FIFA, a position he would hold for a record 33 years. During the First World War Rimet fought as an officer in the French army and was awarded a Croix de Guerre. Rimet organised the first World Cup finals tournament in 1930. He chose Uruguay as the venue after the Uruguayan Football Association offered to pay the travel expenses of all the other teams. Rimet himself travelled to the finals on board the SS *Conte Verde* with the newly created World Cup trophy in his hand luggage.

1949: World heavyweight boxing champion Joe Louis (aka the Brown Bomber) announces his retirement from the sport at the age of 34. His reign as champion had lasted 140 consecutive months and included 26 successful defences of his title – the most for any heavyweight boxer.

1958: The West Indies declare their first innings closed at the end of day four of the third Test against Pakistan at Kingston in Jamaica. Twenty-one-year-old Gary Sobers remained unbeaten on 365 which was, at the time, the highest Test match score of ever.

2 March

1672: Musselburgh Links in East Lothian, Scotland, is acknowledged as the oldest golf course in the world. The first definite record of play taking place there was on this date, although names and results have been lost over time.

1949: Birth of legendary Welsh rugby full-back J.P.R. Williams (John Peter Rhys Williams). He started his career as John Williams, and only changed to using his initials when J.J. Williams (also John) started playing for Wales.

1969: Phil Esposito scores for the Boston Bruins to become the first player in NHL history to score 100 points in a single season. By the end of the season he had thrashed the previous record, with a total of 126 points.

2004: Death of Gaelic footballer Cormac McAnallen at the age of just 24. As well as being a highly successful Gaelic footballer, McAnallen was a very good hurler, and also won awards while at school in junior basketball. He died of Sudden Adult Death Syndrome, from an undetected heart condition.

3 March

1875: The first-ever final of the Inter-Hospital Challenge Cup, now the oldest rugby cup competition in the world. The match is played at The Oval. Guy's Hospital beat St George's Hospital by one goal and one try to two tries (in modern scoring that is 12 points to 10). This cup has been played for without interruption since that first final.

1883: Having beaten Wales a few weeks earlier England complete what is now recognised as a Triple Crown by beating Scotland in Edinburgh by two tries to one. England exploited gaps in the Scottish defence by fielding six backs to the five of Scotland.

1924: At the age of 17 years and 157 days Frank Hewitt becomes the youngest player in the Five Nations rugby championship (now the Six Nations) – a record which remains unbeaten. Not only did Hewitt start at fly-half for Ireland against Wales in Cardiff, he even scored the opening try in a narrow Irish victory.

2005: Death of Dutch footballer and coach Rinus Michels, named by FIFA as the 'Coach of the Century'. Michels was the genius behind the expansive approach commonly known as 'Total Football'.

2011: Atlético Claypole's home soccer fixture against Victoriano in Argentina ends prematurely and in utter chaos. Fighting and ill discipline had been present throughout the game until it finally erupted. The referee Damián Rubino decided enough was enough – and issued 36 red cards … all 22 players on the pitch and the full set of seven substitutes for both teams.

2018: American cyclist Chloe Dygert sets a new world record for women in the 3,000m individual pursuit. At the World Championships in the Netherlands, she sets a time of three minutes and 20.060 seconds.

4 March

1897: Birth of influential baseball coach Lefty O'Doul. As coach of the San Fransisco Seals he coached a young Joe DiMaggio, although he refused to claim any credit for DiMaggio's skills, simply saying 'I was just smart enough to leave him alone'.

1913: In establishing a training camp in Bermuda, the New York Yankees become the first baseball team to train outside of the United States.

1971: Benjamin Odeje becomes the first black player to represent England at football. Born in Nigeria of Jamaican parents, Odeje moved to England at a young age and became a naturalised citizen.

Scoring 400 goals in three years at schoolboy level brought him to the attention of the powers that be, and he was selected to play the schoolboy international against Northern Ireland at Wembley.

1993: Basketball legend Michael Jordan and tennis star Monica Seles become the first winners of the ESPY Awards (Excellence in Sports Performance Yearly).

2008: Manchester United midfielder Darren Fletcher has to miss a couple of weeks with a head injury and mild concussion. This was not a football injury. Fletcher was sitting down minding his own business (or doing his own business) in a public toilet, when the door fell off its hinges and hit him on the head.

2009: Peter Lovenkrands scores the first goal for Newcastle to put them 1-0 up against Manchester United, breaking United goalkeeper Edwin van der Sar's incredible run – 1,311 minutes in the Premier League without conceding a goal (that's more than 14 matches).

5 March

1870: The first international football match is organised by the Football Association between England and Scotland. This was also the first time that teams had changed ends at half-time. Robert Crawford became the first international goalscorer to give Scotland the lead, before Alfred Baker equalised. In the Scotland team was the MP W.H. Gladstone, who was the son of the sitting Prime Minister William Gladstone.

1949: Day two of the four-day match between South Australia and Victoria in Adelaide in a Sheffield Shield match. Resuming on 57/3 South Australia were bowled out for 154, with Don Bradman top scoring with 30. This would turn out to be Bradman's last first-class innings. Sports journalist Vivian Jenkins reflected: 'If W.G. Grace put cricket on the map, Bradman held it there and made it glow with incandescent heat. What a man, and what a record.'

1977: On lap 22 of the South African Grand Prix, Renzo Zorzi suffers engine failure in his Shadow Ford and pulls over to the side of the track. Two stewards raced across the track with fire extinguishers. Sadly Fredrik van Vuuren misjudged his run and was hit by Welsh driver Tom Pryce (in the other Shadow Ford), and was killed in the collision. In a freak accident the fire extinguisher that he had been holding flew out of his hands straight into the face of Pryce who was also killed instantly. Niki Lauda won his first race since his own horrible crash the previous year, but couldn't celebrate, saying 'There was no joy after that.' van Vuuren's body was so badly mutilated that it was only identified by the race director calling all the race stewards in to see who was missing.

1982: Birth of New Zealand All Blacks rugby union fly-half Dan Carter, widely regarded as one of the finest players of all time and the highest point scorer in Test match rugby.

1995: Death of Australian motorbike and touring car racing driver Gregg Hansford. Racing in the Supertouring series in Victoria he lost control of his car and hit a tyre wall. His Ford Mondeo bounced back on to the track where it was hit at full speed by Mark Adderton's Peugeot 405.

2005: The death of Baron Sheppard of Liverpool, better known by sports fans as the Rev. David Sheppard, who played cricket for Sussex and England. He is the only ordained minister to have played Test cricket for England. After retiring from the game he continued in his vocation, reaching the position of Bishop of Liverpool.

6 March

1902: Foundation of Madrid Football Club. Within three years they had won the Spanish Cup, and in 1909 they became one of the founding sides of the Royal Spanish Football Federation. The prefix 'Real' is simply Spanish for Royal – a title granted to the club in 1920 by King Alfonso XIII.

1907: A Canadian ice hockey fixture between Cornwall Hockey Club and Ottawa Victorias degenerates into an on-ice brawl early in the second period. The brawl seemed to centre on Cornwall player Bud McCourt, who was beaten around the head with sticks several times. He was carried from the ice in an unconscious state, and died early the following morning.

1922: Legendary baseball player Babe Ruth signs a new contract with the New York Yankees valued at $52,000 a year. Clearly a relatively small sum in today's market (current equivalent ~$750,000), what marked Ruth's contract out as unique was that it represented 40 per cent of the total value set aside for players' wages by the Yankees.

1963: Coventry City play Lincoln City in the FA Cup. This was an FA Cup third round tie which had actually been scheduled to be played on 5 January. From Christmas Eve Lincoln was buried in snow, so the match was postponed for four days. There was no change in the ground conditions, so it was postponed again. Finally, after 15 postponements and a delay of 63 days they eventually managed to get the game played. Coventry City won 5-1.

2010: Death of Nigerian footballer Endurance Idahor, who played in Sudan for Al-Merreikh and for the U23 Nigerian national team. Idahor collapsed on the pitch playing for Al-Merreikh and died on the way to the hospital. He was just 25 years old.

7 March

1744: Edinburgh City Council agree to the request by Lord Forbes of the establishment of The Honourable Company of Edinburgh Golfers – the first official golf club in the world. Members initially met in Luckie Clephan's tavern at Leith, and set up the first official golf competition, an annual challenge on the Links course at Leith. The winner of that tournament would become 'Captain of the Golf' for the following year.

1857: The organisers and administrators of baseball decree that a match should be decided over nine innings, rather than the first team to score nine runs.

1952: Birth of West Indies batsman and captain Viv Richards, one of the most flamboyant batsmen of all time. To welcome in the new millennium a group of experts named the five greatest cricketers of the 20th century, and Richards was included along with Don Bradman, Garry Sobers, Jack Hobbs and Shane Warne.

1968: Death of Grenville Hair, who had played 443 times for Leeds United in a 16-year career. He was supervising a training session with Bradford City when he just collapsed and died before any help could be summoned. The autopsy revealed he had died of a heart attack. He was just 36 years old.

2009: In the World Cup event in Salt Lake City Shani Davis breaks the record for speed skating over the 1,000m distance in a time of one minute and 6.42 seconds, giving an average speed of 54.20kmh (33.7mph).

2012: Barcelona beat Bayer Leverkusen 7-1, during which Barcelona's Argentinean striker Lionel Messi becomes the first person to score five goals in a match in Champions League history.

2016: American football quarterback Peyton Manning announces his retirement from the sport: 'I've fought a good fight. I've finished my football race and after 18 years, it's time. God bless all of you and God bless America.' Considered as one of the finest ballplayers of all time Manning still holds many NFL records, including passing yards (71,940), Pro Bowl appearances (14) and touchdown passes (539).

8 March

1873: Alexander Morten becomes England's oldest debutant in a football match between England and Scotland – a record he still holds nearly 150 years later (and presumably always will!). Morten was about 42 at the time – his exact age cannot be determined since his date of birth was officially recorded as simply '1831–1832'.

1888: The British and Irish Lions leave Britain to begin their first-ever tour. The tour was particularly significant in terms of the workload, particularly in comparison to modern players. The tour lasted for eight months, and only 22 players were taken – but the team still fitted in 53 matches on their travels!

1924: Eighteen-year-old Tom Hewitt scores a try on his international debut to become the youngest try scorer for Ireland, but he doesn't hold the record for long! Later in the same game his 17-year-old brother Frank also scored a try, also on his debut. Tom's record stood for about 20 minutes; Frank's record is still standing nearly 100 years later.

1971: The 'Fight of the Century'. For the first time ever two undefeated boxers fought each other for the heavyweight title. 'Smokin' Joe Frazier held the WBC and WBA heavyweight titles, with a record of 26 straight wins, 23 by knockout. Muhammad Ali held *The Ring* and the Lineal heavyweight titles after 31 straight wins, 25 by knockout. The fight took place in Madison Square Garden, and Frazier won by the unanimous decision of the judges after 15 rounds.

9 March

1908: Following a split from the Milan Cricket and Football Club (which subsequently morphed into AC Milan), Football Club Internazionale are formed. The name reflected the desire of the new owners to incorporate foreign players into the team, not just locals. Internazionale joined the league the following year, and won it at their first attempt. Virgilio Fossati, who fulfilled the double role of coach and captain, was killed in the trenches during the First World War.

1946: The FA Cup sixth-round tie between Bolton Wanderers and Stoke City attracts a crowd of more than 85,000 people. The oversized crowd pushed and pressed with several falling in the melee, and the teams were taken off the pitch. Tragically 33 people died in the crush. Injured people were shipped off to hospital, while the dead were removed to the edge of the pitch and covered in coats to maintain some measure of dignity. After half an hour the game restarted with sawdust laid down along the touchline to separate the players from the dead bodies which still lay at the side of the pitch. Stoke City legend Stanley Matthews, who was playing, said he was disgusted that the game was allowed to continue.

2007: The official opening of the new Wembley Stadium. The old stadium was demolished in 2003, and the rebuild and redevelopment had taken four years at a cost of £789 million. The new stadium has 90,000 seats, making it the largest stadium in the UK, and has a circumference of 1km (0.62 miles). It also houses a world record 2,618 toilets.

2013: Bernard Hopkins defeats Tavoris Cloud in a unanimous points decision after 12 rounds to claim the IBF world light heavyweight championship. At the age of 48 Hopkins became the oldest ever world boxing champion.

10 March

1300: Official court records of the royal accounts show refunds paid by King Edward I to John de Leek of money he had originally paid to enable Prince Edward to 'play creag and other games' at both Westminster and Newenden (in Kent). Some historians believe 'creag' was an early form of cricket, others think it was more of a 'golf-type game'.

1845: The Crown express a willingness to lease the land of Kennington Common for the use of establishing a cricket club. The lease was £140 per year including tax, and the club's organisers agreed a further expenditure of £300 for turf that was brought over from Tooting Common. Everything was ready within a couple of months, and Surrey County Cricket Club was born.

1926: Birth of basketball legend Marques Haynes, best known as a member of the Harlem Globetrotters. Haynes could dribble a basketball at an astonishing rate of nearly 350 bounces per minute. He played about 12,000 games in more than 100 countries.

1985: The final of the first World Championship of Cricket, a three-week tournament hosted by Australia, with India beating Pakistan by eight wickets. With the World Cup already established organisers did not see the need for an alternative, so the World Championship of Cricket was never staged again.

2012: Death of Canadian ski cross skier Nikola Zoricic in Grindelwald, Switzerland. Zoricic was taking part in a World Cup event when he ran wide on the final jump and fell. He crashed head first into the lining of the course and suffered skull and brain trauma. He was airlifted to hospital but was pronounced dead on arrival.

11 March

1885: Birth of British motor enthusiast and racer Malcolm Campbell (later Major Sir Malcolm Campbell). Campbell held speed records both on land and on water, a tradition that was continued by his son Donald. He was the first car racer to drive in excess of 300mph (480kmh).

1892: The first-ever public game of basketball is played in Springfield, Massachusetts. The game was played at the International Young Men Christian Association training school between the teachers and the students, with the students winning 5-1.

1894: Death of England Test batsman John Selby who, in 1877, becomes the first English batsman ever to be dismissed.

After Australia won the toss in that first Test and elected to bat Selby made his England debut as a wicketkeeper ... because the recognised keeper in the touring party had been arrested and was in jail in New Zealand. Selby died at the age of 44 after suffering a paralytic stroke.

1903: Birth of New Zealand sportsman George Dickinson. After a very successful junior rugby career he was selected to play for the All Blacks on tour at the age of just 19. Dickinson decided to retire from first-class rugby at the age of just 21, opting instead to play the gentler game of cricket as a pace bowler. Later that year he became the first 'double all black' when he represented his country at cricket.

1929: British racing driver Major Henry Segrave sets a new land speed record of 231.4mph (372.5kmh). Segrave held speed records on land and on water at various stages.

1959: The first-ever World Curling Championship takes place over three days in Scotland, with Canada becoming champions. The entire Canadian team were related (brothers and cousins) and were all called Richardson: Wes, Garnet, Arnold and Ernie.

1982: Birth of Pakistan cricketer Hasan Raza. Raza made his Test match debut against Zimbabwe at the age of just 14 years and 233 days, the youngest age ever for a Test cricketer.

1995: Death of 29-year-old Swedish ice hockey player Lars Karlsson. He died after being stabbed by a skinhead with a large knife. The evidence gathered by the police indicated that the attack was probably homophobic.

12 March

1862: The 24th running of the Grand National at Aintree. O'Connell fell at the 15th ('The Chair'). He was led back to the stables but died later of internal injuries. His jockey, Joe Wynne, also died of injuries sustained in the first (and, to date, only) human fatality of the National.

1881: Andrew Watson of Queen's Park is selected to play for Scotland against England – the first black player to represent the Scots. He was handed the captaincy and led his team to a 6-1 victory. The next black player to play for Scotland was Nigel Quashie in 2004 ... 123 years later.

1881: The Welsh rugby union is formed in Neath. Attending sides forming the original union were Bangor, Brecon, Cardiff, Lampeter, Llandilo, Llandovery, Llanelli, Merthyr, Newport, Pontypool and Swansea.

1988: A football match between Janakpur Cigarette Factory Ltd and the Liberation Army of Bangladesh in Kathmandu, Nepal, is interrupted by a hailstorm. The storm was so severe that the vast majority of the crowd fled for shelter. In the ensuing chaos 93 people were trampled to death.

2006: In the one-day international cricket decider Australia post a massive score of 434 in their 50 overs. South Africa scored 438/9 to win with one ball remaining, with Australian bowler Mick Lewis going for 113 runs off his ten overs. He never played for Australia again.

13 March

1873: At a meeting called by representatives of Queen's Park Football Club, the Scottish Football Association is formed. Included in the business of the day was an agreement that the clubs would subscribe for a challenge cup which would be contested annually.

1878: The first-ever varsity golf match sees Oxford beat Cambridge on the neutral territory of Wimbledon Common as guests of the London Scottish Golf Club.

1918: Death of Reggie Pridmore serving as a major with the Royal Field Artillery in Italy during the First World War. Pridmore won Olympic gold with Britain in the 1908 field hockey final in which he scored ten of England's goals in their three matches. He was also a very fine cricketer, playing first-class matches for Warwickshire.

1938: French cyclist Francois Faure becomes the first cyclist to cover more than 50km in one hour when he covers 50.537km at an outdoor velodrome in France.

1991: During the English Amateur Snooker Championship Ronnie O'Sullivan becomes the youngest player ever to compile a maximum 147 break in tournament play at the age of just 15 years and 98 days.

14 March

1765: Death of legendary sumo wrestler Ayagawa Gorōji. Records from the date are sketchy, but it is believed he was about 6ft 7in (~2m) tall and weighed about 23st 8lb (150kg). He was considered the second yokozuna (the highest rank within sumo wrestling).

1939: The fifth Test match between South Africa and England at Durban ends in a draw. South Africa scored 530 and 481 in their two innings, while England replied with 316 and 654/5 before they ran out of time after 218.2 overs. The match was truly unique, having started on the third day and having two rest days … the only Test match lasting ten days (and still not enough time to get a result!).

1986: Birth of Australian paralympic polymath Jessica Gallagher, who represents her country in skiing, athletics and cycling. She was Australia's first female paralympic medal winner, competing in the alpine skiing slalom for visually impaired athletes. Legally blind, Gallagher represented Australia at the 2011 Athletics World Championships, winning a silver medal in the long jump and bronze in the javelin. She was then selected for the cycling team in the 2016 Paralympics. As a junior she also represented her state in both netball and basketball.

1988: Birth of basketball player Wardell Curry II, considered by many to be the greatest shooter of all time. In the 2012/13 season Curry set a new NBA record for three-pointers when he scored 272. Two years later he beat his own record with 286, and then in 2015/16 he scored a totally unprecedented 402.

2017: Scotland's Muirfield, the oldest golf club in the world, finally votes to accept women as members after 273 years as a male-only domain. The owners, The Honourable Company of Edinburgh Golfers, said that 80 per cent of members had voted for the change. The vote, however, was not a belated attempt to get in line with modern society, but a knee-jerk reaction on losing the right to hold the prestigious British Open because of the misogynistic traditions.

15 March

1866: The first cricket Test match begins – England vs Australia played at Melbourne Cricket Ground. Australia won by 45 runs.

1869: The Cincinnati Red Stockings become the first professional baseball team, announcing their professionalism on the day that they beat Antioch 41-7.

1877: James Southerton initially works as a hairdresser from leaving school, and does not begin to play cricket until he is already into his thirties. He was eventually called up to the England Test team – at 49 years and 119 days he is the oldest ever cricket international debutant, and with the increased demands of the modern game that is a record that is unlikely ever to be broken.

1892: Formation of Liverpool Football Club. Up to this point in time Everton had been playing at Anfield, but then got into a financial dispute with the ground's owner John Houlding. Unable to find a resolution Everton moved out and relocated to Goodison Park, which left Houlding with an empty stadium; so he decided to set up his own team which he called Liverpool. It was just nine years later that this team formed from absolutely nothing went on to win their first Division One title.

1971: Death of Jean-Pierre 'Jempi' Monseré, the Belgian road cyclist. The reigning world champion, he was racing in Retie near Antwerp in the Grote Jaarmarktprijs when he collided with a car being driven on the course and died.

2015: Max Verstappen lines up in 11th place on the grid for the Australian Grand Prix. At 17 years and 166 days the Toro Rosso Renault driver was the youngest man ever to start a Formula One race.

16 March

1872: The first-ever Football Association Challenge Cup Final (now known as simply the FA Cup) – making it the oldest cup competition in the world. The final was between Wanderers and Royal Engineers. Wanderers won 1-0 with a goal from Morton Betts (who for some reason, which has been lost over time, was playing under the name A.H. Chequer). Betts was a full-back who had just wandered forward and scored a tap-in. He gained one England cap, as a goalkeeper, and played first-class cricket for both Middlesex and Kent. Sadly the Wanderers did not get to lift the cup … because it wasn't ready! They were given a special reception at a Pall Mall restaurant about a month later at which they were presented with the trophy.

1876: New York is the scene of the first-ever all-female boxing match. The protagonists were Irishwoman Nelly Saunders and Rose Harland from England. They were persuaded to give the public spectacle with a lure of a $200 prize and a silver plate. Saunders won by one point, and the two women left the stage with their arms around each other.

1941: Death of footballer Bob Compton. He played more than 500 times for Blackburn Rovers over a period of 23 years, and was in his second spell as their manager when he had a heart attack in the dugout during a home game. He was rushed to hospital but died later that evening.

1994: Death of baseball pitcher Eric Show at the age of 37. He played his entire career for the San Diego Padres, playing in their first World Series team. Upon retirement he struggled with addiction to alcohol and drugs, and stayed at a drug rehabilitation centre where he was discovered by staff one morning dead in his room.

2002: The Division One match between Sheffield United and West Bromwich Albion is abandoned in the 83rd minute in rather unusual circumstances. Sheffield United had already had three players sent off when Michael Brown limped off … but they had already used all three substitutes, so now had just seven players on the pitch. Another five minutes and Robert Ullathorne was carried off. It was at this point that the referee invoked Law 3 of the IFA guidelines, which recommends 'that a match should not continue if there are fewer than seven players in either team'.

2013: Larry Chloupek II completes the Washington DC Rock and Roll Marathon in a record five hours, 37 minutes and 43 seconds – a marathon record for anyone with just one leg, using crutches. Chloupek had been an amputee since the age of seven having lost one leg to bone cancer.

2018: Canadian boxer David Whittom passes away. Whittom was knocked down in a bout with fellow Canadian Gary Kopas and immediately suffered a brain haemorrhage and was rushed into hospital. He then spent ten months in a medically induced coma before dying, never regaining consciousness. The fight actually took place on 27 May 2017.

17 March

1874: Death of Kincsem, the most successful thoroughbred racehorse ever, with a record of 54 wins from 54 starts. She was foaled in Hungary (Kincsem is Hungarian for 'My Precious'), and won races throughout Europe. In attempting to win the Grosser von Baden in Germany for the second time the judges ruled it a dead heat, so the two horses had to have a run-off to decide the winner!

1876: Englishman Marshall Brooks, an amateur athlete, becomes the first person ever to clear 6ft (1.83m) at the high jump. Brooks, an Oxford Blue, also won one international cap for England playing full-back in rugby union.

1954: Spain and Turkey draw 2-2 in a World Cup qualifying round match. Spain then became the first team ever to be eliminated from the World Cup on the toss of a coin.

1974: The first match is played in the inaugural women's hockey World Cup.

1958: Death of John Boland, a Member of Parliament representing the Irish Nationalist Parliamentary Party between 1900 and 1918. Before politics Boland had been one of the stars at the first modern Olympics in 1896, winning two gold medals in tennis. In the doubles, with no British tennis players available, he joined up with German Friedrich Traun, who was more of an athlete than a tennis player, competing in the 800m and the long jump. This 'united team' surprised everyone by winning the gold medal. When the Union Jack and the German flag were hoisted up the flagpole together Boland was indignant, insisting he was Irish and informing everyone 'It's a gold harp on a green ground, we hope.'

18 March

1877: Birth of Australian cricket batsman Clem Hill. In 1902 Hill became the first batsman ever to score 1,000 runs in a calendar year – a feat that would not be matched until 1947. During the Ashes series of 1901/02 Hill bore the unique (and unfortunate) distinction of scoring 99, 98 and 97 in consecutive innings.

1949: Birth of Northern Ireland snooker legend Alex 'Hurricane' Higgins. Higgins was always a crowd favourite due to the flair with which he played the game. He originally left Belfast and came to England intent on becoming a jockey, but was too heavy so returned home deciding to focus on snooker instead. Higgins won the 1983 UK Championship in one of the most remarkable finals on record. Steve Davis won the first session 7-0, and Higgins slowly clawed the deficit back to eventually win 16-15.

1963: Day three of the third Test between New Zealand and England. England bowled New Zealand out for 159 – the lowest ever total for any international team in which a player scored a century. New Zealand captain John Reid scored exactly 100, an impressive 62.9 per cent of his team's total.

2007: Death of Bob Woolmer in Jamaica where he is coaching the Pakistani cricket team in the World Cup. Woolmer had watched his team surprisingly knocked out of the tournament at the hands of Ireland. Given his age and fitness, and the extraordinary result of the match, local police suspected foul play and opened an investigation. Eventually they recorded an open verdict, stating there was not enough evidence to confirm the cause of death.

2018: The conclusion of the World Cup skiing event sees Norwegian cross-country skier Marit Bjørgen awarded overall first place and the gold medal. Immediately after the competition she announced her retirement from competition just three days short of her 38th birthday. She had won an impressive 15 Olympic medals (eight gold) and 26 World Championship medals (18 gold). But it was at the annual World Cup skiing that her record was most amazing, with 126 podiums including 84 victories.

19 March

1843: The first known public skiing competition takes place in Tromsø, Norway. While clear documentary evidence of the competition exists there is no known record of the result.

1938: The Calcutta Cup game between England and Scotland is the first international rugby game ever to be shown live on television. Since both teams had already beaten Wales the game had an added significance in ensuring the Triple Crown. In perfect conditions Scotland won 21-16.

1943: World featherweight champion Willie Pep loses to Sammy Angott – the first defeat in his entire career after 62 straight victories. The modern era of boxing sees most professionals fighting just two or three bouts a year, which marks Pep's record as quite remarkable. He fought for 26 years, accumulating 241 fights, an average of a fight roughly every 40 days. In this period he had 229 victories (65 by knockout), and the result against Angott was his only defeat with 11 no results.

1972: The final of the first-ever AIAW (Association for Intercollegiate Athletics for Women) women's basketball tournament. Immaculata, the private Roman Catholic University from Pennsylvania, were crowned the first national champions, beating West Chester State University 52-48.

1990: The start of the inaugural IIHF (International Ice Hockey Federation) women's world championship. The opening fixture saw the hosts and eventual winners Canada thrash Sweden 15-1.

20 March

1940: The World Snooker Championship final concludes with the closest finish ever. World number one Joe Davis beats his younger brother Fred 37-36 in the final.

1966: In preparation for the World Cup tournament being held in England, the iconic Jules Rimet trophy is placed on display at Westminster Central Hall. On this date the trophy was stolen, although the exact method of the theft remains uncertain. The trophy was recovered just seven days later by a dog called Pickles. It was wrapped in newspaper and lying under a garden hedge in South London.

1976: In a Division One match at Filbert Street Aston Villa claim a 2-2 draw away to Leicester City. What marked the result out as unique was the goalscorer … all four goals were scored by Aston Villa's centre-back Chris Nicholl.

1990: Death of Soviet goalkeeper Lev Yashin, aka the 'Black Spider'. Frequently regarded as the best goalkeeper of all time, he saved a record 150 penalty kicks. In 1963 he won the Ballon d'Or – the only goalkeeper ever to win the award.

2010: Tom Prydie makes his debut for the Welsh rugby team in the Six Nations Championship against Italy. Prydie was just 18 years and 25 days old, and his inclusion in the team was a surprise – he had made his professional debut just three months earlier and had only played 167 minutes for the Ospreys.

21 March

1935: Birth of Brian Clough, the legendary English football manager, remembered as being highly controversial but influential. He was such a purist when it came to the style of play and avoiding the long ball game that he once said, 'If God had wanted us to play football in the clouds, he'd have put grass up there.'

1964: The first world championships for the trampoline are held in the Royal Albert Hall. Representatives from 12 different countries took part, with American Dan Millman winning the men's title and the gold medal. American Judy Wills won the women's event.

1992: Sheffield United opt to kick off against Chelsea, and immediately Chelsea hardman midfield player Vinnie Jones launches into a typical bone-shaking tackle. Jones therefore became the recipient of the fastest yellow card in English league history … after three seconds.

2010: Eritrean long-distance runner Zersenay Tadese takes the world record for a half-marathon, completing the 21km race in Lisbon in a time of 58 minutes and 23 seconds.

22 March

1866: The first Nottingham derby sees Notts County play against the newly formed Nottingham Forest, initially founded as a multi-sport organisation. As well as forming a football team Forest also became British baseball champions in 1899. In 1886 Forest gave their old kit to Arsenal to help get them started (Forest had just purchased a new kit) – which is why Arsenal play in red.

1888: The first step towards the formation of an English football league. William McGregor, director of Aston Villa, wrote to the directors of the football clubs of Blackburn Rovers, Bolton Wanderers, Preston North End, Stoke and West Bromwich Albion suggesting an annual competition where everyone played everyone in a league format – guaranteeing a set number of fixtures each year.

1896: The first officially recognised marathon race. With Greece preparing for the Olympic Games, athletics fever had gripped the nation. Of special interest was the proposed new marathon – with literally dozens of men wanting to run the race. Realising they needed to restrict numbers, the organisers introduced qualifying heats … and this date marked the first heat, won by Charilaos Vasilakos in a time of three hours and 18 minutes. Vasilakos therefore qualified for the Games where he won the silver medal. Spiridon Louis, who won the Olympic gold medal, came through the second qualifying heat. The Olympic final itself attracted 17 competitors – 13 of whom came from Greece.

1929: The 88th running of the Grand National at Aintree sees the largest ever field for the event, with 66 runners and riders. The race was won by 100-1 outsider Gregalach.

1934: Day one of the first-ever Masters Tournament held at the Augusta National Golf Club in Georgia. For the first five years of tournament play it was officially called the 'Augusta National Invitation Tournament', but was commonly referred to as the Masters from the beginning. American Horton Smith won this inaugural event by one stroke, claiming the first prize of $1,500.

1987: Race one of the first World Touring Car Championship. Fifteen car and driver combinations were entered, despite promoter Bernie Ecclestone setting a $60,000 registration fee. The opening race was at Monza in Italy, and featured all 15 championship teams and a lot more who were simply entering the race but not the championship. Indeed, the winning championship entry actually came sixth in the race.

1989: During an ice hockey game between Buffalo Sabres and St Louis Blues, Uwe Krupp and Steve Tuttle clash heavily near the goal. Tuttle's skate rammed into Clint Malarchuk's neck as he fell, severing his jugular vein and puncturing his carotid artery. Malarchuk bled heavily, but still managed to walk off the ice – causing three players to be sick on the ice, 11 spectators to faint and two to have heart attacks. Malarchuk later explained: 'All I wanted to do was get off the ice. My mother was watching the game on TV, and I didn't want her to see me die.' He lost 1.5 litres of blood, and needed 300 stitches on the wound, but was back on the ice just ten days later.

2012: New York Yankees relief pitcher Joba Chamberlain is injured and is not able to play again until August. This was very frustrating for the Yankees because Chamberlain had only recently signed a new one-year contract for $1.675m. But it wasn't baseball that laid him low – Chamberlain dislocated his ankle while bouncing on a trampoline with his children.

2015: The winner of the Lisbon half-marathon, Mo Farah, becomes the first British runner to break the one-hour barrier for the distance. Farah crossed the line with a time of 59 minutes and 32 seconds. Unfortunately he got tangled up in the winner's tape and ended up falling over and cutting his knee.

23 March

1929: Birth of English middle-distance runner Roger Bannister, the first man to break the four-minute barrier in running a mile, a feat he accomplishes in Oxford in 1954 with an exact recorded time of 3.59.4. He would later confess that his preparations had actually been inadequate as he was too busy in his day job as a neurologist. When asked whether the four-minute mile was his proudest achievement he replied that he felt that was rather insignificant compared to his work in academic medicine.

1952: Ice hockey star Billy Mosienko breaks a world record. Playing for the Chicago Black Hawks in the NHL, Mosienko scored a hat-trick against the New York Rangers in just 21 seconds. He almost scored four in 45 seconds, but his fourth shot hit the post.

1962: Birth of Steve Redgrave, the British rower who won gold medals rowing in the coxless pairs and coxless fours in five consecutive Olympic Games. He also won three gold medals at Commonwealth Games, and a further nine golds in world championship events.

Sir Steve Redgrave

Born: 23 March 1962

British rower who won gold medals at five consecutive Olympic Games

1963: Death of American boxer Davey Moore at the age of 29, who collapses just a few seconds after being knocked out by Sugar Ramos. The fight was shown live on national television. In the tenth round Moore was eventually knocked down by a series of blows, but unfortunately fell with his neck landing on the bottom rope, injuring his brain stem. Despite Moore managing to get back to his feet the referee stopped the bout. Back in the dressing room, Moore quickly slipped into a coma. He died 75 hours later having not regained consciousness.

1980: It is rare for a cricketer to score a century in both innings of a match, but Australian captain Allan Border goes one better against Pakistan in scoring a century and a half in both innings. On this date he was dismissed for 153 in the second innings to go with his unbeaten 150 from the first innings.

1991: The first games in the newly formed World League of American Football (later renamed the NFL Europe League). Seven of the ten teams were based in North America, with the other three from Europe. On this opening day of fixtures London Monarchs beat Frankfurt Galaxy 24-11, Sacramento Surge won at Raleigh-Durham Skyhawks 9-3 and Montreal Machine beat Birmingham Fire 20-5. The NFL Europe League disbanded in 2007.

1997: The Rugby World Cup Sevens tournament final sees Fiji beating South Africa 24-21 to claim the title. This was the final major sporting event played in Hong Kong under British rule before it was handed back to China.

2002: Death of England cricket all-rounder Ben Hollioake at the age of just 24, the youngest age at which any England Test cricketer has passed away. He had only recently begun to establish himself in England's team alongside his brother Adam – the siblings made their Test debuts in the same match. The Hollioakes were born in Australia, and Ben was visiting family before the cricket season restarted. He lost control of his Porsche and hit a wall returning from a family celebration.

2014: In the Plumstead Club in London, table tennis star Daniel Ives and his father Peter break the world record for the longest table tennis rally when they knock the ball between them for eight hours, 40 minutes and ten seconds.

24 March

1877: The 34th University Boat Race between Oxford and Cambridge finishes as a dead heat for the first and (to date) only time in the race's history. The Oxford crew, and many observers, believed they had triumphed. This controversy was underlined when race judge John Phelps allegedly declared the race was a 'Dead heat ... to Oxford by six feet.'

1909: Death of Australian jockey Tom Clayton. His horse, All Blue, was one of a dozen horses to fall at Rosehill Racecourse in New South Wales. Clayton suffered a compound fracture of the pelvis, several broken ribs and internal injuries, and died four days later.

1932: The first world championships for marbles take place in the grounds of the Greyhound pub in Tinsley Green, West Sussex. The event involved teams of six in a knockout tournament. The first world champions were an English team who called themselves 'Black Horse' (presumably after the pub they frequented).

1965: In the quarter-final of the European Cup Liverpool are drawn against Köln, the tie to be played over two legs. Both legs finished goalless, so a decider was played in Rotterdam in the Netherlands, and finished 2-2. The authorities needed some way of deciding who should progress to the semi-finals, in the days before penalty shoot-outs. Liverpool progressed to the semi-final when their captain won the toss of the coin.

1974: The final of the inaugural women's hockey World Cup in Mandelieu in France. The Netherlands beat Argentina 1-0 to become the first world champions.

1993: Nottingham Forest goalkeeper Mark Crossley saves a penalty taken by Matt Le Tissier of Southampton. The save is noteworthy since Le Tissier took 49 penalties in his career – and scored the other 48.

2007: The first football match to be played at the new Wembley Stadium sees England U21 draw 3-3 with Italy U21. The first goalscorer in the new stadium was Italian Giampaolo Pazzini after just 28 seconds, and he was also the first player to score a hat-trick there.

25 March

1882: The Old Etonians beat Blackburn Rovers 1-0 to win the FA Cup Final through a goal by William Anderson. The match was played at The Oval, and marked the last time that an amateur football club won the FA Cup. They reached the final again the following year but lost 2-1 to Blackburn Olympic.

1891: Notts County, the oldest professional football team in the world, reach the FA Cup Final for the first time, losing 3-1 to Blackburn Rovers at The Oval. Just seven days earlier County had defeated Blackburn 7-1 in the league.

1994: Day one of a Test match between Australia and South Africa. Australia were captained by Allan Border in his final Test match – playing in his 153rd consecutive Test.

2005: The baseball match between Colorado Rockies and Arizona Diamondbacks ends with the unusual result of 'bees stopped play'. The players of both sides were forced off the field by a swarm of hundreds of angry bees. After a break the players tried to resume play, but by then there were even more bees 'covering the entire field'. After a brief discussion the match was abandoned with the humans fleeing to safety. Incredibly in a crowd of 8,029 there was not one reported bee sting.

2006: Immediately after the match between Sachsen Leipzig and Hallescher FC, Leipzig's Nigerian midfielder Adebowale Ogungbure is arrested by the local police. His crime was making an offensive gesture in the form of a Nazi salute at the crowd. Such gestures are illegal in Germany, but potential criminal proceedings were dropped when the police learned that this gesture was in retaliation to significant racist abuse he was enduring throughout the match.

26 March

1839: Henley Regatta (later Henley Royal Regatta) is established, an annual rowing event on the River Thames close to the town of Henley-on-Thames. Captain Edmund Gardiner was the man who proposed the regatta hoping it would 'be a source of amusement and gratification to the neighbourhood, and the public in general'. The regatta gained the title 'Royal' in 1851 when HRH Prince Albert agreed to become patron of the organising group.

1916: Birth of Middlesex and England cricketer Bill Edrich. His sporting career was put on hold in the Second World War when Edrich served in the RAF, rising to the rank of Squadron Leader as a pilot for Bomber Command. Having survived the horrors of the war he approached cricket with a new zeal, stating: 'No bowler is too fast to hook; no score too large to defy.'

1992: World boxing heavyweight ex-champion Mike Tyson is sentenced to ten years in prison having been found guilty of the rape of Miss Black Rhode Island, Desiree Washington.

2006: Death of IndyCar racing driver Paul Dana at the age of 30. Dana had a fatal accident in a practice session for the first race of the 2006 IndyCar season, when he ploughed into a competitor's stricken car while travelling at about 176mph (283kmh). Even more tragically, on the morning of Dana's accident his wife found out she was carrying their first child, but she never got the chance to tell him.

2016: At Vars in France, observing strict France Ski de Vitesse rules, the downhill skiing speed records are broken. Italian Ivan Origone was measured at 254.96kmh (158.4mph). On exactly the same date his compatriot Valentina Greggio took the women's record, clocking 247.08kmh (153.5mph).

27 March

1855: The British military have a long and proud association with sport. The first recorded rugby game in the British Army was played at Balaclava between the Cavalry and the Guards, right in the middle of the Crimean War, just five months after the Charge of the Light Brigade.

1871: Scotland host England in a rugby match in Edinburgh, at Raeburn Place, the home of Edinburgh Academicals. This match was widely accepted as the first official international sports fixture. The match was 50 minutes each half, and played as 20-a-side. Scotland's Angus Buchanan scored the first-ever international try, so-called because it enabled the team to 'try' to kick a goal. That goal was successfully kicked (or converted) by William Cross: 1-0. Then both Cross and England's Reg Birkett achieved tries, but these goals were missed, so the match finished 1-0. The try was awarded by the umpire Dr Almond who, after the match, made an incredible admission: 'Let me make a confession: I do not know whether the decision which gave Scotland the try from which the winning goal was kicked was correct in fact. When an umpire is in doubt, I think he is justified in deciding against the side which makes the most noise. They are probably in the wrong.'

1983: The United States Grand Prix West produces one of the most dominant performances in the history of Formula One. The race was won by British driver John Watson in a McLaren-Ford … having started in 22nd place on the grid. Watson's teammate Niki Lauda took second place, 28 seconds behind Watson, having started from 23rd. The final podium place was claimed by the

Ferrari of René Arnoux, a full 73 seconds behind Watson having started in second on the grid. Arnoux was the only driver on the same lap as the McLarens.

1994: Michael Schumacher, in his Benetton-Ford, wins his third Grand Prix on the Interlagos circuit in Brazil. Remarkably Schumacher is the only driver to finish on the lead lap, with even runner-up Damon Hill, in the Williams-Renault, having been lapped by the German.

28 March

1668: One court ruling which was, perhaps, very much a foresight of the time to come. The session in Maidstone decreed that the customs and excise department could not claim tax duty on alcoholic drinks sold at 'kricketing', and that match promoters had the rights to sell ale to spectators.

1891: The first-ever world weightlifting championship is held in London. The organisers had a relatively straightforward job planning the event – only seven athletes applied to compete from six nations, and everyone was in the same category with no allowances or penalties for weight. Briton Edward Levy won the event, becoming the first world champion weightlifter.

1953: Death of American all-round athlete Jim Thorpe. In 1912 Thorpe won Olympic gold medals in both the pentathlon and decathlon, thus becoming the first Native American to win Olympic gold (he was a member of the Sac and Fox Nation). However, he was stripped of his gold medals because he had previously been paid for two seasons of semi-professional baseball, breaking the rules on amateurism. Thorpe also played professional American football and basketball. Sadly his retirement from competitive sport coincided with the Great Depression and he struggled to find employment. He slipped into alcoholism and struggled to support his three ex-wives and eight children. He spent his last year with failing health living in poverty.

1962: Lance Gibbs produces a devastating spell of bowling to give the West Indies victory over India in their Test match. In India's second innings Gibbs removed the last eight batsmen in a final spell of eight wickets for six runs.

2018: Australian cricket captain Steve Smith and vice-captain David Warner are banned by Cricket Australia for their leadership during the infamous ball-tampering scandal during the tour of South Africa. Fielder Cameron Bancroft, who was the man found guilty of actually tampering with the ball, was banned for nine months. Bancroft had sticky tape in his pocket with sharp dirt embedded with which he scraped the surface of the ball to alter its condition.

29 March

1893: Welsh international brothers David and Evan James become the first rugby players suspended by the rugby union for professionalism as they were found guilty of receiving payments for playing for Broughton Rovers.

1927: Briton Henry Segrave, driving a Sunbeam Mystery 1000hp, becomes the first driver to clear a speed of 200mph. On the speed test track at Daytona Beach in the US he is clocked at 203.79mph (327.97kmh).

1981: British runner Joyce Smith becomes the first woman in history to break two and a half hours for the marathon, when she runs 2.29.57 at the London Marathon.

1981: Finland's Tiina Lehtola becomes the first woman to jump more than 100m on skis when she clears 110m (361 feet) on Rukatunturi in Kuusamo, Finland.

2014: Bayern Munich are held to a 3-3 draw at home to 1899 Hoffenheim in the Bundesliga, ending a run of 19 consecutive victories – the longest straight run of wins by any team in professional football. The run formed part of an unbeaten run of 53 games, made up of 46 wins and seven draws.

2014: Two teams calling themselves Walang Iwanan and Bounce Back complete their marathon basketball match at the Meralco Gym in Metro Manila in the Philippines. The match had started on the 24th and lasted for 120 hours, one minute and 7.8 seconds.

30 March

1883: The 45th running of the Aintree Grand National in Liverpool sees the smallest ever field for the event, with just ten runners and riders.

1912: The 69th University Boat Race between Oxford and Cambridge is officially declared as a 'No race' for the first and (to date) only time in the race's history. In poor conditions Oxford went into an early lead, although both boats took on a lot of water. At one point the Oxford crew rowed into the shore and got out so they could empty the boat. However, on getting back in they were approached by the umpire who informed them that Cambridge had sunk, and he was declaring a 'No race'. Oxford rowed on anyway, slowly paddling to a finish. The two crews agreed to row again two days later and Oxford won by six lengths.

1946: Day two and, as it turns out, the final day of the Test match between Australia and New Zealand in Wellington. Australia declared their first innings 157 runs ahead. They then bowled New Zealand out for a second time for just 54 in 32.2 overs to win by an innings and 103 runs. The entire Test match was finished by 3.30pm on the second day.

1954: Day one of the fifth Test between the West Indies and England at Kingston in Jamaica, a match that England would go on to win by nine wickets. The match was noteworthy as it was the Test match debut of cricketing legend Garry Sobers.

1969: Death of Belgian racing car driver Lucien Bianchi. In 1968 he won the 24 Hours of Le Mans with Pedro Rodriguez in a Ford GT40. While testing for the 1969 Le Mans, hoping to defend his title, he spun and hit a telegraph pole, dying just a few minutes later.

1970: Birth of American thoroughbred racehorse Secretariat (aka Big Red). In 1975 Secretariat won the American Triple Crown, the first horse to do so for a quarter of a century. Remarkably he set speed records in all three races. In the official list generated by trainers, owners and experts he was named as the second greatest racehorse of the 20th century, behind only Man o' War.

1993: Football hardman Vinnie Jones is due to attend yet another FA disciplinary hearing, but fails to show up. Wimbledon's chief executive Dave Barnard tried to track him down but failed, and commented: 'It's not like Vinnie – he certainly knows his way here!' Jones did turn up – thinking the meeting was for 2.30pm (it was for 12.30), by which time the FA executive had banned him indefinitely. A new date was rearranged for the following week when the ban was reduced to four matches with a hefty fine. When the press asked Jones to comment as he left he reflected: 'The FA have given me a pat on the back. I've taken violence off the terracing and on to the pitch.'

31 March

1878: Birth of Jack Johnson (aka the Galveston Giant), the first African American boxer to win the world heavyweight title, which he does at the age of 30. He held on to the title for eight years. In a sport packed with memorable moments and heroic exploits, it is Johnson's 1910 bout with James Jeffries which has been dubbed the 'fight of the century'.

1909: The MLB, the organisation overseeing the running and organisation of baseball, decide to take a firm stand on player contracts. All contracts must be honoured, and a player may only move either by mutual agreement with their employers, or once their contract has expired. Any player trying to break their contract was banned from the sport for five years.

1915: Death of British athlete Wyndham Halswelle, gold medal Olympian in 1908 in winning the 400m race – the only athlete ever to win an Olympic gold by walkover. Leading his men in the Battle of Neuve Chapelle during the First World War, he was hit by shell fragments and shrapnel. He refused to be evacuated and insisted on being bandaged up to continue to lead his men. Attempting to rescue an injured fellow officer, he was shot and killed by a sniper.

1931: Death of Norwegian-American football player and coach Knute Rockne, the man primarily responsible for popularising the forward pass in football. Having visited his sons at boarding school the aeroplane on which he was travelling literally fell apart, crashing near Kansas City and killing Rockne and the seven others on board.

1973: Ken Norton becomes one of just five men who beat the legendary Muhammed Ali, winning on a split decision. While most sportsmen developed their skills and their passion as children, Norton did not set foot in a ring until he was in his twenties as a US Marine.

1980: Death of legendary American athlete Jesse Owens, winner of four Olympic gold medals with numerous world records. At the Berlin 1936 Olympic Games he was credited with 'single-handedly crushing Hitler's myth of Aryan supremacy'. Following his death United States president Jimmy Carter paid tribute to him: 'Perhaps no athlete better symbolised the human struggle against tyranny, poverty and racial bigotry.'

1997: Martina Hingis of Switzerland replaces the German Steffi Graf as the world number one WTA tennis player. At 16 Hingis became the youngest player to hold the title, where she would remain for 80 weeks.

2017: Death of British road endurance cyclist Mike Hall after being struck by a car near Canberra in Australia. He was cycling in second place in the 3,300-mile Indian Pacific Wheel Race. The race was cancelled as a mark of respect.

APRIL

1 April

1924: Death of British racing cyclist Lloyd Hildebrand, whose greatest success comes in the 1900 Olympics when he wins the silver medal in the 25km race … for France! Despite being born in North London he had moved to France and married a French woman so decided to race for France.

1924: Death of Australian sprinter Stan Rowley, who wins four medals at the 1900 Olympics. Rowley won a bronze medal in each of the 60m, 100m and 200m sprints. The 5,000m team race was just between Great Britain and France; no one else entered. The teams had to enter five men, each of whom ran 5,000m, and the team with the lowest overall position ranks won. Britain had only four runners, so a couple of his English friends persuaded Rowley to join them! 5,000m was hardly ideal for a sprinter – he didn't even finish because the organisers grew tired of waiting and stopped him after about 3,000m, telling him he had finished and was last. However, his willingness to take part legitimised the British team, and the excellent performance of the four official runners gave them the gold medal despite his weak individual performance.

1967: Wales play a rugby union fixture against France in Paris. The French won the tie 20-14. Making his international debut for Wales was 19-year-old scrum-half Gareth Edwards, who would also play the next 52 Welsh internationals. All of Edwards's 53 caps came in one unbroken spell.

1996: Major League Baseball umpire John McSherry collapses during the first game of the 1996 season. The 1869 Cincinnati Red Stockings were hosting Montreal Expos and McSherry had been assigned home plate. Just seven pitches into the first innings McSherry felt unwell and called a timeout. He signalled for a colleague to replace him and made his way off the pitch – but never made it. He stumbled and fell on the outfield and the emergency services were called so he could be rushed into hospital.

He never regained consciousness, passing away within an hour at the Cincinnati University Hospital.

2 April

1915: In a Good Friday Division One fixture relegation-threatened Manchester United beat mid-table Liverpool 2-0, both goals coming from George Anderson. However, the outcome was soon overshadowed by a betting scandal in which seven players were found guilty of betting on the 2-0 scoreline. The referee had noted the evident lack of effort from some Liverpool players, and suspicions were further aroused when they missed a penalty. All seven players were initially banned for life, although the bans for all but one were lifted during the First World War. Enoch West had his ban lifted in 1945 at the age of 59.

1926: Birth of Australian racing car driver Jack Brabham, three times Formula One world champion, and the only man to win the F1 championship in a car bearing his own name.

1927: Birth of Hungarian footballer and football manager Ferenc Puskás, considered one of the finest footballers of all time. A very prolific goalscorer – he netted 84 times in 85 international matches for Hungary, and 514 goals in 529 in the domestic leagues in Hungary and Spain, winning five league championships in each country.

1932: Johnny Weissmuller's first film is released: *Tarzan the Ape Man*. Weissmuller won five Olympic gold medals for swimming in the 1920s, and a bronze for water polo, as well as setting about 50 world records at various points in his career. He auditioned for the role of Tarzan since the role demanded strong swimming ability.

1951: Swindon Town become the first league side to install permanent floodlights at their ground, and this date marks the first time the lights are used – in a friendly fixture against Bristol City.

3 April

1597: Willem Barentsz's crew are stuck at Nova Zembla during their ongoing exploration of the Arctic Ocean. Crew member Gerrit de Veer recorded in his diary: 'Den 3. April wast moy claer weder met een n.o. wint ende stil, doen maeckten wy een colf toe om daer mede te colven, om also onse leden wat radder te maeckten, daer wy allerley middelen toe zochten' (tr. '3 April: the weather was nice and clear with a north-easterly wind and quiet; then we made a golf [club] to play golf with, and thus make our limbs more loose, for which we sought every means.')

1905: A group of young Italian lads who have immigrated to Argentina with their families come together to find a club to join to play football and other sports. Unable to find one, they decided to form their own, which they called Boca Juniors. The club started playing minor fixtures immediately, and gained admission to the Argentine Primera Division in 1913, where they have remained ever since.

1938: One of the most controversial football matches of all time. The footballing context was that Austria had just qualified for the FIFA World Cup later that year in France, led by their inspirational captain Matthias Sindelar. The political context was that Nazi Germany had invaded and annexed Austria, and had announced that the Austrian team would be dissolved and the best players would play for Germany. But before that happened there was to be one final match – Austria against Germany. The controversy started before kick-off with Sindelar leading his team out in their traditional red and white kits rather than the black and white in which they had been instructed to play. There were rumours that the Austrian team had been ordered to lose. Towards the end of the game Germany were leading 2-0, until Sindelar pulled a goal back. He deliberately celebrated in front of the VIP box full of high-ranking Nazi officers. Germany hung on for a 2-1 victory. After the match Sindelar announced his retirement due to age and injury, incurring the wrath of the German hierarchy. Sindelar died just nine months later allegedly of accidental carbon monoxide poisoning, although several questioned whether this was actually an accident or recompense.

1993: To date the only time that the Grand National has been declared void. The start of the race was shambolic, so the starter aborted it and recalled the runners and riders to start again – but the message didn't get out to the field, and 30 of the 39 horses carried on. Seven completed the 'race that never was', with Esha Ness finishing in what would have been the second fastest time ever. Bookmakers had to refund around £75m in stake money.

1994: Death of legendary greyhound Ballyregan Bob. His coat was brindle (aka tigerstripe), and he was whelped in May 1983. Ballyregan Bob took the world record for 32 consecutive race wins in 1984/85.

2005: It is a common sight to see Formula One drivers removing their helmets at the end of a race and see them pouring with sweat, even in cold weather. Not surprising given the cramped cockpit, the proximity of the engine and the layers of fireproof clothing. Spare a thought then for the drivers at the 2005 Bahrain Grand Prix. The average race temperature was 42.5°C (108.5°F).

4 April

1897: Death of Bert Harris, the first professional cycling champion of England, and widely regarded as the fastest short-course cyclist of his day. He crashed during a race in Aston and went over the handlebars, hitting his head on the hard surface. He passed away a couple of days later in hospital.

1930: England cricketer Andy Sandham becomes the first batsman ever to score a triple century in an international fixture when he scores exactly 300 in a Test match against the West Indies in Kingston, Jamaica.

1959: George Amick becomes the first fatality at the Daytona International Speedway circuit during a race. During the Daytona 100 his Bowes Seal Fast car hit a rail and flipped over, travelling upside down before coming to rest. Amick was killed instantly, before anyone got to him.

1988: Day three of the first Test between Pakistan and the West Indies sees Pakistan finish their innings on 435. The second-highest score for Pakistan as Extras, with a world record 74 (21 byes, 11 leg byes, four wides and 38 no-balls).

5 April

1884: Death of cricketer John Wisden, who has a successful career with Kent, Middlesex and Sussex, predominantly as a bowler. Wisden is best known for his eponymous Cricketers' Almanack, which he initially compiled himself starting from his retirement in 1864 until his death 20 years later.

1902: Scotland host England in an international football match at Ibrox Park in Glasgow. Half an hour into the game one of the wooden stands collapsed, leading to the deaths of 25 supporters and injuries to at least 500 others. The teams replayed later at Villa Park, with money raised going to a relief fund for families of the victims of the original tragedy.

1962: Death of Pat 'Kangaroo Kicker' O'Dea. Australian by birth and attending college in the United States, he had a successful career in both Australian Rules football and American football. The *New York Times* obituary specifically referred to his incredible 110-yard punt in a gridiron game against Minnesota in 1897.

1967: Celtic beat Inter Milan 2-1 in Lisbon to win the European Cup, becoming the first team from the British Isles to win Europe's premier football competition. The match marked the end of Celtic's season in which they scored a record 196 goals in all competitions.

2017: British equestrian Nick Skelton retires from competitive sport after 41 years as a show jumping champion. He won his first individual Olympic gold medal at the 2016 games in Rio de Janeiro at the age of 58, competing in his seventh Olympic Games.

2018: Death of five-time darts world champion Eric Bristow (aka the Crafty Cockney). Bristow was attending a Premier League Darts event in Liverpool, doing promotional work, when he collapsed and was rushed to hospital. He was dead on arrival. His death aged 60 was announced that evening at the event during a match between Daryl Gurney and Peter Wright.

6 April

1893: Andy Bowen and Jack Burke fight the longest known boxing match, a bout which lasts for 110 three-minute rounds. The total fighting time was seven hours and 19 minutes until the referee stepped in and declared a 'no contest', with both boxers physically incapable of continuing.

1896: The opening ceremony and day one of the first modern Olympic Games. This was the first Games since Roman emperor Theodosius I banned the Games in AD 393 as part of a Christian campaign against paganism. Fourteen nations took part – Australia, Austria, Bulgaria, Chile, Denmark, France, Germany, Great Britain, Greece, Hungary, Italy, Sweden, Switzerland and the United States. It couldn't exactly be considered a level playing field – Greece used 169 athletes throughout the week-long competition, while the other 13 nations had brought 76 athletes between them. Australia, Bulgaria, Chile, Italy and Sweden each entered with just one athlete.

1951: Birth of Jean-Marc Boivin, one of the true pioneers of extreme sports – extreme skier, mountaineer, hang glider, paraglider, diver and BASE jumper. (BASE jumping is extreme parachuting off a fixed object, which may be a **B**uilding, an **A**ntenna, a **S**pan or bridge, or the **E**arth – from a cliff.) He was the first man to paraglide from the summit of Mount Everest, the first to ski down the east face of the Matterhorn (with slopes exceeding 60°), the first to climb solo the north face of the Eiger and the first man to paraglide more than 30km (actual distance: 31.5km/19.6 miles) off Mount Maudit. Tragically he lost his life BASE jumping off the tallest waterfall in the world, Angel Falls in Venezuela.

1970: Death of basketball star Maurice Stokes at the age of 36, a player with the Cincinnati Royals. During the final game of the routine 1957/58 season Stokes was knocked over, banged his head on the floor and was knocked unconscious. After brief medical assistance he came round, and even returned to the game. Three days later on a plane journey he suffered a seizure and was left permanently paralysed. The medical diagnosis was post-traumatic encephalopathy, a brain injury from his previous fall. He was just 24 at the time, and was left quadriplegic and unable to communicate other than by blinking. He was cared for by his Royals teammate Jack Twyman until his situation eventually deteriorated such that he required full-time care. He died in hospital of a heart attack.

1986: Official golf rankings are introduced for the first time, with German golfer Bernhard Langer the first official number one ranked player.

1996: The very first match is played in the newly formed Major League Soccer. FIFA had been very keen to see football (or soccer as the US prefer to call it) promoted within the States. San Jose Clash beat DC United from Washington DC 1-0.

2014: Shakey Jakey, considered by many to be the fastest racing greyhound in the world, wins race six at Wentworth Park by an incredible 22 lengths. Despite the overwhelming margin this was actually the only race that Shakey Jakey ever ran. Immediately after the race the owner David Pringle was offered $700,000, then $1m, but turned both offers down. Instead he simply retired him and put him out to stud, figuring he was more valuable producing several top dogs than just racing.

7 April

1896: The first modern Olympics features a few somewhat bizarre events, one of which is the one-handed weightlifting, similar to a snatch, and the contestant has to lift using each hand. Briton Launceston Elliot won the gold, lifting 71kg with each hand.

1906: Mount Vesuvius erupts, devastating Naples and creating difficulties throughout Italy. A great deal of money was needed for the region, so Rome immediately withdrew from holding the 1908 Olympic Games to divert cash where it was needed. The Games were then awarded to London, who had come second in the original voting, leaving them just two years to build the White City Stadium and prepare other facilities. The stadium was certainly unique – in the middle of the running tracks, as well as the unusual facilities for field events, there were platforms for gymnastics and wrestling, as well as a swimming pool with diving boards.

1968: Britain's Jim Clark, twice Formula One champion, is killed in an accident driving his Lotus-Cosworth in a Formula Two race at Hochkenheim in Germany. The car was travelling at about 170mph when it left the track, turned over and hit a tree in a remote part of the Hockenheim circuit. Clark suffered a broken neck and fractured skull, and was dead before he got to the hospital. The cause of the accident was never confirmed. The stunned crowd were informed of the death at the conclusion of the race.

1976: The finals of the fifth European Badminton Championships are held in Dublin. England's Gillian Gilks had a very busy day, winning the women's singles title, the women's doubles title and the mixed doubles final. Gilks was the last person to win all three available titles in a single year.

2002: The final matches in the first-ever women's Six Nations rugby championship. France had already been confirmed champions two days earlier by beating Ireland 46-0. On this final day England were confirmed as runners-up by beating Spain 53-14, while Scotland beat Wales 31-3.

8 April

1907: Manchester United and Scotland defender Tommy Blackstock collapses and dies in a match against St Helens, immediately after heading the ball. The precise cause of death was never established.

1935: The second Masters Tournament in golf is concluded. Gene Sarazen won the tournament to become the first player of all time to win all four major tournaments, the Career Grand Slam.

1963: Birth of Surrey and England batsman and wicketkeeper Alec Stewart. Stewart scored 8,463 Test runs for England – an odd coincidence given that his date of birth is 8/4/63.

1982: Birth of Kazakhstani boxer Gennady Gennadyevich Golovkin (aka GGG), reputed to be one of the finest middleweight boxers of all time. In his full career (amateur and professional) of nearly 400 fights he was never knocked out or even knocked down.

1992: Retired tennis great Arthur Ashe, winner of three major tournaments, announces he is suffering from AIDS. For a clean-living man who had tried to remain active after retirement the announcement was a shock. Ashe had undergone heart bypass surgery, and he was infected with the HIV virus in a blood transfusion. He founded the Arthur Ashe Foundation for the Defeat of AIDS, and spent the remainder of his life funding research and educating the public about the illness.

2014: Three American brothers set the record for the highest team trampoline bounce of all time in New York City. Sean, TJ and Eric Kennedy bounced to a height of 6.7m (22ft 1in).

2015: Golfing legend Jack Nicklaus achieves his first-ever hole-in-one at the Augusta National Golf Club while playing in the

Masters Par Three Contest. Incredibly Nicklaus was 75 when he achieved this milestone.

9 April

1910: Death of MLB baseman Bob Addy (aka The Magnet). Addy is one of those sportsmen who very few have heard of – but probably should have done because of his contribution to the sport. Addy was the player who introduced the slide into baseball, having the triple advantage of avoiding the fielder, avoiding overshooting a base and increasing the speed of the final metre or two of the run. Addy also attempted to start up a new form of baseball which would be played on ice, but it never quite took off.

1957: Birth of Spanish golfer Seve Ballesteros, one of the most iconic and popular golfers of all time. He was still playing at the age of 50 when form deserted him, and he was diagnosed with a malignant brain tumour the following year. Sadly he lost his battle with the cancer just three years later.

1976: Glenn Burke makes his MLB debut for the LA Dodgers, the first openly gay player to play MLB. While his colleagues seemed to have no issue with this, the Dodgers' general manager Al Campanis offered him $75,000 to get married. Burke responded, 'I guess you mean to a woman?' He declined the offer. On an entirely unrelated subject Burke is the man who invented the 'high-five'. After his Dodger teammate Dusty Baker had hit his 30th home run, Burke rushed on to congratulate him and he raised his hand over his head and Baker slapped it, 'inventing' the high-five. It rapidly caught on – the Dodgers started doing it immediately, and that spread through baseball and then beyond.

2009: South African golfer Gary Player tees off in the US Masters at Augusta for the 52nd and final time, which is a record in the tournament. He first played as a 21-year-old in 1957 and played every year since, except for 1973 when he was recovering from an operation.

10 April

1896: The first modern Olympic Games, held in Greece, features eight different gymnastics events. One of these was rope climbing – competitors simply attempted to climb up a 14m rope. Just five competitors entered. Local gymnasts Nikolaos Andriakoloulos and Thomas Xenakis were the only two entrants to climb the full 14m, and Andriakoloulos was awarded gold since he completed it faster and with 'greater style'. German Fritz Hofmann took bronze after managing 12.5m.

1916: Thirty-five enthusiastic individuals form the Professional Golfers Association of America (PGA) at a meeting in New York City.

1929: Birth of Mike Hawthorn, Great Britain's first-ever Formula One world champion (in 1958). He also won the 1955 24 Hours of Le Mans. As soon as his world title was confirmed Hawthorn announced his retirement. A few months later he was diagnosed with a terminal illness, but died in a car accident a couple of months later before the illness could really take hold.

1965: Death of American racing driver Lloyd 'Lucky' Casner. His overwhelming desire was to win the 24 Hours of Le Mans. Sadly he was testing his Maserati for the Le Mans race when he had a fatal accident.

1973: Birth of legendary Brazilian defender Roberto Carlos (birth name Roberto Carlos da Silva Rocha), considered by many as the best left-back in the history of the game. He was nicknamed El Hombre Bala (The Bullet Man) due to his powerful and accurate free kicks, which have been timed at 105mph (169kmh).

2004: Day one of the fourth Test between the West Indies and England. The West Indies batted first and reached an enormous 751/5, before declaring late on the second day as soon as captain Brian Lara had reached 400 – a new record individual Test score.

11 April

1497: The court accounts clearly show a sum of money 'giffen to Jame Dog to by fut ballis to the King' (in modern English: 'given to James Doig to buy footballs for King James IV').

1917: Death of Herbert Wilson, one of the finest British polo players of all time. Wilson was a key member of the British polo team which took the gold medal at the 1908 Olympics. He was killed in action serving his country in the Royal Horse Guards during the First World War.

1959: England beat Scotland 1-0 at Wembley through a goal by Bobby Charlton. England captain Billy Wright became the first international footballer to reach 100 caps. He would go on to secure 105 caps for his country, a record 90 of them as captain.

2001: A local derby between Kaiser Chiefs and Orlando Pirates in Johannesburg, South Africa, sees 43 people tragically crushed to death due to overcrowding in the stadium. The match was abandoned while victims were laid out on the pitch for identification and medical attention. This came just ten years after a stampede at a match between the same two teams in which 42 people were killed.

2002: The fastest recorded cricket delivery at that t time. Bowling in a one-day international against New Zealand, Shoaib Akhtar of Pakistan was the first man to clock 100mph when he was officially measured at 161kmh (100.04mph).

2009: Bristol Academy and Leeds Badgers finish their record-breaking football match – 36 hours without a break. Players went without sleep, although repeated subs were allowed to let players rest. Squads of 18 were allowed, and each player had to play at least 18 hours. Leeds won 285-255, with Adam McPhee scoring 75 goals. The players raised £10,000 for the Meningitis Trust.

2017: One of the most bizarre cricket scorecards of all time in the Bangladeshi Dhaka league, in a match between Lalmatia Club and Axiom Cricketers. Batting first Lalmatia scored just 88 runs, leaving Axiom needing 89 to win. They achieved this total in the first over and in just 17 minutes. Sujon Mahmud bowled 65 wides and 15 no-balls, while the Axiom batsmen achieved 12 runs from the four legitimate balls that were bowled. It was later revealed that Mahmud's bowling was an act of protest against what was perceived biased umpiring both in this game and in earlier matches.

12 April

1539: Work is sanctioned and paid for by King James V for a Caitch Court (Real Tennis) in the grounds of the Falkland Palace in Fife, Scotland. The court took nearly two years to complete, and it remains the oldest tennis court anywhere in the world which is still in use today.

1858: Detroit in Michigan hosts the first-ever billiards championships.

1930: England finish the fourth Test match against the West Indies at Kingston in Jamaica. At the age of 52 years and 165 days England legend Wilf Rhodes becomes the oldest man ever to play in a Test match. His longevity brought Rhodes various cricketing records, including the most first-class matches (1,110) and the most wickets taken (4,204).

2009: Rugby union is rocked with a controversy which becomes known as 'Bloodgate'. The event occurred during a Heineken Cup quarter-final match between Irish side Leinster and English team Harlequins. Harlequins winger Tom Williams came off the field with a blood injury, and was replaced by Nick Evans. Evans had started the game, but had himself gone off injured – meaning he could not return to play as a 'normal' substitute, but could be used in the case of injury. Williams's injury was in fact fake, simply to enable Evans to return to the game – he had bitten into a blood capsule he had been given. An investigation revealed that this was the fifth time that Harlequins had faked a blood injury to enable a tactical substitution. Leinster won the game 6-5 and went on to pick up the cup.

2017: Fergal O'Brien from Ireland is locked at 9-9 with England's David Gilbert in a best-of-19-frame match. At stake was the last place in the world snooker finals, and it was now one frame takes all. The deciding frame, won by O'Brien, was the longest frame of snooker ever recorded – at two hours, three minutes and 44 seconds.

13 April

1314: Football is banned in London, by order of King Edward II: 'Forasmuch as there is great noise in the city caused by hustling over large balls from which many evils may arise which God forbid; we command and forbid, on behalf of the King, on pain of imprisonment, such game to be used in the city in the future.'

1927: The controversial NHL Stanley Cup Final between the Ottawa Senators and the Boston Bruins. Bruins defenceman Billy 'Wild Beaver' Coutu initiated a bench-clearing brawl, apparently at the instruction of his coach Art Ross, during which he attacked the referee. Coutu was banned for life and fined $100 – a vast sum of money for 1927.

1936: Luton Town beat Bristol Rovers 12-0 in a Division Three (South) fixture. Ten of their goals were scored by striker Joe Payne, setting a British record that still stands to this day.

1986: Jack Nicklaus wins the US Masters – his sixth, and his 18th and final win in a major tournament. At the beginning of the day's play he was lying in joint ninth place at two under par, four shots off Greg Norman's lead. After a steady first eight Nicklaus finished the final ten holes seven under par, with six birdies and an eagle. At 46 Nicklaus became the oldest winner of a major tournament.

1997: The 61st Masters tournament at Augusta National Golf Club in Georgia is won by Tiger Woods. At 21 he became the youngest person ever to win a major, and the first non-white player to win at Augusta.

2003: At the London Marathon Paula Radcliffe sets a time of two hours, 15 minutes and 25 seconds – the fastest time ever by a woman over this distance.

14 April

1905: England officially joins FIFA, bringing the number of member nations up to eight.

1929: The Monaco Grand Prix is the first to be run in the principality. It was established by the cigarette magnate Antony Noghès, who had set up the Automobile Club de Monaco. Sixteen invited participants turned out to race for a prize of 100,000 French francs. There was no qualifying, grid positions being drawn out of a hat.

1968: Roberto de Vicenzo loses the Masters golf tournament – by his own carelessness and stupidity. On the penultimate hole of the final round Vicenzo's playing partner wrote a 'four' on his scorecard, when he had actually holed out in three. This gave him a round of 66, despite going round in 65. Did it matter? His cumulative score for the four days was 278, putting him into second place, one shot behind Bob Goalby. So if he had recorded his score correctly he would have tied with Goalby, gone into a play-off and therefore possibly won.

1990: Legendary snooker player Alex Higgins loses his first-round match at the World Snooker Championship at the Crucible Theatre in Sheffield. After several years of decline, failing health and growing alcoholism, Higgins had to qualify for the tournament. After the defeat Higgins was clearly very unhappy and punched one of the tournament officials, Colin Randle, before going into the press conference. He pre-empted any potential ban or sanction by announcing his immediate retirement: 'You can shove your snooker up your jacksy, no more snooker for Hurricane Higgins.' Several spectators observed that he had apparently drunk 27 vodkas during the match.

1991: The final of the first-ever women's rugby World Cup is played in Cardiff. The United States beat England 19-6 in the final.

15 April

1588: The first marbles world championship is held in Tinsley Green in West Sussex. Teams of six players competed for the title and a trophy. Since 1932 the championship has been held in the grounds of the Greyhound pub and has attracted competitors from across the world.

1865: Perhaps the most significant date in the history of boxing, when John Sholto Douglas, the Ninth Marquess of Queensberry, draws up new rules of boxing. The 'Queensberry rules' are still in use today, and totally transformed the sport at the time.

1889: The first-ever substitute used in an international football match. Wales were playing Scotland at Wrexham, and had (as usual) named Preston North End's Jim Trainer as their goalkeeper. Preston refused to release Trainer – but didn't let Wales know until the day of the match. They quickly called up Sam Gillam for his international debut – playing for Wrexham, he was the only one who might have been able to get there on time! But he was late, so Wales started with amateur Alf Pugh in goal, substituting Gillam on after 20 minutes when he arrived.

1947: Jackie Robinson smashes the colour divide when he becomes the first African American to play in Major League Baseball, making his debut at first base for the Brooklyn Dodgers against the Boston Braves. He went on to have a long and distinguished career, as well as make significant contributions to the civil rights movement. Robinson's contribution to the game was so significant that every MLB team retired the number 42 shirt when he stopped playing as a mark of respect … except for matches played on 15 April which, since 2004, has been known as 'Jackie Robinson day', when every player on every team wears the number 42.

1970: The European Cup two-legged semi-final between Celtic and Leeds United is dubbed the 'Battle of Britain'. The leg at Celtic Park was all-ticket, and boasted an attendance of 136,505 – a record both for any UEFA competitive match, and for Britain. Over the two legs Celtic defied the odds to progress to the final.

1992: Death of legendary thoroughbred racehorse Nijinsky. Many racing experts consider Nijinsky as the greatest flat racehorse of all time in Europe, as well as one of the most versatile, capable of winning races by huge distances on different courses and in different conditions.

16 April

1878: Birth of Tip Foster, who holds a unique place in British sport as the only man to have captained England in both cricket and football. Foster played cricket for Worcestershire, as did his six brothers. In 1903 he made his Test debut, scoring 287 – which remains the highest Test debut innings.

1938: Death of Stephen Bloomer, one of the most prolific England goalscorers of all time, scoring 28 goals in 23 international appearances. He also played baseball for Derby County Baseball Club, helping them to become British champions three times. His career was punctuated by the First World War, during which he was imprisoned in the civilian Ruhleben detention camp in Germany.

1994: Day one of the fifth Test between the West Indies and England in Antigua. The West Indies won the toss and decided to bat, and took almost half the time allocated for the Test in their first innings in reaching 593/5, with Brian Lara reaching a then world record 375 – 63 per cent of the team's total.

1998: Death of Fred Davis, three times world snooker champion and twice world billiards champion, at the age of 84. Davis turned professional when he was still 15, and played to within five years of his death – a professional career lasting 64 years.

2001: The Division Three game between Southend United and Mansfield Town at Roots Hall ends prematurely and tragically when referee Mike North collapses during the game of a suspected heart attack in the 42nd minute. The players left the field, and the game was quickly abandoned with the score still at 0-0. North was rushed to hospital, but died shortly afterwards.

17 April

1860: Farnborough in Hampshire is the venue for the bare-knuckle boxing match between Englishman Tom Sayers and American John Heenan. The referee stopped the fight after 37 rounds and declared the match a draw. After an analysis of the fight by the experts Heenan was declared the 'world boxing champion' – the first time this title had ever been used.

1888: The Football League is formally founded at a meeting of eight clubs in Manchester. William McGregor of Aston Villa, who convened the meeting, suggested the organisation should be called 'Association Football Union', but this was rejected because it was felt it sounded too similar to 'Rugby Football Union'. Major William Sudell suggested 'The Football League' as an alternative, and this was quickly accepted and adopted.

1909: The Scottish Cup replay between Celtic and Rangers ends in catastrophe. The match ended in a draw and 6,000 fans invaded the pitch. Fights broke out between the two sides, and between fans and police. The goalposts and fencing were destroyed and supporters lit fires which took almost three hours to get under control. The

Scottish FA abandoned any thought of a second replay and simply cancelled the cup for the season and withheld the medals.

1971: The French town of Hazebrouck hosts the first official women's international football match. France ran out 4-0 winners against the Netherlands, almost 100 years after the first men's international.

2001: Despite Pakistan still remaining short of their set target, England cricket captain Alec Stewart concedes the game at Headingley due to the behaviour of some so-called fans who left Stewart with little alternative. As England strolled towards defeat some supporters became increasingly unhappy and restless which led to pitch invasions. The final straw was the vicious attack on one of the stewards who was left with broken ribs and a dislocated shoulder.

2016: Steve Davis announces his retirement from professional snooker. One of the finest players of all time, he won the World Championship six times.

18 April

1809: The first-ever running of the 2000 Guineas Stakes, a one-mile flat race at Newmarket which would become one of Britain's five Classic races and the opening leg of the Triple Crown (with the Derby and the St Leger). The race was named for the initial prize fund of 2,000 guineas (one guinea = 21 shillings = £1.05). This inaugural race was won by Mr Clift on Wizard.

1942: Birth of Jochen Rindt, the Austrian Formula One racing car driver who was born in Germany. Famously he was the first person to win the Formula One world championship posthumously in 1970, having previously won the 24 Hours of Le Mans in 1965.

1958: Birth of West Indian cricketer Malcolm Marshall. His Test bowling average was 20.94 – the best of any Test bowler in history who had taken 200 or more wickets.

1973: Birth of Ethiopian middle- and long-distance runner Haile Gebrselassie. He competed internationally at distances from 800m up to the marathon, setting 27 different world records at various times. His most successful distance was the 10,000m, for which he won two Olympic gold medals and four World Championships.

1999: New York Rangers against Pittsburgh Penguins in Madison Square Garden marks the retirement of Canadian ice hockey legend Wayne Gretzky, often considered the greatest player of all time. At the time of his retirement he held 61 NHL records including most goals and most assists. He was also the only player to score 200 points in a season – which he did four times! He was so dominant behind the opponent's goal that the region became nicknamed 'Gretzky's office'.

2001: With table tennis players constantly improving, and rallies lengthening as a consequence, the scoring for a game changes from 21 points to 11.

19 April

1592: The council minutes for the city of Edinburgh lists golf as one of the leisure pursuits which should not be performed on the Sabbath.

1897: The first running of the Boston Marathon, the longest continuously running marathon in the world – it is even run through the two world wars to ensure its annual continuity. The first Boston Marathon was 24.5 miles (39.4km), and was won by local John 'JJ' McDermott in a time of 2.55.10. Fifteen competitors entered this inaugural race. The course was extended to the standard marathon distance in 1924.

1986: Despite being more than a stone lighter than his opponent, Michael Spinks beats Larry Holmes in Las Vegas to retain the IBF heavyweight boxing world title. The pair had fought once before, with Spinks winning a unanimous decision, one that Holmes hotly disputed. With that history this fight was dubbed the 'Vindication in Vegas'. This fight also lasted the distance and went to the judges, and Spinks won it on a split decision. This was unsurprising – Spinks landed 296 punches to Holmes's 293. Holmes announced his decision to retire immediately after the bout: 'It's over, this is it, I don't need it, I don't need the aggravation.'

2010: Death of Venezuelan boxer Edwin Valero, who is the WBA super-featherweight and WBC lightweight world champion at the time of his death. Just 29 when he died he had fought 27 times, winning all 27 bouts by knockout. He was arrested on suspicion of murdering his wife, and was found hanging in his jail cell the next day.

20 April

1851: Birth of Scottish golfer Tom Morris (generally referred to as Young Tom Morris, to distinguish him from his father Old Tom Morris, another golfer). Morris Jr won his first Open Championship in 1868 while still just 17 years old, and he remains the youngest ever winner of a major tournament. He got £6 prize money for his efforts. (The runner-up that year was Old Tom Morris, winning £4.) Morris Jr also won the next three Open Championships, and remains the only player in history to have won the same major tournament four times in a row.

1908: Death of Henry Chadwick, the baseball pioneer who wrote the first-ever rule book for the game. Often dubbed the 'Father of Baseball', he created box scores and the statistics of batting average and earned run average.

1949: Bill Shoemaker (aka The Shoe) wins his first race on Shafter V in California at the age of just 17. This was the first win of a career total of 8,833. His nickname was only partly due to his surname. He was born very prematurely weighing just 38oz (1.1kg) and was not expected to survive the night. Those first few nights he was wrapped up in a shoebox to keep warm.

1997: Ronnie O'Sullivan achieves the fastest ever 147 maximum break in the World Championship during his second round tie with Mick Price. The break was timed at five minutes and 20 seconds. O'Sullivan has since broken this record himself ... for the same break! World Snooker decided there was some ambiguity regarding when a break was officially deemed to begin, and confirmed it should be from the moment a player struck the cue ball for the first time. Since the match had been televised the authorities were able to rewatch it and retimed it, and O'Sullivan's record now stands at five minutes and eight seconds.

2008: Danica Patrick, driving for Andretti Green Racing, becomes the first woman ever to win an IndyCar race, winning the Indy Japan 300. Of the 200 laps Patrick only led three of them – but they were the ones that mattered.

21 April

1892: Birth of Frederick Dixon, aka Flying Freddie. Dixon designed a motorbike and sidecar combination that was suitable for driving on America's banked circuits and made turning easier. He remains one of the very few who had racing success on two wheels, three wheels and four wheels.

1980: Rosie Ruiz wins the Boston Marathon in a time of 2.31.56, a time which immediately brings her under suspicion. This was more than 25 minutes faster than she had ever run before. She was barely out of breath, she couldn't remember any split times or any events on the track, and none of the other runners could remember seeing her. Yet Ruiz continued to protest her innocence. Then two students came forward to say they had seen her bursting out of a group of spectators about half a mile from the finish line. A freelance photographer then claimed to have met her on the subway when Ruiz had claimed she was going to the first aid area because she had been injured. It was then firmly believed that

Ruiz had run the first mile or so before hopping on to the subway. Alighting near the finishing tape, she waited until other runners were approaching before bursting on to the track and sprinting the last half mile. She was disqualified from the race. At the time of writing Rosie Ruiz is still alive – and still denies any form of cheating, insisting she won the race fairly.

1986: West Ham United beat Newcastle United 8-1, with England defender Alvin Martin scoring a unique hat-trick. Martin scored his first against Newcastle's goalkeeper Martin Thomas, and shortly after this Thomas was carried off injured. Defender Chris Hedworth took over between the sticks, and Martin scored his second. The Newcastle manager was concerned that Hedworth's performance in goal was unimpressive, so switched and put attacker Peter Beardsley in goal … and Martin scored again. So a genuinely unique hat-trick – three goals scored, each one against a different goalkeeper.

1996: In the first round of the World Snooker Championship Ronnie O'Sullivan caused controversy when he beat Alain Robidoux 10-3 playing left-handed. Robidoux refused to shake O'Sullivan's hand, accusing him of showing 'disrespect' by this action, but an unrepentant O'Sullivan countered stating that he was 'better left-handed than [Robidoux] was right-handed'.

2009: The highest altitude sports fixture ever as two full teams, complete with reserves, play a game of T20 cricket on the Gorak Shep plateau in the so-called 'Everest Test match'. The plateau chosen was 5,164m (16,942ft) above sea level (more than halfway up Everest, about 350m taller than the peak of Mont Blanc). The project was more than two years in the planning – training, organisation and fundraising. The teams raised more than £100,000 for charity. As well as the cricketers, the party included four doctors, three qualified umpires and a team of 'trektators'. Perhaps the most monumental task was carrying the two tons of kit and equipment that they took.

22 April

1823: R.J. Tyers patents his new invention – roller skates.

1884: American immigrant Tom Stevens sets off from San Francisco to take his place in the record books as the first man to cycle around the world. He arrived in America in 1871 as a 15-year-old, and did not learn to ride a bike until 1877. His choice of bicycle for his epic journey was a penny-farthing. He arrived back in San Francisco in January 1887.

1906: The opening of the Games which are now generally referred to as the Intercalated Games in Athens in Greece. The organisers at the time called it an Olympic Games, planned for the tenth anniversary of the first modern Games. Medals were distributed as if it were an official event. Unlike most of the early Olympics the event was pushed into a few weeks and not spread out over months, seemingly a forerunner of the modern Games. The javelin and the pentathlon were new to the Games, as was an opening ceremony with competing nations parading in behind their national flags. That pattern has been followed ever since. The Games were won by France with 15 gold medals.

1947: The first-ever official basketball championship final sees Philadelphia Warriors beat Chicago Stags by four games to one. Several sources listed this as the first NBA championship final, but the NBA didn't exist at the time; this competition was organised by the BAA (Basketball Association of America).

1968: At 1.43pm John Clifton serves at West Hants Tennis Club in Bournemouth … the first-ever service in the Open Era of Tennis. The first Open Era champions were the sisters Christine and Nell Truman in the women's doubles in this British Hard Court Championship. The first men's champion was Ken Rosewall, and the first women's champion was Virginia Wade, who was not eligible for the prize money since she was still an amateur.

1991: Jahangir Khan beats Jansher Khan in the final of the British Open Squash Championships. This marked ten years since Jahangir had lost in the British Open, his last defeat being in the final of the 1981 tournament.

23 April

1898: The Old Peacock Ground, the home ground of Holbeck Rugby League Club, hosts its first-ever football match, with Hunslet beating Harrogate 1-0 in the West Yorkshire Cup Final. By the beginning of the next season a new stand was built, and over time Leeds City began using it for their home fixtures. Eventually it was used exclusively for football, and changed its name to Elland Road. This history explains why Leeds United are nicknamed the Peacocks. The original Peacock of the ground name was the Peacock pub just opposite the main entrance.

1914: The first-ever baseball game played at Weegham Park in Chicago – the ground now known as Wrigley Field. Work didn't actually begin on forming the baseball pitch until two months before the scheduled opening game, but the builders met their target. The Chicago Federals (aka Chi-Feds, now the Chicago Whales) beat the Kansas City Packers 9-1 in their opening match.

1927: Cardiff City beat Arsenal 1-0 in the FA Cup Final, the only time the FA Cup has been won by a team outside England. The match was played at the old Wembley Stadium, called the Empire Stadium at the time. The final was preceded by a concert which included the hymn 'Abide With Me', which then became the traditional hymn for the final and has been sung at every one ever since.

2012: Death of LeRoy Walker, the first black president of the United States Olympic Committee. He had given up a six-figure salary to take the unpaid role of president.

24 April

1738: The first-ever reference to women playing golf. A newspaper report told of two married women playing a match in Edinburgh, with their husbands acting as caddies. The article was very complimentary about their play, without actually mentioning their names, other than the fact that 'Charming Sally' won.

1801: The first known dead heat in a horse race when Worthy and Sorcerer tie for first place in the King's Plate at Newmarket. In these early days the race was decided by the horses running a second (shorter) race – which Worthy won.

1897: Following the breakaway two years earlier of 20 northern rugby teams from the RFU, this date sees the first playing of the Northern Rugby Football Union Challenge Cup (now the Rugby League Challenge Cup). The final saw Batley defeat St Helens 10-3 to pick up the cup at Headingley in Leeds. One of the unusual aspects of this match was the kit. While Batley turned out in their neat white rugby jerseys, St Helens did not have a kit at this stage – so all the players played in their own kit … a random mix of nine different shirts, including two white ones, with one player taking the field in cricket whites.

1902: Official formation of Manchester United. Newton Heath Football Club had recently been relegated, and were now facing a winding-up order from the courts, with debts of £2,670. Four Manchester businessmen took over both the club and the debts and renamed the team as Manchester United.

1932: A routine Brazilian league match between Bonsucesso and Carioca turns into a moment of history when Leônidas da Silva performs a bicycle kick – the first time this is known to have been done. One of da Silva's nicknames was the 'Rubber Man' due to his agility and flexibility.

1973: Birth of Indian cricketing legend Sachin Tendulkar. His followers have dubbed him the God of cricket, although he himself has said: 'I am not the God of cricket. I make mistakes, God doesn't.'

1996: Seventeen-year-old Eiður Smári Guðjohnsen plays in Iceland's 3-0 away win in Estonia. After 62 minutes he was substituted off … to be replaced by his father, Arnór Guðjohnsen.

25 April

1901: One of the finest comebacks in the history of sport. In their first major league game the Detroit Tigers were hosting the Milwaukee Brewers in front of more than 10,000 of their own fans. They entered the ninth and final innings trailing 13-4 and looking certain for a defeat. However, having scored just four runs in their first eight innings, the Tigers managed to score ten runs in their ninth innings to win 14-13.

1932: Birth of Meadow Lemon III, who became famous as Meadowlark Lemon, the 'Clown Prince' of the legendary Harlem Globetrotters with whom he played for 22 years, featuring in more than 16,000 games. After retirement he worked as a church pastor and occasional gospel singer.

1982: The San Marino Grand Prix is run at Imola in Italy. Several of the teams decided to boycott the race due to political situations off the track. Only seven teams actually started the race. With a few laps remaining Ferrari held one–two, so they therefore ordered their drivers to slow down. Leader Gilles Villeneuve interpreted this to mean hold track position, but Didier Pironi overtook his furious teammate on the final lap. Villeneuve was so unhappy he vowed never to talk to his teammate again – a statement which became sadly prophetic when Villeneuve died in a qualifying crash for the next Grand Prix two weeks later in Belgium.

2007: Death of Alan Ball, the youngest member of England's World Cup-winning team. Ball died of a heart attack while working in his garden.

Meadowlark Lemon

25 April 1932–27 December 2015

Basketball legend, best known as the 'Clown Prince' of the Harlem Globetrotters, for whom he made more than 16,000 appearances.

2012: Lock forward Mark Spencer makes his international rugby debut for Qatar against Uzbekistan in the HSBC Asian Five Nations tournament in Dubai. (The title Five Nations is a misnomer – there are actually 19 nations involved in five different divisions – Qatar and Uzbekistan were with Jordan and Lebanon in Division Four.) Spencer became the oldest debutant in world rugby … and the oldest player ever at international level at 57 years and 340 days. Despite Qatar's 74-13 victory Spencer was never selected to play for Qatar again.

26 April

1897: Birth of American sportsman Eddie Eagen, who holds the unique distinction of being the only person in history to win an Olympic gold medal in both a Summer Games and a Winter Games in different unrelated sports. In 1920 Eagen won gold for boxing in the light-heavyweight division. Twelve years later he got his second gold in the Lake Placid Winter Olympics with the US four-man bobsleigh team.

1909: Death of Michael 'Doc' Powers, so nicknamed since he is a qualified doctor as well as an MLB catcher. On 12 April Powers was injured playing for Philadelphia Athletic against Washington Senators. Chasing a ball he ran headlong into a wall, sustaining internal injuries which required surgery. Two weeks and three surgeries later he became the first MLB player to die from injuries sustained on the field of play.

1918: Birth of Dutch athlete Fanny Blankers-Koen, aka the Flying Housewife. During the 1948 London Olympics she gained four gold medals as a 30-year-old mother of two – the 100m, 200m, 80m hurdles and 4x100m relay. Her success helped to eliminate the myth that age and motherhood were barriers to success in women's sport. In 1999 the IAAF elected her as the 'Female Athlete of the Century'.

1952: In the Richmond Open, Patty Berg scores 64, the lowest round of golf ever scored by a woman. She credited her success to her new putter, which she had only bought the previous day.

2016: Belgian cyclist Femke Van den Driessche is stripped of her European Cyclo-Cross Championship title (and the corresponding Belgian title) after being found guilty of cheating. She was also banned from all competition for another five years after a court found her guilty of mechanical doping – a form of technological fraud where the cyclist uses a hidden motor to help to propel the bike along.

27 April

1901: Tottenham Hotspur win the replay of the FA Cup Final 3-1 at Burnden Park in Bolton. This was the first cup final filmed by Pathé News. It was also the only FA Cup competition to be won by a non-league football club.

1908: The first-ever FA Charity Shield (now called the FA Community Shield). Since 1930 the match has been contested between the Division One winners (now the Premier League winners) and the FA Cup winners, but that was not the case for the first few years. The first-ever Charity Shield was competed between Manchester United, winners of the Football League, and Queens Park Rangers, champions of the Southern Football League. The match was held at Stamford Bridge, and finished 1-1. Manchester United won the replay 4-0.

1956: Thirty-one-year-old world heavyweight boxing champion Rocky Marciono retires from the sport, the only heavyweight champion to remain undefeated through his entire career – 49 fights, 49 wins, of which 43 were by knockout. He had decided he wanted to spend more time with his family. He was drafted into the US army when he was 20 and began boxing simply as a way of getting out of kitchen duties.

1975: In finishing sixth in the Spanish Grand Prix, Italian racing driver Lella Lombardi becomes the first (and currently only) female driver to finish in the points in a Formula One race. The race distance had to be shortened due to the death of five spectators after an accident so Lombardi only received 0.5 points.

2009: Women's international football result: Kyrgyzstan 4 Palestine 1. In this fixture Alina Litvinenko, at the age of 13 years and 131 days, became the youngest ever international goalscorer … and the youngest to score a hat-trick!

28 April

1883: The first-ever rugby sevens tournament is held at Melrose Football Club in Scotland. The idea of having a tournament was purely a money-making exercise; rules were adapted to sevens to enable several games to be played in a single afternoon.

1923: The first FA Cup Final to be staged at Wembley Stadium, with King George V in attendance to present the trophy to the winners. Bolton Wanderers entered the final with the unique distinction of having won every single round 1-0 on the way to the final – with David Jack scoring the goal on every occasion! Jack continued his run in the second minute when he opened the scoring, with Jack Smith scoring a controversial second later on. So Bolton ran out 2-0 winners against West Ham United, completing the rare statistic of winning the cup without conceding a single goal in the competition. Wembley Stadium had been designed to cater for 125,000, although some estimates claim as many as 300,000 were there. This historic event is sometimes referred to as the 'White Horse Final' since one of the iconic images was of a policeman mounted on a white horse trying to move the crowds back.

1967: Muhammad Ali appears in Houston to answer the call for him to be drafted. Four times he refused to step forward when his name was called, despite being threatened with prison and fines. He cited compassion on humanitarian grounds and his own personal faith as the reasons, but would later explain: 'Man, I ain't got no quarrel with them Viet Cong. Why should they ask me to put on a uniform and go ten thousand miles from home and drop bombs and bullets on brown people in Vietnam while so-called Negro people in Louisville are treated like dogs and denied simple human rights?'

1999: Death of Sir Alf Ramsey, the man who guides England to their 1966 football World Cup Final victory as manager.

29 April

1899: Belgian driver Camille Jenatzy is the first driver ever to clear 100kmh, when he is clocked at 105.88kmh (65.79mph).

1911: Broughton Rangers beat Wigan 4-0 to win the 15th Rugby League Challenge Cup Final in Salford. This was Broughton's second and last win in the Challenge Cup. The 4-0 scoreline represented the lowest winning score and the lowest aggregate score in any Challenge Cup Final – records that still stand.

1951: Birth of American NASCAR driver and team owner Dale Earnhardt, winner of 76 Winston Cup races, including the 1998 Daytona 500 as well as seven NASCAR championships. His aggressive style behind the wheel earned him the nicknames 'The Intimidator' and 'The Count of Monte Carlo'. Earnhardt was killed instantly in a crash in the 2001 Daytona 500.

1978: Welshman Ray Reardon becomes the oldest snooker world champion of the modern era at the age of 45 years and 203 days, beating South African Perrie Mans 25-18 in the final. Interestingly, the record could actually have been even higher since both losing semi-finalists were older than Reardon. Reardon had beaten 48-year-old Eddie Charlton in the semi-final, while Perrie Mans had overcome 64-year-old Fred Davis.

2013: Death of Greek Cypriot pole vaulter Marianna Zachariadi, silver medallist at the 2009 Mediterranean Games and the 2010 Commonwealth Games. Sadly at the age of 23 she lost her battle with Hodgkin's lymphoma.

30 April

1977: Derby County are entertaining Manchester City in a Division One match at the Baseball Ground. The pitch was in a dreadful state, which became clear as soon as Derby were awarded a penalty and nobody could see the penalty spot. So both sets of players (and obviously all the fans) had to wait a few minutes while groundsman Bob Smith appeared with a bucket and a tape measure to measure the 12 yards and paint a new penalty spot.

1993: Monica Seles, the Yugoslav-born American tennis star, is stabbed in the back by an assailant. Seles was playing a quarter-final match in the Hamburg Open in Germany. A man came out of the crowd with a nine-inch knife and stabbed her in the back. The attacker, Günter Parche, was an obsessive fan of Steffi Graf who despised Seles's rise to the top and particularly beating his hero. Seles was rushed to hospital and would not return to the tennis court for two years. She refused to ever play in Germany again.

1994: Death of Austrian racing driver Roland Ratzenberger who dies during qualifying for the San Marino Grand Prix, driving for Simtek-Ford. He damaged his front wing, meaning he couldn't turn into the Villeneuve Corner and drove straight into a wall at nearly 200mph. He was airlifted to hospital and pronounced dead on arrival. The following morning, before the race the drivers voted to reform the Grand Prix Drivers' Association under a joint directorship of Ayrton Senna, Gerhard Berger and Michael Schumacher. Tragically Senna would be dead just a few hours later. Dying at the same race weekend as the great Ayrton Senna, sadly Ratzenberger's death is too often forgotten.

2016: The longest ever competitive badminton match at the semi-final of the Badminton Asia Championsips in Wuhan in China. The Japanese pair of Naoko Fukuman and Kurumi Yonao surprisingly beat the third seeds from Indonesia, Nitya Krishinda Maheswari and Greysia Polii. The final score was 13-21 21-19 24-22. Very few matches go much beyond an hour, and no match in history had gone beyond two hours previously … but this match lasted two hours and 41 minutes.

2017: In Reading Matthew Prouse throws a dart at a dartboard, hitting the bullseye, from a record distance of 6m (19ft 8.2in).

MAY

1 May

1850: Although women are not allowed to register as professional jockeys or ride on licensed tracks, Victoria in Australia hosts the first day of racing exclusively for amateur female jockeys.

1935: Murder of Henri Pélissier, winner of the 1923 Tour de France. Pélissier was known as a difficult and volatile man. His reputation was such that when he died the newspaper *Paris-Soir* led with the headline 'The Tragic End of Henri Pélissier surprises no one'. Having had a lot to put up with, his wife took her own life in 1933. Pélissier took in a new partner called Camille. One day she ran to the bedroom and got the very gun that Pélissier's wife had taken her own life with and shot him five times.

1958: The first-ever Inter-Cities Fairs Cup Final. Barcelona won this inaugural competition, bizarrely playing a team that didn't technically exist. England entered the competition with a team called London XI featuring, among others, Tottenham Hotspur's Danny Blanchflower, Chelsea's Jimmy Greaves, Johnny Haynes of Fulham and Arsenal's Vic Groves.

1974: Sir Alf Ramsey is sacked as the manager of the England football team. Ramsey died in 1999, leaving clear instructions that England and the FA should have nothing to do with the funeral since he had never forgiven them for his sacking.

1994: Death of Brazilian Grand Prix driver Ayrton Senna. He was actually born Ayrton da Silva, but decided to race under his mother's maiden name. Senna died during the San Marino Grand Prix which was held on the Imola circuit in Italy. He took pole position for the 65th and last time, but he felt his car wasn't handling well. His friend and compatriot Rubens Barrichello crashed in qualifying, breaking his arm and nose. Austrian rookie Roland Ratzenberger had a fatal crash in qualifying. On lap seven Senna left the racing line at turn seven, doing about 307kmh (191mph), and drove directly into a concrete retaining wall. He was airlifted

Ayrton Senna

21 March 1960 –1 May 1994

Brazilian Formula One driver, three times world champion,
considered by many to be the finest driver of all time.

to hospital, and his death was announced at 6.40pm. When his car was searched it was found to contain a rolled-up Austrian flag. Senna believed he would win, and intended unrolling the flag on the podium in honour of Ratzenberger.

2 May

1962: Birth of popular snooker player Jimmy 'Whirlwind' White, one of the three stars who have claimed the title 'The People's Champion' (along with Alex Higgins and Ronnie O'Sullivan – all flair players, and all three rather maverick). White holds the unique (and unwanted) record of having reached the final of the World Snooker Championship six times without ever winning the title.

1969: The birth of legendary West Indian batsman the Honourable Brian Lara (aka the Prince of Port of Spain). He holds the record for the highest individual innings in history (501*) as well as the highest individual Test innings (400*).

1970: Mike Mangeanello wins the Kentucky Derby on board Dust Commander. Back in 15th place was Fathom, with jockey Diane Crump becoming the first woman to race at the historic meeting.

1985: Death of Italian rally driver Attilio Bettega. Driving in the World Rally Championship stage four in Corsica, he lost control of his car and drove into a tree with such force the steering column was forced through the car into his chest, killing him instantly. Bettega was driving a Lancia with the racing number 4. Exactly a year later to the very day Henri Toivonen was driving Lancia #4 when he was involved in an accident. The car erupted into a fireball, killing Toivonen and his co-driver Sergio Cresto.

2015: The first-ever final of the European Champions Cup is an all-French affair. Europe's premier club rugby competition had replaced the Heineken Cup. Toulon beat Clermont 24-18.

3 May

1886: Death of Mary Outerbridge at the age of just 34. She is credited with taking tennis to the States. Outerbridge was visiting Bermuda and was introduced to the sport by soldiers posted there. On returning home she set up the first tennis court on the grounds of Staten Island Cricket and Baseball Club in March 1872. In 1880 the club hosted the first 'Tournament for the Championship of America'. This was won by O.E. Woodhouse, an Englishman who was visiting New York at the time.

1956: The first-ever World Judo Championships are held in Tokyo in Japan. Only four people entered the championship, won by Japan's Shokichi Natsui.

1977: The first-ever IBF (International Badminton Federation) world championships begin in Malmö in Sweden. Denmark's Flemming Delfs won the men's singles competition. Fellow Dane Lene Køppen beat England's Gillian Gilks to win the women's title. The pair met again in the final of the mixed doubles with the same result, when Køppen and Steen Skovgaard defeated Gilks and Derek Talbot.

1978: Final day of the final Test in the series between the West Indies and Australia. Although the West Indies had already won the series by winning three of the first four Tests, Australia set the West Indies a target of 369 to win. They managed to take nine West Indies wickets at a cost of just 258. Vanburn Holder was the ninth out, and slapped his gloves on his thigh in frustration – but the crowd misinterpreted that as meaning he believed the umpire had wrongly dismissed him … and so rioted. Chairs, stones, bottles and anything else was hurled on to the ground and the Australian team ran to the safety of their dressing room. The umpires abandoned the match and declared it a draw, depriving the Australians of victory.

1998: Yiannis Kouros of Greece takes a new world record in one of the greatest supermarathon events – the 24-hour road race.

Running in Basel, Switzerland, Kouros ran a total of 290.2km (180.3 miles) in the 24-hour period.

4 May

1924: The opening of the eighth Summer Olympic Games in Paris, France. The cost was estimated at about ten million francs, which represented a net loss of more than four million francs.

1928: Anticipating parking problems at the forthcoming Amsterdam Games in the Netherlands, the organisers come up with a method of showing visitors where they can park – a large white capital P on a blue background. Now the international symbol to indicate parking, this was the first time this sign was used.

1949: The Superga air disaster occurs when a plane owned by Italian Airlines crashes into a large retaining wall on the hill of Turin. The plane was carrying the entire Torino football team. The accident occurred on the journey home from Portugal. All 31 people on board lost their lives, including 18 players. Between them these players had won 57 league championships, and gained 78 international caps (71 for Italy, five for France and two for Czechoslovakia).

2018: Death of South African footballer Luyanda Ntshangase. Playing in a friendly game for Maritzburg United on 1 May, he was struck by lightning during the game. He was taken to hospital with burns on his chest and placed in an induced coma, but passed away three days later. He was just 21 years old. This was the third tragedy the club had faced in just two years; midfielders Mondli Cele (aged 27) and Mlondi Dlamini (20) had both died in unrelated car accidents.

5 May

1863: Joe Coburn is officially crowned Boxing Champion of America after knocking out Mike McCoole. As well as the title he earned $2,000. The bout lasted one hour and ten minutes, with McCoole knocked out in the 63rd round.

1904: Birth of British jockey Gordon Richards, considered by many to be the greatest jockey of all time. Through his career he won 4,870 races, and was named British flat-racing champion 26 times.

1912: The official opening of the fifth Olympic Games in Stockholm in Sweden (the football and shooting takes place eight weeks later). These games were the last time that the winners' medals were made of solid gold. Japan became the first Asian nation entering. Electronic timing was used for the first time. Figure skating, which had been a Summer Olympic sport, was removed as the hosts wanted to promote the Nordic Games. Stockholm also did not feature boxing, since the organisers disagreed with the sport on principle.

1915: Death of England rugby captain Ronnie Poulton-Palmer, who had scored four tries in a match against France just a year earlier. He was killed in action in Flanders, one of 26 England international rugby players killed in the Great War.

1992: The semi-final of the French football cup competition. Bastia on the isle of Corsica were drawn at home to Olympique de Marseille, who were the league leaders. The Bastian management thought they would maximise the opportunity for profit, and built a large additional stand to pack in more fans. Just ten minutes before the game was due to begin this whole new structure collapsed. Eighteen people died with more than 2,300 injured. The game was immediately abandoned, and was never replayed. For the first time in its history the Coupe de France was abandoned with no final and no trophy awarded as a mark of respect to those who perished.

6 May

1733: The first international boxing match sees Britain's Bob Whittaker beating the Greek fighter Tito di Carni.

1939: Death of Mick the Miller, the first world famous greyhound. He only raced for three years, but is considered iconic to followers of the sport.

1951: Willie Mays is selected for Major League Baseball with the New York Giants. Bizarrely he learned of his selection while at the cinema in Iowa. The Giants tracked him down to the cinema, and then persuaded the movie theatre to flash a message on the screen which read 'Willie Mays, call your hotel'.

1954: At a race meeting in Oxford, London-born Roger Bannister becomes the first man in history to run a mile in under four minutes, with an official time of 3.59.4.

2001: Souleymane Mamam becomes the youngest player ever to play in a World Cup qualifying match when he turns out for Togo against Zambia at the age of 13. Togo won the game 3-2.

7 May

1725: One of the earliest references to cricket concerns a club which no longer exists, playing on a ground which no longer exists, owned by an army unit which no longer exists! The Artillery Ground in Finsbury was owned by the Honourable Artillery Company, and one set of early minutes comments on the use of their land by the London Cricket Club, specifically the 'abuse done to the herbage of the ground by the cricket players'.

1877: The Victorian Football Association (VFA) is formed from eight existing football clubs, for the 'promotion and extension of football throughout the colony'. Within three years more than 100 additional clubs were formed in Melbourne and the surrounding district, and 60 more elsewhere in Victoria. Australian Rules football was taking off very rapidly.

1986: In the Champions Club Cup Barcelona play Steaua Bucharest, ending in one of the most woeful performances of penalty taking ever seen. The first four penalties were all missed before Steau converted their third. Barcelona then missed and Steau scored again. When Barcelona missed their fourth it was all over – Steaua had won 2-0 on penalties with six of the eight penalties missed.

1995: The greatest finish in NBA history. In the Eastern Conference semi-finals the New York Knicks were leading the Indiana Pacers by six points with just 18.7 seconds remaining. In the next nine seconds the Pacers scored eight points (a standard basket followed by two three-pointers). All eight points were scored by Reggie Miller, writing his name into history.

2011: Death of Spanish golfing legend Seve Ballesteros, winner of a record 50 European Tour titles. He died at home of a brain tumour.

8 May

1899: Klondike (born John Haines) becomes the first 'Black Heavyweight Champion of the World'. With blacks barred from competing for the standard titles due to the offensive colour bar, many of the best sportsmen set up titles such as the 'Coloured Boxing Champion'. After defeating the Coloured Heavyweight Champion of the World, Jack Johnson, Klondike claimed the title Black Heavyweight Champion of the World – an unofficial title that had never previously existed.

1945: German international footballer Julius Hirsch is declared dead – his actual date of death is unknown, the date declared being decided by a German court in 1950. Hirsch was the first person of Jewish origin to play for the national German football team. He also served Germany throughout the First World War, even earning the Iron Cross. Yet none of that was enough to save him – as a Jew he was taken to the Auschwitz concentration camp in March 1943 and was never heard of again.

1977: Team Formula One debut for Williams Grand Prix Engineering Limited, founded by Frank Williams and engineer Patrick Head, marking the beginning of a team that has won seven driver's titles and nine team titles.

1982: Japanese athlete Kenicho Ito breaks a world sprint record by running the 100m in 15.71 seconds on his hands and feet.

1982: Death of Canadian Formula One driver Gilles Villeneuve. He died during qualifying for the Belgian Grand Prix at Zolder following a high-speed collision with Austrian driver Jochen Mass.

1994: The Colorado Silver Bullets play their first game. The Bullets were the first all-female professional baseball team since the folding of the All-American Girls Professional Baseball League in 1954. Sadly the ladies were thrashed 19-0 by the Northern All-Stars.

9 May

1867: Foundation of the first South American football team – the Buenos Aires Football Club in Argentina – formed by immigrants from northern England who were construction workers on the railways.

1936: Casuals player Bernard Joy (actually playing for Arsenal at the time, but still registered with Casuals) plays for England against Belgium – the last amateur to play for England.

1965: Birth of Steve Yzerman, the longest-serving captain in the history of the NHL. He led the Detroit Red Wings hockey team for more than 1,300 games, leading them to five league titles and three Stanley Cup wins.

2001: The two biggest teams in Ghana's domestic football league are meeting, so the police are anticipating trouble. Accra Hearts of Oak had scored two late goals to beat their rivals, Asante Kotoko, by a score of 2-1. Kotoko fans were unhappy and launched missiles on to the pitch in protest. The police responded using tear gas, resulting in a stampede that led to the loss of the lives of 129 fans. One fan, Abdul Mohammed, was pulled out from the wreckage and moved to the morgue for burial. However, in the cramped and hectic morgue someone accidently stepped on his foot which brought him round again – he had only passed out, and very narrowly avoided being buried.

2013: Death of British sailor Andrew 'Bart' Simpson, Olympic gold medal winner in 2008 in the Star class as part of the British team. Simpson died when his catamaran capsized in San Fransisco Bay, while training for the America's Cup. The yacht flipped over and broke into pieces, with Simpson trapped under the hull for about ten minutes. The cause of the accident was unknown, but the cause of death was drowning.

10 May

1870: Englishman Jem 'The Gypsy' Mace defends his heavyweight boxing crown against the Irish champion Joe Coburn. Despite the fight lasting one hour and 17 minutes neither boxer actually lands a punch.

1967: Death of Italian Formula One Ferrari driver Lorenzo Bandini. He was running second in the Monaco Grand Prix on lap 82 when he lost control of his Ferrari at the harbour chicane. The car overturned and rammed into straw bales before catching fire. The fire was worsened by the straw catching alight. Bandini was pulled from the fire, but had 70 per cent burns over his body and died of his injuries three days later in hospital. After this straw and hay bales were removed from Formula One circuits, initially replaced with extended rails and more recently by tyre walls.

2011: Death of 24-year-old American jockey Michael Baze. Despite his young age he had already ridden 918 winners. His body was found in his car at the stables where he worked. Blood tests revealed an overdose as the cause of death, which was presumed to be accidental.

2018: When Spaniard Rafael Nadal beats Argentine Diego Schwartzman 6-3 6-4 at the Madrid Open, the match represents his 49th and 50th consecutive set victories on clay. This breaks the record for successive unbeaten sets on a single surface, beating John McEnroe's record of 49 on carpet.

11 May

1875: Philadelphia White Stockings pitcher George 'Charmer' Zettlein pitches the first-ever nine-inning shutout – bowling throughout all nine innings without conceding a single run throughout.

1900: Ten thousand people turn up to see James J. Jeffries knock out James J. Corbett in the 23rd round to win the heavyweight boxing title. The fight was briefly held up because the referee refused to enter the ring until he had received his $500 match fee.

1919: The Polo Grounds V is the venue for the baseball fixture between the New York Yankees and the Washington Senators. The match was played over 12 innings in front of a crowd of 3,000, and the final score was 0-0. (So credit must go to the pitchers Jack Quinn and Walter Johnson.)

1924: Birth of Newcastle and England soccer legend Jackie Milburn, one of the most prolific goalscorers of all time. Milburn was offered a trial at Newcastle as a 19-year-old and scored twice. In his second match he came on as a second half substitute and scored six times. The first time he ever wore the coveted Newcastle number nine shirt, he scored a hat-trick. Milburn was a cousin of Jack and Bobby Charlton.

1985: The day should be one of rejoicing for Bradford City and their fans, who are facing Lincoln City in their final home fixture of the English League Division Three season. Before kick-off the team were presented to the crowd as the Division Three champions, and were handed the trophy in their Valley Parade stadium. The main stand had already been condemned and was due for destruction. Just before half-time a small fire was reported in the main stand, and due to the windy conditions within four minutes this had engulfed much of the main stand. Fifty-six people died in the fire, with another 265 injured.

2008: Death of Portuguese racing cyclist Bruno Neves. Neves was racing in the Classica de Amarante in his home country and was wearing the leader's jersey when he was involved in a bad accident. It was initially believed that he had died from injuries sustained in the accident, but the post-mortem revealed that he had actually had a heart attack while cycling and had caused the accident himself.

12 May

1890: The first official County Championship cricket match starts in Bristol between Yorkshire and Gloucestershire. Yorkshire became the first winners of a county match, while home batsman James Cranston was the first century maker. In the inaugural season the scoring was very simple – one point for a win, and minus one for a loss. Sussex would finish bottom of the league with minus ten points, having won just one game and lost 11.

1925: Birth of baseball catcher Yogi Berra, who played 18 consecutive seasons for the New York Yankees. Incredibly he was chosen for the League All-Star team in all 18 seasons. The media loved him since he invariably produced something bizarre, e.g. 'I really didn't say everything I said.'

1927: The final day of the inaugural professional snooker championship sees Joe Davis beat Tom Dennis 20-11 in Camkin's Hall in Birmingham. This championship becomes the World Championship eight years later. The final was best of 31 frames so Davis was unbeatable when he reached 16-7, but for many years finals were always played to the maximum number of frames as the players shared the final eight frames.

1957: Death of Spanish aristocrat Alfonso de Portago. Portago and his co-driver Edmund Nelson were killed driving in the Mille Miglia. Travelling at about 150mph (240kmh) a tyre blew and he lost control of his Ferrari which spun into the crowd. As well as the driver and co-driver, nine spectators were killed, including five children. Portago had once predicted (wrongly): 'I won't die in an accident. I'll die of old age or be executed in some gross miscarriage of justice.'

1976: Riding King of Swat, American jockey Steve Cauthen makes his riding debut at the age of 16. Having ridden successfully on both sides of the Atlantic he remains the only jockey to have won both the Kentucky Derby and the Epsom Derby.

2012: Australian golfer Rhein Gibson manages a world record score of just 55 (16 under par) at the River Oaks Golf Club in Edmond, Oklahoma.

13 May

1909: The first Giro d'Italia takes place in Italy, won by local cyclist Luigi Ganna. 127 riders started the inaugural race at (bizarrely) seven minutes to three in the morning (2.53am). Forty-nine of the riders completed the three-week race, with Ganna winning 5,325 lire.

1914: Birth of boxer Joe Louis (aka the Brown Bomber). Louis became the world heavyweight boxing champion in 1937, and then held on to the title for more than 11 years through 26 successful defences of his crown. He was widely considered the first African American to achieve cult status in the States.

2002: Andrew Rivett arrives at Land's End having run from John O'Groats in a time of nine days, two hours and 26 minutes.

2007: Britain's Chris Hoy sets a new cycling time trial record in the Flying 500m at La Paz in Bolivia, with a time of 24.758 seconds.

14 May

1754: Formation of the Royal & Ancient Golf Club of St Andrews in Scotland. Twenty-two 'noblemen and gentlemen' chipped in together to purchase a silver club to be awarded annually for a special competition.

1870: The first known game of rugby to be played in New Zealand is a match between Nelson College and Nelson Football Club.

1900: The beginning of competition for the Games of the II Olympiad in Paris. Unlike modern Games, this 1900 Olympics would run until the end of October, and 997 competitors took part in 19 different sports. Since the Olympics were competed as part of the World's Fair, some competitors didn't even realise they had competed in the Olympics. Sailor Hélène de Pourtalès became the first female Olympic champion. These Games featured, for the only time, cricket, croquet, a swimming obstacle race, underwater swimming, ballooning, car racing and motorbike racing. They were also the only Games which used live targets, when pigeons were used in the shooting.

1938: The England national football team play an end-of-season 'friendly' game … in Berlin against Nazi Germany. Over a hundred thousand packed into the ground to see England win 6-3. The British Ambassador to Germany, Sir Neville Henderson, controversially suggested that the team offered a Nazi salute before kick-off as a mark of respect, which they duly did. In attendance were Nazi leaders including Rudolf Hess, Hermann Goering and Joseph Goebbels.

1989: The first-ever Tour de Trump, which folded in 1996. The vision was to have an American cycle race on a par with the Tour de France, and was named for its initial sponsor, businessman Donald Trump. The inaugural winner was Norwegian Dag Otto Lauritzen.

2016: Brazilian surfer Gabriel Medina becomes the first person ever to land a backflip in competition.

15 May

1828: The Epsom Derby finishes in a dead heat for the first time. Cadland won the run-off against The Colonel.

1874: The first game formally recognised as American football is played between Harvard and McGill, featuring the oval ball for the first time, and allowing players to run with the ball or throw it … but only if being actively pursued by an opponent. If not, or if the opponent gave up his pursuit, he then had to stop and kick it! Five hundred spectators paid 50c each for the spectacle.

1912: Major controversy at the baseball game between New York Highlanders and Detroit Tigers in New York. One fan, Claude Lueker, had been consistently heckling baseball legend Ty Cobb. Eventually Cobb had enough and climbed into the stand to sort him out. However, Lueker was disabled – which the rest of the crowd were quick to point out, but Cobb replied: 'I don't care if he's got no feet.' Cobb was thrown out of the game, fined $50 and suspended indefinitely.

1974: The official start date of the British and Irish Lions tour of South Africa, which would become the Lions' most successful tour of all time, winning 21 of their 22 matches, drawing the fourth and final Test against the Springboks. The Lions were captained by Irish lock Willie John McBride, on his record fifth Lions tour.

1986: Death of Italian Formula One driver Elio de Angelis following an accident while testing at the Paul Ricard circuit in France. Very popular with fans and opponents alike, he had been called Formula One's 'last true gentleman'. After the rear wing of his car became detached his car span and flipped. The accident itself only resulted in a broken collar bone and friction burns on his back, but Angelis was unable to get out of his car and was trapped for several minutes before stewards arrived at this distant point of the long circuit. He was eventually removed and airlifted to hospital where he died 29 hours later from smoke inhalation.

16 May

1924: Death of baseball pitcher Candy Cummings, the man credited with inventing the curveball. Having initially had the vision behind the curveball Cummings had to wait a few years before using it in gameplay. Most catchers at the time stood well back from the batsman, making it impossible to pitch the curveball. It was not until Brooklyn Excelsiors bought Nat Hicks, who stood directly behind the batter, that Cummings was able to utilise his new weapon.

1955: Birth of Belarusian gymnast Olga Korbut. Nicknamed the 'Sparrow from Minsk' due to her petite and dainty frame, she was considered primarily responsible for shifting gymnastics away from its ballet roots to greater energy, acrobatics and technique. She was also considered the main contributor towards the popularisation of gymnastics.

1973: AC Milan of Italy beat England's Leeds United 1-0 to win the European Cup Winners' Cup in Greece. Once the final whistle went the Greek crowd threw missiles at the Milan team on their lap of honour, disgusted at what they perceived to be cheating by both Milan and the referee. Milan's goal was scored directly from an indirect free kick, Leeds's Norman Hunter was sent off and Leeds were denied at least three obvious penalties. Although UEFA refused to consider a replay, the Greek FA did look into the refereeing, and found him guilty of accepting bribes from Milan. UEFA banned him from refereeing, although they still insisted the original result stood.

1998: New Zealand women's rugby union team beat their American counterparts 44-12 to win the women's rugby World Cup in Amsterdam. This was the third women's World Cup in rugby, but the first that was officially sanctioned by the International Rugby Board.

2013: Death of American race driver Dick Trickle, championship racer in ASA, NASCAR, All Pro and other formats. He logged more than a million laps in about 2,200 races, of which he won more than 1,200.

2018: Death of footballer Ray Wilson after a long battle with Alzheimer's disease. Wilson played left-back for England in the 1966 World Cup Final. While the majority of his teammates from that famous victory worked as coaches, pundits or in the media, Wilson walked away when his playing days were done, setting up as an undertaker in Huddersfield, retiring in 1997.

17 May

1859: The first set of rules are created for Australian Rules football. Melbourne cricketer Thomas Wentworth Wills believed that a football club should be formed to keep his teammates fit during winter. The Melbourne Cricket Club agreed to the idea and appointed a committee to produce a set of rules. The main rule was players could handle the ball, but were not allowed to run farther than was necessary to kick it.

1875: The first running of the Kentucky Derby. Aristides won, ridden by Oliver Lewis.

1886: Formation of Motherwell FC, created from the amalgamation of two ironworks football teams – Glencairn FC and Alpha FC. The team had little opposition available for matches and when they did play, they frequently began with a man or two short, with players still working their shifts in the local works.

1955: Death of West Indian pace bowler Leslie Hylton. Hylton was hanged for the murder of his wife, and was the only Test cricketer to be executed. His defence at trial was that he was trying to take his own life through depression, intending to shoot himself, but he missed.

2007: Leroy Rosenior achieves a quite remarkable record due to a very bizarre set of circumstances. Torquay United had been struggling both financially and on the pitch. A couple of board members were briefed to find a new manager. They appointed Rosenior. Meanwhile, other directors were negotiating with a consortium with regard to a takeover. By freak coincidence the takeover was confirmed on the same day as Rosenior's appointment … but the new owners wanted their own man in charge – so sacked Rosenior. Rosenior therefore holds the record of having been the manager of a league football team for literally ten minutes.

2009: At an athletics meet in Manchester, UK, Usain Bolt wins the rarely run 150m sprint. The unusual distance did produce one outstanding world record. Allowing the first 50m to get up to speed, Bolt ran the last 100m in 8.70 seconds, the fastest time ever over 100m, equivalent to 25.7mph (41.4kmh).

18 May

1918: The final of the earliest known women's football competition. In an attempt to raise national spirits towards the end of the war, the ladies working in the munitions factories of the north-east of England set up a cup competition – the Tyne Wear & Tees Alfred Wood Munition Girls' Cup (aka The Munitionettes' Cup). After a draw, Blyth Spartans won the replayed final against Bolckow Vaughan 5-0 in Middlesbrough in front of a crowd of 22,000.

1924: The final of the Olympic rugby tournament sees France playing against the USA. On paper it certainly looked like a bit of a mismatch – France had one of the finest rugby teams ever put together, while the majority of the American team had not touched a rugby ball until less than a year earlier. In front of a screaming and drunken crowd in Paris, America shocked everyone, winning 17-3. An early tackle left French star Adolphe Jauréguy badly injured and needing to be carried from the field of play. At that moment the crowd turned. Rocks and bottles were hurled on to the field, fighting broke out in the stands and US reserve player Gideon Nelson was left unconscious after an assault by a spectator with a walking stick. At the final whistle the French crowd invaded the pitch, and the French team had to join the police in trying to protect the Americans.

1946: Joe Davis wins the World Snooker Championship Final at the Royal Horticultural Hall in London. The final was a best-of-145 affair so the result was decided when he was leading 73-62, but all 145 frames had to be played to give the audience value. Davis beat Horace Lindrum 78-67 to claim his 15th and final World Championship win.

1978: Retirement of Belgian road and track cyclist Eddy Merckx, often considered the finest cyclist of all time. He is one of only three cyclists to have won all five 'monuments' – Milan to San Remo (the sprinter's classic), the Tour of Flanders (the cobbled classic), Paris to Roubaix (the 'Hell of the North'), Liège to Bastogne and back to Liège (the oldest classic), and the Giro di Lombardia in Italy (aka the Race of the Falling Leaves).

19 May

1536: Death by execution (beheading) of Queen Anne Boleyn, second wife of King Henry VIII. While a huge crowd gathered to watch the spectacle, the King didn't attend. News was brought to him while he was playing tennis at Hampton Court.

1890: Death of South African cricketer Gus Kempis. In March 1889 Kempis was selected to play in South Africa's first-ever Test match. The following season he took 41 wickets at an average of just 12.42. Sadly, however, he contracted a virus and died of a fever in Mozambique at the age of just 24.

1935: Following a proposal from a couple of members, the NFL votes to adopt an annual college draft. The first draft took place in 1936, and has become an annual event.

1958: Death of English racing driver Archie Scott-Brown, famous for battling both disability and prejudice. He won 71 different races in various categories. He died fighting for the lead in a sports car race at Spa-Francorchamps when he skidded on a wet surface, suffering massive injuries and dying the following day in hospital at the age of just 31. Nevertheless, his achievements still stand as truly remarkable for a man who only had one hand.

20 May

1734: The first-ever jockey club forms in South Carolina in the States.

1878: British athlete Ada Anderson completes her remarkable record in the sport of pedestrianism. Anderson started her challenge on 8 April, aiming to complete 1,500 miles in 1,000 hours. But this was not just an endurance event, it was also a challenge of sleep deprivation – the record involved doing 1.5 miles every single hour over the 43 days.

1902: London dentist Jack Marles creates the first-ever mouth guard for boxers. At the time of the creation they were never intended to be used in fighting, but to simply protect the mouth during training and sparring.

1911: Death of E.M. Grace, older brother of W.G. Grace. E.M. played for Gloucestershire, and made one Test appearance against Australia in 1880, when both W.G. and another brother Fred were also playing. In 1862, while still aged only 20, E.M. produced one of the most remarkable cricketing performances of all time. Playing for the MCC against Kent he carried his bat for 192* out of a total of 344. He then bowled, achieving 10-69. This is not an official record since the game was 12-a-side.

1973: Tragedy strikes at the Monza racing circuit in Italy. Monza was lined by steel barriers which motor enthusiasts felt improved safety standards for both car racers and spectators – but the barriers reduced safety for motorbikes. On the very first lap of the Nations Grand Prix, Renzo Pasolini's bike lurched sideways and hit one of these barriers, killing him instantly. He was thrown from the bike and his bike bounced back across the circuit, hitting leader Jarno Saarinen from Finland on the head and he was also killed. The incident caused a massive accident involving 14 other bikes.

21 May

1866: First-class cricket debut of Fred Grace at the age of just 15 years and 159 days. Grace was the youngest brother of the cricketing family featuring Henry, Alfred, E.M. and the legendary W.G. W.G. played in his brother's debut match, both representing the 'Gentlemen of England XI' against Oxford University.

1891: San Francisco plays host to the much-vaunted boxing match between two of the finest boxers of the day – James J. Corbett and Peter 'Black Prince' Jackson. The referee stepped in and declared a draw – after 61 rounds.

1904: Foundation of FIFA (Fédération Internationale de Football Association) meeting in Paris. The founding members were France, Belgium, Denmark, the Netherlands, Spain, Sweden and Switzerland. England had been invited to be a founding member, but were hesitant to commit for political reasons and would not join for another 11 months.

1980: Ian Rush makes his international debut for Wales against Scotland in Glasgow. The remarkable thing was that he still had not made his debut for Liverpool but had been restricted to a few matches with the second XI.

1989: Death of motor racing driver Don Williams at the age of 42. Williams was involved in a multi-car pile-up in the NASCAR Sportsman 300 race on 17 February 1979, suffering permanent brain damage and miscellaneous other injuries. He remained in a coma until passing away a little more than ten years later.

22 May

1907: Bowling for Middlesex against Somerset Albert Trott takes seven wickets. Remarkably all seven wickets came in just two overs, separated by a lengthy gap. He took four wickets in four balls fairly early on in the innings, and then claimed a hat-trick later on in the same innings.

1922: A British expedition led by General Charles Bruce and Lt-Col Edward Strutt makes the first serious attempt at conquering Mount Everest. Although the attempt is unsuccessful they are the first climbers ever to reach a height in excess of 8,000m. They are forced to turn back when they reach 8,170m (26,800ft).

1953: The FA Cup Final, the so-called Matthews final, sees Blackpool winning the cup with a 4-3 victory over Bolton Wanderers. With two minutes to go Bolton were leading 3-2, but a last-minute goal by Stan Mortenson and an injury-time winner by Bill Perry brought the cup to Blackpool. Mortenson's 89th minute goal completed his hat-trick – the only time a hat-trick has been scored in a Wembley FA Cup Final. It is indicative of how impressive Stanley Matthews was that this final invariably carries his name and is not known as the Mortenson final, despite his heroics.

1955: The Monaco Grand Prix witnesses one of the most extraordinary events in the history of Formula One racing. Italian driver Alberto Ascari lost control of his car and opted for what he considered to be the safest path ... straight through the barriers and into the sea. Panic surged through the crowd as the car made its way to the bottom of the Mediterranean until Ascari's blue helmet resurfaced and he was pulled to safety.

1966: McLaren Racing Limited make their Formula One debut at the Monaco Grand Prix, the first race of the new season. The team only entered one car, driven by Bruce McLaren himself.

1987: The first rugby union World Cup tournament begins in New Zealand. As hosts the All Blacks had the right to open the tournament and on day one they entertained Italy, thrashing them 70-6.

23 May

1883: A truly bizarre baseball game was played at Recreation Park in Philadelphia, advertised as the Snorkeys against the Hoppers. The Snorkeys were named after a one-armed soldier in the stage play *Under the Gaslight* because each member of the team only had one arm. The Hoppers only had one leg – some had primitive prosthetics but the majority relied on crutches. The Snorkeys beat the Hoppers 33-17.

1908: American Jay Gould II wins the Olympic gold medal in the Jeu de Paume competition (aka real tennis) – the only time it has been a competitive Olympic sport.

1941: Buddy Baer is disqualified in the seventh round of a heavyweight bout against Joe Louis. The fight nearly didn't happen. It was an outdoor arena and heavy rain in the morning meant that many people assumed the fight wouldn't go ahead – including referee Arthur Donovan who went out drinking and became rather intoxicated. On learning the fight was happening he had a bit of a struggle trying to sober up. Louis had floored Baer twice in the sixth round, stirring up the crowd who became so loud that Louis didn't hear the bell. As Baer staggered to his feet Louis hit him again – now well after the bell. Baer's manager and trainer argued that Louis should be disqualified, so they refused to leave the ring for the next round. The referee disqualified their man for their actions.

2002: Death of American golfer Sam Snead (aka Slammin' Sammy). The man renowned for his 'perfect swing' won a world record 82 PGA tour titles, including seven majors. Snead was also the only man to achieve a top ten finish in a major tournament in five different decades. Perhaps his most bizarre claim to fame was in 1962 when he won the Royal Poinciana Plaza Invitational – becoming the only man ever to win an LPGA Tour event (Ladies Professional Golfers' Association). He claimed his philosophy of life was 'Keep close count of your nickels and dimes, stay away from whisky and never concede a putt.'

24 May

1843: The first confirmed college sports club is the Yale University Boat Club, established on this day when a group of Yale students purchase a small rowing vessel called *Whitehall*.

1964: The Estadio Nacional disaster in Lima is the biggest catastrophe in the history of association football. Peru were hosting Argentina in the build-up to the Tokyo Olympics football tournament. Argentina led for much of the match but Peru equalised with just six minutes remaining. The Uruguayan referee disallowed the goal, triggering a pitch invasion by the home fans. The police retaliated with tear gas and the crowd rushed to the exits. Unfortunately the exits were tunnels leading to the streets, sealed at the ends with corrugated steel shutters during matches. As the crowds rushed down the tunnels they hit a dead end, but those following on behind didn't realise this and kept coming. In the initial press down the tunnels 328 people lost their lives, mainly through asphyxia or internal haemorrhaging, with many more injured.

1979: Somerset face Worcestershire in the final round of group matches in the limited overs Benson & Hedges Cup, the outcome of which would determine which teams would progress through to the quarter-finals. The group containing these two teams was remarkably close – if Worcestershire could beat Somerset, and Glamorgan won their game, then these three counties would all be level on points, and progression would come down to bowling strike rate ... for which Somerset held a healthy lead. So on winning the toss Somerset captain Brian Close decided the best thing he could do was to preserve the strike rate advantage – by minimising the amount of work his bowlers had to do. He therefore opted to bat, and declared after just one over with the score on 1-0. Worcestershire required ten balls to score the two runs they needed. The match was over in 18 minutes – 16 deliveries producing three runs and no wickets … and Somerset were through to the quarter-finals. However, the TCCB met the following week and expelled Somerset from the competition for 'sacrificing all known cricketing principles by deliberately losing the game'.

2014: The 22nd Champions League Final is an all-Madrid affair as Real Madrid beat Atletico Madrid 4-1 in Lisbon!

25 May

1868: The Surrey Gentlemen host the Australian Aboriginal cricket team, who are beginning their first tour of England.

1896: Loughborough footballer James Logan dies after developing pneumonia while playing. Logan was the first person to score a hat-trick in an FA Cup Final while playing for Notts County against Bolton Wanderers.

1935: The Big Ten Championships, a large intercollegiate athletics meet, in Michigan. What happened next no one could have foreseen – frequently referred to as the 'most incredible 45 minutes in the history of sport'. At 3.15pm Jesse Owens ran the 100 yard dash in 9.4 seconds, equalling the world record. Ten minutes later he jumped 8.13m in the long jump, setting a new world record despite the fact he only had one attempt at this due to his commitments on the track. At 3.34pm he was back on the track running the 220-yard (200m) dash – in another world record time of 20.3 seconds. At 4.00pm Owens achieved another world record – 22.6 seconds in the 220-yard (200m) low hurdles. Forty-five minutes, four gold medals, three new world records and one equalled world record.

1956: Althea Gibson of the US beats Britain's Angela Mortimer to win the women's singles title at the French Championships. Gibson became the first black athlete to win a tennis Grand Slam title. In the 1960s she became the first black player to compete on the women's professional golf circuit.

1967: Celtic become the first British team to lift the European Cup, beating Internazionale (aka Inter Milan) 2-1 in the final in Lisbon. The most astonishing fact associated with their victory, particularly in the context of modern football, is that 14 of the matchday squad of 15 were born within ten miles of Celtic's ground in Glasgow – the other was born 18 miles away!

2002: Another incident to prove that cheats sometimes prosper. In the closing moments of rugby's Heineken Cup Final at the Millennium Stadium in Cardiff, Leicester Tigers were leading Munster 15-9 with just moments to go, but faced a scrum on their own five-metre line. With Munster scrum-half Peter Stringer preparing to put the ball into the scrum, Leicester's England flanker Neil Back, on the blind side of the referee, knocked the ball out of Stringer's hand into the scrum on Leicester's side. They successfully recycled the ball, punted into touch and won the game. The incident was missed by the match referee and the Irishmen were justifiably furious, but the result stood and Leicester were the champions.

26 May

1875: George Bechtel and Bill Craver become the first baseball stars ever to be sold by one club to another when they move from Philadelphia Centennials to Philadelphia Athletics for $1,500. Bechtel soon became the first person in MLB history to be suspended for life for deliberately losing games for cash. The evidence came when he sent a message to a teammate: 'We can make $500 if you lose the game today. Tell John [manager Jack Chapman] and let me know at once.' The teammate wired back to say he wasn't interested, and passed the note to the authorities.

1923: The beginning of the first 24 Hours of Le Mans race. The original plan was to have three 24-hour races a year, with the winners being the ones who drove the furthest over the three races combined. That was changed five years later to become the more familiar single 24-hour race. The 1923 race was won by French drivers André Lagache and René Léonard, driving for the Chenard-Walcker team, having covered a distance of 2,209.5km (1,373 miles).

1955: Death of Italian motor racing champion Alberto Ascari, twice winner of the Formula One World Championship. Just four days after the Monaco Grand Prix, Ascari travelled to Monza to watch his good friend Eugenio Castellotti test drive the Ferrari 750 sports car that they were to co-drive in the 1,000km Monza race. After watching his friend he asked if he could have a go – so wearing his shirt, tie and suit he set off wearing Castellotti's helmet. On his third trial lap he lost control and the car catapulted and threw Ascari on to the tarmac where he died moments later.

1989: Death of Don Revie, erstwhile football manager of Leeds United and England, after a battle with motor neurone disease. Revie was manager of England before controversially leaving for a lucrative contract in the Middle East. But it is with Leeds United that his name will be forever synonymous. A Leeds player who took over as manager when the team were languishing in the lower half of Division Two, Revie turned them into one of the most successful and feared teams in Europe. He had a very basic philosophy to success: 'You get nowt for being second.'

2010: Retirement of football coach Ivor Powell. He coached and/or managed several teams, finishing at Bath City. He finally took his retirement … at the age of 93, after coaching for more than 55 years.

27 May

1719: The first use of the term 'boxing' referring to a prize fight in a bare-knuckle championship. The winner of this first 'boxing' match was James Figg; the loser's name has been lost over time.

1908: Foundation of Belgian soccer club Anderlecht (official name: Sporting Club Anderlechtois). Their first match was against Institut Saint-Georges, and Anderlecht won 11-8.

1943: Death of American Olympic distance runner Louis Zamperini ... who died in 2014! Zamperini became famous for his performance in the 5,000m at the 1936 Berlin Olympics. He passed the bell well adrift of the field, but refused to give up and ran the last lap in an amazing 56 seconds as he attempted to catch the others in the field. He finished eighth, but his last lap heroics caught the eye of Adolf Hitler who asked to meet him. Zamperini served in the Second World War, and while on active duty the plane he was in was shot down over the Pacific. His parents were sent a letter listing this as his 'official date of death', and a personal letter of condolence from president Franklin D. Roosevelt. But he hadn't died. He drifted on a raft for 47 days before being captured by the Japanese who imprisoned and tortured him. He remained a prisoner of war, and presumed dead, until the end of the conflict. Louis Zamperini actually died at home in Los Angeles from pneumonia on 2 July 2014, at the age of 97.

2013: Death of Cullen Finnerty, the NCAA quarterback. He played in the NFL with the Baltimore Ravens and the Denver Broncos, then spent some time playing Aussie 4es, and finally Canadian football. He then took some time off, and went on a fishing trip to recuperate. At one point he telephoned both his wife and her brother, claiming he was being stalked by two men who wanted to hurt him. Two days later his body was found in an open clearing near the road, with absolutely no mark, cut or bruise anywhere on his body. Toxicology tests were clear. The cause of his death remains unknown.

28 May

1888: The long-term enemies of Scottish football, Celtic and Rangers, play for the first time in what is termed a 'friendly encounter' shortly after Celtic have been founded, with Celtic winning 5-2. In these early days Celtic didn't wear their famous green and white hoops; they wore white shirts with a green collar, black shorts and green socks.

1912: For many Test cricket bowlers achieving a hat-trick (three wickets in three balls) is something that they can only dream of. Many of the world's finest bowlers never achieved it – Dennis Lillee, Muttiah Muralitharan, Malcolm Marshall, Fred Truman, Richard Hadlee … the list goes on. Indeed it has only happened 43 times in the first 140 years of Test cricket. Only three players have managed to achieve this feat twice. Therefore the achievement of Australian Jimmy Matthews must rank as one of the greatest sporting feats of all time. Bowling for Australia against South Africa at Old Trafford in Manchester, England, Matthews achieved two hat-tricks … on the same day. Responding to Australia's score of 448, South Africa were bowled out for 265, with Matthews removing Rolland Beaumont, Sid Pegler and Tommy Ward in consecutive balls. South Africa followed on and were skittled out for just 95, with Matthews claiming the consecutive wickets of Herbie Taylor, Reggie Schwarz and Ward (again!)

1927: Wally Hammond scores his 1,000th run of the season, after just 22 days.

1993: The first-ever game of three-sided football (aka 3SF) is played on Glasgow Green. Played on a hexagonal pitch with three teams all playing each other with standard football goals, the winner was the team which conceded the fewest goals. The game was devised by Danish professor Asger Jorn to explain his theory of triolectics, and was organised by the London Psychogeographical Association. The first 3SF World Cup was played in May 2014, with Silkeborg KFUM from Denmark crowned as the first world champions.

29 May

1646: The earliest known reference to a single wicket cricket match see two players from Coxheath playing against four men from Maidstone on Coxheath Common. The result of the game is unknown.

1900: The day of the equestrian events at the Paris Summer Olympic Games, comprising five events. The equestrian events have certainly changed over time: Aimé Haegeman from Belgium won the horse jumping event, Frenchman Dominique Gardères and Italian Gian Trissino shared first place in the horse high jump, while Constant van Langhendonck won the gold medal for the horse long jump. Louis Murat of France won the 'Hacks and Hunter Combined', while Belgian Georges Nagelmackers took gold in the 'mail coach' event.

1977: A.J. Foyt wins the Indianapolis 500. Fellow American Janet Guthrie became the first woman to compete in the race but she was forced to retire on lap 27.

1985: The European Cup Final between England's Liverpool and Juventus of Italy at the Heysel Stadium in Brussels, Belgium. In the build-up to the game both sets of fans were openly hostile to the opposition with missiles thrown and threats made. Then about an hour before kick-off the Liverpool fans charged the Juventus fans, who retreated backwards towards a wall. Many people near the wall were crushed, and the stampede continued until the wall collapsed. Thirty-nine people were killed, the majority of whom were from Juventus, and more than 600 were injured. The blame was laid exclusively at the feet of Liverpool. Twenty-six of their fans were extradited, 14 of whom were found guilty of manslaughter. UEFA took the step of banning all English clubs from European competitions for 'an indeterminate period of time' (which turned out to be five years, six years for Liverpool themselves).

2003: Death of British motorcycle racing driver David Jefferies. Jefferies died during practice for a race on the Isle of Man, losing control on a corner, hitting a garden wall of an adjacent house and being killed immediately on impact. At the end of the weekend the organisers hosted a parade lap of honour, and literally thousands of bikes joined in, filling the 37-mile circuit.

2005: An iconic moment in the history of the Indy 500 race, when Danika Patrick takes the lead and heads the race for a few laps – the first time that a woman has led the famous race.

30 May

1911: Nearly two years since it is first considered open, the famous Indianapolis oval race track finally sees its first official race after radical restructuring. The track had seen testing in 1909, but most drivers and officials were unhappy at the visible degradation. The owners decided to relay the entire surface with bricks – more than 14,000 tonnes of them! Incredibly each brick was laid by hand over a two-inch cushion of sand, levelled out, and gaps were filled with mortar. The final brick was laid by the state governor, and was made of gold. The track soon became known as the brickyard – and three feet (0.91m) of the original bricks still remain at the start/finish line. The first race was a 500-mile race (hence Indy 500) (800km) won by Ray Harroun, averaging 74.6mph. Harroun gained a significant weight advantage over the rest of the field by driving solo. The other 39 competitors carried a mechanic to tell the driver what was going on around them, particularly immediately behind. Harroun gathered this information himself by sticking a mirror on the windscreen to see behind – the first-ever rear-view mirror.

1955: Death of the American motor racing driver William 'Vuky' Vukovich Sr., twice winner of the Indianapolis 500. In the 1955 race Vukovich had built up a 17-second lead and was trying to pass three backmarkers to lap them. One of these, Johnny Boyd, was pushed into Vukovich's path and hit him; Vukovich became airbourne and spun, landing upside down. He then hit a low wall and his car burst into flames – although medics stated that Vukovich was already dead before the fire started having been partially decapitated.

1962: Geoff Hurst, England's 1966 World Cup hero, makes his debut … for Essex County Cricket Club against Lancashire. It turned out to be his only first-class match for Essex, although he did play several matches for their second XI.

1964: Death of the highly successful American racer Dave MacDonald at the age of just 27, and of fellow competitor Eddie Sachs. In a four-year racing career MacDonald competed in 118 races, with 52 wins and another 23 podium finishes. Overtaking Walt Hansgen MacDonald, just clipped the back of his car and lost control. Hitting a wall his car erupted in flames. Sachs drove into him, and his car also caught fire. Sachs died immediately. MacDonald was brought out of his car and rushed to hospital, but succumbed to his injuries two hours later. For the first time in the history of the Indianapolis 500 the race was stopped due to the accident.

31 May

1787: Thomas Lord plays in his first recorded cricket match, turning out for Middlesex against Essex. (It is believed he probably played for a few years before this time, but no records exist for this period.) The 9th Earl of Winchilsea (George Finch) and the 4th Duke of Richmond (Charles Lennox) ran a cricket team called the White Conduit Club. They wanted a cricket ground which could be their exclusive venue, and approached Lord to design and build such a ground, which he did. The finished ground bore his own name (hence Lord's), and the first match to be played here was the Middlesex vs. Essex match. The Earl and the Duke rehoused the White Conduit at Lord's, and the club soon evolved into the new Marylebone Cricket Club (MCC). The ground still exists today, known as the 'Lord's Old Ground'.

1868: The first known official bicycle race takes place at the Parc de Saint Cloud in Paris, over a distance of 2km. The race was actually advertised as a 'velocipede' race – an early form of bicycle with pedals cranked through to the front wheel. The winner was a Dr James Moore of the UK.

1975: Day one of the county cricket match between Derbyshire and Lancashire, in many ways the most bizarre county match of all time. In Buxton on a gloriously hot summer's day, Lancashire batted first, hitting a big and rapid 477/5 in just over two sessions before declaring. In the remaining time they were able to remove two Derbyshire wickets for 25. On day two there was no play … because following the heatwave Derbyshire woke up to four inches of snow! On the third and final day the snow had melted, but the day was cool, damp and overcast – a treat for the bowlers. The Lancashire bowlers took the final eight wickets for just 17 runs. Clive Lloyd enforced the follow-on and Derbyshire were dismissed for 87, leaving Lancashire the winners by an innings and 348 runs.

2002: Patrick Tillman, an American football player with the St Louis Cardinals, turns his back on his sporting career to enlist with the US army. Tillman and his brother Kevin were so enraged at the 11 September attacks that they decided to join the war on terror, serving in both Iraq and Afghanistan. Tillman actually turned down a three-year $3.6m contract extension from the Cardinals to serve. Tragically Tillman was killed in action on 22 April 2004.

2003: The conclusion of the Zürich Premiership, England's top league for rugby union. This was the 16th season of the Premiership – but the first time the title had been decided by a play-off after Leicester Tigers and Saracens finished level at the top of the league. To maintain neutrality, the play-off was played at Franklin's Gardens, the home of Northampton Saints. The game went into extra time, with the Tigers eventually winning 27-20.

JUNE

1 June

1899: Day one of the first Test between England and Australia at Trent Bridge in Nottingham. The match was highly significant in terms of England cricketing legends – it was the final Test match for Dr W.G. Grace, and the first for Wilf Rhodes.

1925: Lou Gehrig takes his place in the starting line-up for the New York Yankees, replacing Wally Pipp. This was the first of a record 2,130 consecutive games for Gehrig.

1964: Birth of United States Paralympic swimmer Trischa Zorn. Blind from birth, Zorn would go on to become the most successful Paralympian of all time with an incredible haul of 41 gold medals, nine silver and five bronze.

1983: Jockey Lester Pigott wins the Epsom Derby in Surrey riding Teenesco, to claim a record ninth victory at the historic race. The 'Long Fellow' (as Pigott is often referred) is widely considered the finest flat-racing jockey of all time. The derby has been run since 1780, and was named since it took place on Epsom Downs and the earliest races were sponsored by the 12th Earl of Derby.

2002: Death of South African cricketer and erstwhile captain Hansie Cronje. Despite being a magnificent cricketer with a wonderful record he is invariably best remembered for his lifetime ban from the game in April 2000 for match-fixing allegations. Cronje died in a plane crash at the age of just 32.

2 June

1935: Briton Fred Perry defeats German Gottfried von Cramm 6-3 3-6 6-1 6-3 to win the French Championship in tennis (now the French Open). In so doing Perry became the first male player of all time to win a 'Career Grand Slam' – winning all four major tournaments. Uniquely he was also the table tennis world champion in 1929.

1941: Death of baseball legend Lou Gehrig, aka the Iron Horse. Gehrig played his entire career of 17 seasons for the New York Yankees, hitting 493 home runs and having 1,995 runs batted in. After 2,130 consecutive games Gehrig surprised everyone, taking himself out of the starting line-up to break the streak. The reason, unknown to others at the time, was that he was beginning to struggle badly with his health, suffering from an incurable neuromuscular disease called amyotrophic lateral sclerosis (a form of motor neurone disease, now frequently referred to as Lou Gehrig's disease). The illness led to his premature death just two years later.

1965: Brazil beat Belgium 5-0 in a friendly football international in Rio de Janeiro. The match marked Pelé's seventh and final hat-trick in international football.

1970: Death of New Zealand racing car driver, engineer and designer Bruce McLaren, best known as the founder of his eponymous racing car company which has gained considerable success, particularly in Formula One in which it has gained eight constructors' championships and 12 drivers' championships. Bruce McLaren died at the age of just 32 when the Can-Am car he was testing crashed at Goodwood in England.

2004: In the CONMEBOL World Cup qualifying group Brazil beat Argentina 3-1 in front of 60,000 fans in Belo Horizonte. All three Brazilian goals were scored by Ronaldo – all three from the penalty spot.

2007: The UEFA European football championship qualifying game between neighbours Sweden and Denmark ends in controversy. With the teams locked at 3-3 going into the last minute Danish midfielder Christian Poulsen punched Swedish striker Markus Rosenberg in the abdomen – inside the penalty box. The German referee took the correct course of action in awarding a penalty and issuing a red card, upon which a drunk Danish fan came out of the crowd and assaulted the referee before being restrained. The referee ordered the teams to the dressing rooms and abandoned the match, awarding it to Sweden with a 3-0 scoreline.

3 June

1887: The formation of the oldest football club in the Americas, Club de Gimnasia y Esgrima La Plata in Argentina. The formal establishing of a soccer club was very impressive given that the city of La Plata was only founded in 1882.

1899: W.G. Grace plays his last Test match for England in Nottingham, scoring just one in his final innings. At 50 years and 320 days he remains the second oldest person ever to play for England. The only Englishman to play Test cricket who was older than W.G., Wilf Rhodes, made his Test debut in the very same Test in which W.G. bowed out!

1927: Play gets under way in the first Ryder Cup competition at the Worcester Country Club in Massachusetts. In the early years of play it was simply USA against Great Britain, and was just a two-day competition. USA captain Walter Hagen led his team to a resounding 9½-2½ point victory over the British team led by Ted Ray. Sadly the visionary founder Samuel Ryder was unable to attend the inaugural competition due to ill health.

1932: New York Yankees legend Lou Gehrig becomes the first Major League Baseball player to hit four home runs in one game since the modern era began.

1941: Death of Polish international football striker Antoni Łyko, a member of the Polish squad for the 1938 World Cup tournament. Łyko was arrested by the Gestapo and taken to the Auschwitz concentration camp where he was shot.

1993: England cricket captain Graham Gooch is dismissed in the Ashes Test against Australia 'handled the ball'. He had scored 133 by the time of his dismissal.

2015: In the preliminary round of the Danish FA Cup Sundsøre IF and Nykøbing Mors are level after extra time and so go to a penalty shoot-out. Sundsøre IF won the marathon shoot-out by a record score of 20-19.

2016: Death of boxing champion and legend Muhammad Ali, the man frequently considered not only the greatest boxer but the greatest sportsman of all time. Born Cassius Clay, he changed his name to Muhammad Ali at the of 22 shortly after winning the world title for the first time. He had converted to Islam and now considered Cassius Clay his 'slave name'. In 1984, just three years after his retirement, he was diagnosed with Parkinson's disease. His condition slowly but steadily deteriorated over the next 32 years. He died in hospital, officially of septic shock.

4 June

1913: The Derby is severely disrupted when suffragette Emily Davison walks on to the track during the race and attempts to interfere with Anmer, the horse of King George V. She deliberately targeted the monarch's horse for political publicity to promote the suffragettes' plight. Jockey Herbert Jones and Davison were both taken to hospital. She had a fractured skull and never regained consciousness, dying four days later.

1923: Death of horse trainer, stableman and part-time jockey Frank Hayes while racing at Belmont Park in New York State, in one of the most bizarre stories ever in the history of sport. Hayes was riding the 20-1 shot Sweet Kiss when he suffered a fatal heart attack, but his body remained in the saddle for the remainder of the race. Sweet Kiss crossed the line first. Race regulations at the time stipulated that a jockey had to be in the saddle for a horse to win – but made no reference as to whether the jockey was still alive at the time – so the result stood! This was Frank Hayes' first race win, the only jockey known to have won a race after death.

1957: England declare their second innings closed on 583/4 against the West Indies. The vast majority of the runs were scored in the fourth wicket stand of 411 between captain Peter May, who remained unbeaten on 285, and Colin Cowdrey, who scored 154. West Indies off-break bowler Sonny Ramadhin took 2-179 off a world record 98 overs.

1987: Danny Harris wins the 400m hurdles in a meeting in Madrid, with Ed Moses coming in second. That was Moses's first defeat in the event after a winning streak of 122 races, which started in September 1977 in Düsseldorf, West Germany.

1995: Boy Scouts in Germany are attempting a world record, a tug of war with 650 Scouts involved. The rope snapped, leading to the deaths of two of the boys with another 29 injured, five seriously.

2012: German freediver Tom Sietas breaks the world record for underwater breath holding when he remains submerged for 22 minutes and 22 seconds in China.

2016: The Oxford University Polo Club beat their own 105-year varsity record when they beat Cambridge University 19-0 at Guards Polo Club in Windsor.

5 June

1909: The first-ever event at the Indianapolis speedway circuit bizarrely has nothing to do with motorsport – it doesn't even have anything to do with the famous oval circuit, which has not been completed at this time. Forty-thousand people packed into the grounds to watch the start of a helium gas-filled balloon race. Nine balloons took part, with Universal City winning the challenge, landing 382 miles away in Alabama.

1938: Pole Ernst Wilimowski becomes the first person ever to score four goals in a match at any World Cup finals tournament. He achieved this in the first round of the tournament in France, but Poland still lost the match 6-5 to Brazil, after extra time.

1968: Tottenham Hotspur midfielder Alan Mullery is sent off in the final minute of England's semi-final of the Euro '68 tournament in Italy, against Yugoslavia. This was the first time any English player had been sent off in an international. Yugoslavia won the tie 1-0 before losing to Italy in the final.

1985: The 206th Derby is run on Epsom Downs. The race was won by Steve Cauthen on board Slip Anchor, a horse trained by Henry Cecil. Having won stateside seven years earlier, Cauthen remains the only jockey to have won both the Kentucky Derby and the Epsom Derby.

2016: During the Copa America, Uruguay are playing against Mexico. As usual before kick-off the two teams lined up for the anthems. The Mexican song passed off without incident, and the band started the Uruguayan anthem – much to the utter confusion of the team. By some bizarre event the band had actually been handed the national anthem for Chile, and it was that which they were playing.

6 June

1946: The Basketball Association of America meet for the first time in New York City and allocate franchises to major cities around the US.

1953: Gordon Richards wins the Epsom Derby aboard Pinza, winning by four lengths. The prize was £19,118 and ten shillings. Richards started racing in 1921, and enjoyed enormous success – in 1942 he won four of the five classics – but the Derby always eluded him. So, remarkably enough, this marked Richards's first Derby win after more than 30 years in the saddle and more than 20 attempts at the Derby. Through his career Richards rode 4,870 winners, which remains a British record, and he is still the only flat jockey to have been knighted.

1992: Russia plays its first-ever international rugby game, beating the Barbarians 27-23. The lateness of the date was due to the Soviet government failing to recognise rugby as an official sport.

1994: The final day of the County Championship cricket match between Durham and Warwickshire. Responding to Durham's 556/8 declared, Warwickshire declared their first innings closed on 810/4 to leave the match drawn. West Indian Brian Lara finished on a world record 501 not out.

1995: England beat Canada 3-2 in their opening World Cup finals group game at Helsingborg in Sweden. Clare Taylor made her England debut in this fixture, completing a remarkable double. Taylor was also a member of England's winning World Cup cricket team in 1993.

7 June

1952: Day three of the Test match between India and England sees India starting their second innings. The first over of the innings was bowled by England debutant Fred Truman – it was a maiden, and Truman removed Roy. The second over was bowled by Alec Bedser – another maiden with the loss of Gaekwad. Truman's second over was also a maiden, and he clean bowled both Mantri and Manjrekar; three overs; 0 for 4 – the worst ever start to a Test match innings.

1955: Birth of motor racing pioneer Tim Richmond. In moving from IndyCar to NASCAR he became one of the first people ever to change from open wheel racing to stock cars. By 1987 he was struggling with his health as his immune system was shutting down with AIDS. He stopped racing in the August of that year, and died of the condition two years later.

1987: Soviet athlete Natalya Lisovskaya puts the shot a distance of 22.63m to set a new women's world record, throwing in Moscow.

2015: Sir Bradley Wiggins breaks the 'hour record' – the furthest distance cycled in one hour on a velodrome. In his one hour Wiggins cycled 54.5km (33.9 miles).

8 June

1913: The Deutsches Stadion (tr. German Stadium) is formally dedicated in front of 60,000 people, with the release of 10,000 pigeons. The stadium was to have been the centrepiece for the 1916 Olympics. Berlin had won the right to host the Olympics, but the Games were eventually cancelled due to the Great War. Not wishing to waste their efforts the Germans decided to host a 'winter sports week', with ice hockey, figure skating, speed skating and Nordic skiing – the concept of which laid very early foundations for the Winter Olympics.

1961: Eddie Matthews, Hank Aaron, Joe Adcock and Frank Thomas score a record four consecutive home runs for the Milwaukee Braves in the seventh innings. Remarkably in light of this, Cincinati Reds still managed to beat the Braves 10-8 after all nine innings.

1979: After failing to finish in the Monaco Grand Prix, James Hunt calls a press conference and announces his retirement from the sport with immediate effect. A dynamic and flamboyant driver who had taken the world Formula One title in 1976, Hunt had simply become disillusioned with the sport, although his decision was blamed on the team's inability to provide him with a competitive car.

2003: Death of Leighton Rees of Wales, the first-ever World Professional Darts champion, beating John Lowe 11-7 in that inaugural world final in 1978.

2012: The fourth round of the Wuxi Classic qualifiers sees the most points ever scored in a single frame of snooker – 192, as Peter Lines of England beats Welshman Dominic Dale 108-84. Dale conceded 14 fouls in the frame to a value of 60 points, while Lines made six errors conceding 36 points.

9 June

1934: The final day of the US Open golf tournament. Bobby Cruikshank of Scotland began the day in second place, one shot behind American Gene Sarazen. He started the final round well, and he was challenging for the lead. His approach shot to the 12th was quite remarkable, and he was so thrilled he threw his club in the air in celebration. Then the club came down again … on his head, knocking him out! On recovering he insisted he was fine to carry on, but the incident seemed to have a negative effect on his play. Cruikshank bogeyed five of the remaining seven holes to finish in joint third, two shots behind the winner. Analysing the scores of the whole field up to and including the 11th hole (pre-injury) Cruikshank was in the lead, two shots clear of his nearest challenger. He never won a major, and threw away his best opportunity in this moment of stupidity.

1949: The first World Championship race under the auspices of the FIM (Fédération Internationale de Motocyclisme) is the 350cc Junior TT race on the Isle of Man. Ben Drinkwater swerved near the 11th Milestone marker trying to avoid another competitor. He came off his bike and was killed on impact with the track. The S-bend where he had come off was subsequently renamed Drinkwater's Bend.

1973: The 105th Belmont Stakes is run in New York City, and is won by Secretariat by a record-breaking margin of 31 lengths. His winning time of 2.24 remains the fastest time ever for 1.5 miles run on a dirt track.

1991: The first-ever World Bowl – the final of the World League of American football – played at Wembley Stadium. The London Monarchs beat the Barcelona Dragons 21-0 to take the first world title.

2017: Tennis star and former world number one Venus Williams runs a red light in Palm Beach, Florida, causing an accident injuring 79-year-old Jerome Barson. Tragically he died two weeks later of his injuries.

---

10 June

1829: The first University boat race between Oxford and Cambridge at Henley-on-Thames. Two school friends from Harrow – Charles Wordsworth of Christ Church College in Oxford and Charles Merrivale of St John's in Cambridge – met together in Cambridge and went rowing on the River Cam. It was at that point the two friends thought up the challenge – the two universities row against each other on the River Thames. On 10 February a letter was sent: 'that the University of Cambridge hereby challenge the University of Oxford to row a match at or near London, each in an eight-oared boat during the ensuing Easter vacation.' Oxford won this inaugural race comfortably. (Charles Wordsworth was the nephew of the famous poet William Wordsworth.)

1944: Bossuet, Brownie and Wait a Bit finish in a dead heat in the Carter Handicap at the Aquaduct Racetrack in Queen's, New York. This is the first known triple dead heat in horse racing history.

1965: Leeds United centre-back Jack Charlton makes his debut for England just four weeks short of his 30th birthday. With Bobby Moore confirmed as the ball-playing centre-half captain for the national side, manager Alf Ramsey wanted a 'no nonsense' centre-half to play alongside him. England were held to a 2-2 draw by Scotland – a good result given that England played a long period with nine men due to injuries. England's opening goal was scored by Jack's brother Bobby Charlton, with Jack providing the assist.

---

11 June

1907: In a County Championship game in Gloucester, Northamptonshire are bowled out for 12 runs – the lowest championship score of all time. Northamptonshire followed their 12 up with a second innings of 40/7 when the weather intervened. Gloucestershire bowler George Dennett took eight wickets for nine runs in the first innings, and had taken all seven second innings wickets – giving him match figures of 15-21.

1919: Three-year-old Sir Barton wins the Belmont Stakes to become the first horse in history to win the American Triple Crown – the Kentucky Derby, the Preakness and the Belmont Stakes, all in the space of just 32 days. Even more remarkably the Kentucky Derby was his first professional race, and he was only entered for the race by his stable as a pacemaker for Billy Kelly.

1955: The worst accident in the history of motorsport, during the Le Mans 24 Hours race. A large crash resulted in the death of French driver Pierre Levegh, and the flying debris killed 83 spectators and injured another 180. The accident was so severe that Mercedes-Benz pulled out of all motorsport immediately, a self-imposed exile that lasted for 34 years. Levegh swerved to avoid an accident, but hit a kerb causing his car to disintegrate and ignite. He was thrown from the car and died immediately, while flaming bits of car showered the crowd. The bonnet itself remained intact and flew into the crowd, and was described by one witness as 'decapitating tightly jammed spectators like a guillotine'.

1967: The day that would change the face of motorsport forever. Dan Gurney had just won the 24 Hours of Le Mans (with A.J. Foyt), and came to the podium for the awards. After getting his cup he picked up the champagne bottle, which was always placed for the competitors to celebrate, and rather than drinking it he shook it up and sprayed it everywhere. The action was purely spontaneous, and started a custom which is now standard in most brands of motorsport.

2016: Arsenal's Granit Xhaka lines up for Switzerland against Albania in their opening fixture at the Euro 2016 tournament in France. On the Albanian team was French-born Taulant Xhaka, Granit's brother, who qualified for Albania since their parents were Kosovo Albanian immigrants. For the record Switzerland won the tie 1-0.

12 June

1880: Bowling for the Worcester Worcesters (arguably the least imaginatively named team in the history of sport) against the Clevelands, Lee Richmond pitches the first perfect game (a feat which has only been achieved 23 times in the history of MLB). A perfect game is when no opposing player reaches base in a minimum of nine innings, meaning that the pitcher cannot allow any hits, walks or anything else, which allows the batsman to reach first base – 27 pitches, 27 players out. Richmond had only graduated from college the previous day, so had been up until gone 6am celebrating before his historic game.

1938: With the World Cup finals being the very pinnacle of football performance, hat-tricks in the tournament are rare. However, when Sweden beat Cuba 8-0 in the quarter-final in France, Gustav Wetterström and Harry Andersson both scored hat-tricks for the Swedes.

1981: Larry Holmes beats Leon Spinks in the third round on a technical knockout in a fight for the WBC heavyweight boxing title. The fight was billed as a tribute to boxing legend Joe Louis who had died two months earlier. Holmes earned $1.9 million from the bout, while Spinks made $490,000. The referee stepped in to stop the fight almost simultaneously with the moment that Spinks's corner threw in the towel.

1994: Nicole Brown Simpson, the ex-wife of NFL running back O.J. Simpson, and her friend Ron Goldman are found murdered. Simpson, one of the best-known sportsmen in the States, was arrested and charged with their murders. The trial was lengthy and, given O.J.'s popularity and fame, televised across the States. In the criminal trial O.J. was found not guilty, but in a separate civil action brought by the families of the victims he was found responsible for their wrongful deaths and fined $33.5m.

13 June

1897: Birth of Paavo Nurmi, the Finnish middle-distance and long-distance runner, probably the most consistent and successful runner in history. He set 22 world records for races between 1,500m and 20km. He entered 12 events in Olympic Games finals, and won nine gold medals and three silver medals. He was unbeaten in cross-country events and 10,000m races through his entire career, and had a winning streak of 121 races in all events.

1915: Birth of American tennis player Don Budge, widely considered to have the finest backhand in the history of the sport. Budge won ten major tournaments, including a record six consecutive Grand Slams. He was the first person ever to win a calendar Grand Slam.

1953: British runner Jim Peters becomes the first man to run a marathon in under two hours 20 minutes, when he clocks 2.18.40.4 at the Polytechnic Marathon.

1956: The first-ever European Cup Final sees Real Madrid of Spain beat the French side Reims 4-3 at the Parc des Princes, Paris. There were no criteria for qualification for this or any of the next four years, participating sides being chosen by the French football magazine *L'Equipe*. Chelsea were selected to represent England, but the FA would not allow them to participate in what they considered an 'irrelevant distraction' to the domestic season.

1978: During a world record attempt in Pennsylvania, the tug of war rope snapped with 2,300 participants on it. Two-hundred people were injured, with six fingers and thumbs needing to be amputated.

1982: Death of Italian motor racing driver Riccardo Paletti. Formula One race eight was in Canada, and was the first time Paletti took his place on the starting grid. At the front of the grid Didier Pironi stalled his Ferrari just as the lights went green. Most cars managed to avoid the stricken Pironi, but Paletti just ploughed into the back of the Ferrari at about 180kmh (~110mph). Paletti was unconscious with severe chest injuries as the car had concertinaed, and then his car caught fire. He was airlifted to hospital but died shortly after arriving. His mother was in the stands – she had come to watch the race and then go out to celebrate his 24th birthday later in the week. Paletti therefore holds the unwanted record that his entire Formula One race career lasted about 80m.

1986: In a World Cup finals group game Uruguay are held to a goalless draw by Scotland. The Uruguayan coach had cited Gordon Strachan as the danger man for Scotland, and told his team to watch him closely. José González clearly took the advice to heart, launching a reckless tackle on Strachan that earned him a red card … after 56 seconds, a record for a World Cup game.

14 June

1927: Death of Italian cyclist Ottavio Bottecchia, the first Italian winner of the Tour de France, at the age of just 32. Eleven days before his death he had been found at the roadside with a cracked skull and several broken bones. His bike lay nearby but appeared totally untouched with no sign of an accident. He was taken to a nearby inn where a priest gave him the last rites. From there he was taken on a cart to hospital where he eventually died without regaining consciousness. Exactly what happened on that fateful day has never been established.

1969: Birth of German tennis legend Steffi Graf, winner of 22 Grand Slam singles titles and the only person ever to achieve the Golden Slam – all four Grand Slam tournaments in the same calendar year plus an Olympic gold medal (1988). Graf was ranked number one in the world for a record 377 weeks.

1974: Chile's Carlos Caszely becomes the first person ever to be red-carded in a World Cup football match when he is sent off against West Germany.

1987: Welsh lock Huw Richards gets the first-ever red card in the rugby World Cup in Wales's defeat to New Zealand.

2005: FC United of Manchester is formally registered with the Manchester County Football Association. The club was founded by a group of Manchester United supporters who were unhappy with the takeover of their club by the American Malcolm Glazer. Open trials were held to get a squad together. The club's first signing was Jonathan Mitten, whose great uncle Charlie Mitten played 142 times for Manchester United in the five years after the war.

15 June

1909: Representatives of the cricket teams from England, Australia and South Africa meet at Lord's Cricket Ground and form the Imperial Cricket Conference (the forerunner of the International Cricket Council). It was agreed that future membership would be restricted to Test-playing countries who were members of the British Empire (obviously since changed!) New Zealand, India and the West Indies were elected as full members in 1926. Nowadays the ICC has 12 full members who play Test cricket, and 92 associate members.

1958: Driving a Maserati in the Belgian Grand Prix, Maria de Filippis becomes the first woman to drive in Formula One.

1958: In a World Cup group game in Sweden, Brazil beat the Soviet Union 2-0. The significance of the game was that it marked the debut in a Brazilian shirt of the 17-year-old Pelé.

1998: A terrorist plot is uncovered at the FIFA World Cup in France, leading to the arrest of more than 100 people from seven different countries. The plot was organised by the Algerian Armed Islamic Group, supported by al-Qaeda. The central focus of the attack was to be the Stade Velodrome in Marseille during the evening when England were playing Tunisia, with a view to attacking both players and spectators.

2014: Argentina beat Bosnia and Herzegovina 2-1 in their World Cup group match in the Maracaná Stadium. The opening goal was scored by Sead Kolašinac in just two minutes and ten seconds – not the fastest goal in the World Cup finals, but certainly the fastest own goal.

16 June

1950: Rio de Janeiro All-Stars beat São Paulo All-Stars 3-1 in the first-ever match at the newly constructed Maracaná Stadium. The organisation committee claimed the stadium could seat 200,000 but that figure has always been doubted. The building was slightly behind schedule so although the match went ahead with a large crowd, parts of the ground rather resembled a building site.

1983: One of the most controversial boxing matches of all time takes place between Luis Resto and 'Irish' Billy Collins. Resto took the televised bout by a unanimous points decision after ten rounds. Collins's father shook hands with Resto, and felt his gloves were too thin and demanded an investigation. It was discovered that the gloves were each missing an ounce of padding – the blame falling on Resto's trainer, Carlos 'Panama' Lewis. Lewis was banned from boxing for life with his licence permanently revoked. He was sentenced to six years in prison for his actions, and Resto got three years.

1999: American Maurice Greene becomes the first man in history to break the 9.8-second barrier for the 100m sprint. Running at a meet in Athens he clocked 9.79 seconds.

1999: Russian athlete Maksim Tarasov beats the outdoor pole vault record, with a leap of 6.05m (19ft 10in) in Athens. That record has not, in 2019, been beaten.

2008: Death of 28-year-old Neath scrum-half Gareth Jones. Jones was badly injured in an accident during a Premiership match against Cardiff on 20 April. He had several operations and a lot of treatment to try to overcome the damage, but passed away eight weeks later.

17 June

1902: The final of the British League Cup – a competition set up between English and Scottish league sides to raise funds to support the families of those who died in the Ibrox disaster earlier in the year. The final saw Celtic beat Rangers 3-2 after extra time thanks to a hat-trick by Jimmy Quinn.

1956: Death of American race car driver Bob Sweikert, the only man to have won the Indianapolis 500, the National Championship and the Sprint Car Championship in a single season. Sweikert died after crashing a sprint car at the Salem Speedway.

1962: Twenty-two-year-old Jack Nicklaus wins his first major tournament, beating Arnold Palmer by three shots in a play-off for the US Open in Oakmont, Pennsylvania. The play-off extended the tournament to a fifth day as Nicklaus and Palmer played a full round against each other. The extra effort was rewarded as both were given an additional $2,500 on top of their prize money as a share of the gate receipts.

1976: The NBA merges with the ABA to produce one basketball 'superpower'. The only difficulty was that there was not sufficient time or space to fully incorporate the ABA into the NBA – six ABA teams would have to go. The teams based at Memphis, San Diego, Utah and Virginia all rapidly folded, leaving just two more to be sacrificed. John Brown, owner of the Kentucky Colonels, was paid $3.3m to close his team down … one more to go. Next in the firing line was the Spirit of St Louis, owned by brothers Ozzie and Daniel Silna. They rejected a similar offer, asking for a small percentage of television revenue instead. But nobody could foresee how popular NBA would become, nor how much television revenue would be pumped into the sport. By 2006 the Silnas were earning more than $10m a year for owning a team that had not played basketball for more than 30 years. By 2014 the NBA decided to cut their losses and bought the brothers out of their contract … for $500m. Overall the Silna brothers received about $800m for the privilege of not owning a team.

2018: The conclusion of the 24 Hours of Le Mans, which is won by Toyota Gazoo Racing driven by Sebastien Buemi, Kazuki Nakajima and Fernando Alonso. This was Alonso's first attempt at the Le Mans race, and he joined Mike Hawthorn, Phil Hill and Jochen Rindt as the only drivers to have won both this and the Formula One world championship.

18 June

1724: The first cricket match to be played at The Oval, built on what was Kennington Common. The Oval has been the home of Surrey Cricket Club since 1845, and a Test cricket ground since 1880, but the earliest known match there was between London and Dartford. There were very few matches during the first 100 years since the ground was regularly used for public hangings.

1927: The first race to take place at the original long course Nürburgring is one of motorcycles and sidecars, won by Toni Ulmen on his 350cc Velacette. The full Gesamtstrecke was an incredible 20.8km (12.9 miles) long and contained 174 bends. The short course was opened in 1984.

1932: Foundation of FIBA (Fédération Internationale de Basketball Amateur). FIBA defined the rules of basketball, oversaw transfers, equipment and facilities, and appointed international referees. In 1989 the Federation dropped the word 'amateur' from its title, but maintained the acronym FIBA since it was so well known worldwide. FIBA currently has 213 national federations as members.

1952: Death of British motor engineer Cameron Earl. A technical consultant for the ERA (English Racing Automobiles), he was testing the R14B in Nuneaton, Warwickshire, when the car flipped over. He died in hospital from a fractured skull, becoming the first person to die driving a Formula One car.

1967: Caserta is the scene of a horrific accident in an Italian Formula Three race. Beat Fehr, Franco Foresti and Andrea Saltari were involved in a bad crash. Fehr managed to jump out of his car and run back down the track to try to warn oncoming vehicles, but was tragically hit by another car and killed. Geki Russo was the first car to arrive, but was unable to stop in time and he ploughed into the wreckage and lost his life. Tiger Perdomi also hit the wreckage and was taken to hospital where he died eight days later.

1990: Hale Irwin wins the first-ever sudden death play-off at the US Open Golf Championship in Illinois. Afte Irwin and Mike Donald finished level with each other after four rounds the pair played an additional round – in which they were also level … so they started sudden death. Irwin only needed one extra hole as he managed a birdie on the first (the 91st hole of the competition) to win the tournament.

2010: Thomas Gronnemark of Danish side FC Horsens gets his name into the record books with the longest ever football throw-in when he launches the ball 51.3m. The throw was a demonstration throw, not part of a match.

19 June

1846: The first baseball match is played under a firm set of rules, written nine months previously (the so-called 'Cartwright rules'). The game was played in New Jersey, and the New York Nines beat the New York Knickerbockers 23-1.

1870: Nottinghamshire cricketer George Summers dies after being hit on the head by a short-pitched delivery from John Platts of the MCC. He was carried from the field and seemed to recover, returning home by train. However, he died of his injuries four days later. With concerns about fast bowling, and with the safety helmet not being in use, the next batsman, Richard Daft, came out to bat with his head wrapped in a towel.

1932: The end of the 24 Hours of Le Mans sees French racing driver Odette Siko finishing in fourth, the highest position ever achieved by a woman in the famous endurance race.

1949: Sara Christian becomes the first woman ever to compete in NASCAR when she drives at the Charlotte Speedway. Driving a Ford, she qualified in 13th but unfortunately could not finish the race itself. Her teammate Bob Flock lost his car on the 38th lap with engine trouble – so he took over her car. At the next race three weeks later she became the first woman to complete a NASCAR race, when she finished 18th in Daytona Beach.

1958: FIFA World Cup quarter-final: Brazil 1 Wales 0. The only goal of the game was scored by Pelé who, at 17 years and 239 days old, became the youngest ever goalscorer in a World Cup finals tournament.

1960: Death of British Formula One motor racing drivers Chris Bristow and Alan Stacey in unrelated incidents at the Belgian Grand Prix. Bristow, the 'wild man of British club racing', rolled his car and was thrown into barbed wire, killing him instantly. Literally a few minutes later Stacey died at the same corner, but in most extraordinary circumstances. Travelling at about 120mph in his Lotus he was actually hit directly in the face by a bird. His car climbed the embankment through thick hedges and he fell into a field. Medics were split as to whether the force of the bird had actually broken his neck, or whether he was unconscious and had died during the accident.

1984: The day of the NBA draft – a day that one or two teams would certainly regret. Houston Rockets got first pick – and opted for the Nigerian Hakeem Olajuwon. Portland Trail Blazers went second and chose 7ft 1in Sam Bowie. Third up were the Chicago Bulls – and they selected Michael Jordan.

2011: The conclusion of the 111th US Open at the Congressional Country Club in Maryland. The event was won by Rory McIlroy of Northern Ireland with a record score of 16 under par, eight shots ahead of the field.

20 June

1904: Official formation of the FIA (Fédération Internationale de l'Automobile). The organisation, best known for their oversight of Formula One, was created to represent the interests of motoring organisations and motor car users, and not only for sporting events. They also promote road safety worldwide.

1954: Hungary thrash West Germany 8-3 in the World Cup group stages in Switzerland, with inside-right Sándor Kocsis scoring four goals. Just three days earlier the Hungarians had beaten South Korea 9-0, with Kocsis weighing in with three goals. He therefore became the first person to score two hat-tricks at the same World Cup finals tournament – scoring seven goals in three days. Kocsis scored a brace in the quarter-finals, and two more in the semi-finals, bringing his tournament total to 11. However, he failed to score in the final when West Germany took their revenge, beating Hungary 3-2.

1976: Possibly the most remarkable penalty kick of all time. In the final of the 1976 European Championship Czechoslovakia were locked at 2-2 with West Germany after extra time, so the European Championship would be decided by a penalty shoot-out for the first time. After four penalties each Czechoslovakia were leading 4-3. Step forward Antonin Panenka – if he scored, Czechoslovakia won. He raced forward as if he was going to blast it into the side of the goal, causing the German goalkeeper Sepp Maier to dive to his left. Seeing the keeper committed, Panenka simply delicately chipped the ball down the middle into the empty net.

1987: New Zealand beat France 29-9 in the first-ever rugby union World Cup Final. The match was played in Auckland on New Zealand's North Island in front of 48,035 supporters.

2015: Death of Romanian football manager Angelo Niculescu. Niculescu invented tiki-taka (to use its official name), the delaying tactics where one team keeps possession in their own half by using a series of short passes to keep the ball moving and away from the opposition to disrupt the opponent's plan and destroy their patience.

21 June

1925: Sport has always had its rivalries – the All Blacks against the Springboks, the Russian ice hockey team against Canada, Boston Red Socks against the New York Yankees, Liverpool against Everton and many more. Yet all of these surely pale into insignificance compared to the exhibition baseball game played in Kansas. One team was the Wichita Monrovians, a semi-professional African American team that played in negro leagues (in those sad days of racial segregation). The Monrovians were taking on a team from Lodge Six of the Ku Klux Klan. The game was considered a political move by both teams, each hoping to demonstrate they were superior to the other. Surprisingly (and delightfully) the game took place without incident on the field or in the stands. For the record the Monrovians won 10-8.

1970: Death of British Formula One driver Piers Courage, who died following an accident at the Dutch Grand Prix. Something failed in his car causing him to fail to turn in a chicane. He drove up an embankment and the car literally disintegrated before bursting into flames. One of the wheels broke free and hit Courage on the head, breaking his neck and killing him instantly.

1975: The final of the first cricket World Cup tournament (originally called the Prudential Cup '75). It was the first major limited overs ODI cricket tournament. The final was contested between the West Indies and Australia at Lord's, with the West Indies winning by 17 runs.

1982: In the World Cup Kuwait are trailing 3-1 to France when, in the dying minutes, they concede the fourth. However, the players were convinced they had heard the referee's whistle during the build-up to the goal and several of them stopped playing. The referee ignored the players' remonstrations, until the president of the Kuwaiti FA, Sheikh Fahid Al-Ahmad Al-Sabah, came out of the stands and on to the pitch to argue with the referee. After a heated exchange, and possibly to avoid some diplomatic incident, the referee relented and chalked the goal off. There was still time for France to score their fourth and win the match 4-1. The referee lost his status as an international referee after the match.

1998: Romanian Daniela Petrescu becomes the first woman to run the 3,000m steeplechase in under ten minutes when she clocks a time of 9.55.28 in Bucharest.

22 June

1865: First-class cricketing debut of the 16-year-old William Gilbert Grace (aka W.G. Grace), playing for the Gentlemen of the South against the Players of the South. Grace took 13 wickets in the match (for 84 runs), leading to his selection for the national Gentlemen against Players game later that year.

1915: American boxer Mike Glover loses his title as world welterweight boxing champion to compatriot Jack Britton. The significance of the result was that it brought to a close the shortest ever reign as a boxing world champion – Glover had won the title just 21 days earlier on 1 June, beating Matt Wells.

1981: The Wimbledon first round tennis match between John McEnroe and Tom Gullikson is one of the most memorable matches in SW19 history, but for all the wrong reasons. After a Gullikson serve McEnroe's return was called long at which he screamed at the line judge 'You cannot be serious'. This led to a heated exchange between McEnroe and the chair umpire Edward James in which McEnroe argued that everyone could see a puff of chalk dust. He called James 'the pits of the earth' and 'an incompetent fool'. The tournament referee was called and he gave

McEnroe a point penalty, but Gullikson was unimpressed: 'If it was the 120th player in the world, they would have defaulted him.'

1986: One of the best-known 'goals' ever in World Cup competition as Diego Maradona scores with his hand in a 2-1 win against England in Mexico City. With Maradona claiming 'divine intervention', this subsequently became known as the 'Hand of God' goal. With a long ball bouncing forward Maradona jumped against England goalkeeper and captain Peter Shilton, and realising he was just coming up short he nudged the ball over Shilton with his hand. Both the Tunisian referee and the linesman missed it, and the goal stood, and is about all anyone remembers from the tie. That in itself is a shame because Maradona, just four minutes later, scored one of the finest goals ever seen in a World Cup. Congratulations for honesty to England goalscorer and future captain Gary Lineker who, when asked if he would have owned up (as all the commentators were saying Maradona should have done), just laughed and gave an unequivocal 'No'.

2002: As the St Louis Cardinals are warming up for the game against the Chicago Cubs, team management notice that their pitcher Darryl Kile is missing. They contacted the team hotel to check he hadn't been left behind. Hotel staff entered his room to find Kile lying on the bed, dead from a heart attack. He was the first MLB star to die during the regular season for 23 years.

23 June

1889: In the MLB American Association, Louisville Colonels beat St Louis Browns 7-3 to bring to a close a losing streak of 26 consecutive games. This remains the longest winless run in professional baseball, unchallenged after nearly 130 years.

1894: Formation of the International Olympic Committee (IOC), a non-governmental organisation based in Lausanne in Switzerland, which is the authority responsible for the modern Olympic Games.

1917: Playing against Washington Senators, Boston Red Sox pitcher Babe Ruth only pitches to one batsman. There then developed a heated argument between Ruth and the umpire, the theme of which was never revealed. At the conclusion of the row Ruth punched the umpire and was ejected from the field.

1951: During the 24 Hours of Le Mans race Jean Larivière loses control of his Ferrari 212 Export C, which hits a sand bank with such force it literally launches into a neighbour's garden. Unfortunately for some reason the neighbour had a taut wire stretched across the garden, which decapitated Larivière.

2003: Michael Schumacher is appointed Ambassador-at-large for the Most Serene Republic of San Marino.

24 June

1911: Birth of Juan Manuel Fangio, the Argentinian racing driver who is the first Formula One megastar and believed by many to be the best driver of all time. Fangio was nicknamed El Chueco (tr. the bow-legged one). He was the first person ever to win the Drivers' World Championship five times, a feat he accomplished driving for four different teams: Alfa Romeo, Ferrari, Mercedes-Benz and Maserati. Fangio only won 24 races, competing in 53, with a winning percentage of 46 per cent which remains a Formula One record.

1927: Tommy Armour plays perhaps the most remarkable hole of golf ever. During the Shawnee Open Armour recorded the first-ever archaeopteryx (the technical term for any score of 15 or more over par). On the par-5 17th hole Armour took an incredible 18-over-par 23. So was this just some incompetent amateur? Not exactly – just seven days earlier Armour had won the US Open!

2007: Death of Canadian professional wrestler Chris Benoit. On the day of his death he was due to challenge for his third world title, with WWE. The autopsy revealed severe brain damage after years

Juan Manuel Fangio

24 June 1911–17 July 1995

The first Formula One superstar, who set the standards by which
all drivers would be measured

of abuse in the ring, a condition which was greatly exacerbated by severe depression. On 22 June, while in a particularly low state, he murdered his wife and son, before hanging himself two days later.

2010: American John Isner and Nicolas Mahut from France conclude their first-round singles match at Wimbledon – a match that has begun on the 22nd, and lasts 11 hours and five minutes. Wimbledon has a long and proud history of not using a tiebreak in a deciding set – it is simply played out until one player has a two-game cushion. Both the third and the fourth sets went to tiebreaks so it looked like this would be tight, but no one foresaw a fifth set which would be won by Isner 70-68.

2017: Mount Kilimanjaro in Tanzania hosts the highest altitude football match of all time. A squad of 30 players representing 20 different nations climbed to an altitude of 5,714m (18,747ft) supported by a referee and assistants, and a small crowd. They took with them goalposts and nets as well as bags of flour that they used to mark out the pitch. Trekking poles were used as corner flags. The pitch surface was volcanic ash, and the match featured several current and past internationals ranging in age from 18 to 66. The teams, calling themselves Volcano FC and Glacier FC, played out a goalless draw.

25 June

1892: The foundation of what is now the oldest international sports federation that comes under the umbrella of the Olympic movement. FISA was the Fédération Internationale des Sociétés d'Aviron (tr. International Federation of Rowing Associations), and was formed by representatives from France, Italy, Switzerland, Belgium and Adriatica (which is now a part of Italy).

1947: Death of American boxer Jimmy Doyle, who passes away in hospital 17 hours after being knocked out by Sugar Ray Robinson. The pair were contesting the world welterweight title. In a supremely sad moment of irony Robinson had actually tried to pull out on the morning of the fight, because he had suffered a nightmare the previous night about killing an opponent in the ring. A priest had persuaded him to go on with the bout.

1966: In establishing an annual NFL–AFL championship, Lamar Hunt, the owner of the Kansas City Chiefs, writes to football commissioner Pete Rozelle about the game saying, 'I have kiddingly called it the Super Bowl, which obviously can be improved upon.' Obviously nobody could improve upon it, and so the Super Bowl earned its name.

1966: The first-ever Great Knaresborough Bed Race, which has since become an annual event. Highly decorated beds with at least one occupant were wheeled around a gruelling 2.4-mile course. Proceeds from the event went towards local charities and community needs. Being a street circuit, the race was restricted to 90 entrants. Just to increase the challenge for competitors and the fun for spectators, organisers included crossing the River Nidd at a width of ~30m. The vision of a bed race has now spread across the globe, but Knaresborough 1966 was where it all started.

2006: The infamous 'round of 16' match between Portugal and the Netherlands in the Germany-based FIFA World Cup. The match, which Portugal won 1-0, saw 16 yellow cards issued and four red. The match was so feisty that it has since been dubbed the 'Battle of Nuremberg'.

26 June

1969: Certainly not the most significant football match in history – but probably the match with the biggest consequences. Honduras and El Salvador were drawn against each other in a FIFA World Cup qualifier. Both teams won their home legs, although both matches were marred by violence in the stands. FIFA decided the two should play off in Mexico City. On the day of the match El Salvador dissolved all diplomatic ties with Honduras, stating that since the second leg more than 11,000 Salvadorans had been forced to flee Honduras. They further claimed that the Honduran government was complicit in the awful treatment of their citizens. El Salvador won the game 3-2 after extra time, but then 18 days later declared war on Honduras, launching a military attack. The Organisation of American States managed to negotiate a ceasefire four days later – which is why this is sometimes called the '100 Hour War', but is also referred to as the 'Football War'.

1999: Grand opening of the Stadiwm y Mileniwm in Cardiff (tr. The Millennium Stadium, known since 2016 as the Principality Stadium). Initially built for the 1999 Rugby World Cup at a cost of £121m, it is the home of Welsh rugby and where they play all their home games, but has also hosted some Welsh football matches and some FA Cup finals while Wembley was being rebuilt.

2003: Death of Cameroonian international footballer Marc-Vivien Foé. A combative midfielder, he played for Lens, West Ham United and Lyons, ending his time on loan at Manchester City. Foé was playing for Cameroon in the Confederations Cup. In the semi-final of the tournament Cameroon were playing against Colombia when Foé collapsed in the centre circle in the 72nd minute. No other player was near him at the time. The manager had actually tried to substitute him a few minutes earlier, saying he looked tired, but Foé had said he was fine. Medics worked on him on the pitch for 45 minutes before he was moved to the medical centre. He died shortly afterwards. The autopsy revealed cardiac arrest brought on by hypertropic cardiomyopathy, a hereditary and previously undetected heart condition.

2016: Swiss cyclist Francesco Russo sets a new distance record in one hour, when he covers 92.432km at the Dekra Lausitzring in Germany.

27 June

1890: George Dixon knocks out Englishman Nunc Wallace in 18 rounds to be officially recognised as the world bantomweight champion, making him the first black boxing world champion for any weight. He was nicknamed 'Little Chocolate' since he stood just 5ft 3in (1.61m) and weighed just 6st 3lb at the start of his career. Dixon was also credited with inventing shadow boxing.

1906: Ferenc Szisz, driving for Renault, wins the inaugural Grand Prix de l'Automobile Club de France (aka the French Grand Prix). The race began the previous day on closed public roads around Le Mans. The organisers planned a circuit which was 103.2km (64.1 miles) long, and would be lapped six times on each day (so the total race distance would be 1,238.2km or 769.4 miles). Overall the total race time was a little over 12 hours.

1960: Death of Lottie Dod, all-round athlete and five-time winner of the women's singles Wimbledon title. She helped to set up the England women's national field hockey team, and played for them twice. She also won the British Ladies' Amateur Golf Championship, as well as winning a silver medal in archery at the 1908 Summer Olympics.

1988: Mike Tyson knocks out Michael Spinks in Atlantic City in just 91 seconds. Prior to the fight both men were undefeated. Tyson held the WBC, WBA and IBF heavyweight titles, while Spinks held the Ring title and was the lineal champion. Tyson earned $20m for the bout, while Spinks got $13.5m. Only ten punches were landed in the entire fight – eight by Tyson and two by Spinks. Immediately after his defeat Spinks announced his retirement from the sport and never fought again.

2001: Legendary Ethiopian runner Haile Gebrselassie sets a new world record for the one-hour run when he completes 21,285m (13.2 miles) in just 60 minutes. The record was achieved in Ostrava in the Czech Republic.

28 June

1922: Eighteen-year-old Ralph Samuelson of Minnesota becomes the first person to come up with the idea of using skis on water being towed behind a boat, thereby inventing waterskiing.

1958: The third-place play-off for the World Cup sees France beat West Germany 6-3 in Gothenburg. French forward Just Fontaine netted four times to take his tally to 13 in just six matches – not only winning the Golden Boot, but also the highest tally ever in a World Cup finals tournament.

1976: Soviet runner Tatyana Kazankina becomes the first woman to run the 1,500m in a time under four minutes, when she completes the distance in 3.56.0 in Podolsk in the Soviet Union.

1995: British doubles pairing Tim Henman and Jeremy Bates become the first players to be disqualified at Wimbledon in the Open Era. Tournament referee Alan Mills ruled that they had committed a code violation and were ejected from the competition. After Henman made a mistake he lashed out in frustration, hitting the ball he was holding, which unfortunately hit a ballgirl hard on the side of the head. She initially collapsed, then ran back to her position in tears and a doctor was called. Henman took the disqualification on the chin: 'It's a complete accident, but I'm responsible for my actions.'

1997: One of the most anticipated ... and notorious professional boxing matches in history. Dubbed 'The Sound and the Fury', this was the rematch between Evander Holyfield and Mike Tyson. The original match eight months earlier had been won by Holyfield after the referee stopped the fight in the 11th round. The controversy was a headbutt by Holyfield which opened a cut above Tyson's eye but that the referee ruled accidental. The rematch was eagerly anticipated, but was stopped in the third round when Tyson bit off part of Holyfield's ear. In fact Tyson came out of his corner without his mouthguard, but the referee noticed this and made him put it in. But just two minutes later the two protagonists were in a clinch when Tyson struck – biting fully through the ear and cartilage and spitting the severed portion on the floor of the ring. Almost unbelievably the referee sought the doctor's opinion on Holyfield's fitness – and when he decreed Holyfield was fit to continue the referee ordered the fight to restart. But on seeing a second bite the referee did finally stop the fight and award the bout to Holyfield.

29 June

1709: The earliest known cricket fixture which definitely features teams representing counties is the invitation match between Kent and Surrey played at Dartford Brent for a prize of £50.

1958: The FIFA World Cup Final with Brazil beating Sweden 5-2. At 17 years and 249 days old, Pelé became the youngest ever winner of the World Cup Final. To further raise his personal profile Pelé scored two of Brazil's five goals.

1966: England beat Norway 6-1 in a friendly international in preparation for the forthcoming World Cup tournament. Jimmy Greaves scores four of the goals.

2001: Russian swimmer Roman Sludnov becomes the first swimmer ever to swim 100m breaststroke in under a minute. In competition in Moscow, Sludnov completed the distance in 59.97 seconds.

2002: AFC Wimbledon hold player trials to establish a team for the newly formed club. This followed the decision to move Wimbledon Football Club to Milton Keynes for financial reasons (since renamed Milton Keynes Dons, aka MK Dons). Wimbledon supporters were obviously very unhappy at the move, losing access to their local team, so initially decided to protest, and then to start the club up again from scratch. Two hundred and thirty hopefuls showed up, from whom a squad was assembled.

2003: Barrie Dewsbury makes his international soccer debut for Sark against Gibraltar ... at the age of 52 years and nine months! Particularly given his age he must have wondered whether it was worth the effort when Sark lost 19-0.

30 June

1927: The Wimbledon semi-final between the second seed American Bill Tilden and seed four Henri Cochet of France is one of the greatest tennis comebacks of all time. Tilden was leading 5-1 in the third set having won the first two sets, and serving for the match. Cochet then won the next six games to take the set, and took the remaining two sets to claim the match 2-6 4-6 7-5 6-4 6-3.

1975: Muhammad Ali beats Joe Bugner by a unanimous decision of the judges after 15 rounds in Kuala Lumpur in Malaysia. The bout represented Ali's third defence of both his WBC and his WBA heavyweight titles, and earned him $2m. Bugner got $500,000 for his role.

1985: Birth of American swimmer Michael Phelps, the most decorated Olympian of all time with 28 medals, 23 of which are gold. Overall, in long course competitions Phelps has won 82 international medals, 65 of which are gold – including Olympics, World Championships and Pan Pacific Championships. He is considered by many to be the best swimmer of all time.

2012: A golden set in tennis is one in which the player not only wins all six games but does so without conceding a single point in any of the games (i.e. 50-0 0-50 50-0 0-50 50-0 0-50). This has only been accomplished a few times in professional tennis, and only once at Wimbledon – the first set by Kazakhstani Yaroslava Shvedova against Italian Sara Errani.

2018: Nineteen-year-old Kylian Mbappé becomes only the second teenager to score twice in a World Cup finals game as France beat Russia 4-3 in Russia. The only other teenager to manage this was Pelé 60 years earlier.

JULY

1 July

1903: The first-ever Tour de France begins in the village of Montgeron, with Maurice Garin winning this first stage, and eventually winning overall. The race was actually set up by the French newspaper *L'Auto* simply as a method of increasing circulation.

1905: Chelsea buy goalkeeper Willie Foulke. At 6ft 4in and 24st he certainly took up a lot of the goal. Not only did Chelsea hope they were getting a goalkeeper, but as he was a big crowd pleaser, they hoped it would boost gate receipts. To emphasise his size even more, Chelsea would place two small boys behind the goal to make him appear even bigger. Sometimes when the ball went out of play the boys would run to retrieve it and get the game moving again … and so the concept of a ballboy was born.

1951: The French Grand Prix is one of the oddest Formula One races of all time. Alfa Romeo's lead driver Juan Manuel Fangio qualified in pole position with Italian teammate Luigi Fagioli back in eighth. After just ten laps of the 77-lap race Fangio came into the pits complaining of misfiring and engine problems. Fagioli came in ten laps later for what he thought would be a routine pit stop … but the Alfa Romeo bosses ordered him out of the car, and gave the car to Fangio who headed off. Fangio brought Fagioli's car home in first place. With just eight points for a win in those days, the race organisers decided to give four points each to Fagioli and Fangio, and the official race classification lists first place as 'Fagioli and Fangio'. Immediately after the race Fagioli quit racing and never got into a Formula One car again.

2001: Spencer Prior transfers from Manchester City to Cardiff for the sum of £878,000 … but this is no ordinary transfer. Cardiff City owner Sam Hammam inserted two rather bizarre clauses into Prior's contract – for no apparent reason other than his own amusement. Prior was contractually obligated to eat a sheep's brain and testicles one day before a match, and he had to 'have a physical liaison with a sheep'. Several witnesses have testified that he did have the meal, but no mention was made of the other part of the deal.

2011: MLB slugger Roberto Bonilla signs a fresh contract with the New York Mets guaranteeing an annual payment of $1.19 million a year for the next 25 years. Bonilla actually retired ten years earlier – this was for unpaid salaries from the time when he was playing!

2017: During the Space Coast three-event competition at Palm Bay in Florida, Canadian Ryan Dodd breaks the world record for the distance achieved during a waterskiing jump. Dodd cleared a remarkable 77.4m (254ft).

2 July

1943: Death of Dutch gymnast Lea Nordheim, gold medal winner at the 1928 Summer Olympics. As a Jew in the war she was captured and placed in the Sobibor extermination camp where she was murdered along with her husband and ten-year-old daughter.

1985: Death of British Formula One motor racing driver David Purley at the age of 40. Purley is best remembered for his part in the 1973 Dutch Grand Prix. Roger Williamson had a very large crash and Purley immediately abandoned his own race and, showing scant regard for his own safety, did everything he could to put out the fire and get Williamson out of the car. Sadly Williamson died, but Purley was awarded the George Cross for his efforts. After retiring from Formula One the adrenaline junkie began a career in aerobatics. He died when his plane crashed into the English Channel in one display session.

1994: Death of Colombian footballer Andrés Escobar, nicknamed 'The Gentleman' due to his clean style of play, gentlemanly conduct and sense of calm. On 22 June 1994 Colombia played the United States in their second group match of the World Cup in the USA. Colombia had already lost their opening fixture, and then lost to the hosts 2-1, the first US goal being an own goal from Escobar. Colombia won their final fixture, but it was too little too late and the team were eliminated and flew home on 27 June. Just five days after arriving home Escobar was shot and killed. Although never proved, it was widely claimed that he was murdered in retaliation for his own goal.

2000: Death of Northern Irish motorcycle former world champion Joey Dunlop, three times a winner of the Isle of Man TT. Still riding at the age of 48, Dunlop had already won both the 600cc and 750cc of the meeting at Tallinn, Estonia, and was competing in the 125cc race on the Pirita-Kose-Kloostrimetsa Circuit. In wet conditions he lost control of his bike, hitting a tree. He was killed immediately on impact.

3 July

1959: The end of the British Open, played at Muirfield in Scotland. South African Gary Player won his first-ever major tournament, his four under par giving him the title and the £1,000 prize money (despite finishing three over par on the first day).

1987: Australian Pat Cash defeats Ivan Lendl of Czechoslovakia 7-6 6-2 7-5 to win the Wimbledon men's singles title for the first time. This was the second successive Wimbledon singles final that Lendl had lost.

1988: Despite her tremendous record in the major singles tournaments, German Steffi Graf only ever won one major doubles title. Partnering Argentinean Gabriela Sabatini, the pair beat Larisa Savchenko and Natasha Zvereva 6-3 1-6 12-10 to win the ladies' doubles at Wimbledon.

2017: Beginning of the Little Swan World Cup – a professional but non-ranking team snooker tournament where the teams represent nationalities. The tournament was played in Wuxi in China and was won six days later by the local team of Ding Junhui and Liang Wenbo, who beat the English pair of Judd Trump and Barry Hawkins by four frames to three.

4 July

1910: Jack Johnson knocks out Jim Jeffries in the 15th round to be formally recognised as the world heavyweight boxing champion. His victory prompted race riots across America which saw at least 26 people die.

1919: In what is at the time one of the greatest shocks in the history of boxing Jack Dempsey defeats Jess Willard to claim the heavyweight title of the world. Willard, nicknamed the 'Pottawatemie Giant', stood at 6ft 6.5in (1.99m) – a full six inches taller than Dempsey, and weighed 17st 7lb (111.1kg) to Dempsey's 13st 5lb (84.8kg). Willard had been the world heavyweight champion for just over seven years, and had never been knocked down in his entire career. Dempsey knocked him down seven times in the first round alone. After the fight the medic attending reported that Willard had a broken jaw, a broken cheekbone and several missing teeth.

1938: Death of French tennis player Suzanne Lenglen, regarded by many to be the greatest female tennis player of all time. Recently diagnosed with leukaemia, she passed away from pernicious anaemia. Her tennis record is unlikely to ever be matched. Her overall win percentage was 98 per cent (just seven losses from 348 matches ... the best from the Open Era is Chris Evert's 90 per cent).

1964: Australian Roy Emerson beats compatriot Fred Stolle to win the men's singles title at Wimbledon, becoming the first (and to date the only) man in history to win a Career Grand Slam in both singles and doubles.

1984: NASCAR legend Richard Petty wins his 200th and final race, the Firecracker 400, which is part of the Winston Cup Series. The race was started by President Ronald Reagan, who gave the famous 'start your engines' command.

2006: The Italian Federation's prosecutor calls for very severe sanctions to be brought against five top Italian teams after a far-reaching investigation into match rigging. Juventus were considered to be the most guilty, so their punishment was the most severe. They were relegated to Serie B for the next season, and started there on minus nine points. Their league title was awarded to second-placed Inter Milan. They were also stripped of the title from the previous year, but this was not reallocated.

5 July

1900: Foundation of West Ham United. In 1895 workers of the largest and last surviving shipbuilder on the River Thames formed a football team, Thames Ironworks FC. Five years later there was infighting over control of the club and dwindling finances, so the club folded and almost straight away West Ham United were built from the ruins. This explains the iron hammers on the club's badge, as well as the 'Irons' nickname.

1958: Having lost the first Test match, this is viewed as a 'must win' rugby league game for the Great Britain touring team in Australia. The game was only four minutes old when British captain Alan Prescott broke his arm making a tackle. Since this was in the days before substitutes, Prescott decided to play on, leading his team to a 25-18 win.

1981: Retired miner Reg Mellor sets a new world record in the bizarre sport of ferret legging – how long can the competitor keep a live ferret down their trousers? Miller lasted five hours and 26 minutes at the Annual Pennine Show in Yorkshire.

2002: Death of American baseball player Ted Williams who played for Boston Red Sox for 19 seasons, a career only interrupted by serving for the States in both the Second World War and the Korean War. His on-base percentage remains the highest of all time.

2012: Death of Belgian road racing cyclist Rob Goris. Before becoming a cyclist he had represented Belgium in ice hockey.

Having turned professional he planned to enter the 2013 Tour de France. To get a feel for the event he visited the 2012 Tour, but died of a heart attack in his hotel room in Rouen. He was just 30 years old.

6 July

1849: Death of Norwegian-Danish army officer Olaf Rye, who dies a hero during the Danish war. A passionate skier, he was the first person known to have performed a ski jump when he launched himself 9.5m in the air in 1808 with fellow soldiers as his audience. He was just 17 at the time.

1913: Jean Bouin from France breaks the world record for the one-hour run when he runs 19,021m (11.8 miles) in an hour in Stockholm. His record would stand for almost 40 years.

1993: Death of Croatian basketball player Drazen Petrovic. Petrovic had a successful career in several European countries before hitting the big time in the NBA with the New Jersey Jets. He was visiting family in Croatia, out driving on the motorway with his girlfriend and a friend, when a truck crossed the central passageway and hit him head on. He was killed immediately.

2002: Bison Dele decides to celebrate his early retirement from the NBA in style as he sets off for an ocean voyage on board a catamaran called *Hakuna Matata*, with his girlfriend, the ship's captain and his brother Miles Dabord. Dele was an early draft in 1991 under his birth name of Brian Williams. By 1998 he was gaining increasing success with the Detroit Pistons, and changed his name to Bison Dele to reflect his 'African and Native American ancestry'. In 2002 he walked away from basketball, turning down a contract offer of $36m and headed off on his travels. The group regularly checked in as expected, until 8 July when radio contact went silent. Then two weeks later on 20 July the *Hakuna Matata* arrived in Tahiti – Miles Dabord was the only person on board. Dabord was interviewed but there was no evidence of a crime, so he was released while investigations continued. A couple of days after his release Dabord's body was found on a beach in Mexico. He had died of an overdose. Police now believe Dabord had murdered his brother Bison Dele and the other two on board and dumped their bodies overboard. The motive appears to have been jealousy of Dele's success.

7 July

1775: In a cricket match played between Players of Hampshire and Gentlemen of Surrey, John Small of Hampshire scores 136 runs – the earliest known century in first-class cricket.

1896: Volleyball is played for the very first time, initially as an exhibition sport.

1898: W.G. Grace may be a genius cricketer, but he is not renowned for either sportsmanship nor for his humility. He was also almost certainly the only batsman to have been out three times in three balls! Star bowler for a 'Gentlemen's XI' Charles Kortright trapped him lbw with a delightful delivery. Grace stood his ground, and glared at the umpire who crumbled and ruled him not out. Off the very next delivery he was caught behind, but again refused to walk, barking at the umpire 'Play on, man. They've come here to see me bat, not to see you umpire.' With the next delivery Kortright clean bowled Grace with sufficient pace to knock two of the stumps clean out of the ground. Grace realised he had pushed his luck far enough and reluctantly began to walk back to the pavilion. Kortright called after him: 'Surely you're not going, Doc? There's still one stump left standing.'

1912: The pentathlon event at the Stockholm Olympics in Sweden. Gold was awarded to Jim Thorpe who was registered as representing the United States, but he proudly proclaimed he was a member of the Sac and Fox Nation, a tribe of Native Americans. Thorpe not only won the gold medal, he won four of the five individual events. The only event he did not win was the javelin

– basically because he had never thrown one before in his life, but he still came third! Thorpe also took gold in the decathlon – until the organising committee discovered that he had played two seasons of semi-professional baseball for which he had been paid. This violated existing rules on the necessity of amateurism in the Olympics, and they stripped him of both titles.

1999: Moroccan Hicham El Guerrouj breaks the world record for running a mile in a time of 3.43.13 in Rome.

2011: Tragedy strikes at a baseball match between Texas Rangers and the Oakland Athletics in a most bizarre manner. Texas firefighter Shannon Stone was attending the game with his six-year-old son. When the ball went to the outfield Stone called to the fielder Josh Hamilton to throw him the ball, which he did. Stone overreached and fell over the railing, falling 20 feet head first on to concrete. He was able to talk to the paramedics who attended him, but he died on the way to the hospital.

8 July

1805: The first known transatlantic boxing bout sees American Bill Richmond knock out the British fighter Jack Holmes, in Kilburn Wells, England.

1924: American DeHart Hubbard wins the long jump title at the Paris Olympics with a jump of 7.445m, and leaps into the record books. Beating 33 other athletes from 22 countries, Hubbard becomes the first African American to win an individual gold medal at the Games.

1990: The final of the Italian World Cup sees West Germany beat Argentina thanks to a late penalty. The German manager Franz Beckenbauer becomes only the second person in history (after Brazilian Mario Zagallo) to win the trophy as both a player and a manager, having captained his nation to victory in 1974.

2012: The first-ever Quidditch World Cup is held in Oxford. The final of the tournament saw the United States beat France 160-0. The victorious US team played an exhibition match the following day against the UK as part of the Olympic torch relay ceremony in Oxford.

2018: Tommy Charlton makes his footballing debut ... at the age of 72. More than 50 years since his older brothers Jack and Bobby were in the victorious England World Cup team, the youngest Charlton was picked to play for the England Over-60s team against Italy.

9 July

1877: The start of the first tennis tournament held at The All England Croquet and Lawn Tennis Club in Wimbledon, London, widely recognised as the first official lawn tennis competition, and the first Grand Slam tournament. Lawn tennis had been promoted since 1875 to try to compensate for the waning interest in croquet. The only competition at the inaugural Wimbledon was the Gentlemen's Singles, played for by 22 players who each paid one guinea to enter. The final was on 19 July, played in front of a crowd of 200 who each paid a shilling to be there. The first Wimbledon champion was Spencer Gore in a match that lasted just 48 minutes. He got 12 guineas in prize money and a silver trophy.

1904: Stage three of the Tour de France is around the Loire region near to the home of Ferdinand Payan, the popular French rider. Payan had been disqualified in the first stage for allegedly being towed by a car, and his supporters were furious. As the other riders made their way on the route they were pelted with rocks, and roads were barricaded. Other roads were strewn with broken glass and nails. Because of this it would be nearly 50 years before the Tour would head back to the Loire.

1966: Jack Nicklaus rallies on the last day to overturn a two-shot deficit and win the British Open golf tournament at Muirfield in

Scotland, to become only the fourth person in history to win a Career Grand Slam (all four majors).

2006: The final of the FIFA World Cup in Germany sees Italy beat France. Italy won 5-3 on penalties in a shoot-out after the match had finished 1-1 after extra time. Before the final French legend Zinedine Zidane announced his retirement from playing, confirming this would be his final competitive match. With just ten minutes remaining Zidane head-butted Italian defender Marco Materazzi in the chest, and immediately became the first player to be sent off in a World Cup Final. So what did Materazzi say that provoked such a reaction? Zidane claims Materazzi said unpleasant things about his mother – which he felt justified his reaction. When someone later suggested a line should be drawn under the event and everyone move on, Zidane stated he would rather 'die than apologise'. Materazzi claimed that the Frenchman had said that he could have his shirt at the end of the game … to which Materazzi replied, 'I'd rather have your sister.' He confessed he wasn't exactly proud of what he said, but feels that the reaction was disproportionate to the comment. Which version is correct? I don't suppose we will ever know.

2018: LeBron James, considered by many to be the finest basketball player of all time, signs for the Los Angeles Lakers in a four-year deal worth $154m.

10 July

1912: Hawaiian-born Duke Kahanamoku wins the gold medal for the US at the Olympic Games. One of the last people born in the Kingdom of Hawaii, he became a naturalised US citizen. Kahanamoku was one of the forerunners of popularising the ancient Hawaiian sport of surfing.

1949: The NASCAR race at the Daytona Beach road course is a race of three 'firsts'. Sara Christian became the first woman to complete a NASCAR race. In being joined on the grid by Ethel

Mobley and Louise Smith, this was the first NASCAR race to feature three women. And with Frank Christian also racing, it was the first time a husband and wife team had raced against each other.

1978: Death of snooker and billiards player Joe Davis, winner of the first 15 consecutive World Snooker Championships. He was also World Billiards champion four times.

1980: Birth of American NASCAR driver Adam Petty – the first-ever fourth generation NASCAR racer (son of Kyle Petty, grandson of Richard Petty and great-grandson of Lee Petty). Sadly the youngest Petty died while still just 19 years old, killed instantly in a crash in a practice session for the Busch 200 race at the New Hampshire Motor Speedway.

11 July

1836: The first of what would, for many years, become an annual fixture when the North of England play the South of England at Lord's. In the 18th century cricket had been a very southern sport, but as more northern districts started playing, it was decided to have a north–south play-off. In the first fixture the North surprisingly beat the South by six wickets. The last North of England v South of England match was played as recently as 1961.

1924: Scotsman Eric Liddell wins the 400m gold medal at the Paris Olympic Games. Liddell had become famous just five days earlier when the heats for the 100m were run on a Sunday, and he refused to run because it conflicted with his Christian faith.

1968: England begin their third Test match against Australia at Edgbaston in Birmingham. England captain Colin Cowdrey became the first player in the history of Test cricket to play in 100 Tests, and he celebrated in style, scoring 104 in England's first innings. Cowdrey opted not to bat in the second innings. He would go on to play in 114 matches for England.

1982: Italian goalkeeper Dino Zoff leads his team to victory over West Germany in the World Cup Final in Spain. At 40 years, four months and 13 days he is the oldest ever winner of football's premier competition.

1996: There is a certain irony in a boxing match ending up in a fight, but this is what happens immediately after Riddick Bowe is awarded victory over Polish heavyweight boxer Andrew Golota. At Madison Square Garden, Golota was deemed to have delivered a series of low and illegal blows which led to his disqualification. This led to a fight between the two corners and soon spread to the crowd.

12 July

1817: Inventor Karl von Drais demonstrates his new invention, the draisine (an early form of bicycle). Drais actually called his invention a running machine, since there were no pedals and propulsion was by a running motion while seated on the saddle. On a long run on this date he completed 'without much effort 13 to 15 kilometres per hour, that was a sensation'. Drais advertised his draisine as: '1. The machine goes uphill on good country roads, as fast as a human being in a strong step. 2. On the plain, even immediately after a heavy rainstorm, like the squadrons of the sentries. 3. On the plain, with dry footpaths, like a galloping horse. 4. Downhill, faster than a horse in Carrière [racetrack].'

1932: The final day of the County Championship cricket fixture between Yorkshire and Nottinghamshire at Headingley. After a period of rain the pitch was challenging, and Yorkshire brought England's slow left-arm bowler Hedley Verity into the attack. The first nine overs he bowled were all maidens. As the pitch dried out Verity managed to generate an incredible amount of spin, and took seven wickets in his next three overs. By the end of the innings Nottinghamshire had been dismissed for 67 with Verity claiming 10-10, the best bowling analysis in the history of cricket.

1936: The São Paulo Grand Prix is one of the few historically to feature a female racing driver, Hellé Nice from France. Nice had a bad accident when she was running in second place, her car catapulting up in the air and flying into the grandstand. She was thrown from her car and landed on a soldier who broke her fall and saved her life. The soldier wasn't so fortunate and died on impact. Her car continued into the crowd, killing four spectators and injuring more than 30 others.

1977: England football manager Don Revie uses the press to advertise the fact that he is resigning as manager of England and will be taking over as manager of the United Arab Emirates. The FA immediately suspended Revie for ten years on a charge of bringing the game into disrepute. Revie decided to contest this through the courts and won, after the judge found that the FA had overreached its powers.

2009: Australian driver Mark Webber wins the German Grand Prix in the Red Bull-Renault. This was Webber's first Grand Prix victory ... at his 130th attempt!

13 July

1751: The earliest confirmed reference to a cricket match played in Somerset is a memorial fixture in memory of Frederick, Prince of Wales, who had died just three months earlier. Prince Frederick had been an enthusiastic patron of the sport.

1912: Armas Taipale of Finland wins the two-handed discus throw gold medal at the Stockholm Olympics, the only time the event is held as an Olympic sport. Competitors threw the discus three times with their right hand and three times with their left, and the longest throw from each hand was added together for their score.

1930: The first two World Cup football matches take place simultaneously in Montevideo in Uruguay. The United States beat Belgium 3-0, while France won against Mexico 4-1. Thirteen teams entered this inaugural competition – Argentina, Belgium, Bolivia, Brazil, Chile, France, Mexico, Paraguay, Peru, Romania, the United States, Uruguay and Yugoslavia.

1972: Aristeidis Moumoglou scores the world record for the number of individual points in a basketball match. Playing for Iraklis against VAO, Moumoglou scored 145 of his team's total, in a 172-94 win. The match was in the Greek Basket League.

2007: Death of American professional free solo climber Michael Reardon. He had just finished climbing down the 180m Fogher Cliff in County Kerry, Ireland, when he was hit by a freak wave and swept out to sea. A search was launched immediately, but he was never seen again.

14 July

1930: The first player ever to be sent off in a World Cup match is Romanian defender Plácido Galindo against Peru.

1951: Argentine racing driver José Froilán González wins the British Grand Prix at Silverstone, giving Ferrari their first-ever Formula One victory.

1981: Birth of Australian motorcycle stunt rider Robbie Maddison, aka Maddo. In 2004 he won the gold medal at the X Games for completing 13 backflips. In 2009 Maddison demonstrated his immense ability by jumping his Yamaha YZ 250 on to the top of the Arc de Triomphe in Paris Las Vegas, a jump of 29m (96ft), landing cleanly on the top. He then lowered gently on to a lower stage, before safely dropping the bike 24m (80ft) to the ground. Maddo's motto is 'Face your fears – live your dreams'.

2012: Death of Swedish cross-country skier Sixten Jernberg. In a 13-year career Jernberg took part in 363 races, ending on the podium for 263 of them, 124 of which were victories. He also won four world titles and nine Olympic medals (four gold).

15 July

1850: The first known instance of a bowler taking all ten wickets in an innings occurs when John Wisden achieves the feat bowling for the North of England against the South of England. Remarkably all ten wickets were clean bowled.

1912: Death of Portuguese champion marathon runner Francisco Lázaro, who dies while taking part in the marathon in the Stockholm Olympics. Before the race Lázaro, a very experienced marathon runner, allegedly stated 'Either I win or die'. The temperature was very hot, and Lázaro went down on the 30km mark. Initially it was thought he had died from dehydration due to the heat, but the truth was more bizarre than that. Lázaro had apparently decided that to make himself more streamlined, and to prevent sunburn, the best thing he could do would be to cover his body with suet. But the suet prevented him perspiring, causing him to overheat internally and creating severe electrolyte imbalance which was the cause of death.

1938: Kent batsman Arthur Fagg scores 202 (in 170 minutes) against Essex in Colchester, to become the only batsman ever to score two double centuries in the same match, having scored 244 in the first innings.

1986: Death of harness driver Billy Haughton. Winner of the Hambetonian four times, the Little Brown Jug five times and the Messenger Stakes seven times, he finished his career with 4,910 wins. He was still racing up to his death at 62, dying from injuries sustained from a fall at Yonkers Raceway.

2000: The Stadium Australia in Sydney boasts the largest crowd ever for an international rugby match as 109,874 turn out to see the hosts narrowly lose to New Zealand 35–39.

16 July

1900: The tug of war contest takes place for the Paris Olympic Games. Originally this was to be a contest between France and the United States, but several of the American team were unavailable since they were taking part in the hammer throw. Organisers accepted a late entry just to ensure a competition went ahead – a team from Scandinavia comprising of three Swedish athletes, two Danish athletes and a Danish journalist. Despite the late entry and the evident lack of coordination, the mixed team took the gold medal with the French taking silver; there were no other entries.

1900: American athlete Ray Ewry wins three gold medals at the Paris Olympics. All three medals were won on the same day, all three were for jumping events and all three were for events that are no longer contested: the standing high jump, the standing long jump and the standing triple jump.

1950: The World Cup Final, in Rio de Janeiro, sees the hosts surprisingly beaten 2-1 by Uruguay. But the final was famous for another reason – the largest official attendance at a football match as 173,850 tickets were sold. Unofficial figures, however, suggest the attendance was closer to 210,000 as people were packed in to watch the match.

1984: Jay Aldous and Matt DeWaal complete their round-the-world cycle ride in Salt Lake City in the US. The 14,290-mile (22,997km) journey had taken 106 days, travelling in an easterly direction through 15 different countries.

17 July

1912: Seventeen nations join together and form the International Amateur Athletic Federation (now the International Association of Athletics Federations (IAAF)). The organisation oversaw all aspects of athletics. The change of name was forced by governing an increasing element of professionalism.

1937: Death of Scotsman Leslie Balfour-Melville. He was the captain, opening batsman and wicketkeeper for the Scottish cricket team, even leading them to a victory over Australia in 1882. He won the second Scottish Open tennis tournament in 1879. He played rugby for Scotland against England in 1872. In 1895 he won the amateur golf championship at St Andrews. He was the Scottish billiards champion. He was also excellent at the long jump, ice skating and curling.

1980: The Netherlands win the inaugural world championship for underwater hockey. The week-long competition was held in Canada.

2015: Death of French Formula One driver Jules Bianchi, nearly ten months after the accident that leaves him comatose. Bianchi had a serious accident in the 2014 Japanese Grand Prix. Conditions were poor on 5 October with intermittent heavy rain and fading light, when Bianchi lost control of his Marussia on the Dunlop Curve and crashed into a tractor crane. He was treated at the site before being transferred to hospital. He never left hospital and died from the injuries sustained – the first direct Formula One death for more than 20 years.

2016: Sweden's Henrik Stenson claims victory in The Open tournament played at Royal Troon with a record-breaking 20 under par, just three shots ahead of America's Phil Mickelson, but 14 ahead of third place J.B. Holmes.

18 July

1588: The story of Sir Francis Drake playing bowls at the beginning of the Spanish Armada is one that is often repeated. When the Spanish ships were spotted Drake said to his fellow players, 'We still have time to finish the game and to thrash the Spaniards too.'

Indeed, he and his party finished their game (Drake lost), before sailing off to 'thrash the Spaniards'.

1884: Maud Watson becomes the first-ever Wimbledon singles ladies champion. Thirteen women entered the competition, all from Britain, dressed in white corsets and petticoats, and it was 19-year-old Watson who came out victorious to win the title and a silver flower basket. In the final Maud beat her older sister Lilian 6-8 6-3 6-3.

1848: Birth of William Gilbert Grace, invariably known by just his initials. W.G. Grace was a cricketer who captained England, Gloucestershire and the MCC. He played first-class cricket for 44 seasons and yet he never became a professional, preferring to continue with his day job as a medical doctor. Grace was also a champion hurdler over 440 yards, played football for The Wanderers, and was a very good and enthusiastic curler, golfer and lawn bowler.

1932: Yorkshire County Cricket Club dismisses the visiting touring Indian team for just 66 in Harrogate – the lowest innings total ever which includes a half century! Nazir Ali scored 52 runs, an incredible 79 per cent of the innings total, while his ten colleagues managed just nine runs between them.

1976: At the Summer Olympics Romanian gymnast Nadia Comăneci scores an unprecedented perfect score of ten for her 30-second routine on the uneven bars. Comăneci was just 14 at the time. Not only had nobody ever achieved this score, but nobody had anticipated it happening, nor prepared for the possibility – the scoreboard only had three digits for scores such as 9.90 or 9.35. Therefore, to the initial confusion of the crowd, the scoreboard flashed her score as 1.00.

1999: Paul Lawrie wins the 128th Open Championship at Carnoustie Golf Links in Scotland to round off the most unlikely golfing victory in history. At the start of this final day's play Frenchman Jean van de Velde was leading the field on even par. Lawrie was almost out of sight on ten over. He completed his

W.G. Grace

18 July 1848–23 October 1915

Amateur England cricketer, widely considered one of the finest
players of all time, who played competitively for a remarkable 44
seasons while still practising as a doctor.

round on four under par, giving him a net six over. Van de Velde came to the final tee just three over, until he triple-bogeyed on the 18th to give a three-way tie for the lead, and the three men headed off to a play-off. Lawrie won the play-off to complete an extraordinary comeback, and seal the only major win of his career.

19 July

1908: Following a meeting in the Manchester Hotel in London, FINA (Fédération Internationale de Natation [Swimming]) is formed for overseeing competition in water sports including swimming, open water swimming, artistic swimming, diving, high diving and water polo. Founding members were Belgium, Denmark, Finland, France, Germany, Great Britain, Hungary and Sweden, but FINA now represents more than 200 nations.

1922: Olympic swimmer Johnny Weissmuller (star of several *Tarzan* films) becomes the first swimmer ever to swim 100m freestyle in under a minute. Weissmuller completed the distance in 58.6 seconds in California.

1952: The opening of the Helsinki Summer Olympics in Finland. Helsinki had originally been chosen to host the 1940 Games which had to be cancelled because of the Second World War. It became the northernmost city to host the Olympics. Several countries made their Olympic debuts in Helsinki, including the Soviet Union. The People's Republic of China also debuted, although only one member of their team (swimmer Wu Chuanyu) arrived in time to take part! Their involvement led to the withdrawal of the Republic of China (Taiwan).

1980: The opening of the 22nd Olympic Games in Moscow, Soviet Union (now Russia). These were the first Games held in Eastern Europe, and the first in a socialist nation. Only 80 nations attended the Games, the smallest number since 1956, primarily due to the boycott organised by US president Jimmy Carter due to the Soviet invasion of Afghanistan. Some athletes from the

66 boycotting countries decided to compete anyway, competing under the Olympic flag.

2009: Death of 18-year-old Henry Surtees, son of the legendary driver John Surtees. He was driving at Brands Hatch in a Formula Two race when Jack Clarke had an accident and hit a wall. Unfortunately one of his wheels broke its tether and bounced across the track, hitting Surtees. He was taken to hospital but died shortly afterwards, with his death attributed to the impact of the wheel rather than the subsequent crash.

20 July

1859: New York beat Brooklyn 22-18 in a baseball game staged on a racetrack on Long Island. The crowd of 1,500 became the first to pay to attend a baseball fixture, paying the princely sum of 50 cents each.

1976: The opening day of the fencing at the 1976 Olympics features Soviet fencer Boris Onischenko, who had won the silver medal at the 1972 Olympics. Some contestants noticed that Onischenko appeared to be gaining points even when they were certain he had not made contact with his foil. After an investigation it was discovered that he had managed to rig the scoring machine with an electronic trigger which he could set off by hand without needing to waste time on trivialities like hitting your opponent. He was rapidly thrown out of the competition.

1984: German Uwe Hohn, competing in East Berlin in East Germany, throws the javelin 104.80m. This was the first time that a javelin had been thrown more than 100m. This record is one athletics achievement that will never be surpassed. With the athletics governing bodies increasingly concerned about safety as more athletes were throwing ever longer distances, the men's javelin was redesigned in 1986 to reduce the distance it could be thrown.

2003: The British Grand Prix at Silverstone is won by Rubens Barrichello driving a Ferrari. But the race is most memorable for

Catholic priest Neil Horan managing to get on to the track. On the 11th lap of the race Horan managed to get on to the track and walked towards the cars waving large religious banners. Several of the cars had to swerve to avoid him. He was tackled by one of the stewards and removed to a safe area where he was charged with endangering lives. He was given a two-month jail sentence.

21 July

1904: Louis Rigolly from France is the first driver to clear 100mph when his Gobron-Brillie is paced at 103.56mph (166.66kmh).

1909: Belgian cyclist Karel Verbist dies while racing on the Bruxelles track after colliding with his own pacemaker motorbike. The accident became the subject of a rather macabre folk poem, which may be translated as 'Verbist, if you hadn't ridden your bike, you may not have ended up in a coffin'.

1943: Death of American athlete Charley Paddock. Paddock won the gold medal for the 100m in the 1924 Olympics, adding a second gold for the 4x100m relay, and was dubbed the 'world's fastest human' at the time. Paddock was also a veteran of both world wars. He died in a plane crash while on active duty in the second conflict aged just 42.

1978: Alan Minter and Italian boxer Angelo Jacopucci have a boxing match for the European middleweight title, a fight which would change the face of boxing. Minter won in the 13th round, by which time Jacopucci was totally destroyed. After graciously joining in Minter's celebration Jacopucci felt very sick so went back to his hotel. There he slipped into a coma and was taken to hospital, where he was declared dead the following morning at the age of just 29. The Boxing Board of Control immediately made changes including no fight going beyond 12 rounds, and every boxer would have to have mandatory CT scans. Five years later the ringside doctor from the fight was found guilty of second-degree murder for failing to take proper action and given an eight-month suspended sentence as well as having to pay $14,000 in damages to Jacopucci's widow.

2002: Michael Schumacher wins the French Grand Prix in his Ferrari, and in so doing is crowned Formula One world champion for the fifth time, matching Juan Manuel Fangio's 40-year record. No one else before or since has become world champion while there are still six races remaining on the calendar.

22 July

1912: The end of the Games of the V Olympiad, held in Stockholm, Sweden. This was the last time medals of solid gold were presented, and the first time any Asian nation had joined in the Games, with Japan's debut. It was also the first international sports event to utilise electronic timing of events. Both boxing and figure skating were banned – boxing because the Swedes felt it incompatable with the aims of the Games, and figure skating because the hosts wanted to promote the Nordic Games.

1951: Brazilian team Palmeiras win the first-ever Copa Rio after a two-legged final against Italian giants Juventus. This was the first intercontinental football club tournament – the precursor to the FIFA Club World Cup which began in the year 2000.

1996: The final of the Open Greco-Roman wrestling competition at the Atlanta Olympics is won by Russian Aleksandr Karelin. Karelin's Olympic record is certainly unique, a victim of political machinations. Karelin won Greco-Roman gold at the 1988 Olympics representing the Soviet Union. He repeated the success four years later for the 'Unified Team' ... so now he won his third gold medal at three successive Olympics, with each medal ceremony celebrated under a different flag. Karelin is usually considered the finest Greco-Roman wrestler of all time, with a professional record of 887 wins from 889 bouts.

2006: Canada beat the United States 15-10 in the World Lacrosse Championship, ending the States' record of 38 straight wins in the competition, a record going back nearly 24 years.

2010: Sri Lankan bowler Muttiah Muralitharan delivers his final ever Test match delivery, and has Indian cricketer Pragyan Ojha caught by Mahela Jayawardene. In so doing he became the first bowler in history to reach a total of 800 Test wickets.

23 July

1849: Day one (of three) of what is generally considered to be the first-ever Roses Cricket Match. Hyde Park in Sheffield staged the match between Sheffield and Manchester, but it was billed as 'Yorkshire versus Lancashire'. Yorkshire won the fixture by five wickets.

1868: The All England Croquet Club is founded in Wimbledon. In 1876 the club began to host Sphairistikè tournaments (Sphairistikè was the forerunner of lawn tennis, invented by Major Clopton Wingfield). The following spring the club changed its name to 'The All England Croquet and Lawn Tennis Club'.

1881: The European Federation of Gymnastics is founded in Liège in Belgium, initially comprising of just Belgium, France and the Netherlands. It would be another 40 years before non-Europeans were welcome to join, at which point the organisation changed its name to the Fédération Internationale de Gymnastique.

1908: British athlete Wyndham Halswelle wins the gold medal in the 400m at the London Olympics … hardly surprising since he is the only person in the final. Halswelle was blocked in the first final, so the organisers decided on a rerun between Halswelle and the men who finished first and second to decide on the medals. William Robbins and John Taylor were both from the US and decided that they would not contest the final since they disagreed with the rerun – which left Halswelle as the only competitor, producing the only walkover in Olympic history.

1942: Surrey and England cricketer (and England footballer) Andy Ducat dies suddenly while playing a match at Lord's. He was actually playing for his Home Guard unit against another unit. The match was immediately abandoned. Ducat remains the only person to have died playing a match at Lord's.

1976: The equestrian events begin in the Canada Olympics, with HRH Princess Anne becoming the first member of the British royal family to compete in the Olympics. She was also the first female athlete who was not made to undergo a gender test – historically this was compulsory due to concerns of men disguising themselves as women and having an advantage (thankfully this archaic and somewhat patronising practice has since been stopped).

24 July

1908: Italian Dorando Pietri wins the marathon at the 1908 London Olympics, leading the field of 56 competitors. He actually ran the first half of the marathon at quite a leisurely pace before accelerating through the remainder of the race, eventually gaining the lead near the 24-mile mark. He carried on to build a big lead. The effort had taken its toll and with the end in sight he collapsed. He was helped back to his feet and carried on before collapsing again. He collapsed five times, each time being helped back up – the final 350m took nearly ten minutes, but he still crossed the line first. American Johnny Hayes finished second, and the American team immediately lodged a complaint about the help Pietri had received. The complaint was upheld and Pietri was disqualified with Hayes taking the gold.

1978: Birth of American surfer Andy Irons, three times world champion, twice Rip Curl Pro Search winner and with 20 elite tour victories. He was the only surfer to have won at least one title at every single ASP (Association of Professional Surfers, now the World Surf League) venue.

1980: In the pentathlon event in Moscow, Olga Kuragina completes the final event (the 800m) in a time fast enough to set a new world record for the total points in the pentathlon. Just behind her on the track was Olga Rukavishnikova, whose time also set a new world record for the pentathlon. Her joy was short-lived, however, as the next person to complete the race was Nadezhda Tkachenko – with another new world record total for the pentathlon, and the gold medal. So Kuragina ended up with bronze – and the title of world record holder for 1.4 seconds, while Rukavishnikova took the silver having held the record for 0.4 seconds … the shortest time for which anyone has ever held a world record.

2010: Death of Alex 'Hurricane' Higgins, the Northern Irish snooker player who is probably more responsible than anyone for the popularising of the game and turning it into a global spectator sport. Higgins originally came to England as a 14-year-old to train as a jockey before specialising in snooker. The 'People's Champion', it is estimated that Higgins earned more than £3m in his career but spent most of his retirement in poverty due to his addictions to alcohol and gambling. By the time of his death he was living off disability living allowance.

25 July

1938: In the fourth Ashes Test between England and Australia at Headingley, Australia win by five wickets. In the Australian first innings Don Bradman scored 103, becoming the first (and to date only) batsman to score a century in six consecutive Test matches.

1970: The end of the British Commonwealth Games in Edinburgh. While there were previous events, such as the British Empire Games, this was the first use of the new title. It was the first significant athletics event in which metric units were used rather than imperial. Australia won the event with 36 gold medals.

1992: The opening of the Games of the XXV Olympiad, the Barcelona Summer Olympics in Spain. The Games marked the last time that the Summer and Winter Olympics were held in the same year after a decision by the IOC to alternate the Games every other year. South Africa competed for the first time since

1960 after a lengthy ban because of their apartheid policy. To demonstrate the spirit of the Games and the change in South Africa, white South African Elana Meyer and 10,000m winner black Ethiopian Derartu Tulu ran a lap of honour hand in hand. Germany entered as a single nation for the first time since 1964. Baltic nations Estonia, Latvia and Lithuania entered for the first time since 1936. Following the dissolution of the Soviet Union the region sent a 'Unified Team', made up of modern-day Armenia, Azerbaijan, Belarus, Georgia, Kazakhstan, Kyrgyzstan, Moldova, Russia, Tajikistan, Turkmenistan, Ukraine and Uzbekistan.

2012: The women's football match between North Korea and Colombia, as part of the London Olympics, begins with offence rapidly followed by chaos. The players stood on the pitch just before the game at Hampden Park in Glasgow. As the announcer ran through the team each individual's picture and key statistics would be flashed on to the large screens alongside the national flag. Due to an extraordinary gaffe the North Koreans were clearly displayed as intended … alongside the South Korean flag. The team stormed off the pitch and initially refused to play, eventually being persuaded to do so more than an hour after the advertised kick-off time.

26 July

1745: The first recorded women's cricket match, which takes place 'between 11 maids of Bramley and 11 maids of Hambledon, all dressed in white'. It would, however, be another 142 years before the first official women's cricket club was established – the White Heather Club in Yorkshire.

1920: Oscar Swahn of Sweden becomes the oldest ever Olympic medal winner when he gains a silver in the Running Deer shooting team at the age of 72 years and 280 days.

1921: American motor racing driver Jimmy Murphy (aka Gentle Jimmy) wins the French Grand Prix on a road circuit just south of Le Mans. Relations between the nations were strained when the victory banquet began with a toast to Frenchman Jules Goux who finished third. The American team walked out and went to a nearby café to enjoy a lunch of ham and eggs.

1930: The first-ever football World Cup semi-final sees Argentina thrash the USA 6-1, but does contain one marvellous moment of pure comedy. The Americans were unhappy with the refereeing. One of the US trainers rushed on to the field to remonstrate with the referee. He became so irate that he threw his bag down, shattering a large bottle of chloroform, and promptly passed out from the anaesthetic.

1970: The start of the third Commonwealth Paraplegic Games (also, rather patronisingly, called the 'Little Games') – 197 athletes competed from 14 commonwealth countries.

2009: World Wrestling Entertainment hosts the Night of Champions, a spectacular of numerous significant bouts and titles in Philadelphia, Pennsylvania. The event featured the World Heavyweight Championship, the WWE Championship, the Unified WWE Tag Team Championship and several other competitions.

2024: The IOC Organising Committee have announced that the 2024 Olympic Games will begin on this date in Paris, closing on 11 August. It will mark exactly 100 years since Paris last hosted the Games.

27 July

1952: Emil Zátopek of Czechoslovakia wins his third gold medal of the Helsinki Olympic Games. He had already won the gold medals in the 10,000m and the 5,000m races when, buoyed by his success, he decided he might as well have a go at the marathon. He wasn't on the original competitor list but his team managed to get him an entry. So Zátopek was entered and won his third gold medal, beating the rest of the field by two and a half minutes, the first time he had ever run a marathon in his life.

1996: Domestic terrorist Eric Rudolph plants a pipe bomb in the Centennial Olympic Park in Atlanta, Georgia, on day eight of the Olympic Games. The bomb went off, killing one person and injuring more than 100 others. A second person suffered a heart attack from shock and died later in the day. The damage could have been substantially worse but security guard Richard Jewell discovered the bomb prior to detonation and managed to clear most of the crowds to safety.

2001: The Australian team win the 4x200m freestyle relay at the World Aquatics Championship in Japan. For team member Ian Thorpe this was his record-breaking sixth gold medal at this Games. He had taken gold in the individual races of the 200m freestyle, 400m freestyle and 800m freestyle, with a world record time in each.

2007: Death of British heavyweight boxing champion James Oyebola. The 6ft 10in (2.08m) boxer won the bronze medal at the Commonwealth Games in 1986 in the super-heavyweight division. He was meeting a friend for a drink in the Chateau 6 Club in Fulham when he witnessed an argument between some staff and four customers. He wandered over to help and was shot in the neck and the back. He died four days later in hospital.

28 July

1928: The ninth Olympic Games starts in Amsterdam in the Netherlands. The opening marked the first time that the Olympic flame was lit during the Olympics, although the torch relay was not established until eight years later. It was also the first time that the parade of nations started with Greece and finished with the host nation, a tradition which continues today. It established the pattern of 16 days of competition – the majority of its predecessors had been stretched out over several months.

1936: Birth of West Indies cricket legend Garry Sobers, widely considered to be the best all-rounder in the history of the game.

1948: The first-ever Stoke Mandeville Games for the paralysed is held in the UK, the forerunner of the modern Paralympics. The first Games were the brainchild of neurologist Sir Ludwig Guttmann who wanted a sporting competition for World War II veterans to motivate them towards rehabilitation, and he deliberately timed it to coincide with the opening ceremony of the 1948 London Olympics. These first Games were restricted to those in wheelchairs, and involved just one event – archery. Fourteen ex-servicemen and two ex-servicewomen entered.

1973: The first-ever women's cricket World Cup – one of the few sports in which the women's version predates the men's. Seven teams competed in a round-robin tournament – hosts England, Australia, New Zealand, Trinidad and Tobago, Jamaica, an international XI and Young England. England won the league, and hence the World Cup, with Australia runners-up.

1984: The 23rd Olympic Games open in Los Angeles. After the US-organised mass boycott in Moscow at the previous Games, 14 Eastern Bloc countries retaliated by boycotting these Games, led by the Soviet Union and East Germany.

29 July

1751: The first-ever world title prize fight saw Jack Stack of England beat Frenchman M. Petit in 29 minutes. There were no rounds – just a continuous fight until one of the men simply could no longer continue.

1874: Major Walter Copton Wingfield patents a portable tennis court, which he called 'The New and Improved Court for Playing the Ancient Game of Tennis'. The game he marketed was enclosed in a box containing rubber balls, a net with poles, court markers and an instruction manual. The idea was that the game could be set up on croquet courts for 'healthy exercise and social amusement'.

1948: The opening of the Games of the XIV Olympiad – the London Summer Olympic Games. London had been timetabled to host the 1944 Games but this was cancelled due to the Second World War, so London was automatically awarded the new peacetime Games. Lord Burghley gave the welcoming address, beginning: 'Your Majesty: The hour has struck. A visionary dream has today become a glorious reality. At the end of the worldwide struggle in 1945, many institutions and associations were found to have withered and only the strongest had survived.'

1973: Death of British racing driver Roger Williamson during the Dutch Grand Prix, only his second professional race. On the eighth lap one of his tyres burst causing the car to flip over, whereon it burst into flames with Williamson trapped inside. Marshals were poorly trained and ill-equipped and didn't help him. Fellow driver David Purley driving behind immediately quit his own race and stopped and made a very brave attempt to help him. All his efforts failed, and Williamson died where he lay. Sadly the race continued – eventually won by Jackie Stewart.

2013: Death of Ecuadorian striker Christian Benitez (aka Chucho), one of the most prolific goalscorers in Ecuador's history. During the close season he went to hospital with abdominal pain, and died a few hours later of a heart attack at the age of just 27. Ecuador attempted to retire Benitez's number 11 jersey as a mark of respect, but due to petty FIFA regulations they had to reinstate the jersey for the 2014 World Cup.

30 July

1914: Tragic death of cricketing legend Albert Trott. Bizarrely he held the unique distinction of playing Test cricket for both Australia and England. He was very popular with the crowd – he would regularly field on the boundary so he could have a beer with supporters while the game progressed. He was one of only two players ever to have taken two hat-tricks in the same innings. In his own testimonial he got four wickets in four balls, and then a hat-trick later on. Sadly because of his heroics the match was rather brief, so he didn't raise much money! (He later claimed to have 'bowled himself into the poorhouse'.) Despite his records and his popularity he retired into poverty. He wrote his will on the back of a laundry ticket, leaving his wardrobe and the sum of £4 to his landlord, before heading out to a park in Middlesex where he took his own life by shotgun.

1930: The first-ever football World Cup Final in Uruguay. In the final of this inaugural tournament the hosts met their South American neighbours Argentina and beat them 4-2.

1966: The World Cup Final at Wembley Stadium sees England beat West Germany 4-2 after extra time. There has been so much discussion in football about the need for goal-line technology. Such technology introduced in 1966 may have produced a different result! The sides were locked at 2-2 after the 90 minutes. Then in the 11th minute of extra time Hurst scored his second, and England's third – or did he? Most fans believe that the ball did not cross the line – but the linesman gave it and the rest, as they say, is history. Right on full time Hurst scored his third to become the first person in history to score a hat-trick in the World Cup Final.

1980: The Moscow Olympics are, in many ways, possibly the most unpleasant in history. The whole vision of the Olympic movement appeared to be forgotten among the Soviet fans who jeered and booed non-Soviet athletes with remarkable frequency.

31 July

1899: Albert Trott hits what is probably the biggest six in the history of cricket, although it is never measured. Batting for England against Australia he clobbered a delivery with such force that he managed to clear the huge Lord's pavilion and the ball went out of the ground – the only person who has ever managed that at Lord's.

1956: The end of the England against Australia fourth Test match in Manchester, in which Jim Laker achieves 10-53 in the second innings – the best Test match bowling performance of all time. Laker had taken 9-37 in the first innings, finishing that innings by taking seven wickets for eight runs off 22 deliveries. England won the Test by an innings and 170 runs.

1983: British motorcycle Grand Prix at Silverstone. When the weather broke the bikers slowed down. Norman Brown went back to the pits and, after a little work on the bike, was sent out again – but still travelling significantly slower than other bikes. Other bikes flew past him, except for Swiss rider Peter Huber who was unsighted and drove into Brown at pace, both drivers coming off their bikes and hitting the tarmac. The organisers insisted that the race had to go on – but lost that battle when the majority of the other bikers came into the pits and parked out of respect and concern for their colleagues. Tragically both riders died of their injuries.

2012: Zara Tindall (nee Phillips – daughter of Princess Anne and Captain Mark Phillips, granddaughter of Queen Elizabeth II) finishes her own contribution to the equestrian event at the Olympics aboard her horse High Kingdom. As a key member of the British eventing team she became the first member of the British royal family to win an Olympic medal, as the British team won silver. Mrs Tindall's medal was presented to her by her mother.

AUGUST

1 August

1715: Actor Thomas Doggett establishes a prize for watermen in their first year of apprenticeship, a solo skull race on the Tideway on the River Thames. Now over 300 years old, it is the oldest continuous sporting fixture in the world. The Doggett Coat and Badge prize brought fame but little fortune, with the winner eligible to man the royal barge on state occasions.

1856: Birth of George Coulthard. He was suspended from Australian Rules football for a year for fighting and using bad language. He never played the game again, focusing instead on his cricket career. As well as playing in one Test against England, he also excelled as an umpire – the first one to dress in white, setting a trend for all future umpires. Coulthard also fought a bare-knuckle bout against national boxing champion Jem Mace (aka The Gypsy), and survived a shark attack in Sydney harbour. He died of tuberculosis at the age of 27, having packed an awful lot into his brief life.

1909: François Faber of Luxembourg becomes the first non-Frenchman to win the Tour de France. This seventh Tour is made up of 14 stages over a total of 2,794 miles (4,497km). Faber won six of the stages, and won the overall title easily.

1955: Legendary racehorse Camarero loses a race for the first time since 19 April 1953, a record-breaking winning streak of 56 races.

1976: Reigning Formula One world champion Niki Lauda suffers a near fatal accident at the German Grand Prix, the last time the race is run at the extended version of the Nürburgring. Before the race Lauda had complained to the authorities about the safety conditions at the circuit, particularly given the threat of rain. He attempted to arrange a boycott of the race at the drivers' meeting, but was outvoted by a solitary vote. During the race his Ferrari spun and hit an earth bank, bouncing back on to the track in flames. Harald Ertl and Brett Lunger both hit the stricken Ferrari and stopped, while Arturo Merzario and Guy Edwards stopped voluntarily. The four drivers managed to pull Lauda from the flames, but not before he had suffered severe burns. He fought for his life for the next few days before his condition stabilised and he eventually came through his ordeal. Lauda surprised many by returning to the sport, and even won back his world drivers' title in 1977.

2 August

1907: The first stanchion is laid in position by Lady Desborough for the building of the Great Stadium (later renamed the White City Stadium). In was officially opened ten months later by King Edward VII in readiness for the 1908 Summer Olympics. The stadium was demolished in 1985.

1932: The final of the men's 3,000m steeplechase at the Los Angeles Olympics, won in a time of 10.33.4. The time appeared to be remarkably slow, particularly for an Olympic final, so an investigation was launched. It was discovered that one official remarkably miscounted the laps, and the runners did an extra one … the 3,000m steeplechase inadvertently became the 3,460m steeplechase.

1963: The beginning of the first-ever World Netball Championships, held in Eastbourne, England. Eleven teams entered, playing in a round-robin format. The very first match saw New Zealand thrash Northern Ireland 112-4, with Colleen McMaster scoring 86 points. Australia would become the first world champions nine days later.

1978: Death of businessman and motor racing fanatic Antony Noghès. In 1911 he helped to create the Rallye Monte-Carlo. In 1929 he became the founder of the Monaco Grand Prix. Noghès was also the man who suggested the international adoption of the chequered flag to end all motor races.

2001: The women's British Open golf tournament tees off at Sunningdale in Berkshire. It replaced the Canadian du Marier Classic as the fourth and final major of the ladies' season; 144 women entered the tournament which was won by Se-Ri Pak of South Korea at 11 under par, two strokes ahead of the field.

2016: Death of Australian polymath Forbes Carlisle. He was a true pioneer in elite training methods including stress training, heart rate tests, pace clocks, logbooks, interval workouts and T wave studies.

3 August

1852: The first official organised inter-college sport takes place when three boat crews from Yale and Harvard meet on Lake Winnipesaukee in New Hampshire over a two-mile course. Harvard's boat *Oneida* came first and her crew were presented with a pair of black walnut oars as a trophy.

1880: Foundation of Leicester Football Club, the original name of the rugby club. The club was formed by the merger of three existing minor sides – Leicester Societies AFC, Leicester Amateur FC and Leicester Alert. They moved to Welford Road in 1892.

1921: The day after the players implicated in the Black Sox scandal are acquitted of all legal charges, the independent commissioner Kenesaw Landis hands out his own verdict. The governing authorities of baseball had appointed Landis, a federal judge and baseball fan, to carry out an internal investigation to see whether any punishment should be meted out internally. Eight players of the Chicago White Sox were given a life ban from the sport.

1958: Death of British racing driver Peter Collins, who died during the German Grand Prix just two weeks after he had won the British Grand Prix. Collins lost control of his car which flipped over, throwing Collins into a tree from which he sustained serious injuries. His teammate Mike Hawthorn went on to win the drivers' crown that year, but was so deeply upset by Collins's death that he retired at the end of the season and never drove again.

1968: The end of the first-ever Special Olympic Games in Chicago, an international sporting competition for athletes with intellectual disabilities. The Games lasted a fortnight and involved thousands of athletes competing in 32 Olympic-style sports.

1992: The Olympic weightlifting competition is the tightest it has ever been, with three men tied in first place having lifted exactly the same weight. Olympic rules stated that in the event of a tie the determining factor would be the competitors' weights. That left USSR weightlifter Ibragim Samadov with the bronze medal as the heaviest, just 0.05kg heavier than the silver medallist. Samadov was understandably furious, since nobody had lifted more than he had. At the medal ceremony he refused to lean forward to accept his medal – he simply took it in his hand, glanced at it … and then dropped it on the podium and walked off.

2017: Brazilian forward Neymar (full name Neymar da Silva Santos Júnior) signs for Paris Saint-Germain from Barcelona for a world record €222 million (~£200 million). He was offered €45 million (~£40.7 million) a year pre-tax to sign on a five-year deal.

4 August

1936: The favourite for the women's 100m sprint at the Berlin Olympics is Polish runner Stanisława Walasiewicz (who becomes Stella Walsh in 1947 when she becomes an American citizen). However, she was comfortably beaten by American sprinter Helen Stephens in an event which yielded not one but two extraordinary follow-on stories. The first concerned the medal ceremony, which was best described by Stephens in her own words: 'Hitler … gets hold of my fanny [bottom] and begins to squeeze and pinch, and hug me up. And he said, "You're a true Aryan type. You should be running for Germany." So after he gave me the once over and a full massage he asked me if I'd like to spend the weekend in

Berchtesgaden.' Stephens refused. Walasiewicz's team were so shocked by Stephens's speed they were convinced she was too fast to be a woman, so demanded that she was checked. A medical examination proved she was a woman, and Walasiewicz had just been beaten by a better woman. Fast forward to 1980 and Stella Walsh (as she had become) was shot dead while out shopping in Cleveland. A full autopsy yielded a major surprise – Walsh was in fact intersex (or a congenital eunuch as she would have been called in 1936, or hermaphrodite as it would be termed in 1980).

1957: Juan Manuel Fangio becomes the oldest ever Formula One world champion at the age of 46 at the German Grand Prix. With the increasing physical demands on racing drivers it is extremely unlikely that this record will ever be beaten.

2012: When Ian Millar takes to the individual jumping course on board Star Power he breaks an Olympic record, despite only finishing joint 42nd. The 65-year-old equestrian first represented Canada during the 1972 Olympics, and therefore became the first athlete to appear in ten Olympic Games. (It would have been 11 Games but for the Canadian boycott in 1980.)

2015: Swiss-Brazilian Laso Schaller beats the world record for a high dive when he dives from a board set at a height of 58.8m (192ft 10in) in Ticino, Switzerland.

5 August

1900: The finals of the shooting events in the 1900 Paris Olympics. Shooting remains a very popular sport within the Olympic movement, but back in the day the event was rather different. Live pigeons were released from traps just in front of the shooters, and the winner was the one who killed the most birds. Once any competitor had missed two birds they were out. The results were not recorded in the official Olympic records – because the IOC considered their inclusion somewhat embarrassing. By 1904 the US had introduced the clay pigeon.

1970: The first-ever penalty shoot-out in any professional football match in England takes place in the semi-finals of the Watney Mann Invitation Cup tie between Hull City and Manchester United. George Best became the first player to take a penalty in a shoot-out and the first to score, Denis Law was the first to miss, and Manchester United won.

1976: Death of thoroughbred racing horse Dr Fager. He set the record for the mile at the Washington Park Handicap with a time of 1.32.4, averaging 39.0mph.

1998: Death of the Standardbred horse Albatross. One of the first horses to earn more than $1m, it was as a sire that he was most financially successful. His 2,546 foals won more than $130m.

6 August

1926: Gertrude Ederle from New York becomes the first woman ever to swim the English Channel. Ederle, a former five-time world record holder for various swimming events and an Olympic gold medal winner, swam from Calais to Dover in just over 14 hours – beating the times of the five men who had already accomplished the feat by more than an hour.

1997: The final day of the first Test between India and Sri Lanka at Colombo, debatably one of the least thrilling Test matches ever, simply because it never came close to being a competition. India spent the first two days batting before declaring on 537/8. In reply Sri Lanka just kept on batting, closing their innings at the end of day five on 952/6, a record innings score for Test cricket. As a result nobody even started a second innings and the match was drawn.

2006: Travis Pastrana is famous as a motorcycle racer, performer and stunt rider. During the X Games Pastrana became the first person ever to land a double backflip in competition, a stunt that has never (as of 2019) been bettered.

2012: Death of American professional basketball player Danny Roundfield who spends a dozen years in the ABA and NBA, most notably with the Indiana Pacers. He was named in three All-Star teams. Tragically he died in Aruba in the Dutch Caribbean. He was involved in a boating accident, and lost his life through drowning while helping his wife to safety.

7 August

1932: The marathon at the Los Angeles Summer Olympics is won by Juan Carlos Zabala of Argentina. But it was Finn Paavo Nurmi who made the headlines. He was the favourite for the event. But the day before the marathon was due to be run Nurmi was banned for professionalism. He protested that he had turned down the opportunity to become professional on more than one occasion. The Olympic officials, led by Swede Sigfrid Edström, said that he was professional because he had claimed too much in travelling expenses and this constituted pay. Nurmi presented a petition signed by every marathon entrant appealing for his reinstatement, but the officials stood firm. This incident was the catalyst to Finland refusing to participate in the usual annual Finland–Sweden athletics challenge, and the event did not happen again until 1939.

1947: Batting for Essex against Derbyshire, Peter Smith scores a magnificent 163 runs – the highest score ever achieved by a number 11 batsman. (The first ten runs of his innings were actually scored on the previous day.)

1993: American Gerald McClellan beats compatriot Jay Bell to claim the WBC middleweight championship. At 20 seconds this was the shortest world title bout in history.

1995: Britain's Jonathan Edwards breaks the world triple jump record twice in the same competition in Gothenburg, Sweden. Early in the competition he became the first man to clear 18m with a leap of 18.16m (59ft 6.75in). His final jump in the competition was a staggering 18.29m (60ft 0in).

2016: The International Paralympic Committee's Governing Board votes unanimously to ban the whole Russian team from the 2016 Summer Paralympics, citing the Russian organising committee's inability to enforce the World Anti-Doping Code – stating that this is a 'fundamental constitutional requirement'. They further stated that the Russian government had 'catastrophically failed its Para athletes'.

8 August

1922: The first meeting of what would become a regular sporting event, the Jeux Olympiques Féminins (tr. women's Olympic Games). These first Games were held in Paris, the first-ever track and field event for women, lasting for just one day. Seventy-seven athletes from five nations took part – Czechoslovakia, France, Great Britain, Switzerland and the United States.

1970: Death of thoroughbred racehorse Citation, the first horse in history to gain more than $1m in prize money.

1979: Disaster strikes on day three of the 28th running of the Royal Ocean Racing Club's Fastnet race, a biannual yachting race around the seas off the south coast of Britain, the climax of the Admiral's Cup. On day three a raging storm created chaos. Of the 306 yachts in the race five sank, 77 were turtled at least once and more than 100 were knocked down at some stage. Tragically 18 lives were lost – 15 race contestants and three rescuers. The Royal Navy, the RAF and even a nearby Dutch warship intervened to prevent greater losses.

2015: As Australia thrash Barbados 83-16 in a netball World Cup group game, goal shooter Caitlin Bassett scores 30 goals … from an unbelievable 30 shots.

2016: Kazakh ice hockey defenceman Damir Ryspayev, playing for Barys Astana against Kunlun Red Star, starts a brawl that is both exhaustive and entirely unprovoked. And ridiculously early, in just the third minute of an exhibition match. Having hit several opponents, seemingly at random, he started on the substitutes. He was eventually ejected from the game (which was cancelled in the chaos), and ten days later received a lifetime ban from the sport. The Council of Directors stated that they simply could not allow their rules to be 'systematically and grotesquely violated'.

9 August

1886: Andrew Stoddart scores 98 runs in a day batting for Middlesex. Two days earlier he had scored 207 for Hampstead. And just three days before that he had scored 485 in a single day for Hampstead against Stoics – a world record score at the time. His total of 790 runs in a week remains a world record. Stoddart played cricket for England, as well as representing both England and the British Isles in rugby union.

1936: At the Berlin Olympics the United States sprint relay team become the first team ever to break the 40-second barrier. The 4x100m team comprised of Ralph Metcalfe, Foy Draper, Frank Wykoff and the legendary Jesse Owens. On the morning of the competition the US team made changes to the line-up by removing Sam Stoller and Marty Glickman – who were the only two Jewish athletes in the US Olympic team. Apparently the US committee leader had done this to avoid any potential offence to Adolf Hitler with Jews winning gold medals. That being the case then it was perhaps an unusual step to replace these two with Jesse Owens and Ralph Metcalfe … replacing two Jewish runners with two black runners may not have fully appeased the wrath of the Führer!

2012: Having already successfully defended his Olympic 100m title, Usain Bolt repeats this feat in the 200m final in a time of 19.32 seconds. Yohan Blake and Warren Weir ensured it was a Jamaican clean sweep on the podium. After crossing the line he then did five press-ups – one for each of his five Olympic gold medals (to that point – he eventually retired with eight). And in an interview just after the race he modestly proclaimed: 'I'm now a legend. I'm also the greatest athlete to live.'

2015: Racing in the Alpe Adria Road Racing Championship, Slovenian Berto Camlek suffers a fatal accident, becoming the first person ever to die racing on the Hungaroring circuit in Hungary. The Hungaroring was the first Formula One Grand Prix circuit behind the Iron Curtain.

10 August

1874: Birth of American jockey Tod Sloan. Well known on both sides of the Atlantic, he is perhaps referred to more frequently than any other sportsman, although most people are unaware they are even mentioning him. The cockneys used his name for rhyming slang – as in 'He's on his Tod Sloan' meaning that he is on his own; so every time the phrase 'He's on his tod' is used it is a reference to the jockey!

1900: The first International Lawn Tennis Challenge. The idea for a match between the UK and the US was generated in Harvard. Once the two associations had agreed, one of the players, Dwight Davis, designed the format and purchased a trophy out of his own money. America won the inaugural competition 3-0 in Boston. After Davis's efforts and generosity, just a couple of years later the tournament became known as the Davis Cup.

1932: The men's tumbling competition takes place as part of the gymnastics programme in the Los Angeles Olympics. This was the first and indeed only time that tumbling was included as an Olympic sport. Only four gymnasts actually entered – so István Pelle from Hungary holds the unique (and bizarre) record of being the only person ever to enter an Olympic tumbling event without winning a medal.

1954: Legendary jockey Sir Gordon Richards retires with a record of 4,870 wins.

1984: One of the most iconic and memorable moments of track athletics when South African-born British barefoot runner Zola Budd collides with American runner Mary Decker in the 3,000m at the Los Angeles Olympics. Decker fell and was out of the race, while Budd stumbled and could only finish in seventh place. Budd was booed loudly through the remainder of the race for her part in the demise of the local heroine.

11 August

1711: Ascot Racecourse in Berkshire is officially opened by Queen Anne and hosts its first race, 'Her Majesty's Plate'. Seven horses competed for the plate, run in three separate four-mile heats.

1929: Babe Ruth (real name George Herman Ruth) scores an unprecedented 500th home run in Cleveland, Ohio, batting for the New York Yankees against the Cleveland Indians.

1991: Death of experienced NASCAR driver J.D. McDuffie, who started NASCAR racing in 1963, and died during a race 28 years later. McDuffie collided with Jimmy Means on the fifth lap of the 'Budweiser at The Glen' race and was killed by a broken neck. His death was one of the major factors in the future production of the HANS (head and neck support) device, now compulsory in all motorsport events.

2012: At the London Olympics the Jamaican sprint relay team break the world record in the final of the competition. Nesta Carter, Michael Frater, Yohan Blake and Usain Bolt clocked a time of 36.84 seconds in the 4x100m race.

2014: The Swedish national football team for the intellectually disabled want to go and play in the International Sports Federation for Persons with Intellectual Disability World Football Championships in Brazil, but they are unable to raise the necessary funds of $51,000 to attend. Swedish stars Johan Elmander, Kim Källström, Per Nilsson and Andreas Isaksson gave the squad autographed shirts so they could auction them off to raise some funds, but Swedish captain Zlatan Ibrahimović was a little scathing of their efforts: 'What the h*ll are you going to do with a shirt? How much is it to go?' On hearing the amount, Ibrahimović paid them the full amount from his own pocket so they could go.

2016: Death of Pakistan cricketer Hanif Mohammed, who represented his country in 55 Test matches. Hanif was actually the middle of five sons. Older brother Wazir, and the younger pair of Mushtaq and Sadiq, all also played cricket for Pakistan. Hanif is best remembered for the 499 runs he scored for Karachi against Bahawalpur in 1959 – the highest ever score by an individual in a cricket match, a record which stood until 1994.

12 August

1900: Australian Frederick Lane wins the 200m obstacle race at the Paris Olympics – the only time the event is held. The event was even odder than it sounded … because it was a swimming event. Twelve competitors from five nations swam 200m, clearing three obstacles along the way. First they had to go over a pole suspended just above the water, then they had to scramble over a row of boats, and finally they had to swim under another row of boats.

1936: At the age of 13 years and 268 days Marjorie Gestring becomes the youngest winner of an event at the Olympic Games, winning gold for her performance in the 3m springboard diving.

1970: The youngest of modern football's 'superpowers', this date marks the formation of Paris Saint-Germain, created by merging Paris FC and Stade Saint-Germain. Paris FC had only been formed the previous year to try to address the issue of having no top French football team based in the capital.

1975: New Zealander John Walker becomes the first man to break 3.50 for the mile at a meet in Gothenburg in Sweden. His official time was recorded as 3.49.4.

1978: Death of English motorcycle racer John Williams, who dies in an accident in the first-ever Ulster TT Formula One race. Earlier that day he had won the Ulster Grand Prix, making him the only motorbike racer to die on the same day as a race victory.

1984: The final day of the Los Angeles Olympics in California sees the introduction of the most oxymoronic sport in the world. Many people struggle with synchronised swimming being classified as a sport – is it truly sporting or just a dance competition underwater? This date saw the first Olympic competition for solo synchronised swimming. How was that possible? With whom were they synchronised?

1989: Death of Nigerian midfielder Samuel Okwaraji. He was playing a World Cup qualifying game against Angola when he collapsed on the pitch and died within minutes. A post-mortem revealed he had an enlarged heart and very high blood pressure.

13 August

1887: Scottish football team Hibernian become the first winners of the 'Football World Championship'. Incorporating the word 'world' into the title may be a little misleading – in truth this was simply a play-off between the Scottish champions and the English champions! The first few championships were played by the cup winners of the respective nations before switching to the league champions in 1895. In the very first final Hibernian beat Preston North End 2-1 in Edinburgh.

1944: The end of the unofficial 'POW Olympics', staged by Polish prisoners of war in the Woldenberg Oflag POW camp, with the permission of their German captors. The prisoners made an Olympic flag from a bed sheet and pieces of coloured scarves, and various events were staged. The event was considered a demonstration of the Olympic spirit transcending war.

2000: Sheffield Wednesday host Wolverhampton Wanderers in one of the earliest games of the new Championship season. Almost immediately Wolves poured forwards and Wednesday goalkeeper Kevin Pressman came out to try to intercept and break up the attack. He was, however, adjudged to have deliberately handled the ball outside of his area. Pressman was therefore given a red card after just 13 seconds – the fastest ever in the English league.

2016: The American swimming team win the 4x100m medley relay in the Rio Olympics. For one of the team, Michael Phelps, this marked his fifth gold medal at this one Olympic Games, and his record-breaking 23rd and final Olympic gold medal overall.

14 August

1894: Death of Australian steeplechase jockey Tommy Corrigan. He suffered severe brain damage when his horse Waiter fell during the Victoria Amateur Turf Club Grand National Steeplechase, and died three days later without regaining consciousness. His funeral procession was led by 150 jockeys and trainers on foot.

1909: The first-ever motorsport event is held on the famous Indianapolis oval circuit with seven motorcycle races.

1920: The opening ceremony for the Olympics of Antwerp, Belgium. This particular ceremony was significant in being the first one at which the Olympic flag was flown, the first when the Olympic Oath was said, and the first in which doves were released to symbolise peace.

1948: Czechoslovakian gymnast Eliška Misáková is diagnosed with polio shortly after arriving at the Olympic Games in London, and so is admitted to a local hospital. She died during the competition while her teammates, including her sister Miloslava, won the gold medal. During the medal ceremony the Czech team raised a national flag with a black border as a sign of mourning. Misáková became the first, and so far only, athlete in the history of the Olympics to be awarded a medal posthumously.

1996: Russian runner Svetlana Masterkova breaks the women's world record for running a mile in a time of 4.12.56 in Zürich.

2017: Leon Walraven destroys the world record for the most basketball hand bounces in a minute, when he completes 609.

15 August

1903: The New Zealand All Blacks rugby team play their first-ever rugby Test match, against Australia's Wallabies at the Sydney Cricket Ground. Despite this being their first match the All Blacks won comfortably 22-3.

1936: The Berlin Olympics is intended (to his mind, at least) to be Adolf Hitler's opportunity to flex his political muscle, and to demonstrate to the watching world his Aryan master-race. Clearly the Indian field hockey team hadn't read the script, as they thrashed Germany 8-1 in the Olympic hockey final.

1972: England off-spinner Pat Pocock takes a hat-trick with the first three deliveries of an over, bowling for Surrey against Sussex. The fourth ball was uneventful, and he then took wickets with the remaining two deliveries – becoming the only bowler in cricket history to take five wickets in an over.

2004: One of the most bizarre disqualifications in the history of the Olympics. Iranian judoka Aresh Miresmaili had a big issue with the IOC's recognition of the State of Israel. And then he was drawn to fight Israeli Ehud Vaks. But judo is a sport of integrity and honour, so he didn't want to do anything controversial. He appealed to his management team to be allowed to refuse to fight, but they declined. So he was running out of options – so the day before the contest he decided to binge eat, eating as much as he could possibly cram in within a 24-hour period ... and was disqualified for being overweight!

16 August

1743: English boxing champion Jack Broughton publishes the very first official rules of the sport of boxing. Entitled 'Rules of the Ring', the code carried the subtitle 'Rules to be observed in all battles on the stage'. The booklet listed seven clear regulations, and was an attempt to safeguard against increasing brutality and general lawlessness, which were creeping into the sport. Broughton was painfully well aware of the need for regulation having killed George Stevenson in a bout two years earlier. These rules would be the guiding principles for the sport for more than 100 years.

1860: Birth of Martin Hawke, better known as Lord Hawke, the England and Yorkshire cricketer. Hawke was appointed captain of Yorkshire while just 22, and held on to the position for 27 years. He was appointed as Yorkshire club president aged 38 while still playing, and held on to the presidency for 40 years until his death.

1930: The opening ceremony to commence the very first British Empire Games (now called the Commonwealth Games). The inaugural Games were held in Ontario in Canada and featured just six sports – athletics, boxing, lawn bowls, rowing, swimming and diving, and wrestling. Canadian triple jumper Gordon Smallacombe had the distinction of winning the first-ever gold medal. England won the first Games with 25 gold medals.

2008: Jamaican Usain Bolt becomes the first man in history to break the 9.7 second barrier for the 100m sprint. Running at a meet in Beijing in China he clocked 9.683 seconds.

2009: Usain Bolt takes the 100m world record in Berlin, Germany, in a time of 9.58 seconds. Bolt declared himself delighted with the record, but dissatisfied with the time, convinced that a time under 9.5 seconds is possible.

17 August

1869: The first transatlantic rowing race sees Oxford beat Harvard on the River Thames.

1920: Death of Cleveland Indians shortstop Ray Chapman at the age of 29. Carl Mays, pitching for the New York Yankees, hit him directly on the head and he passed away 12 hours later – the first, and currently only, MLB player to have died as a direct result of an in-game injury. After the pitch Chapman didn't move, he just slowly fell to his knees and then fell to the ground with blood gushing out of his left ear. After a while he was able to get up and walk off the field, but his speech was incoherent. As he was walked off, his knees gave way and he had to be helped the rest of the way. Chapman died in New York City, at about 4.30am.

2012: Day one of the 'World Alternative Games'. With London hosting the UK Olympics and very little happening in Wales, some passionate Welshmen were unhappy with this state of affairs and proposed that the little town of Llanwrtyd Wells in Powys in the middle of the principality should host this alternative event – a fortnight of quirky fun. Events for the games included a man vs. horse marathon, the world bog snorkelling championships, the wife-carrying championships, French cheese rolling, underwater hockey, the bathtubbing championship, worm charming, chariot racing, a French cockerel throwing competition, and … believe it or not … world championship finals for both rock-paper-scissors, and for Pooh sticks.

2017: The relatively new discipline of Twenty20 cricket has proved incredibly popular among fans, encouraging batsmen to swing the bat. This has, of course, proved rather costly to bowlers – some more than others! Bowling for Northamptonshire against Yorkshire at Headingley, Ben Sanderson saw his full allocation of four overs smashed for 77 runs – an average of more than three runs for every delivery!

18 August

1920: Great Britain beat the Netherlands in the final of the tug of war competition at the Olympic Games in Belgium. Originally a standard event in the Games, this was the last time that the tug of war featured as an Olympic sport.

1948: Legendary Australian batsman Don Bradman plays his last ever Test match in an Ashes fixture at The Oval. In his final innings Eric Hollies bowled the great man out for a duck, leaving the Don frustratingly with a Test match batting average of an unprecedented 99.94. Nobody in history has even come close to this, a record sometimes referred to as the greatest achievement by any sportsman in a major sport. If he had scored just four runs he would have hit an average of 100 (or if he had opted not to bat!)

1951: The final day of the fifth and final Test between England and South Africa at The Oval. England's opening batsman Len Hutton became the only person in the history of Test cricket to be dismissed 'obstructing the field'.

1962: Denis Law makes his debut for Manchester United after a record British transfer fee of £115,000 secures his services from Torino. Law got off to a dream start on his debut against West Bromwich Albion, scoring after just seven minutes. The match finished 2-2.

1964: South Africa are banned from competing in all forms of Olympic competition due to their policy of apartheid.

2005: Death of American professional wrestler Christopher Bauman Jr, known in the ring as Chri$ Ca$h. Ca$h is best known as the Combat Zone Wrestling World Tag Team champion. He died in a motorbike accident at the age of just 23.

19 August

1909: After the hot air balloons and the motorcycles, the Indianapolis circuit finally sees cars on the track for the first time. Despite the fact it was only a practice session nearly 20,000 people turned up, paying $1 each for the privilege – as much to see the circuit as the cars. The surface was slowly disintegrating, and needed to be repaired overnight for the second day of practice. Wilfred Bourque's rear axle broke, resulting in the car flipping, with Bourque and his mechanic Harry Halcomb becoming the first fatalities on the famous track.

1951: Dwarf Eddie Gaedel becomes the shortest player ever to participate in a Major League Baseball game when he turns out for the St Louis Browns against the Detroit Tigers. Back in the days before political correctness this was (sadly) a gimmick rather than a genuine team selection. Gaedel stood at 3ft 7in (1.09m). As if to underline the gimmick, he was given shirt number $^1/_8$. This was his only plate appearance ever, and he was walked on four consecutive pitches – under strict instructions not to make any attempt to swing for the ball.

1975: A good goalkeeper needs many attributes – bravery, flexibility, agility, reflexes, vision … and ideally a good loud voice for commanding his or her defence. Unfortunately for Manchester United goalkeeper Alex Stepney his voice was not quite loud enough, and he ended up dislocating his jaw by screaming too much and missed the next couple of matches.

2006: Ronnie O'Sullivan whitewashes Dominic Dale 6-0 in the semi-final of the Northern Ireland Trophy at the Waterfront Hall in Belfast. During the six frames O'Sullivan compiled breaks of 65, 64, 84, 75, 67, 63, 106 and 63 at his usual pace, while Dale only managed 29 points. The entire match was over in just 53 minutes.

20 August

1900: The last day of the final of the Olympic Games cricket tournament … and the only game of cricket ever played in the Olympic Games. This was due to be a tournament between four teams, but the Netherlands and Belgium both pulled out shortly before the tournament, leaving Great Britain and France to compete a final which Britain won by 158 runs. Neither team were strictly a national side. Britain were represented by the Devon and Somerset Wanderers, while the French team were basically British expats calling themselves the French Athletic Club Union. The British team were awarded silver medals and the French team were awarded bronze, with all players given miniature statues of the Eiffel Tower. The medals were upgraded to gold and silver in 1912.

1938: Melbourne in Australia hosts the first-ever international netball fixture. At the time the sport was actually called 'women's basketball'. Australia beat New Zealand 40-11.

2000: Tiger Woods wins the PGA Championship in a play-off against Bob May. Having already won the US Open and The Open Championship he became the first player for nearly 50 years to win three majors in the same calendar year. At the beginning of 2001 he won the Masters Tournament so he was holding all four major titles simultaneously.

2006: Day four of the fourth Test match between England and Pakistan at The Oval. Umpires Darrell Hair and Billy Doctrove charged the Pakistan bowlers with ball-tampering, and awarded five penalty runs to England. Pakistan refused to accept the charge, and refused to come out to field after tea unless the ruling was changed. The umpires waited half an hour, and then declared Pakistan had forfeited the match. The result was overturned by the ICC in July 2008, and recorded as match abandoned in the records – but then the ICC reversed their decision six months later and the match was re-awarded to England.

2009: In an athletics meeting in Berlin, Germany, Usain Bolt takes the world record for the 200m with a time of 19.19 seconds. This historic run was just four days after he had taken the world record for the 100m.

21 August

1848: The year that cricket great W.G. Grace was born witnesses one of the most extraordinary games of cricket of all time – a match for which Grace would not have been eligible. More than 2,400 people turned up at The Priory Ground in Reigate, Surrey, to watch the match advertised as 'Eleven One-Armed Men v Eleven With One Leg'. If this does not seem bizarre enough this was a rematch of a fixture from 1796, although details of that match have been lost over time. The players were all ex-servicemen injured in the line of duty, who played in their veterans' uniforms. At the conclusion of the match the two teams headed off together to the local pub behind a marching band, where they were given a free drink to toast Her Majesty's health and ten shillings for their efforts.

1894: Death of French cyclist 21-year-old Pierre Froget who is competing in a tandem race at the Velodrome of Vichy. He was involved in a bad accident in which he sustained head injuries and died in hospital six days later. His fellow rider escaped with minor injuries.

1965: The English Football Association sanctions substitutions in matches from the start of this season for the first time. Keith Peacock of Charlton became the first substitute used in the 11th minute of the match against Bolton Wanderers.

2001: San Diego Padres pitcher Adam Eaton needs surgery on a wound in his stomach which brings his season to a rather premature end. The cause of the injury? Unfortunately it was self-inflicted – he managed to stab himself with a kitchen knife while trying to remove the shrink-wrap off a DVD.

2014: Tony McCoy wins aboard Arabic History at Newton Abbot – his 100th winner of the National Hunt season. McCoy breaks the speed record for 100 winners in a season, completing the achievement in just 116 days.

22 August

1851: *America*, owned by the New York Yacht Club (NYYC), wins the inaugural Royal Yacht Squadron Cup. She raced against 15 yachts of the Royal Yacht Squadron in a 53-mile regatta around the Isle of Wight. Six years later the surviving crew members donated the cup they had won to the NYCC to be used as a challenge trophy between friendly nations – hence 'America's Cup'.

1950: Althea Gibson becomes the first black competitor in the United States National Championships (now the US Open). United States Tennis Association rules banned racial and ethnic discrimination, but qualification for the major tournaments was through the accumulation of points in minor competition, many of which were held at whites-only clubs. Gibson was awarded wildcard entry after retiring champion Alice Marble published a scathing attack in the magazine *American Lawn Tennis*. She made her national debut on her 23rd birthday, winning her first-round tie.

1972: Following a vote by the IOC members (International Olympic Committee), Rhodesia (now called Zimbabwe) are banned from competing in the summer's Munich Olympics ... just four days before the Games are due to start. The vote was only narrowly carried by 36 to 31. Several African nations had threatened to boycott the Games if Rhodesia were allowed to compete. The argument concerned the white minority rule within the country and the abuse of black residents.

2000: Ashton Gate in Bristol hosts the 2-2 draw between Bristol City and Brentford ... and a world record for injury time (now termed 'time added on for stoppages'). During the first half there was a broken leg and a dislocated shoulder. The dislocation was so severe that an ambulance had to be driven on to the pitch. The fourth official signalled 13 minutes of injury time. In that period two goals were scored, and another player was concussed – leading to another delay. In the end 23 additional minutes were played, with the first half ending 68 minutes after it started.

2004: The Olympic Games has a historical reputation of individuals going beyond normal human achievement and pushing themselves into superhuman performances. Therefore the rowing final of the women's eight in Greece was certainly unusual. In the latter stages of the race one of the Australian rowers, Sally Robbins, said she felt exhausted … so she simply stopped rowing. She even allowed her oar to drag in the water, and at one stage lay down backwards on to teammate Julia Wilson's lap. Unsurprisingly the Australian team finished last. Robbins was heavily criticised across the globe for her actions.

23 August

1926: Death of French track cyclist Gustave Ganay who dies after a fall racing on the Parc des Princes. Ernest Hemingway explained the accident rather graphically (but apparently quite accurately) in his *A Lovable Feast*: 'where we saw that great rider Ganay fall and heard his skull crumple under the crash helmet as you crack a hard-boiled egg against a stone to peel it on a picnic.'

1938: Day four of the fifth Test between England and Australia at Lord's sees England close their first innings with a record Test score of 903/7. Several other world records were broken during the innings, one of which remains to this day – the most expensive Test bowler, as Chuck Fleetwood-Smith laboured through 87 overs for figures of 1-298.

1986: The final of the 1,500m freestyle at the FINA World Championships sees West German swimmer Rainer Henkel take the gold medal. Russian swimmer Vladimir Salnikov (aka the Leningrad Express) came fourth – not a position he was particularly used to, having won his previous 61 1,500m freestyle races, a record dating back to 1977.

2008: The bronze medal fight for the open weight class in the taekwondo competition at the Olympics ends in disgrace. Ángel Matos from Cuba was disqualified from the contest. He was so unhappy with this decision that he kicked the referee in the face, leading to an immediate disqualification and a subsequent lifetime ban for both Matos and his coach. After the fight, Yang Jin-suk, the secretary general of the World Taekwondo Federation, apologised: 'This is an insult to the Olympic vision, an insult to the spirit of taekwondo and, in my opinion, an insult to mankind.'

2014: Death of Cameroonian footballer Albert Bodjongo. Bodjongo was playing in the Algerian top division for JS Kabylie and was leaving the field after a 2-1 defeat against USM Alger when he was struck on the head by a projectile thrown from the crowd. He immediately collapsed and was taken to hospital where he died a couple of hours later. The post-mortem results showed that the cause of death was not the projectile but a severe beating he had received just a day or two before the game. The exact circumstances of and reason for the beating were never established, and the culprits were never apprehended.

24 August

1892: Everton formally open their new ground Goodison Park, the first purpose-built stadium in the country. Bizarrely for such a momentous occasion the crowd of 12,000 were treated to … no football. The club decided to host an athletics event followed by a firework display. Football was first played at Goodison nine days later when Everton, donning their new salmon and navy striped shirts, entertained Bolton Wanderers in an exhibition match which Everton won 4-2. Their first league game in their new ground was the very next day, a 2-2 draw with Nottingham Forest.

1961: Death of show jumping horse Huaso (originally named Faithful). He started his career as a racing horse, but was too jittery to be successful and so was sold with a view to being converted to dressage. Huaso holds one of the longest-held sporting records having high-jumped to a height of 2.47m (8ft 1in) in Chile in 1949.

1963: Argentinian football legend Alfredo Di Stéfano is kidnapped at gunpoint by Venezuelan revolutionaries – the Armed Forces of National Liberation. He was touring South America with Real Madrid at the time. Bizarrely he was released two days later totally unharmed without any ransom being paid, and was keen to emphasise that the kidnappers had treated him well.

2015: Death of British motor racing driver Justin Wilson. Wilson was a past winner of the International Formula 3000, and of the 24 Hours of Daytona. At the time of his death he was driving a Honda for Andretti Autosport in the IndyCar Series. Wilson was racing in the Pocono Raceway when he was struck on the head by a car nose cone after race leader Sage Karam had a big crash. Wilson was removed from the car in a comatose state and airlifted to hospital but died the following day.

25 August

1875: Captain Matthew Webb becomes the first man to swim across the English Channel. He swam from Dover in Kent to Calais in a time of slightly less than 22 hours.

1930: Death of Italian-American boxer Frankie Campbell. Campbell was fighting heavyweight champion Max Baer, and was knocked unconscious in the fifth round, after which he was taken to hospital. He died a few hours later. An autopsy revealed that the punch was so ferocious that his brain had been separated from the connective tissue of the skull.

1960: The beginning of the Games of the XVII Olympiad in Rome, Italy, more than 50 years after the city was first awarded the

Games! In 1905 Rome was successful in its bid to host the 1908 Games, but the following year Mount Vesuvius erupted which drained the nation of funds and facilities, so the 1908 Games were given to London. Rome finally got a Games of their own!

1991: Michael Schumacher, who is contracted to the Mercedes racing team, makes his Formula One racing debut ... for the Jordan-Ford team, in the Belgian Grand Prix at Spa-Francorchamps. Eddie Jordan signed Schumacher as a temporary replacement for his driver Bertrand Gachot. Gachot was unavailable since he was serving a prison sentence after spraying CS gas at a London cabbie in a case of road rage.

2004: During the Olympic Games in Athens Hossein Rezazadeh from Iran sets a new world record in weightlifting for the clean and jerk when he lifts 263kg (41st 5lb).

26 August

1960: Death of Danish cyclist Knud Jensen during the Rome Olympics. Participating in the 100km team time trial, one of the Danish cyclists dropped out after the first lap suffering with sunstroke – meaning the remaining three all had to finish. Jensen told his teammates he wasn't feeling well, and they supported him for some time, one on each side. They also sprayed him with water to try to help. When they temporarily let go of him he immediately collapsed and cracked his head on the pavement. He was taken to a military tent, but died in the afternoon. The physicians who examined him concluded that the head injury was not the cause of his death but that he had died from heatstroke.

1995: The IRB (International Rugby Board) declares rugby union to be an 'open' game, removing all restrictions on payments and benefits paid to players. The decision was borne of necessity with clubs and players trying to find legal ways to work around the law to entice and reward players – so-called 'shamateurism'. The IRB therefore openly embraced professionalism to maintain control over the sport.

2017: Floyd Mayweather and Conor McGregor fight their super-middleweight bout. The referee stepped in during the tenth round to award the fight to Mayweather. Mayweather announced his retirement after the fight, becoming one of the very few boxers in history to retire undefeated. He made around $100m from this final bout, while McGregor earned $30m. Mayweather also got a sizeable share of the TV rights. Overall he actually earned a world record $178,041 per second!

27 August

1902: Death of Manchester City and Wales full-back Di Jones. Ten days earlier Jones had been playing in a pre-season friendly for Manchester City when he fell on some broken glass on the pitch. The wound became infected and Jones died of tetanus and blood poisoning. Tragically, since this was a pre-season friendly, City argued that Jones wasn't actually 'working' and hence refused any liability, so his widow and children received absolutely nothing.

1908: Birth of Australian cricketer Don Bradman. Bradman was discovered as a young man playing bush cricket, and his rise to stardom was meteoric. His influence was such that even 50 years after his retirement Australia's Prime Minister John Howard called Bradman the 'greatest living Australian'. And when he was stricken with appendicitis one of his Test teammates took a telephone call from the private secretary to King George V requesting that the king was kept informed of his health.

1960: John Devitt of Australia is awarded the gold medal for the 100m freestyle in the Rome Olympics, in very controversial circumstances. Lance Larson of the United States was given the silver medal in a very close finish. Back in those days there were no television replays for close races – results were decided by eye by the finish judges – and they decided that Devitt was the winner. However, individuals were also timed for the record books by three timers, with the average taken. The three timers for Devitt timed

Sir Don Bradman

27 August 1908–25 February 2001

Australian cricketer widely regarded as the finest batsman ever.
His Test batting average of 99.94 is one of the finest sporting
achievements of all time.

him at 55.2, 55.2 and 55.2 – the consistency seemed to indicate the timing was pretty accurate. Larson was timed at 55.1, 55.1 and 55.0 – so Devitt was awarded the gold medal despite not having the fastest time in the race.

1975: The start of the 95th US Open, the first time the tennis major had not been played on grass. The tournament took place on the outdoor clay courts at Forest Hills in Queens, New York. The tournament would only be played here for three years before moving to its permanent home on the hard courts at Flushing Meadows.

2004: German kayaker Birgit Fischer wins the gold medal in the K-4 500m class at the Athens Olympics. In so doing she became the first woman in any discipline to win gold medals in six different Olympic Games.

28 August

1624: The earliest definite record of a cricket match, with Horsted Keynes hosting West Hoathly. Both teams represented Sussex villages. The result of the match is not known.

1845: The laws of the game of rugby football are clarified at Rugby School, with 37 resolutions passed as to how the game shall be played. It was actually written over four days by William Arnold, W.W. Shirley and Frederick Hutchins, all of whom were students at the school. The majority of these laws made sense and are still used today, or an adaptation of them.

A few, however, were significantly more bizarre, including:

- 'A player standing up to another may hold one arm only, but may hack him or knock the ball out of his hand if he attempts to kick it, or go beyond the line of touch' (Law 16)
- 'A player having touched the ball straight for a tree, and touched the tree with it, may drop from either side if he

can, but the opposite side may oblige him to go to his own side of the tree' (Law 18)

● 'No strangers, in any match, may have a place kick at goal' (Law 25).

1978: The beginning of the 98th US Open, the first time the 'fourth major' has been played at the USTA National Tennis Center In Flushing Meadows, New York, and the first time it has been played on hard courts. The singles tournaments were won by Americans Jimmy Connors and Chris Evert.

1978: Don Vesco becomes the first motorbike racer to clear 500kmh. At Bonneville in America Vesco is clocked at 509.8kmh (318.6mph) on his 2,030cc Lightning Bolt streamliner.

29 August

1895: At a meeting in Huddersfield 20 rugby clubs from Yorkshire, Lancashire and Cheshire resign from the RFU and form the NRFU (Northern Rugby Football Union), participating under slightly different rules. It was not until 1922 that this breakaway group would call themselves the 'Rugby Football League'.

1904: The beginning of the Games of the III Olympiad in St Louis, Missouri, the first time the Olympic Games (in any form) have been held outside of Europe. The Games themselves would only last six days, but they were part of a wider sports festival in Missouri which lasted for five months. Due to various worldwide political issues, combined with the difficulties of reaching St Louis, 589 of the 651 athletes came from the US or Canada. In fact in 53 of the 95 events the US were the only country to enter any competitors.

1993: The final of the fourth women's hockey Champions Trophy sees the first penalty shoot-out in the history of the tournament. Australia and the Netherlands battled through to the final and drew 1-1. Australia won 4-2 on penalty strokes to win the trophy for the second consecutive time.

2004: Hitting the final 7km of the marathon in the Greek Olympic Games, Brazilian Vanderlei de Lima was in the lead and looking very likely to win. He was then suddenly and without warning attacked by an Irish protestor called Neil Horan. The attack took 15–20 seconds off his lead, and left him badly shaken and in some discomfort. He was therefore overtaken and only finished third. While he accepted his bronze medal with dignity and humility he knew what everyone else knew – without this attack he would probably have won. What was particularly bizarre was that there was no known relationship (past or present) between de Lima and Horan, and while he described himself as a protestor, whatever message he was trying to protest against was never very clear. Horan is a defrocked Roman Catholic priest who regularly protests at various events – see also 20 July 2003.

30 August

1882: The birth of the term 'The Ashes' to refer to Test cricket matches between England and Australia. England had just lost a Test match at home to Australia – their first defeat on home soil. *The Sporting Times* wrote a mock obituary for English cricket, which concluded with the line 'The body will be cremated and the ashes taken to Australia'. For some reason that vision really appealed to the public, and soon everyone was talking about 'The Ashes'. A few weeks later the English team set off to Australia to play with captain Hon. Ivo Bligh, vowing to come back with 'The Ashes', and Australian captain W.L. Murdoch vowing to keep hold of them. During an invitation match Bligh was given a small urn symbolic of the ashes. Bligh kept the urn on his mantelpiece until the day he died when it was bequeathed to the MCC in his will.

1977: Day two of the US Open sees Virginia Wade play Renee Richards. Ms Richards was playing her first match in the women's singles ... but not her first match in the US Open. Richards actually first played in the US Open in 1960 (when it was called the US National Championship) ... as Richard Raskind in the men's singles before he underwent gender reassignment surgery. Richards lost in straight sets to Wade 6-1 6-4. The gender change didn't appear to have any effect on the tennis ability – Raskind lost to Neale Fraser in straight sets 6-0 6-1 6-1.

1992: The Belgian Grand Prix at the Spa-Francorchamps circuit is won by Michael Schumacher in his Benetton-Ford – his first race win in Formula One. His winning margin was more than half a minute.

2001: A college football game between the Cumberland Bulldogs and the Jacksonville State Gamecocks is certainly a world first. During this game the Gamecocks utilised placekicker Ashley Martin – the first woman ever to play and score in an NCAA American football game. Jacksonville State certainly benefitted from her expertise as they beat Cumberland 72-10.

31 August

1769: The earliest known cricket century is the 107 scored by John Minshull of the Duke of Dorset's XI against Wrotham in a minor match in Sevenoaks, Kent.

1968: Captaining Nottinghamshire against Glamorgan, Sir Garfield Sobers becomes the first batsman to score 36 off one over by hitting all six deliveries for six. One of them was actually caught by Roger David, but he unfortunately stepped backwards over the boundary rope in taking the catch. The unfortunate bowler was Glamorgan's Malcolm Nash.

1969: Death of legendary boxer Rocky Marciano, the only world heavyweight champion ever to retire undefeated. On the evening before his 46th birthday Marciano was a passenger on a small private plane. The pilot was attempting to land on a small airfield, but hit a tree on the approach. Marciano, the pilot and a friend of Marciano's were all killed immediately. There were no survivors.

1984: Shortly after the Los Angeles Olympics, Frenchman Thierry Vigneron breaks the pole vault world record with an effort of 5.91m. With the very next vault Soviet Sergey Bubka managed 5.94m – meaning Vigneron had been the world record holder for just 77 seconds.

2001: The third and final day of the Asian Test Championship in Multan. Pakistan declared their innings against Bangladesh closed at 546/3. Only six players batted (three out, one retired hurt and two not out) … and five of the six scored centuries!

2006: Croatian Veljko Rogošić completes his marathon swim across the Adriatic Sea. Rogošić set off from Grado and swam 225km (139.8 miles) to Riccione in 50 hours and ten minutes. This was the greatest distance ever swum in the open sea without the use of flippers or other propulsion aids.

SEPTEMBER

1 September

1920: Derbyshire County Cricket Club lose their final match of the season against Somerset at Weston-super-Mare. The result left Derbyshire with the worst county season record of all time: played 17, lost 17. They were due to play 18 matches, but the game against Nottinghamshire was abandoned without a single ball being bowled. The previous worst was from 1884: played 10, lost 10 ... by Derbyshire!

1946: The first-ever US women's Open Golf Championship concludes at the Spokane Country Club near Washington DC. It remains the only time the women's US Open has been played in match play competition. The field of 39 was whittled down to 32 to begin the match play, reducing it to 16, eight and then four in the next three days. The semi-finals were played over a 36-hole competition, leaving Patty Berg and Betty Jameson in the final. The pair were level after the first round, but Berg dominated the second 18 to win 5 and 4. Berg won the first prize of $5,600 – the highest prize fund awarded at the women's US Open until 1972!

2013: Death of American heavyweight WBO boxing champion Tommy Morrison at the age of 44. His death was the result of multiple organ failure caused by AIDS. Morrison had retired from boxing at the age of 27 when he was first diagnosed with HIV, but returned to the ring ten years later for two further bouts.

2 September

1899: Sheffield Wednesday play their first match at the Owlerton Stadium (which would be renamed Hillsborough in 1914). Their previous ground, Olive Grove, had been purchased for an expansion to the railways. The first match at the Owlerton Stadium was kicked off by the Lord Mayor of Sheffield, and saw Chesterfield take an early lead through Herbert Munday. However, Wednesday came back in style to win 5-1.

1899: Death of British tennis player Ernest Renshaw who, together with his twin brother William, won the Wimbledon men's doubles five times. He also won the singles once. Renshaw died at the age of just 38. According to the post-mortem his death was from the 'effects of carbolic acid'. No explanation or further details have survived.

1937: Death of Pierre de Frédy, Baron de Coubertin, the father of the modern Olympic Games, the founder of the International Olympic Committee and the second president of the IOC. Serving from 1896 until 1925, he remains the longest-serving president of the movement.

1970: A tennis set tie-break is used for the first time ever in a major tournament. The need for change was highlighted two years earlier, after Franklin Robbins had beaten Dick Bell in a match requiring 100 games: 22-20 9-7 6-8 8-10 6-4. The tie-break was the vision of Jimmy Van Alen, who had earlier set up the Tennis Hall of Fame. Initially the tie-break was called the Van Alen Streamlined Scoring System (VASSS), and was different from the modern version in a couple of respects. Firstly it was a best of nine (first to five), rather than the best of 13 (first to seven). Also it was literally first to five, no need to win by two clear points. When the tie-break was in progress the umpire put a small red flag on his table to indicate this was the case. If the tie-break score went to four-all then it was simply next point wins. In this case the umpire put up two red flags – one with the letter S on, and one with a D – standing for sudden death. Most players did not enjoy the high-pressure intensity, but spectators and fans loved it. The very first tie-break was in a first-round tie, and was won by Australian Owen Davidson against Manuel Santana. Interestingly their first three sets went to tie-breaks, with Santana winning the game 6-7 7-6 6-7 6-3 6-4.

3 September

1935: Briton Malcolm Campbell becomes the first man to drive in excess of 300mph. Driving his Campbell-Railton Blue Bird at the Bonneville Salt Flats in Utah, US, he was officially timed at 301.129mph (484.598kmh).

1972: In the German Olympics Mary Peters enters the final event of the pentathlon (the 200m) in the lead. Heide Rosendahl won the race in a time fast enough to set a new points world record for the pentathlon. However, she had to settle for the silver medal as Peters arrived hot on her heels with a time which was not quick enough to take the race but did give her a points total large enough to set yet another new world record. This meant that technically Rosendahl was the world record holder for the event for 1.12 seconds!

1994: Daniel Kimenez of Puerto Rico knocks out Austrian Harold Geier to defend his WBO (World Boxing Organisation) super-bantamweight title in Austria. The bout entered the record books as the shortest ever world championship boxing fight, lasting just 17 seconds.

1994: The Swedish Federation of Kaninhop (aka rabbit show jumping) is established. The sport of Kaninhop started in Sweden in the early 1970s and has grown from there, particularly in Sweden. The Scandinavians have stretched the sporting prowess of rabbits – the long jump record stands at 3.00m (118.1 inches) by Yaboo, and the high jump best was 1.00m (39.4 inches) by Aysel.

4 September

1931: The official foundation of the World Archery Federation (FITA, from the French Fédération Internationale de Tir à l'Arc). It is fairly common practice for a newly formed organisation to set about organising a world championship or cup to spread their fame. Interestingly, archery did it the other way round. The first-ever World Archery Championships were held in August 1931, and it was in running these that it became clear they really needed a governing body! FITA was initially organised by Czechoslovakia, France, Poland and Sweden.

1966: Race seven in the Formula One season is held in Italy. Italian Ludovico Scarfiotti and Briton Mike Parkes made it a Ferrari 1-2. Jack Brabham was forced to retire on lap seven with an oil leak, but given the failure of competitors Graham Hill, John Surtees, Jackie Stewart and Jochen Rindt, he was crowned world champion. Brabham's success was truly historic as he became the first (and to date only) driver to win a world championship driving one of his own cars.

1972: The American swimming team win the 4x100m medley relay in the Munich Olympics. For one of the team, Mark Spitz, this marked his seventh gold medal at this one Olympic Games. He was also a member of the other two relays, as well as taking gold in the 100m and 200m freestyle, and the 100m and 200m butterfly. Incredibly, Spitz set a world record in all seven events.

2011: Death of American footballer Lee Roy Selmon, best known as the defensive tackle for the Tampa Bay Buccaneers over nine seasons. He built his reputation in college football, and so was the first overall pick in the 1976 NFL draft. He stopped playing at the age of just 30 to become athletic director for the University of South Florida. After a few years he gave that up and opened his own restaurant. On 2 September, at the age of 56, he suffered a large stroke, but lost his struggle for life two days later.

5 September

1882: Foundation of Hotspur Football Club, made up of schoolboys who played for Hotspur Cricket Club and were looking for something to do in the winter months. In the early months they accidentally received letters intended for London Hotspur, so in 1884 they changed the club's name to Tottenham Hotspur to avoid further confusion.

1970: Death of Formula One racing driver Jochen Rindt during a practice session for the Italian Grand Prix. Rindt was born in Germany, but drove as an Austrian national. During the practice session his car's brake shift failed, causing him to drive into the guardrails. The heavy impact caused strangulation by the seatbelt and although he was freed from the car he was pronounced dead on the way to the hospital. At the time of the accident he was leading the World Drivers' Championship. In the remaining races his nearest rival Jacky Ickx was unable to secure enough points to overhaul his lead, so Rindt became the first (and as of 2019 the only) driver to be awarded the title of world champion posthumously.

1972: During the 1972 Olympics in Germany, 11 members of the Israeli team are shot dead by the Palestinian terrorist group Black September. The terrorists were demanding the release of 234 Palestinians being held prisoner. German security attempted a rescue which sadly backfired, resulting in the deaths of the Israelis along with a German police officer and five Palestinians.

2015: Len Granger and Jamie Barnett finish the longest ever game of squash. The game was played at Barnt Green in Worcestershire, and lasted 38 hours and 27 seconds. The match was designed as a world record attempt rather than in competitive play – and raised £5,000 for charity.

6 September

1880: The first true superstar of cricket, W.G. Grace, makes his Test match debut for England against Australia at The Oval. Opening the batting he scored 152 in his first innings. Interestingly his opening batsman partner was his brother E.M. Grace, and the pair shared a 91 opening stand. E.M. was also making his debut for England, as was a third brother G.F. Grace. While W.G. went on to a long and illustrious career, neither E.M. nor G.F. ever played for England again.

1910: In Boston, Massachusetts black Canadian boxer Sam Langford becomes the undisputed Coloured Boxing Champion, winning on points over 15 rounds. Langford is regularly credited as the greatest boxer who never challenged for the world title – mainly due to the fact that he was excluded because of the colour bar, and even Jack Johnson (the first African American world heavyweight champion) refused to fight him. He won the coloured title a record five times, but was never given the chance to claim the title he probably deserved.

1913: Woolwich Arsenal (now just Arsenal) play their first match at their new stadium on the opening weekend of the 1913/14 season, winning at home to Leicester Fosse 2-1 in the old Division Two. The club had moved from the Manor Ground in Plumstead, wanting a more modern stadium, and leased ground from St John's College of Divinity in Highbury (the name by which the stadium would rapidly become known). Leasing from a college of divinity did bring conditions – in the early days the club were not allowed to play matches on 'holy days', nor to sell 'intoxicating liquor' at the stadium.

1995: If not the greatest save ever, certainly the most bizarre – from the man who is nicknamed El Loco (tr. the madman). An underperforming England football team were playing a friendly against Colombia. The ball broke to England midfielder Jamie Redknapp who thought he would try his luck from distance. It was a weak shot straight at goalkeeper Rene Higuita for what could (and possibly should) have been a simple catch. Too simple for El Loco. As the ball reached him he launched himself forward kicking his legs up behind him. The ball passed over his head, and as his legs flew upwards he cleared the ball behind his back with his studs – his own unique creation which he called the 'scorpion kick'.

7 September

1892: The first-ever boxing match which is fought by the now familiar Marquis of Queensberry rules. The rules were actually written by John Chambers, but the Marquis (real name John Douglas) provided the sponsorship so it was his name that was carried forward. The match was a world heavyweight bout with gloves, and it ended when James J. Corbett knocked out John L. Sullivan in the 21st round.

1953: Maureen 'Little Mo' Connolly wins the US Open tennis tournament ten days before her 19th birthday, becoming the first-ever winner of the calendar Grand Slam. Sadly just ten months later, a couple of weeks after winning Wimbledon for the third time, she had a horse riding accident which ended her tennis career at the age of 19. Connolly died at the age of just 35, suffering from ovarian cancer.

1956: Top Brazilian side Santos give a debut to their new signing, the 15-year-old Pelé. In a league game against FC Corinthians Pelé opened his account with four goals.

1996: England's Chris Boardman sets a new 'hour record' (the maximum distance cycled in exactly one hour) in Manchester, when he pedals a remarkable 56.375km.

2011: Russian professional ice hockey team Lokomotiv Yaroslavl are preparing for their first match of the season in the Kontinental Hockey League, away to Minsk in Belarus. They chartered a Yak-Service aeroplane and, being the first game of the season, took the entire playing squad and four members of the youth team. For a reason that was never determined the aeroplane left the runway before taking off, hit a tower, burst into flames and crashed about 1km from the air traffic control – 43 of the 45 people on board perished at the scene. Hockey winger Alexander Galimov died five days later in hospital. One aircrew member was the sole survivor of the accident – the entire first team squad of Yaroslavl perished.

8 September

1788: The first formal boat race recorded in England's annual register. Two eight-oared cutters, *The Invincible* and *The Chatham*, raced from Westminster to Richmond-on-Thames.

1888: The first round of matches of the inaugural season of the newly formed Football League. Twelve football clubs had been officially welcomed as members, with none from London or the south. The founder members were Accrington (later Accrington Stanley), Aston Villa, Blackburn Rovers, Bolton Wanderers, Burnley, Derby County, Everton, Notts County, Preston North End, Stoke (later Stoke City), West Bromwich Albion and Wolverhampton Wanderers.

1968: Arthur Ashe beats Tom Okker 14-12, 5-7, 6-3, 3-6, 6-3 in the final of the US Open to become the first (and to date the only) black winner of the championship. This was the first year of professionalism within the sport (the 'Open Era'), but Ashe was still registered as an amateur so was not entitled to the $14,000 prize money, which was given to Okker. After retirement Ashe underwent a heart bypass operation during which he became contaminated with HIV during a blood transfusion. He died from AIDS-related pneumonia in 1993.

2012: Australian Trent Grimsey takes the world record for a cross-Channel swim when he completes the swim from Dover to Calais in six hours and 55 minutes.

2015: England are hosting Switzerland in a qualification match for Euro 2016 at Wembley. They were already 1-0 up through a goal by substitute Harry Kane when, in the 84th minute, they won a penalty. Up stepped Wayne Rooney to become the first Englishman to score 50 international goals, overtaking Bobby Charlton's record of 49 in the process.

9 September

1912: Two days after Manchester City win away to Manchester United (1-0) the United manager Ernest Mangnall becomes the manager of City. His appearance in the United dugout was somewhat controversial at the time since his move to City had already been agreed – and he struggled to hide his delight at City's winner. Mangnall remains the only manager in history to have managed both Manchester clubs.

1964: Sunderland draw 2-2 with Aston Villa at Roker Park. In the Sunderland line-up for the final time was Brian Clough, who was taken off near the end with damage to his anterior cruciate ligament. The damage would prove terminal and he faced retirement from playing at the age of 29. Clough played for Middlesbrough and Sunderland, scoring 251 league goals from 274 starts. With a strike rate of 0.916 goals per game, he remains the most prolific English goalscorer of all those who have played at least 250 matches.

1972: The final of the eighth basketball Olympic competition. The previous seven had all been won by the USA, a record going back to 1936. In fact going into this final the USA had an Olympic record of played 63, won 63. The USA were facing the Soviet Union, and with seconds to go the Soviet Union were leading by one point. Doug Collins was fouled and earned two free throws. He was successful with the first and the scores were level. At the very moment he was going to take the second the hooter sounded to signal the end of the game. Collins scored to make the score 50-49 in favour of the USA, but the ball was still live. While the Soviets tried to get down to the other end, one of the Soviet coaches argued with the scorer's table, stating they had called for a timeout before the free throws that they should have been given. After much consultation the referees decided that the two free throws would stand, and play restarted from under the basket with three seconds remaining. However, the chaos had enabled the Soviets time to plan for this play. They also made a substitution – which they were not permitted to do without the timeout. The Soviets ran the play and got it very wrong, and the horn went and the United States started celebrating – until the referee ordered those final three seconds to be rerun (or re-rerun) because the clock wasn't working properly. In a chaotic three seconds the Russians launched the ball the full length of the court where it was caught by Aleksandr Belov, who dunked the final two points as the horn sounded. Whatever the rights and wrongs the record books show that the Soviet Union won the gold medal by a score of 51-50.

2008: The Bulgarian women's hockey team hit an all-time low with the worst loss in hockey history against Slovakia. The final score, after all three periods, was 82-0. Technically the Bulgarian goalkeeper should also be in the record books – despite conceding 82 goals she still managed to make a record 57 saves, but the international governing body refused to acknowledge this as a record due to the 'farcical' score. So without her it could have been a lot worse!

2014: American Elan Buller successfully scores a basketball shot from a distance of 34.29m (112ft 6in).

10 September

1624: The earliest known cricket fatality. Batsman Edward Tye had hit the ball which had basically gone straight up in the air in a village match. Jasper Vinall moved in for the catch as Tye swung at the ball again to avoid being dismissed (which was allowed then). Unfortunately Tye's bat connected with Vinall's head, who collapsed. He died 14 days later of the injuries sustained.

1858: As Brooklyn entertain New York in a baseball game, home batsman John Holden hits the first recorded home run.

1910: Brazilian football team Corinthians play their first match, away to União da Lapa. The 1-0 defeat was still a very impressive result – União da Lapa were an established team, whereas Corinthians had only been formed nine days earlier by a committee of enthusiasts comprising two decorators, a cobbler, a driver and a labourer. Within just four years Corinthians had claimed its first league championship.

1922: The second Italian Grand Prix is run on the newly opened Autodromo Nazionale Monza. The circuit had only been opened a week earlier, and immediately became home to the Italian Grand Prix, which has been run at Monza every year since, with the exception of 1980.

1961: The Italian Grand Prix is the penultimate race of the season, and this is the last time the race is run over the full Monza track of 10km (6.2 miles). At the end of lap two Ferrari's German driver Wolfgang von Trips lost control of his car and crashed into spectators, killing 15 of them and himself. The race continued because organisers were concerned a cancellation would produce gridlock among people trying to leave the stadium and hamper rescue and emergency vehicles. Von Trips's Ferrari teammate Phil Hill won the race and with it the championship.

1972: West Germany win the hockey gold medal on the penultimate day of the German Olympics – the first time a European team has triumphed for more than 50 years. Sadly their moment of glory was marred by the behaviour of their opponents Pakistan – players, officials and fans. A big pitch invasion at the end got close to becoming a war zone. The Pakistan players refused to wear their silver medals, and turned their backs on the German national anthem at the medal ceremony. The 11 players were banned for life, but this was reduced to two years after a very public and humble apology by the team.

11 September

1839: The Caer Howell Grounds in Ontario hosts the first Canadian track and field athletics meeting.

1978: Death of Swedish Formula One racing driver Ronnie Peterson (real first name Bengt), during the Italian Grand Prix at Monza. Very early in the race he was hit by James Hunt and many other cars were involved in a large melee. Peterson hit the barriers and his car burst into flames and stopped in the middle of the track. Hunt, Clay Regazzoni and Patrick Depailler pulled Peterson out of the car and lay him in the road while stewards put the fire out. At the time it appeared he suffered nothing more than severe burns and the medics spent far longer with Vittorio Brambilla who appeared in worse shape after being hit by a loose wheel and was comatose in his car. Peterson, Brambilla and other injured drivers were taken to the hospital in Milan … and the race was restarted. Once in hospital it was found that Peterson had seven fractures in one leg and three in the other, so he was moved to intensive care. During the night his condition deteriorated, initially showing fat embolism and then renal failure, before he passed away the following morning. For the record Niki Lauda won the Grand Prix.

1983: Jimmy Connors beats Czechoslovak Ivan Lendl 6-3 6-7 7-5 6-0 to win the US Open singles title. This was Connors's 100th ATP singles title. He would win another nine titles before he retired, and remains the only male tennis star to reach the magic 100 milestone.

2001: Death of international cricketer Nezam Hafiz. A middle-order batsman, he played first-class matches for Guyana, and later for the United States, to whom he had become a naturalised citizen. After his cricket career he became a businessman with an office in the World Trade Center, and was one of those who perished in the 9/11 terrorist attacks.

12 September

1885: Arbroath beat Bon Accord 36-0 in the first round of the Scottish Cup, recording the highest score ever in a professional football match. Poor little Bon Accord had only been formed in 1884, and had to play in the Arbroath away kit, having arrived without any formal kit. After the game referee Dave Stormont claimed he had actually felt sorry for Bon Accord and so refereed sympathetically – he wiped off seven further goals for minor misdemeanours that could equally have been given. Eighteen-year-old John Petrie was the star, netting 13 goals. Bizarrely just 18 miles (29km) away in Dundee was another Scottish Cup first round tie, which finished Dundee Harp 35 Aberdeen Rovers 0. The referee had recorded 37 goals, but the club secretary at Dundee Harp had been keeping score and said it was 'only' 35, which the referee accepted and registered. So it was possible that Dundee Harp actually won 37-0 to set a new record, but nobody will ever know.

1895: American Annie Londonderry completes the first-ever round-the-world cycle trip by a woman. The trip took her 15 months and earned her a $10,000 prize. Born in Latvia as Annie Kopchovsky, she changed her name for the ride to gain sponsorship from the Londonderry Spring Water Company. She had never ridden a bicycle until about a week before starting her trek. The money had been put up by two Boston businessmen betting that a woman could not achieve the feat, and she completed her journey in 14 days under the total time allowed for the challenge.

1920: The Games of the VII Olympiad begin in Antwerp, Belgium. This marked a return to the Summer Olympics as the proposed 1916 Berlin Games were cancelled due to the First World War. Because of the war Germany, Austria, Hungary, Bulgaria and the Ottoman Empire were not allowed to compete. Belgium didn't quite host everything – two of the sailing events were in Amsterdam in the Netherlands.

1974: The controversial genius Brian Clough is sacked by Leeds United after just 44 days in charge. An unpopular choice of manager among the squad due to his open criticism of Don Revie, a few days after he was appointed he told the Leeds players they could put all their medals in the bin because (in his opinion) 'none of them were won fairly'. Despite awful performances the club still had to pay off Clough's contract to the tune of £98,000 – a very large amount at the time. Reflecting on his sacking Clough said, 'Resignations are for prime ministers and those caught with their trousers down, not me.'

13 September

1842: Chris Lilley and Tom McCoy compete in a bare-knuckle boxing match in the United States. McCoy was knocked down 81 times during the contest. Then in round 119 he fell again – tragically he was dead. The fight had lasted two hours and 43 minutes.

1893: While primitive derivations of the sport have existed for many years, this date marks the official launch of the sport of badminton as would be recognised in the modern era, formally launched by the newly formed Badminton Association of England.

1949: On the morning of the US women's amateur golf tournament, the Ladies Professional Golf Association (LPGA) forms in New York City.

1970: The running of the first New York City Marathon – 127 competitors entered the race, but only 55 finished, led by local fireman Gary Muhrcke in a time of 2.31.38. It certainly wasn't the great spectator event that it is considered as today, with only about 100 people turning up to watch.

14 September

1891: Billy Heath scores the first-ever penalty in the Football League, scoring for Wolverhampton Wanderers at home to Accrington Stanley. Wolves won the match 5-0.

1957: Birth of Kepler Wessels, who unusually plays both Test cricket and one-day internationals for both South Africa and

Australia. While others have represented more than one country in Tests, Wessels was the first to play one-day internationals for two nations.

1982: Trevor Baxter of England sets a world high jump record, leaping a height of 5ft 5.7in (1.67m) on a skateboard.

2008: The local derby between Socozaki and Nyuki System in the Democratic Republic of the Congo. The eastern part of the Congo houses very superstitious people and, with Nyuki System losing to their neighbours, their goalkeeper headed down the pitch apparently bent on casting a spell on their opponents to influence the outcome of the game. This led to a fight between the teams, and when the police chief attempted to intervene he was pelted with stones from the crowd. Other police officers retaliated by firing tear gas into the crowd, which resulted in a stampede which itself developed into a full-scale riot.

2016: In the FAI World Championship event in Chicago, Swede Henrik Raimer breaks the record for speed skydiving when he reaches a speed of 601.26kmh (373.6mph).

15 September

1873: The earliest known water polo match – a demonstration sport, played during the fourth open air fete of the London Swimming Club, held at the Crystal Palace.

1978: In his 59th professional fight Muhammad Ali beats Leon Spinks by a unanimous decision after 15 rounds. Ali won the WBA, lineal and *The Ring* heavyweight boxing titles in his victory. This would turn out to be his last win in the ring – he only fought twice more, against Larry Holmes and Trevor Berbick, and lost both bouts!

1980: Death of American football offensive tackle Jim Tyrer. He played almost his entire career with the Kansas City Chiefs (called the Dallas Texans until 1963). During those 13 years he was an eight-time All-AFL and seven time AFL All-Star. After playing he declined an offer to work as a scout and went into business, but the businesses failed and he ended up in a lot of debt. Feeling despair he took his gun, killed his wife and then turned it on himself. Just the day before he took his own life he had taken his youngest son, aged ten, to a Chiefs game.

2000: The beginning of the Games of the XXVII Olympiad, the Sydney Olympic Games held in Australia, considered by many people to be the finest Olympic Games of all time. Some 199 nations competed with a record 80 achieving at least one medal. The cost of the Games was estimated at A$6.6 billion. The United States won the Games with 37 gold medals.

2007: O.J. Simpson, best known as the running back for the Buffalo Bills and star of the Pro Bowl for five consecutive years, is arrested following an armed robbery at the Palace Station hotel casino in Las Vegas. He was charged with criminal conspiracy, assault, kidnapping, use of a deadly weapon and robbery. Simpson was found guilty and sentenced to 33 years in prison.

16 September

1869: In the first round of the Open Golf Championship Young Tom Morris hits the earliest recorded hole-in-one. He achieved this distinction at the 166-yard par-3 eighth hole (aka the Station Hole) on the Prestwick course.

1905: The original All Blacks (aka 'The Originals') win their first-ever tour match on British soil when they beat Devon 55-4. This was the first use of the title 'All Blacks'. This was a very long and intense tour in which they played 28 clubs and regional teams from Great Britain as well as Tests against England, Scotland, Wales and Ireland. They then crossed the Channel to play a Test against France before returning home via Canada to play two provincial teams. Overall they played 35 matches, winning 34 of them – setting the standard of All Black performance which still remains to this day. Their only reverse was a 3-0 loss in the Test against Wales at Cardiff Arms Park.

1937: The BBC show the first televised football match. Since this was very experimental and very much a trial run for commentators, camera crew, sound crew, editors, etc., the BBC felt it would be sensible to run a trial on an insignificant fixture – so arranged for a match to be played specifically for this purpose. Therefore the first match ever broadcast was between Arsenal and Arsenal Reserves.

2017: The first season begins of the newly formed Premier 15s, the top league of women's domestic rugby union organised and overseen by the RFU (Rugby Football Union). Most of the teams came from the existing women's Premiership, with a vision to raise standards and increase professionalism. The RFU promised millions to competing clubs to improve facilities and develop professional coaching. To ensure any money invested was not immediately lost there would be no promotion or relegation for the first two seasons.

17 September

1967: The football match between Kayserispor and Sivasspor in the Atatürk Stadium in Kayseri, Turkey develops into a most unpleasant riot, leading to the deaths of 43 people with more than 300 others injured. By half-time Kayserispor were leading 1-0, and their fans began taunting their opponents. This led to ugly scenes with fans of both teams throwing rocks at each other. Some of the hooligans had arrived armed with knives and bats. The ensuing riot spilled out of the stadium and on to the streets and innocent locals were attacked. Vandalism continued for a long time, along with riots in Sivas. The government took the unprecedented step of sealing both cities for a few days to allow things to settle down.

2005: Julio Chavez Sr retires from boxing during a fight against Grover Wiley. He had injured his hand during the bout, and retired in his corner after the fourth round. A disappointing end to an iconic, multi-record-breaking career. At various points in his career Chavez had been world boxing champion at three different weights – super-featherweight, lightweight and light welterweight. Chavez successfully defended his various titles a record 27 times. His 13-year undefeated run is the longest in the history of boxing, with 87 consecutive wins.

2008: Austrian wheelchair athlete Thomas Geierspichler wins the gold medal for the T52-class marathon at the Beijing Paralympics, with a world record time of one hour 40 minutes and seven seconds.

2016: Death of Iranian Paralympic cyclist and erstwhile powerlifter Bahman Golbarnezhad, who is a veteran of the Iran–Iraq War. As a powerlifter he won 12 gold medals in international competition but, wanting a new challenge, he changed to bicycle racing. At the 2016 Paralympics he was the only Iranian in their cycling team. Tragically Golbarnezhad was on a road race when he hit his head on a rock jutting out in a mountainous region. He was treated in situ, and was being transferred to the athletes' hospital, when he suffered a large heart attack and passed away.

18 September

1938: Dora Ratjen sets a new world record for the women's high jump at the European Athletics Championships. But the record would not stand. Dora, who had represented Germany in the 1936 Olympics by order of the Führer, was not Dora Ratjen at all … he was Horst Ratjen who had tightly bound his genitals to avoid detection. Horst later claimed he had been forced to do this by the Nazis who were not confident of their female athletes' ability to take medals.

1960: The beginning of the first official Paralympic Games. The Games were held in Rome, immediately following the Rome Olympics and using the same venues. There had previously been nine similar events called the 'International Stoke Mandeville Games'. Four hundred athletes from 23 nations competed in 57 different events drawn from eight sports. Italy won the inaugural Games with 29 gold medals.

1971: Birth of disgraced American road cyclist Lance Armstrong, who began his competitive sporting career in triathlon as a teenager. He soon became a specialist cyclist, but his early career was cut short when, at 25, he nearly lost his life to testicular cancer. On recovering he hit fame by winning the Tour de France a record seven times. However, in 2012 a United States Anti-Doping Agency investigation found him guilty of using performance-enhancing drugs, and cited him as the leader of 'the most sophisticated, professionalised and successful doping programme that sport has ever seen'. As a result he was stripped of all his records and achievements.

2017: British cyclist Mark Beaumont completes a full circumnavigation of the globe, arriving back in Paris. His time of 78 days, 14 hours and 40 minutes thrashed the previous best time by a full 44 days and ten hours. This was a supported ride with a team providing him with meals, support and a comfortable place to sleep. Beaumont had previously circumnavigated the globe unsupported, a trip that had taken him 194 days.

19 September

1904: American Matilda Howell wins the women's double Columbia round event, the first woman ever to win an Olympic gold. Archery was the only sport women were allowed to enter in the 1904 Olympics, although a few others did appear in demonstration sport, including a display of female boxing – the last time a female boxer was seen at the Olympics until 2012!

1971: New Orleans Saints and Los Angeles Rams play their NFL season opener in Louisiana in a record-breaking 130°F (54°C).

1993: Nigel Mansell, driving a Newman/Haas, wins the penultimate leg of the CART IndyCar World Series on the Nazareth Speedway circuit in Pennsylvania, and is named world champion for the CART series. He was, at this point, still the reigning Formula One world champion. Mansell became the first driver to win the CART series in his debut season, and remains the only driver to hold both the CART and the Formula One world titles simultaneously.

1998: Prairie View A&M Panthers lose 37-7 against the Southern Jaguars in a college American football game. But the match is often remembered for something else a little more surreal – a big brawl at half-time … between the two marching bands of the schools involved! Both bands were immediately suspended for two games.

2000: The heats for the 100m freestyle swimming in the Sydney Olympics. One of the heats featured a swimmer from Equatorial Guinea called Eric 'The Eel' Moussambani Malonga. He was in a heat of just three swimmers, and completed the swim in 1.52.72 – the slowest time ever in Olympic history (for comparison, Dutch swimmer Peter van den Hoogenband later won the gold medal in a time of 48.30 seconds – by which time Eric the Eel would have swum just under 43m assuming constant speed). Bizarrely he actually won his heat because both of his challengers were disqualified for false starts. He also set a personal best – since he had never swum that far before; it was also a national record – since none existed!

20 September

1873: Birth of Hungarian race car driver Ferenc Szisz. Szisz claimed his place in sporting history by winning the race which is recognised as the first-ever official Grand Prix of motor racing – in France, on 26 June 1906.

1973: Bobby Riggs was a fairly mediocre tennis player. He was also ridiculously misogynistic, being very verbal in his criticism of female tennis players ... until Billie Jean King challenged him. The challenge became a national spectacle and was even televised. And when King beat Riggs in straight sets it became a celebration for women everywhere, and an eating of humble pie for Mr Riggs.

1980: The Woodward Stakes in Belmont is certainly one of the oddest horse races in history. Only four horses were registered to race – and three of them dropped out, leaving Bill Shoemaker on Spectacular Bid to run the entire distance on their own to take the victory.

1982: Jalal-ud-Din of Pakistan takes the first one-day international hat-trick against Australia, removing Rod Marsh, Bruce Yardley and Geoff Lawson.

2004: Death of legendary football manager Brian Clough. After a prolific career as a player he became a household name as a manager, most notably of Nottingham Forest who he took to levels of success they had never before reached. He always remained modest and unassuming in his management, once claiming: 'I wouldn't say I was the best manager in the business. But I was in the top one.'

21 September

1901: Birth of Learie Constantine, the West Indian all-round cricketer. Constantine took the West Indies' first-ever Test wicket. On retirement he became Britain's first-ever black peer, influential in the passing of the 1965 Race Relations Act.

1982: The beginning of the NFL players' strike, a strike which lasts for 57 days during which no games take place. The two sides of the dispute hit a stalemate. The deadlock was broken when the authorities agreed to increased wages, and to guarantee retirement packages and long-service bonuses. Having lost 57 days, the season was reduced from 16 games per team to just nine, with the season ending with a 'Super Bowl Tournament' featuring 16 teams (eight from each conference).

1991: One of the most brutal boxing matches on record, certainly under Queensberry Rules. Michael Watson had already fought Chris Eubank once for the world super-middleweight title, which the judges awarded to Eubank. Watson was in control of this rematch until he was hit by a sucker punch in the 11th round and was nearly knocked out. In the final round Eubank sensed his chance and landed a series of hefty punches and Watson could barely move. The referee stopped the fight and Eubank was proclaimed champion again. Watson collapsed in the ring, and remained there for 30 minutes while medics worked on him before getting him into a neurosurgery unit. He spent 40 days in a coma. He was unable to walk, speak or even hear for eight months, and spent more than a year in intensive care and another six in a wheelchair. In court the British Boxing Board of Control was shown to be 'in breach of its duty of care to Mr Watson' who was awarded £400,000 damages. In 2003 Watson completed the London Marathon, raising money for the Brain and Spine Foundation. The run took him six days, sleeping on a support bus. Chris Eubank, now a close personal friend, joined Watson as he crossed the finishing line.

1998: Death of American sprinter Florence Griffith Joyner, aka Flo-Jo. She is considered the fastest woman of all time having taken the world records for both the 100m and the 200m in 1988, records that still stand today. In the 1988 Olympics she won three gold medals, but retired soon afterwards. Flo-Jo died at the age of 38 following an epileptic seizure.

2008: The final game played at the old 1923 Yankee Stadium, the home of the New York Yankees. The ceremonial first pitch was thrown by Julia Ruth Stevens, the daughter of Babe Ruth. The Yankees won this emotional encounter against Baltimore Orioles 7-3. Work was already well underway on the new $2.3 billion stadium adjacent to the old one.

22 September

1908: Possibly the most careless and the most costly error in the history of baseball. 'Merkle's Boner', as the error became known, cost his team the championship and with it a small fortune. Fred Merkle came out to bat for the New York Giants against the Chicago Cubs with the entire game balanced on a knife-edge. This was the final innings of the game; the game was tied 1-1 at that stage, and the Giants were already two out. The mathematics were simple – one more out and the game was drawn, one more run and the Giants win. Moose McCormick was on first base. Merkle, the youngest player in the National League at the time, tapped a single, and McCormick sprinted to third. Al Bridwell came in to bat. He too hit a single, and Merkle and McCormick both set off. McCormick got home comfortably to win the game and the crowd started to invade the pitch. Merkle abandoned his run and headed off to the clubhouse to celebrate. The Cubs' second baseman, Johnny Evers, touched his base with the ball, appealing to the umpire to dismiss Merkle, who had not bothered reaching second. Merkle was out, so McCormick's run wouldn't count – and being the third out meant the game was tied. Incredibly the Giants and the Cubs ended the season tied in first place. The two teams were made to play a rematch for the title – which the Cubs won 4-2.

1927: Almost exactly a year after Gene Tunney has beaten Jack Dempsey to become the heavyweight boxing champion of the world, he successfully defends his title against the same man in Chicago, winning in ten rounds. This particular bout has historically become known as the 'long-count' fight. In the seventh round Tunney hit the canvas, and referee Dave Barry started counting him out, but then stopped because he realised that Dempsey had not returned to his corner. The referee restarted his counting three or four seconds later – and those few extra moments were all the respite Tunney needed to get to his feet. Tunney went on to win the fight, and retired the following year undefeated.

1927: Death of 16-year-old American jockey Sandy Graham at the Polo Park Racetrack in Winnipeg in Canada. Leading the field on board Vesper Lad, the horse stumbled and threw him to the ground. He was kicked and trampled by several following horses, and suffered a broken back and crushed chest. With no ambulance service around he lay on the track until a group of jockeys carried him back to the jockeys' room. His stablemate and friend Tommy Luther tried desperately to get some transport to the nearest hospital but couldn't find anyone to help – fellow jockeys refused since they were contracted to ride and would face severe punishment if they went. Luther tried taking a collection to get a taxi, but couldn't raise enough money. Eventually, at the end of the day's racing, someone did take them to the hospital, but by then it was too late and Graham's injuries were too severe. He died ten days later in the hospital. He had no insurance, and his family were very poor, so he was buried in a pauper's grave in the Brookside Cemetery in Winnipeg.

1989: The International Paralympic Committee is founded in Düsseldorf, Germany, adopting as a mission statement: 'To enable Paralympic athletes to achieve sporting excellence and inspire and excite the world.'

2015: Half-time in the Bundesliga, Bayern Munich are losing 1-0 to Wolfsburg, so the Bayern coach decides to bring on Polish striker Robert Lewandowski. Lewandowski levelled the scores in the 51st minute, and gave Bayern the lead a minute later. Three minutes after this he had his hat-trick. Two minutes later he had his fourth, and just three minutes later a super scissor-kick gave him his and Bayern's fifth. The final score was 5-1 to Bayern, with substitute Lewandowski scoring all five. There was a gap of exactly eight minutes and 59 seconds between his first and fifth goals.

23 September

1771: A match which necessitates rewriting the laws of cricket. Batting for Chertsey against Hambledon, Thomas White came to the crease carrying a bat which was as wide as the wicket, thus making it effectively impossible for him to be bowled. The Hambledon players objected strongly but since it did not contravene regulations White was allowed to continue. In 1774 the laws of cricket were rewritten so that the bat could be no wider than 4.25 inches.

1845: Alexander Joy Cartwright creates and publishes the rules of baseball in a small leaflet entitled 'Rules & Regulations of the Recently Invented Game of Base Ball'. The rule book was immediately adopted by the New York Knickerbocker Base Ball Club, although very rapidly gained a wider ownership.

1926: Ex-marine Gene Tunney beats Jack Dempsey to claim the crown as the heavyweight boxing champion of the world.

1990: The second day (of two) sees Estonian Indrek Kaseorg crowned the world champion in the icosathlon (aka double decathlon) – 20 events of track and field over two days. Due to the intensity of the competition, and wide range of activities expected from competitors, there is an official rule that there must be a full one-hour gap (called a pause) inserted on each day of the competition. The events are the 100m, 110m hurdles, 200m, 200m hurdles, 400m, 400m hurdles, 800m, 1,000m, 1,500m, 3,000m, 3,000m steeplechase, 5,000m, 10,000m, long jump, high jump, triple jump, shot put, discus, javelin and pole vault.

24 September

1844: The first official sporting international is a cricket match between the United States and Canada in Manhattan, billed as 'The United States of America versus the British Empire's Canadian Province'.

1931: New York City's three Major League Baseball teams – the Yankees, the Giants and the Brooklyn Robins (the future Dodgers) – play a round-robin play-off doubleheader against each other, in front of a crowd of 44,119. There was no trophy and no monetary award up for grabs. This was purely for charity, seeking to raise money for the unemployed and the homeless of New York. They raised $48,135 – a vast sum of money for the time.

1984: Vicky Nelson Dunbar and Jean Hepner play an epic match at the Ginny Tournament at the Raintree Swim and Racquet Club in Richmond, Virginia. Nelson Dunbar won 6-4 7-6 in a match which lasted six hours and 22 minutes. The match was decided by a tie-break which itself lasted one hour and 47 minutes, ending 13-11. One single point of the tie-break was a rally of a world record 643 shots, which took 29 minutes.

1989: The third and final day of the 28th Ryder Cup at The Belfry in Warwickshire. Europe and the United States finished level, at 14-14, meaning that Europe retained the cup it had won two years ago. It featured one of the most one-sided singles games in the history of the tournament – the game between Europe's Howard Clark and Tom Kite of the US. The match actually finished on the 11th green with Kite already eight holes up and hence guaranteed victory (written in golf as 8 and 7 – meaning eight holes up with only seven left to play).

2017: Malaysian Lee Chong Wei smashes the shuttlecock at a world record 417kmh (259mph) in the Japan Open badminton final against Viktor Axelsen from Denmark.

2017: Possibly the most bloody battle in the history of world sport. On one side were players of the NFL. Their opponent is president Donald Trump. Over the last few months a handful of black NFL players have knelt before a game during the playing of the national anthem, a silent protest against perceived institutionalised racism and police brutality. Trump stated publicly that these players should be sacked, kicked out of the game for good. This date was chosen to send a message back to the president, where literally hundreds of NFL players across the country of all colours and nationalities chose to show contempt for his comments, and defiance of his position. In some teams the majority of players knelt down. Others stood and linked arms. A few teams even went back to the dressing room for the national anthem. Some team owners and officials, even Trump's close friend Robert Kraft who owns New England Patriots, stood/knelt/disappeared with their teams as a sign of solidarity. Kraft reflected, 'There is no greater unifier in this country than sports, and unfortunately nothing more divisive than politics.'

25 September

1928: Death of Australian cricketer Karl Schneider. Tragically he was just 23 when leukaemia claimed his life. In 1924 he was selected for the Australian second XI tour of New Zealand, but collapsed near the end of the tour while horse riding with what turned out to be the beginning of his illness.

1943: England football legend Stan Mortenson makes his international football debut ... for Wales! Wales were playing against England when Ivor Powell had to come off with an injury, and the Welsh side didn't have a substitute. So Mortenson came on, three years before he made his full debut for the England team.

2011: ODD Grenland are playing Tromsø Idrettslag in the top flight of the Norwegian football league, and are leading 2-1 with just minutes to go. Tromsø desperately wanted at least a draw to keep their title hopes alive. Winning a corner, they sent everyone up, including the goalkeeper. ODD cleared the ball, and a retreating Tromsø defender tried to put the ball back – but only managed to find the head of ODD's Jone Samuelsen who headed it back towards the empty goal. 3-1 to ODD, and Samuelsen enters the record books with the longest ever headed goal at 58.1m (nearly 200 feet).

2016: Death of American golfer Arnold Palmer, the first golfing superstar of the television age. He won his first major (The Masters) in 1958 and continued playing competitively until 2004.

26 September

1909: Birth of American racing car driver Bill France, the man who founded NASCAR (National Association of Stock Car Auto Racing). After years of drivers being abused and used by promoters and event organisers, France decided they needed an organisation under which to stand together, and so NASCAR was born. The immediate changes were driver uniforms, safety, insurance and guaranteed purses.

1934: Murt O'Donoghue compiles snooker's first known maximum break (147).

1959: Death of jockey Manny Mercer, brother of jockey Joe Mercer, and father-in-law of Pat Eddery. At the start of the Red Deer Stakes at Ascot, his horse Priddy Fair threw him from the saddle, and kicked him in the head as he fell. The kick proved fatal.

1983: Australia II, representing the Royal Perth Yacht Club, beat Liberty to become the first non-American winner of the America's Cup. Their victory brought to an end the longest winning streak in sports history as America had successfully defended the title continuously for 132 years.

2004: At the Toronto Marathon, Ed Whitlock becomes the first over-70 to run the distance in under three hours, when he sets a time of 2.54.48.

2006: In the Brazilian league Atlético Sorocaba are leading 1-0 against Santacruzense in the dying minutes when Santacruzense striker Samuel gets into a good position to equalise but sees his shot whistle past the far post. The referee Silvia Regina de Oliveira turned her back to go back towards the halfway line while a cheeky ball boy collected the ball near the goal – and quickly dropped it on to the pitch and tapped it into the net just as de Oliveira turned around again. Despite having clearly watched the ball sailing wide, when she saw the ball in the net she assumed she had been confused … and awarded the goal! The game finished 1-1, and de Oliveira and her linesman were suspended.

27 September

1884: Anfield host their first football match when Everton entertain Earlestown – yes, Anfield was originally Everton's home ground. Just eight years later Everton would move to Stanley Park in an area now known as Goodison Park. Liverpool FC were not formed until 1892, and immediately claimed the newly vacated Anfield as their home. Anfield was named after the region of Annefield in County Wexford, Ireland.

1956: Death of the American sporting polymath Babe Didrikson Zaharias. Her first job after school was in an insurance company – and she was given the job so that she could lead the company's basketball team. The next year she represented the company at the AAU athletics championships where she took part in eight of the ten events, winning six of them. That performance earned her a place on the US team for the 1932 Olympics where she won two gold medals and one silver. Didrikson came to the sport of golf late, but made up for lost time, winning both the US and the UK women's amateur championships. After turning professional she dominated the women's golf scene, co-founding the Ladies Professional Golf Association. Given a prowess in all things sporty, the St Louis Cardinals invited her to pitch the first innings of an MLB exhibition game against the Boston Red Socks. Her later years were beset by health problems. Just three years before she died she won her tenth and final major, the US Women's Open Championship, wearing a colostomy bag! Almost unbelievably given how much she had fitted in, she was still only 45 when she died.

1998: The Baltimore Orioles play their final MLB game of the season against the Boston Red Sox. Cal Ripken Jr voluntarily dropped out of the Baltimore starting line-up. The gesture

Babe Didrikson Zaharias

26 June 1911–27 September 1956

Double Olympic gold medallist, star of basketball and baseball,
and professional golfer who won ten LPGA titles.

brought to an end a quite remarkable run of 2,632 consecutive games stretching back over 17 seasons.

2016: Following allegations of inappropriate behaviour Sam Allardyce leaves the role as manager of the England football team by 'mutual consent'. He had only been in charge for one game (which England won), appointed 67 days previously.

28 September

1884: Death of English left-arm fast bowler Fred Morley. In a 13-year career for Nottinghamshire and England he took 1,274 wickets at an average of just 13.73. He died a typical Victorian death ('congestion and dropsy') at the age of just 33. He was buried with a cricket ball in his left hand.

1919: Polo Ground V hosts the fastest baseball game in MLB history. The New York Giants beat the Philadelphia Phillies 6-1 with the entire game lasting just 51 minutes.

1946: The record for the most international debuts in a fixture comes from England, under extreme circumstances. The Second World War put an end to a great many careers for various reasons, and so when international football restarted after the war many sides found themselves having to effectively start from scratch. England's first competitive match after the war was away to Ireland in the British Championship, and they gave an international debut to nine players. The game was also the first international for manager Walter Winterbottom, appointed despite having no experience at all in football management.

1975: Riding at Bonneville in the United States, Don Vesco is the first racer recorded at driving his motorbike in excess of 300mph, when his 1,480cc Yamaha Silver Bird streamliner is clocked at 302.9mph (487.5kmh).

1986: The Mexico City Marathon sets a new competitor record as 23,000 runners start the race.

29 September

1892: The college American football game between Wyoming Seminary High School and Mansfield University of Pennsylvania is the first game to be played at night under lights. Unfortunately the game was abandoned at half-time with the score at 0-0 after the lights failed.

1937: Death of American jump specialist Ray Ewry. With ten gold medals he was one of the most successful Olympians of all time, with success in the standing long jump, the standing high jump and the standing triple jump over four Olympics.

1962: Peter Lorimer makes his debut for Leeds United against Southampton at the age of just 15. Lorimer earned a reputation for having the hardest shot in football – remembering that he played in the era of the heavy leather ball, one penalty he took was officially recorded at 107mph.

1977: Muhammad Ali beats Earnie Shavers to retain the world heavyweight boxing title. Now 35 years old, the self-styled 'greatest' was a shadow of his former self. Shavers took the champion the full 15 rounds, but lost by a unanimous decision from the judges – and that is where the real history was made. One of the judges was Eva Shain, the first woman ever to referee a world heavyweight bout. Allegedly Ali asked Shain if she minded getting blood on her clothes, to which she coolly replied 'Well, it's not my blood.'

2004: Death of French motorcycle rally driver Richard Sainct. He was killed on the fourth stage of the Pharaohs Rally. Early in the race he took a tumble, but carried on, insisting he was fine. After about 270km of the stage Sainct fell again, and died almost immediately. It is believed he had probably had some internal injury from the first fall, and the excursion probably worsened this.

30 September

1659: The last Dutch director general of the colony of New Netherlands, Peter Stuyvesant, forbids the playing of tennis during religious services – the first mention of tennis in the States. Five years later New Netherlands was ceded to the English and renamed New York.

1915: Death of German weightlifter Heinrich Schneidereit, winner of three medals in the 1906 Intercalated Games – a gold medal in the tug of war, and bronze medals in both the one-handed lift and the two-handed lift. He was killed in action during the First World War.

1916: Boston Braves beat New York Giants 8-3 in an MLB fixture. In the preceding 23 days the Giants had crammed in a staggering 26 matches … and won them all.

1980: The final of the seventh AFC Asian Cup, overseen by the Asian Football Confederation. The tournament was sadly deeply affected by politics when Iraq (who were not in the competition) invaded Iran (who were), and the Iranian team were constantly met with news of hate and death and destruction. Iranian striker Hassan Roshan learned his brother had been killed at home while he was at the tournament.

1980: Birth of Swiss tennis star Martina Hingis. (Although Hingis is world renowned as a top Swiss player, she was actually born in Czechoslovakia.) She spent 209 weeks at number one in the rankings, and 90 weeks in the doubles rankings, holding the two titles simultaneously for 29 weeks.

OCTOBER

1 October

1951: The first time floodlights are used in a competitive football match when Southampton reserves entertain Tottenham Hotspur reserves at the Dell in the Football Combination.

1977: Losing to Ilie Năstase in Aix en Provence is Guillermo Vilas's first defeat after a run of 46 straight victories – a record-winning streak for the Open Era of tennis. All 46 matches were played on clay.

2006: Swiss football club FC Sion enjoy a decent start to the season. They were sitting proudly on top of the Swiss Division One, and had won through the first round of the Swiss Cup. In the second round they were drawn away to FC La Chaux-de-Fonds. At half-time Sion were losing 1-0, and coach Néstor Clausen asked the club president Christian Constantin to join him in the dressing room while he spoke to the players. With players and president assembled Clausen announced his resignation with immediate effect and walked out. The reason for this bizarre step was never clarified. Sion rallied in the second half without a manager and won the game 3-1.

2006: The Chinese Grand Prix is run at the Shanghai International Circuit, and is won by Michael Schumacher in his Ferrari, marking his 91st and last Grand Prix victory – a total that remains a record.

2 October

1909: The first rugby game is played at Twickenham. The home of English rugby is still occasionally affectionately referred to as the 'Cabbage Patch' … because just two years before the inaugural match, that's what the ground was! In 1907 rugby committee members William Williams and William Cail purchased the ten-acre market garden for £5,500, 12 shillings and sixpence. The first match saw Harlequins hosting Richmond. The ground was not used for sport throughout the First World War – so it was used for grazing livestock from the area.

1919: Death of South African cricketer Ernest Halliwell, the man who introduces padded gloves for wicketkeepers. Such things did not exist in his day – so Halliwell used to come out to keep wicket with raw steak stuffed down his gloves to protect his hands.

1976: Blackburn Rovers footballer Dave Wagstaff is sent off against Leyton Orient – the first person in England to be given a red card. (Football fans will be interested to know that the second person to be red-carded in England later that same afternoon was the iconic legend George Best playing for Fulham against Southampton.)

1988: The conclusion of the Games of the XXIV Olympiad, the Seoul Olympics in South Korea. After three consecutive Olympic tournaments with major boycotts these Games featured a then record 159 nations. The medals table was led by the Soviet Union with 55 gold medals, followed by East Germany with 37. It was, however, a last Games for both countries – the Soviet Union and East Germany did not exist in 1992.

3 October

1888: The New Zealand Natives play their first rugby game in Great Britain. This was not an official New Zealand national side; the Natives were organised privately with many coming from Māori roots. They were, however, the first New Zealand representative team ever to wear the now iconic silver fern, to wear an all black kit or to perform a haka. There was an incredible depth of ignorance back in the day – one Scottish reporter wrote that 'one remembers that they were a savage tribe no further back than a generation'. This opening game was against Surrey, with the Natives winning 4-1.

1936: Death of John Heisman, player and coach of American football, baseball and basketball. He was the man responsible for legalising the forward pass. The Heisman Trophy, awarded every year to the season's most outstanding college football player, is named after him.

2011: Australian Cameron Pilley hits a squash ball at an incredible 281.6kmh (175mph) – the fastest a squash ball has ever been hit in open game play.

2014: Tim Brys, Mathieu Foucaud, Pierre de Loof, Hannes Obreno, Thijs Obreno, Thibaut Schollaert, Giel Vanschoenbeek and Arjan van Belle, all from Belgium, complete a marathon 24-hour row on the Watersportbaan in Ghent, Belgium. The eight men rowed 342km (212.5 miles) in the 24 hours.

4 October

1895: The first-ever US Open golf tournament is played at the Newport Country Club in Rhode Island. Newport was only a nine-hole course, and competitors played four rounds on the one day. The tournament was won by 21-year-old Englishman Horace Rawlins, who had come to America just a few months earlier to work at the Newport club. He won $150 cash and a gold medal worth $50.

1933: Gordon Richards wins all six races on the card at Chepstow. Winning additional races on both the day before and the day after gave him a winning streak of 12 consecutive races – a record that still stands to this day.

1970: After Jacky Ickx's failure to win the American Grand Prix, it is officially confirmed that Jochen Rindt will be the 1970 Formula One world champion. Tragically Rindt couldn't celebrate his first world title, having died at the Italian Grand Prix a month earlier.

1981: An international gymnastics competition takes place in Greece. The tournament was significant when local girl Pasakevi

Kouna became the youngest international gymnast at the age of nine.

2012: Formula One legend Michael Schumacher announces his retirement, for the second and final time. After the glory years at Ferrari there were questions as to whether his comeback was sensible. He himself admitted: 'There were times in the past few months in which I didn't want to deal with Formula One or prepare for the next Grand Prix.'

5 October

1887: Ellen Hansell beats Laura Knight 6-1 6-0 in the inaugural US women's national singles championship. The tournament was held on outdoor grass courts set up at the Philadelphia Cricket Club.

1895: The first individual time trial for racing cyclists is held on a 50-mile course to the north of London. The National Cyclists' Union (NCU) had purchased the land and built the course specifically for this purpose. Five years earlier the Union had banned cycle racing on UK public roads, because they feared that if races continued then the government might ban all cycles from roads, which would be unfair to standard users. Many races still continued on roads, with efforts taken to prevent detection. Information sent to competitors was in envelopes headed 'private and confidential' (a habit which continued into the 1960s!), competitors raced alone at staggered intervals and no competitors wore numbers or other distinguishing features.

1997: The final round of races in the season's motorcycle Grand Prix world championship takes place in Victoria, Australia. Italy's Valentino Rossi could only finish sixth, almost 20 seconds behind Japan's Noboru Ueda, but it was enough to confirm his first-ever world title.

2007: Futatsuryū Jun'ichi, the stablemaster of the Tokitsukaze group, is dismissed by the Sumo Association – the first time they have ever dismissed a serving stablemaster. Following the death of junior wrestler Tokitaizan four months earlier, Jun'ichi tried to push for a quick cremation, so Tokitaizan's family demanded an autopsy which revealed a lot of injuries and abuse. Jun'ichi admitted (eventually) to hitting him on the head with a beer bottle, and to pushing him through intense sessions lasting 30 minutes (intense sessions should only last five minutes). He also confessed to allowing other wrestlers to hit Tokitaizan with a metal baseball bat. A spokesman for the Sumo Association said: 'His actions were unbecoming as a stablemaster, he's outraged the public and he's defiled the name of the Sumo Association.'

6 October

1824: Birth of the 'Father of Baseball' Henry Chadwick in Exeter, Devon. He earned his unofficial moniker by developing the first rule book, creating box scores – creating the abbreviation K for a strikeout, and developing the statistics of batting average and earned run average.

1882: The very first World Series game, albeit unofficial, sees the Cincinnati Red Stockings of the American Association beat the Chicago White Stockings of the National League 4-0. The 'series' in this case was just two games, and Chicago won the other game, so honours were even. There were initially plans for a longer series but Cincinnati dropped out following threats from the American Association that they would be expelled if they continued with this 'unofficial' competition.

1974: Death of Austrian motor racing driver Helmuth Koinigg in only his second Grand Prix start. Following suspension failure his car ploughed into the Armco barrier, which should have been a relatively minor accident. Tragically though the barrier failed and the lower half gave way, allowing him to continue through, but the top half stayed put which literally sliced his head off.

1993: Michael Jordan, reputed to be the finest player of his generation, announces he is quitting basketball. Still only 30 he just wanted a new challenge. He had become disillusioned with basketball, and felt rather lost following the murder of his father three months earlier, so signed with the Chicago White Sox to play minor league baseball. His baseball record was disappointing, so 18 months later he was back on the hardwood and re-signed for the Chicago Bulls.

2007: Double world champion Peter Gilchrist of Singapore takes the world record for the highest break ever in billiards – 1,346 during the New Zealand Open.

7 October

1916: Death of Dick Roose, goalkeeper for several football clubs as well as the Welsh national team. Roose was directly responsible for one of the rule changes when the rule book was rewritten in 1912. Renowned for his powerful kick, he took full advantage of the rule at the time allowing goalkeepers to handle the ball anywhere in their own half. The amount of successful attacks he launched led to the rule of goalkeepers only handling in their box. He joined the war effort at the outbreak of the 1914 conflict, serving in France and Gallipoli. His goalkeeping skills came in handy as he became an expert grenade thrower. He was killed in action at the age of 39 towards the end of the Battle of the Somme. His body was never recovered.

1956: Hungarian striker Sándor Kocsis scores his 75th and final goal for Hungary, in a 2-1 friendly victory over France in Paris. His 75 international goals were achieved in just 68 matches.

1991: The ninth race at Belmont, New York, creates only the second ever triple dead heat in thoroughbred racing history. Café Lex, Space Appeal and Scorecard Harry were all officially listed as tied first.

2000: England play their final football match at the old Wembley Stadium before it is to be replaced with the new stadium. England lost 1-0 to Germany in a World Cup qualifying match with

Liverpool's Dietmar Hamann scoring the last international goal at the stadium. So farewell Wembley Stadium, and farewell England manager Kevin Keegan who resigned immediately after the game.

8 October

1818: Padded boxing gloves are used in a fight for the first time. The padded glove was invented by English boxer Jack Broughton 75 years earlier, but had only been used in practice and sparring. Two unnamed English boxers used gloves in a fight in Aix-la-Chapelle in France.

1932: Birth of Welsh snooker legend Ray Reardon, winner of the World Championships six times and one of the most popular players of all time. Reardon decided at a very early age that he wanted to become a snooker player. He was offered a place at grammar school at the age of 14 but turned it down, taking a job down the mines so he could play in his spare time. Having been buried alive for a few hours he quit mining and became a policeman.

1953: An early case of positive discrimination. Jackie Robinson's 'Negro-White All-Stars' baseball team were touring in an attempt to combat racism, but were banned from competing in Birmingham, Alabama … until Robinson agreed to drop white players from his team.

2000: The fastest red card in footballing history. Cross Park Farm Celtic were playing Taunton East Reach Wanderers. Striker Lee Todd was stood in the centre circle waiting for the kick-off with his back to the referee, so was taken by surprise when the referee gave a shrill blast of his whistle – so shrill Todd exclaimed 'F**k me, that was loud.' He was immediately sent off for using foul and abusive language, with his red card officially timed at two seconds. Todd was fined £27 and banned for 35 days. Cross Park, despite having to play the entire game with ten men, still won 11-2.

2011: Irish darts player Brendan Dolan achieves the first nine-dart finish seen on television during his semi-final of the PDC World Darts Championship in Dublin. To make the achievement even more special the tournament also featured a double start rule. Dolan started with double top followed by five treble 20s, leaving him needing 161. He finished with treble 20, treble 17 and bullseye.

9 October

1976: Javed Miandad makes his Pakistan Test debut in the first Test against New Zealand at Lahore. Pakistan were put in to bat, and Miandad managed to score 163 on his first day of Test cricket. He was eventually out off the bowling of Peter Petherick. Petherick then removed Wasim Raja and Intikhab Alam with his next two deliveries to record a hat-trick – on his own Test debut.

1995: Death of Lord Home of the Hirsel, better known as Alec Douglas-Home, the Conservative Prime Minister for a year in the 1960s. Before getting into politics Douglas-Home played cricket for Oxford University, Middlesex and the MCC, making him the only British Prime Minister to have played first-class cricket. He also represented Eton at Fives.

1996: In a World Cup qualifying match Scotland are due for an evening kick-off away to Estonia. However, they were concerned about the floodlights in Tallinn and shared their concerns with FIFA, who agreed and moved the fixture from 6.45pm to 3.00pm. However, they didn't make the decision until the morning of the match! Estonia protested that they were not given enough warning, so didn't show up. The match was awarded to Scotland by a default 3-0 scoreline – but only after they had come out on time in full kit, lined up, stood through the two national anthems, and kicked off! Sadly for Scotland FIFA then had a change of heart and ordered a rematch in a neutral stadium. The two teams drew 0-0 in Monaco a couple of months later.

2006: Death of British snooker player Paul Hunter, winner of the British Open, and the Masters three times. Tragically he suffered from neuroendocrine tumours, which claimed his life five days before his 28th birthday.

2013: The second round Hampshire Senior Cup game between Brockenhurst and Andover Town is level after extra time and so goes to a penalty shoot-out. Brockenhurst won the shoot-out 15-14. The 30th penalty taken was the first one to be missed after 29 successful spot kicks.

10 October

1964: In a poignant gesture Yoshinori Sakai lights the Olympic flame to mark the start of the Japan Olympics. Sakai had been born in Hiroshima on 6 August 1945, the day that the atomic bomb had been dropped on the city.

1965: Death of Swiss Grand Prix motorcyclist Florian Camathias. He was racing as the driver in a motorbike and sidecar race at Brands Hatch when he crashed for no apparent reason. His sidecar partner Franz Ducret was injured but recovered in hospital, but Camathias died at the scene. An inquest ruled that the cause was a simple welding fault that caused the front fork to fracture, recording a verdict of death by misadventure.

2004: The Japanese Grand Prix is the 17th and penultimate race in the Formula One season, and is won by Michael Schumacher in the Ferrari. This was Schumacher's 13th race win of the season despite only 17 races being completed. The final race in Brazil was won by Juan Pablo Montoya in the Williams-BMW with Schumacher struggling back in seventh place, but his record of 13 race wins out of 18 remains the most dominant season for any driver in Formula One.

2007: Atlanta Falcons' Michael Vick is instructed by an arbitrator to reimburse the Falcons to the tune of $19.97m. After six successful years with the Falcons, fans of the sport were horrified when the story broke that Vick was organising, running and financing a dog-fighting ring. The arbitrator concluded that Vick was fully aware that his activities were illegal at the time he had signed his new contract three years earlier, and hence he had brought both the club and the sport into disrepute.

11 October

1937: Birth of England and Manchester United legend Bobby Charlton. With Manchester United he was one of the few who survived the Munich air crash, his life saved when goalkeeper Harry Gregg pulled him clear of the wreckage. He was United's captain in 1968 when they became the first English team to win the European Cup. During a long and distinguished career he set records for Manchester United appearances, Manchester United goals and international goals for England.

1953: Although substitutions are not universally accepted until 1958 some football associations experiment and trial substitutions earlier. The first recorded substitution in an international match was German Horst Eckel being replaced by Richard Gottinger in a World Cup qualifying group match against Saarland. (Saarland was a member of the Council of Europe, but became a district of Germany just two years later.)

1991: During the third round of the Las Vegas Invitational at the Sunrise Golf Course, Chip Beck achieves a Professional Golf Association record score with a 13-under-par 59.

2006: Many baseball teams are reluctant to face Detroit Tigers with their pitcher Joel Zumaya and his reputation for incredibly fast pitches. So they would be delighted when he found himself on the injured list with a severe inflammation in his pitching wrist. What was the problem? Too many fireballs? Not according to his doctor. His injury was caused by too much Guitar Hero on his Playstation.

2011: Death of masked professional wrestler Clemente Nájera, known professionally as Doctor X or latterly Doctor X-Treme. He was shot in the head and died instantly while trying to break up a fight at a party.

12 October

1853: John Morrissey and Yankee Sullivan are slugging it out in a championship boxing match. The match was awarded to Morrissey in the 36th round when Sullivan left the ring to start a fight with some of Morrissey's supporters in the crowd.

1925: Running at Port Chester in the United States, American Albert Michelsen became the first person ever to complete the marathon in less than two and a half hours, with a time of 2.29.01.8.

1972: A plane carrying the Stella Maris College rugby team from Uruguay to Chile crashes in awful weather high in the Andes. The 50 people on board included the whole squad and coaching staff. Seventeen people were killed in the crash, and five more died in the next couple of days. A couple of weeks later there was an avalanche which killed another eight of the survivors. Still freezing and out of food the remaining people (now just 20) decided the only thing they could do to survive was to start eating some of their fallen comrades. A couple of months after the crash nothing had changed and there was no sign of hope, so three of the rugby players decided to head off and try to get help. After hiking for 12 days they finally found help just two days before Christmas, and a helicopter was scrambled. After everything they had been through 16 of the original party survived the ordeal.

2005: France are entertaining Cyprus in a World Cup qualifier, and are leading 4-0 as they enter injury time and looking very comfortable. They brought on substitute Franck Jurietti for his debut. The referee blew the final whistle just five seconds later. Jurietti never played for France again, becoming the footballer with the shortest ever international career.

13 October

1947: The first National Hockey League All-Star Game sees the NHL All-Stars beat the Toronto Maple Leafs 4-3 in Toronto.

1974: The first-ever running of the Berlin Marathon is won by local Günter Hallas in a time of 2.44.53. The women's race was also won by a local, Jutta von Haase in 3.22.01. Over the years Berlin have really maximised the opportunity, turning this into a massive weekend event. On the Saturday thousands complete the course on inline skates. There are also marathons over the same weekend for wheelchairs, for hand-bikers and power walkers. There is also a children's marathon, exactly ten per cent of the marathon length.

1984: John Lowe scores the first televised nine-dart finish at the MFI World Matchplay, and receives prize money of £102,000. There are a few ways of doing 501 in nine darts – Lowe started with two 180 maximums, leaving 141 needed from the last three darts. Lowe scored triple 17, triple 18, double 18. He went on to win the overall competition.

2017: In a competition in Shropshire Mike O'Neill breaks an angling world record by landing a 64lb (29kg) common carp at The Avenue, RH Fisheries.

14 October

1882: Birth of Gloucestershire bowler Charlie Parker, one of the most prolific bowlers in history. He almost achieved a truly unique achievement in his own benefit match against Yorkshire in 1922 when he clean bowled five batsmen in five consecutive deliveries – but the second was called a no-ball.

1909: Birth of German racing driver Bernd Rosemeyer, winner of the European driving championship in 1936. For Rosemeyer driving was only ever a hobby – his official role was serving as a Hautsturmführer (equivalent of captain) in the SS (Schutzstaffel, the Nazi paramilitary organisation under Adolf Hitler). He died at the age of just 28 attempting to break the land speed record when his car catapulted and he was thrown out, dying at the roadside.

1968: Running for the United States at the Mexico Olympics, Jim Hines completes the 100m sprint in a time of 9.95 seconds – the first person ever to complete the distance in less than ten seconds.

1968: The Mexico Olympics are the first Games to use doping tests, and Hans-Gunnar Liljenwall is disqualified on day two of the modern pentathlon competition. He had been randomly selected for a drug test. His sample was shown to have an excess of alcohol. He did confess to drinking 'several beers' just before the fencing started.

1983: Birth of Chinese professional badminton player Lin Dan, widely believed to be the greatest badminton player of all time. By the age of 28 he had completed the 'Super Grand Slam' – winning all of the nine major badminton titles. To date he remains the only person ever to achieve this.

2007: Bernhard Langer wins his first event on the US Seniors Tour (rebranded as the PGA Champions Tour at the start of the 2016 season). The 50-year-old won the Administaff Small Business Classic in Texas with a truly remarkable score of 25 under par.

15 October

1520: King Henry VIII orders his ministers to install bowling lanes at Whitehall for his use and the use of others.

1862: The first-ever confirmed game of Canadian football is played at the Montreal Cricket Ground. Bizarrely neither team are Canadian, but two British military teams serving in Canada. The First Battalion Grenadier Guards beat the Second Battalion Scots Fusilier Guards by three goals and two rouges to nil.

1887: The largest ever scoreline in an FA Cup tie when Preston North End beat Hyde 26-0 in the first round of the competition. (Some people claim this is the origin of the phrase 'Getting a good hyding', but that is unconfirmed.)

1910: Death of Polish-American boxer Stanley Ketchel (aka The Michigan Assassin), one of the finest world middleweight champions of all time. One morning he had taken his ranch hand to task for beating one of his horses. The following morning while he was having breakfast the ranch hand came in to the kitchen with a gun and shot him through the chest. Ketchel was rushed into hospital but died that evening. His final words were, 'I'm so tired. Take me home to mother.'

1927: The final of the inaugural Greyhound Derby at the White City Stadium, organised by the Greyhound Racing Association. The race was won by local entrant Entry Badge from trap five, completing the 500 yards in 29.01 seconds (~35mph). Entry Badge won £1,000 (a vast sum of money for the time) and a gold cup.

1997: Briton Andy Green becomes the first person ever to set a new land speed record at supersonic pace. Driving an adapted Rolls-Royce Spey on the Black Rock Desert in Nevada in the US, he was officially clocked at 763.035mph (1,227.986kmh).

16 October

1962: Birth of basketball player Manute Bol, who played for several clubs in the NBA. Bol was born in the Sudan, the son of a Dinka tribe elder, and was given the name Manute which means 'special blessing'. At 2.31m (7ft 7in) he was the tallest person ever to play in the NBA.

1968: American sprinters Tommie Smith and John Carlos come first and third in the men's 200m race at the Olympic Games in Mexico City. Both runners were members of the Olympic Project for Human Rights, and showed solidarity with the Black Freedom

Movement. To promote the cause both came up to the rostrum wearing black socks without shoes, lowered their heads during the rendition of the 'Star-Spangled Banner', and raised one black-gloved fist throughout the anthem. While most sound-thinking people would be sympathetic to their ideals it was strongly felt that an Olympic medal ceremony was not the correct time or place to take a stand. Both were banned from the Olympic village and suspended from the Games.

2004: For many snooker players the 147 break marks the pinnacle of perfection in the sport. Scotsman Jamie Burnett went one better in the qualifiers for the UK Championships when he compiled a break of 148 against Leo Fernandez. Fernandez played a foul shot leaving Burnett snookered on all 15 reds and thus earning a free ball. He took a brown as the extra red, and then potted the brown followed by all 15 reds with 11 blacks and four pinks followed by all the colours. Burnett won the tie 9-8.

2011: British Sikh Fauja Singh completes the Toronto Waterfront Marathon in a time of eight hours, 11 minutes and six seconds, the record marathon time for someone aged 100 or more. He ran his first marathon aged 93.

2016: Death of Irish rugby union Test player Anthony Foley. As head coach of Munster he had taken his team to Paris to face Racing 92 in the European Rugby Champions Cup. A couple of days before the match he died in the hotel of an acute pulmonary oedema. He was just 42 years old.

17 October

1860: The first-ever Open Championship is held at the Prestwick Golf Club in Ayrshire, Scotland. Just eight golfers took part in a one-day competition. Scotsman Allan Robertson had been widely acknowledged as the world's greatest golfer, but he had passed away in 1859. This tournament was to find his replacement as the unofficial world number one. Willie Park Sr from Musselburgh won by two shots from Tom Morris Sr of Prestwick. The prize, apart from the prestige, was a belt.

1879: Foundation of Sunderland FC, originally called Sunderland and District Teachers AFC. They were elected to the Football League in 1890, the first new club to join the league since its inception.

1919: Leeds City become the first club (and still the only one) to be expelled from the Football League mid-season. They were kicked out for financial irregularities, and were replaced by Port Vale (who were given all of Leeds City's results up to that point). On this date an auction was held at the Metropole Hotel in Leeds city centre, where all the players as well as other assets were auctioned off to raise funds for their debts. The 16 team members up for auction were sold for £9,250 to nine different clubs with Billy McLeod going to Notts County for £1,250. On 31 May 1920 Leeds United were elected to the Football League.

1981: The final race of the 35th season of Formula One racing. Nelson Piquet was crowned champion – technically the first FIA Formula One world champion, as the championships (drivers' and constructors') replaced the World Championship of Drivers and the International Cup for Constructors.

1989: The World Series of 1989 is named the 'Bay Area World Series' as the San Fransisco Giants face Oakland Athletics. Just a few minutes before game three of the series an earthquake hit San Fransisco of magnitude 6.9, sufficient to cause significant damage to the stadium in which the game was due to be played. The game was immediately cancelled, and was not played for ten days, leading to a late finish to the series for the first time in its history. Experts claim that the World Series actually saved lives because a lot of people left work early to watch the game and were not in high-rise offices when the disaster struck.

18 October

1793: Death of the massively successful thoroughbred racehorse Highflyer. Highflyer raced in just 14 races, winning every one, including the 1,400 Guineas Stakes and the Great Subscription Purse. After racing he was the leading sire for 15 years, producing 469 winners.

1862: Death of American baseball player James Creighton, considered by many to be the first true superstar of the sport, playing for the Excelsior of Brooklyn. As a pitcher Creighton revolutionised the entire sport, moving it from a batting, catching and fielding spectacle into a battle royale between batter and pitcher. Bowling at the time was underarm and tended to be lobbed, but Creighton developed a method for delivering the ball flat and at pace. Sadly Creighton was killed by the sport he loved. One day he hit a home run with such force that he ruptured an abdominal hernia and split his bladder. He died four days later from internal bleeding.

1930: Joseph Sylvester becomes the first jockey to win seven races in a single day (off an eight-race card).

1956: Birth of Czechoslovakian-born American tennis player and coach Martina Navratilova. She was one of only three women (with Doris Hart and Margaret Court) to achieve the so-called Career Grand Slam boxset – winning all four major tournaments in singles, women's doubles and mixed doubles. In 1983 her record was 86 wins and one defeat – to the unseeded Kathy Horvath in the fourth round of the French Open, an incredible 98.9 per cent win ratio.

1992: Zimbabwe play their first official Test match, against India in Harare. The country had had a national side for nine years, but it had taken a long time to gain official full Test status. Ten of the team were therefore making their Test cricket debuts, but one of them was an old hand at this. In 1970 John Traicos had played for

South Africa in the three-match series against Australia – the last Test series for South Africa before they were banned from world cricket because of their apartheid stance. Traicos was actually born in Egypt, and the gap between his last Test for South Africa and his first appearance for Zimbabwe was a record 22 years and 222 days.

1995: Death of champion thoroughbred Red Rum, debatably the finest steeplechaser of all time. Red Rum raced in more than 100 steeplechases without ever falling. He is best known for his unequalled record of three Grand National victories – in 1973, 1974 and 1977. The two years in the middle of this run (1975 and 1976) saw him finishing second. Following his death he was buried at the finishing line on his beloved Aintree track.

2003: During a championship cup series practice on the Daytona speedway circuit Bryan Cassell's ThunderBike Ducati is hit from behind by Jeff Tatham who cannot avoid carrying on over the stricken driver. Twenty-eight-year-old rookie Cassell was pronounced dead at the medical centre shortly afterwards.

19 October

1856: In Melbourne Jack Smith and James Kelly fight a bare-knuckle contest which lasts for six hours and 15 minutes. There was no record as to who won.

1962: Birth of Evander Holyfield, the only man who has been undisputed world boxing champion at both heavyweight and cruiserweight. He was also the only man to claim the heavyweight title four times.

1986: The final day of the third Test between Australia and India in Bombay. During his innings Allan Border scored the one millionth Test run.

1988: Simen Agdestein makes his international debut for the Norwegian football team in a 2-1 defeat against Italy at the age of 21. Agdestein is unique among footballers in that he was also a genius chess player – Norwegian champion when he was just 15, an international master at 16 and a grandmaster at just 18.

2014: Peter Biaksangzuala of Bethlehem Vengthlang dies of spinal injuries sustained when he lands badly in the process of performing a goal celebration after netting against Chanmari West.

20 October

1968: American Dick Fosbury takes the gold medal in the Olympic Games high jump competition in Mexico City. Fosbury stunned the crowd, not to mention fellow competitors, with his unusual and unique approach to the jump. While most jumpers had changed from the traditional but outdated scissors jump to the Western roll, Fosbury ran at the bar, turning at the last minute, and went over backwards, arcing his body as he went. Fosbury walked off with the gold medal with a new Olympic record of 2.24m. The technique was soon being universally adopted by all high jumpers and referred to as a 'Fosbury flop' – the name that is still used today.

1982: The UEFA Cup tie between FC Spartak Moscow and HFC Haarlem at the Central Lenin Stadium (now the Luzhniki Stadium) ends in tragedy when 66 of the home fans are trampled to death. In freezing subzero conditions about 16,500 hardy fans turned up to watch their team. Only about 100 fans came from the Netherlands. As the full-time whistle drew near many fans headed for the exits. A woman near the front lost her shoe and stopped to retrieve it leading to a domino effect with more falling, many of whom were trampled underfoot. Of the 66 who died, 45 were adolescents.

2012: Fulham entertain Aston Villa in the Premier League. In goal for Villa was American Brad Guzan, bringing to an end Brad Friedel's record of playing in 310 consecutive matches for Blackburn Rovers and Aston Villa, an ever-present record dating all the way back to August 2004.

21 October

1950: American Patty Berg wins the Hardscrabble Women's Invitational golf tournament in Arkansas – the final event in the first-ever Ladies Professional Golf Association Tour. Berg won the event by two strokes.

1964: Larisa Latynina of the Soviet Union wins the gold medal for the floor exercises at the Tokyo Olympic Games. She later got gold in the team all-round event. This completed a career haul of 18 Olympic medals (14 won individually, four with a team), of which nine were gold. The total remained a record for almost 50 years, until it was overhauled by Michael Phelps in the pool in 2012.

1984: The Portuguese Grand Prix is the 16th and final race of the 1984 Formula One season, leading to the closest finish to any season. Alain Prost in the McLaren-TAG won the Grand Prix, and the nine points awarded took his total to 71.5 points. His teammate Niki Lauda came in second to claim six points, which took his final total to 72 points – so Lauda was proclaimed world champion by a margin of half a point.

2007: The final race of the 58th Formula One championship season sees Kimi Raikkonen crowned champion, just one point ahead of both Lewis Hamilton and Fernando Alonso in Brazil. Not only was the final drivers' table unbelievably close, Raikkonen's victory was very unlikely with just four races to go. The drivers arrived in Belgium with Raikkonen on 74 points, trailing Hamilton (96) and Alonso (95). Yet Raikkonen won three of the last four races, to snatch the victory. Even at this final race, the win seemed unlikely – if Hamilton had finished fifth (he was seventh) or if Alonso was second (he was third) either one of them would have claimed the crown.

22 October

1850: The first Olympian Games, very much the forerunner of the modern Olympics, are established by the Wenlock Agricultural Reading Society for 'the promotion of the moral, physical and intellectual improvement ... especially of the working classes, by the encouragement of outdoor recreation, and by the award of prizes annually at public meetings for skill in athletic exercise.' The first Games were held at Much Wenlock racecourse in Shropshire. Standard athletic and sporting events were competed, along with other things such as quoits and penny-farthing races. The Olympian Games also included odd events such as the blindfolded wheelbarrow race, and one year there was even an 'old women's race' with a first prize of a pound of tea.

1878: The first-ever floodlit rugby game takes place in Salford and sees Broughton beat Swinton by two goals, three tries and three touchdowns to nil. Nearly 10,000 people turned out to watch the spectacle.

1908: The semi-finals of the first officially recognised international football competition at the 1908 London Olympics. In the first semi-final England beat the Netherlands 4-0, with all four goals scored by Henry Stapley. In the second match Denmark thrashed France 17-1. Sophus 'Krølben' Nielsen scored ten goals.

1926: Death of American professional boxer Edward Greb, aka The Pittsburgh Windmill. In a 13-year career he fought an incredible 298 bouts. He died after complications from an operation after suffering a cardiac arrest at the age of just 32.

1989: Long-time Formula One protagonists Ayrton Senna and Alain Prost collided in the penultimate Grand Prix of the season at Suzuka in Japan. Prost was out of the race, but Senna managed to get back to the pits for repairs. Then after a breathtaking drive he regained first place and took the chequered flag, which would have kept the drivers' title open until the final race of the season, with Prost still leading. President of FISA at the time was Frenchman Jean-Marie Balestre, who took the extraordinary and unprecedented step of disqualifying Senna, fining him and finally suspending him. Many years later Balestre admitted that he deliberately intervened and acted in such a way to benefit his compatriot Prost.

1994: 'High Noon in Hong Kong' is a WBO-sanctioned boxing event to be held in Hong Kong Stadium. The mega-event would feature four fights on the card – three of which were for world titles, including Herbie Hide and Tommy Morrison fighting for the heavyweight crown. After months of preparation the event was cancelled at the very last minute due to severe financial difficulties.

23 October

1915: Death of iconic cricketer W.G. Grace. In a 43-year career he dominated the sport and was thought of as an outstanding all-rounder. He was considered the creator of modern batsmanship. Grace died of a heart attack at the age of 67.

1940: Birth of Brazilian footballer Edson Arantes do Nascimento, better known to the world as Pelé. His parents actually wanted to name him Edison after the inventor, but there was a spelling mistake on his birth certificate! Widely considered the greatest footballer of all time, he played in 1,363 games (including unofficial friendlies and tour games), netting 1,281 goals in the process. He played for his country 92 times, scoring 77 goals. His favourite player when he was young was the goalkeeper Bilé – which he consistently mispronounced as Pill-ay, and that is where his nickname came from, although he actually disliked it. His family called him Dico as a child.

2010: Death of American long-distance swimmer Francis Crippen. He had been a pool swimmer initially, changing to open water swimming in 2006. At the age of 26 he was competing in FINA's 10K series in the United Arab Emirates. After the race fellow

Pelé

Born: 23 October 1940

Legendary Brazilian footballer, widely considered
the finest player who has ever lived.

swimmer Alex Meyer noticed that Crippen had not finished. After a lengthy search he was discovered underwater by divers just 500m from the shore and near to the finishing buoy. The exact cause of his death was never established.

2011: Death of Italian MotoGP motorcycle racer Marco Simoncelli. He began racing in the 125cc class world championships at the age of just 15, before moving up to the 250cc class. He died following an accident at the Malaysian Grand Prix in Sepang. Losing control of his bike, he veered across the track and was simultaneously struck by both Colin Edwards and Valentino Rossi. He was taken to hospital, but declared dead less than an hour later of injuries sustained.

24 October

1857: Formation of Sheffield Football Club by Nathaniel Creswick and William Prest, both members of Sheffield Cricket Club. As the first football club in the area, initially they didn't have anyone to play against – so they used to put on exhibition matches playing among themselves, such as 'married against singles' and 'professionals vs. labourers and unemployed'. Sheffield Football Club is still in existence, officially recognised as the oldest football club in the world, although (bizarrely) they now play in Dronfield in Derbyshire.

1971: Detroit Lions substitute wide receiver Chuck Hughes dies while playing against Chicago Bears at the Tiger Stadium in Detroit. Hughes remains the only NFL player to die on the field in the course of a game. With Detroit chasing the game, losing 28-23, they brought Hughes on. With just a minute left Hughes dropped to the turf holding his chest. Medics from both sides worked on him and an ambulance was called to take him to hospital where he died an hour later. He was just 28 years old. The final minute was played out in near silence, and then players waited for the news they were dreading. A post-mortem revealed a previously undiagnosed heart condition, with the cause of death given as myocardial infarction caused by arteriosclerosis.

1996: Hasan Raza makes his Test cricket debut, playing for Pakistan against Zimbabwe at Faisalabad. At just 14 years and 227 days he remains the youngest person ever to play Test cricket.

1998: Perhaps the most bizarre event ever in the history of world sport. Bena Tshadi were playing at home to Basanga in a football league game in the Democratic Republic of the Congo when a storm started. A massive bolt of forked lightening hit the crowd, with 30 people needing treatment for burns. All 11 players from Bena Tshadi were struck and died, while not one player from Basanga was touched. In a region beset by witchcraft many of the locals believed that the club had been cursed.

2007: The Puerto Rican women's football team beat the Cayman Islands 4-0 in an international fixture played on the islands. Making her debut for the Caymans was Alyssa Chin; at 13 years and 17 days old she is the youngest person ever to play international football.

2016: In an attempt to emulate the run of his film hero Forrest Gump, Pete Kostelnick arrives at New York City Hall having raced 3,100 miles from San Fransisco. Averaging 73 miles a day, Kostelnick had run for 42 days, six hours and 34 minutes. He would begin at 3.30 every morning, only taking two fifteen-minute breaks, finishing at 7.00pm. He only sustained a coupled of minor injuries through stumbles – the real casualties were the eight pairs of running shoes he got through on his journey.

25 October

1884: *The Straits Times*, a weekly publication in Singapore, publishes the first known reference to snooker: 'A Darjeeling correspondent sends a copy of the rules of a new game called "Snookere", which he ventures to prophesy will soon supplant both Pool and Pyramids in every club and messroom throughout the northern provinces.'

1947: Before the modern era of sponsorship, televised games, worldwide tournaments and schedules, snooker matches really were marathon affairs. The 1947 World Championship was the first since the retirement of Joe Davis, who had won the previous 15 world finals. Joe Davis's younger brother Fred and Walter Donaldson both won their five-day semi-finals. The final took place in a newly rebuilt Leicester Square Hall in London, which had been badly destroyed by bombing in 1940. Donaldson won the ten-day marathon in October, beating Davis 82-63. With the final being the best of 145 frames Donaldson was technically world champion when the score reached 73-49, but in those days matches were always played through to completion, even after the outcome was already decided.

1964: The Mexican Grand Prix is the tenth and final race in the Formula One season, and there is still everything to play for with three drivers, all British, still in with a chance of the world title. In the end John Surtees finished in second and claimed the title. The win was truly historic as Surtees had previously won the 500cc motorcycle world championship four times. Surtees therefore became the first man (and to date, in 2019, the only man) who has been the official world motor racing champion on both two wheels and four.

2017: The FIFA U-17 World Cup semi-final between England and Brazil is held in Kolkata in India. England progressed to the final thanks to a hat-trick from Liverpool forward Rhian Brewster, giving them a 3-1 win. This was Brewster's second hat-trick for the Three Lions in consecutive tournament games.

26 October

1863: The formation of the Football Association, the oldest governing body of association football in the world. Twelve clubs were invited to join: Barnes, Blackheath, Blackheath Proprietary School, Charterhouse (who sent their captain to the meeting, but turned down the offer to join), Civil Service, Crusaders, Crystal Palace (who soon folded, and have no direct link to the Crystal Palace in the modern game), Forest of Leytonstone (who would later become The Wanderers), Kensington School, NN Club (from Kilburn; 'NN' stood for 'No Names'), Perceval House (a military training school in Blackheath) and Surbiton. Of the 11 founding members of the FA, Civil Service FC are the only club still in existence and playing competitive football.

1869: The first steeplechase horse race is held in America, at the Westchester Course in New York. Prior to this race there had only been hurdle races. One reporter wrote: 'The novelty of the thing struck people, many of whom had not the vaguest idea of what a steeplechase was.' Five-year-old Oysterman won this inaugural steeplechase by a neck.

1951: Rocky Marciano defeats his boyhood hero Joe Louis. Despite the result, Marciano took $44,000 from the fight, while Louis picked up $132,000. It was a clean knockout of which Louis later reflected: 'I saw the right hand coming, but I couldn't do anything about it.' Such was the affection that Marciano had for Louis, he cried in his dressing room after the fight that he had destroyed a legend. Louis never fought again.

1969: Air Marshal Nur Khan of Pakistan sees his idea for a hockey World Cup approved by the FIH. It was agreed that the first World Cup for field hockey would be played in October 1971 in Pakistan – the Air Marshall's 'reward' for the vision. However, given the ongoing Bangladesh Liberation War against Pakistan, and the recent war against India, in March 1971 the FIH decided to move the tournament to Barcelona in Spain.

2000: The very first women's rugby league World Cup competition gets underway in Great Britain with eight teams split into two pools to decide on the semi-finalists. The final would take place four weeks later with New Zealand winning the inaugural contest, beating Great Britain 26-4 in the final.

27 October

1906: Death of Leeds City centre-forward David 'Soldier' Wilson. As a teenager he had been a soldier, serving with Black Watch, and in South Africa during the Boer War. Returning to Britain he played for a few Scottish teams before settling in England with Hull City. Leeds City purchased him for £150. Playing for Leeds against Burnley he left the field complaining of severe chest pains. This was, of course, before the days of substitutions, so when two of his teammates came off injured he was determined to return to the field of play against medical advice. He soldiered on in much pain until he eventually collapsed on the field. He was carried to the dressing rooms where he passed away. The post-mortem revealed he had suffered a heart attack.

1977: Death of Tony Hulman, head of the Hulman empire, controlling, among other things, the Indianapolis Motor Speedway and IndyCar. To many people's surprise his 72-year-old widow Mary picked up the reins of his businesses, including all those associated with motorsport – the first woman to have such an active role in any motorsport organisation. She even took over her late husband's role in calling 'Gentlemen, start your engines' at the 1978 Indianapolis 500 – a role she continued into her nineties!

2000: Spain win the Olympic gold medal for the men's basketball ID competition at the 2000 Paralympics. The ID competition was only competed in very few sports – the competition was for the 'intellectually disabled' (to use the official Olympic wording). Team members must have had an IQ less than 75, and would have corresponding difficulties with spatial awareness, conceptual skills, social interactions and practical skills. In one of the most distasteful forms of cheating ever in any sport it was found that only two in Spain's squad of 12 actually suffered any intellectual disability. They were quickly stripped of their medals, with losing finalists Russia being crowned champions.

2004: Death of 30-year-old Brazilian footballer Serginho, who dropped down dead of a cardiac arrest 60 minutes into a game while playing for São Caetano against São Paulo. It transpired that he had an undetected heart defect – his heart was found to weigh 600g at autopsy, approximately double that which would be expected of a healthy heart.

28 October

1900: The end of the second modern Olympic Games. The Games actually began on 14 May, and so were a long, drawn-out event. So much so that there were several instances of competitors (even winners) taking part in events that they hadn't even realised were Olympic events. There was no opening or closing ceremony, the Games being held as part of the 1900 World's Fair.

1900: The largest crowd of the Summer Olympics turn out to see France beat Great Britain 27-8 in the gold medal rugby game. The British team were actually Mosley Wanderers RFC.

1904: The third modern Olympics are held in St Louis in Missouri, the first time the Games have left Europe. The event would be relatively unrecognisable when compared to the modern Games. The Games lasted almost five months, and featured 651 athletes from 15 nations – although 589 of those athletes came from North America. More than half of the events (53 out of 95) saw competitors from the United States as the only people taking part. Club swinging was introduced as a new event, one of the 11 gymnastics events, all of which were only open to men. The gymnast stood still holding a club in each hand, and then twirled and span them around – the more impressive the routine, the higher the points. The sport was dropped for 1908.

1994: Adam Parore scores 96 runs for New Zealand against India in the Test match at Vadodara. Clearly nothing unique with that – except that Parore's 96 runs were all run – there was not one single boundary in the innings.

2006: Death of Jamaican-Canadian heavyweight boxer Trevor Berbick. Berbick was best known for fighting two of the greatest icons the sport has ever known. In 1981 he was the last boxer ever to fight Muhammad Ali, and beat the aged champion. Then five years later, as WBC heavyweight champion, he faced his first defence of his title – losing to the young Mike Tyson. Berbick was bludgeoned to death in a church in Jamaica with a piece of steel pipe. The assailant was his 20-year-old nephew Harold, along with a friend.

29 October

1877: Birth of Yorkshire and England slow left-arm bowler Wilf Rhodes. As a Test cricketer Rhodes took 127 wickets and scored 2,325 runs. Rhodes holds three cricket records which remain unbeaten – the most first-class matches (1,100), the most wickets (4,204) and the oldest Test cricketer at the age of 52 years and 165 days.

1904: German-American gymnast George Eyser wins six medals in a single day in the St Louis Games, representing the United States, including gold on the parallel bars, the long horse vault and the 25-foot rope climbing. Fifty-six years before the first official Paralympics, Eyser was actually competing with a wooden prosthesis having lost his left leg when he was hit by a train.

1905: Death of Canadian athlete Étienne Desmarteau, winner of the 'weight throwing' at the 1904 Olympic Games. The weight concerned was 56lb (25.4kg), and Desmarteau threw it 34ft 4in (10.46m). He had asked the Canadian police for leave of absence to attend the Olympics but they refused, so he went anyway and was sacked. After he won gold he was given his job back. Desmarteau died the following year of typhoid fever.

1935: Death of Canadian boxer Del Fontaine (born Raymond Bousquet). Fontaine had won the Canadian middleweight boxing crown for the second time in 1931. The following year he decided to head to England to try to make his fortune, leaving his wife and children in Canada. Little is known of his boxing career in England. He met a young lady in Bristol with whom he formed a relationship. Believing he had found evidence of her being unfaithful he shot and killed her, and then shot her mother (the mother survived although Fontaine believed he had killed her). Fontaine was sentenced to death by hanging.

1960: Olympic light-heavyweight boxing champion Cassius Clay (the future Muhammad Ali) has his first fight since turning professional. He beats Tunney Hunsaker after six rounds. Clay received $2,000 for the fight, Hunsaker got $300, and the proceeds from the gate went to the Kosair Crippled Children's Hospital.

30 October

1867: Birth of American baseball star Ed Delahanty, twice batting champion in the Northern League. He played MLB for 15 years and was still playing for the Washington Senators at the time of his death. He was travelling by train when the conductor threw him off for being drunk and disorderly. He was crossing a railway bridge when he slipped. He then either drowned, or died dropping over Niagara Falls. His body was found near the bottom of the Falls about two weeks later.

1960: Birth of Argentinean legend Diego Maradona, considered one of the finest footballers of all time. Maradona tended to play in what was considered a classic number ten position. His home fans called him 'El Pibe de Oro' (tr. The Golden Ball).

1974: The Rumble in the Jungle. Muhammad Ali knocks out George Foreman in the eighth round of their famous fight in Zaire (now the Democratic Republic of the Congo). During the bout Ali adopted a new and unusual technique of retreating to the ropes, covering up and allowing Foreman to hit him to tire him out. Ali retaliated with counterpunches. The technique has since become known as 'rope-a-dope'. The technique worked and Ali easily dispatched a tired Foreman.

2012: Reading are hosting Premier League giants Arsenal in the fourth round of the League Cup, so must have been surprised to be 4-0 ahead after just 37 minutes. Arsenal pulled one back right on the stroke of half-time. Arsenal dominated the second half but could only score once, until hitting two more in the final couple of minutes to send the tie into extra time. Arsenal, having been 4-0 down, ended up winning 7-5.

31 October

1908: The end of the fourth modern Olympic Games, which are held in London. At 187 days this was the longest modern Olympics of all time, having begun on 27 April. The tournament was originally due to be in Rome, but the eruption of Mount Vesuvius meant it had to be moved.

1914: With war raging around them the British troops in the trenches amuse themselves by holding a sports day! Surviving programmes from the day show the soldiers involved in pillow fights, wheelbarrow races and wrestling on mules.

1968: Donald Crowhurst sets sail from Teignmouth in Devon to begin his competition in the round-the-world yacht race, beginning one of the most extraordinary and bizarre sporting performances of all time. Crowhurst set off with good intentions in a substandard boat and by the time he had crossed the Atlantic he believed if he was to continue then he would almost certainly lose his boat. So he landed safely in Chile, and settled down. Since this was before the days of satellite coverage, he decided that nobody needed to know he had stopped, so he periodically radioed in false positions – positions that would soon have him in the lead as far as everyone else was concerned! Realising that he couldn't actually win (because he wasn't racing) he made his radio contacts less frequent, and soon had himself in third place. He then radioed to say he was so far behind Nigel Tetley that there was no point in continuing and he was going home again, only to be told that Tetley had just sunk so he was going to finish second. Running out of options Crowhurst set sail once again, and when he got some way out to sea he leapt overboard, tragically seeing no other way out. His body was found 12 days later.

1986: Retired St Louis Cardinals defensive end Robert Rozier is charged with murder. He would be convicted and sentenced to 22 years in prison. After quitting American football he decided to join the cult called 'The Brotherhood'. As initiation to the group he was required to murder a 'white devil' and return with a body part from the murdered person. Rozier clearly got a taste for this – and murdered seven white men, presenting the cult with an array of body parts. His sentence was lenient after he agreed to testify against The Brotherhood.

2002: The most ridiculous game in the history of football. Stade Olympique de L'Emyrne were the reigning champions in Madagascar and were hoping to repeat their success. They needed to win their penultimate game to keep their hopes alive, but they were held to a draw after the referee gave their opponents a very controversial late penalty. SOL were furious, and were convinced there was a conspiracy to see them fail. Their final match now had nothing riding on it – so by way of protest SOL's manager Ratsimandresy Ratsarazaka told his team to score 'some own goals'. Adema beat SOL 149-0 … all 149 were own goals scored by SOL players!

2008: British boxer Peter Buckley beats Martin Mohammed in Birmingham in what proves to be the last fight of his career. Buckley was thrilled to bow out with a victory, after a record of 256 defeats and 43 no-results from his previous 299 bouts.

2010: In the Romanian Liga 1 Feminin (the women's top division), CFF Olimpia Cluj beat CFF Clujana 13-2. Almost unbelievably Olimpia's striker Cosmina Dușa scored all 13 of her side's goals. Dușa was with Olimpia for just two seasons, and netted 174 goals in her 48 appearances.

2010: England's Lee Westwood is named as the world's number one golfer, bringing to an end a record 281 weeks at the top for Tiger Woods.

NOVEMBER

1 November

1884: The foundation of the Gaelic Athletic Association, formed to promote Irish amateur sports, games and culture. It particularly focused on traditional Gaelic sports such as hurling, camogie, rounders, Gaelic football and Gaelic handball. Members of the police and the army were not allowed to join.

1935: Birth of South African golfer Gary Player, winner of nine major championships, six champions tour championships and three seniors' championships. In 1965 he became the only non-American to win all four majors. Player also owns a stud farm breeding thoroughbred racehorses.

1946: With the basketball franchise still in its infancy the Toronto Huskies host the New York Knicks for the first official game in league history. The Knicks beat the Huskies 68-66.

1947: Death of the American thoroughbred Man o' War. Most of his career was just after the First World War when he ran in 21 races, winning 20 of them. He won $249,465, an enormous sum of money for the period. In 1920 the *New York Times* named Man o' War as the outstanding athlete of the year, a title he shared with Babe Ruth.

1962: Death of Mexican racing driver Ricardo Rodríguez. In 1958 at the age of just 16 he was denied entry to the 24 Hours of Le Mans for being too young. Two years later he did enter with André Pilette and came second, becoming the youngest person ever to stand on the podium at Le Mans. The following year he became the youngest driver to race for the Ferrari Formula One team when he guested for them at the Italian Grand Prix. He signed to drive for Rob Walker's Lotus 24 but died on his first day of testing when he hit the barriers after a suspension failure. He was just 20 years old.

2013: Team American Chunker win the world championship in the sport of pumpkin chucking, setting a new official world record at the same time. The world championships are held annually in Bridgeville in Delaware, and the competition is simply launching a pumpkin as far as possible by any means. More than 100 teams entered using catapults, trebuchets, cannons, slingshots and valves. Team American Chunker launched their pumpkin a distance of 1,430.9m (4,695ft).

2 November

1934: Birth of Australian tennis star Ken Rosewall, winner of 23 tennis majors including eight Grand Slam titles. In 1971 he became the first male player in the Open Era to win a tournament (the Australian Open) without dropping a single set throughout. He still holds the world records for the most matches played (2,282) and the most matches won (1,665).

1969: The inaugural European competition for women's football concludes in Turin, Italy. The competition was deemed unofficial since it was not organised under the umbrella of UEFA, but it was considered the precursor to the UEFA women's championship. Only four teams entered, with Italy beating Denmark 3-1 in the final. Earlier in the day England had beaten France 2-0 to secure third place.

2008: At the Brazilian Grand Prix Lewis Hamilton becomes the first person ever under the age of 24 to become world champion, but he certainly left it late. Going into the last lap of the final race Hamilton was in sixth place with Ferrari's Felipe Massa leading – a position that would have given both drivers the same number of points, and left Massa as world champion having won six races to Hamilton's five. As rain fell towards the end of the race most drivers headed to the pits for intermediate tyres – but Timo Glock decided to stay on his dry tyres, a decision which was risky but nearly paid off. In the last few corners Glock ran wide, allowing Hamilton to overtake him and to take the title by one point. In fact visibility was so poor by then that Glock actually had no idea Hamilton had passed him until after the race had finished.

2012: The New York Marathon is cancelled – just two days before it is due to be run, and only three days after the mayor of New York announces it would be going ahead! It was just a week since Hurricane Sandy had devastated the city. The mayor explained: 'While holding the race would not require diverting resources from the recovery effort, it is clear that it has become the source of controversy and division. We would not want a cloud to hang over the race or its participants, and so we have decided to cancel it.' Entrants were offered the choice of a full refund, or guaranteed and free entry to a future New York Marathon. Many of the entrants who had come to New York from outside actually stayed on for a bit to help the clean-up effort.

2013: Stoke City's Bosnian goalkeeper Asmir Begovic claims two records – the earliest goal scored by a goalkeeper, and the longest distance from which a goal has been scored. In the first minute of the game against Southampton, Begovic hammered the ball home from 91.9m (301ft 6in). The game finished 1-1.

3 November

1899: Heavyweight world boxing champion James J. Jeffries makes the first defence of his title in Brooklyn, New York, beating Irishman Tom Sharkey over 25 rounds. The fight was considered the most physical and brutal that the American audience had ever watched at that point in time. The bout actually lasted a little more than two hours, but the 19,000 crowd stayed to the end, absorbed by the spectacle.

1931: Don Bradman plays as a guest in a friendly fixture between Blackheath and Lithgow to celebrate the opening of Blackheath's ground. The club asked Bradman to play not solely for his genius, but because they knew that his presence would attract a large crowd for the celebration – which it did – and Bradman certainly gave them something to cheer about ... a century in three overs! (This was when there were eight balls in an over, but it still equates to four modern-day overs.) Bradman scored 33 runs off one over, including three sixes and three fours, and took a single off the last ball to keep the strike. He then scored 40 off the next over – four sixes and four fours – but the final boundary meant he lost the strike. His partner then took a single off the first delivery, and Bradman scored two sixes and a single off the next three. Another single from his partner and he finished the over with two fours and a six – 27 runs off the over, and 100 off the three overs (plus two for his partner). Overall, Bradman scored 256, including 14 sixes and 29 fours.

1949: Birth of Larry Holmes, the American heavyweight world boxing champion. Having made 20 successful defences of his various world titles, he is behind only Joe Louis and Wladimir Klitschko. Perhaps his greatest claim to fame was that, while four other men managed to beat Muhammad Ali on points, Holmes was the only man to actually stop him.

2004: Death of Latvian ice hockey player Sergei Zholtok. He was playing for HK Riga 2000 against Belarusian team HC Dinamo Minsk when he was feeling unwell so asked to come off. He was helped to the dressing room by teammate and good friend Darby Hendrickson. In the dressing room he just collapsed on to his friend and died in his arms. An autopsy revealed heart failure caused by cardiac arrhythmia.

4 November

1947: Mike Collins floors Pat Brownson with the very first punch of their Golden Gloves boxing contest. The hit was so effective the referee didn't even bother with a count and immediately awarded the contest to Collins. The fight therefore was officially the briefest boxing match in history, officially timed at four seconds.

1955: Death of baseball legend Cy Young. In a 22-year career Young was the pitcher for five different teams in the major leagues. Young pitched for a world record 511 victories – nearly 100 ahead of his nearest competitor.

1980: Death of boxer Johnny Owens (aka the Merthyr Matchstick), the British and European bantamweight champion who was the first Welshman to hold the Commonwealth title. Owens challenged the Mexican boxer Lupe Pintor for the world title, a bout which would take place on 19 September at the Grand Olympic Auditorium in Los Angeles. The match was initially very well matched but the world champion started to take control in the final few rounds. With just 25 seconds remaining Owens was grounded by Pintor. He never got up. He lay on the canvas for five minutes being treated, before being taken to hospital where he lapsed into a coma. Owens died seven weeks later at the age of just 24.

1999: Death of West Indies pace bowler Malcolm Marshall. Marshall broke into the West Indies team during the days of legendary pacemen Michael Holding, Andy Roberts and Joel Garner, and saw through the transition to Curtly Ambrose and Courtney Walsh ... and Marshall was probably the quickest and most feared of them all. Among Test bowlers who have achieved more than 200 wickets Marshall tops the bowling averages at 20.94. In 1996 Marshall became the coach of both Hampshire and the West Indies, but just three years later it was announced he was suffering from colon cancer. He died a few months later at the age of just 41, weighing only about four stone (just over 25kg).

5 November

1916: Hungary draw 3-3 away to Austria in Vienna. Hungarian forward Imre Schlosser became the first international to win 50 caps.

1935: Birth of English flat-racing jockey Lester Piggott. Named flat-racing Champion Jockey 11 times, included in his 4,493 wins are the 1,000 Guineas (twice), the 2,000 Guineas (five times), the Oaks (six), the Derby (nine) and the St Leger (eight).

1978: Birth of Spanish road racing cyclist Xavier Volpini, who specialises in the mountainous stages of the major races. He became infamous within the sport when he tipped police off about a doping ring in February 2011. He died tragically just three months later when he was crushed between his own car and his automatic garage door while preparing his bike for a training ride.

1994: Forty-five-year-old George Foreman becomes the oldest ever world heavyweight boxing champion, when he knocks out Michael Moorer to claim both the IBF and the WBA belts.

2005: In the Olympic Oval invitation event in Calgary in Canada, Norwegian Eskil Ervik breaks the record for speed skating over the 3,000m distance. He skated the distance in a time of three minutes and 37.28 seconds, giving an average speed of 49.71kmh (30.9mph).

2016: The world's top side, the New Zealand All Blacks, are beaten 40-29 against Ireland at the Soldier Field in Chicago, US. Since beating Australia 41-13 in Auckland on 15 August 2015 the All Blacks had won 18 consecutive matches before this defeat in the exhibition match.

6 November

1869: Rutgers University (the state university of New Jersey) play against the College of New Jersey (now Princeton University) in a 25-a-side match which is generally regarded as the first-ever game of American football. The rules of the match were written by the Rutgers captain William Leggett, and bore little similarity to the modern game. A round ball was used, and players were not allowed to throw or carry the ball – the emphasis was on kicking. Goals were scored by kicking the ball into the opposition's goal. There was no time limit placed on the game – the first team to six goals would win. Rutgers won 6-4.

1933: Trinidad beat Barbados 6-0 in a football match in Port of Spain. In the Barbados team that day were brothers Arthur and Reyn Foster, along with their 42-year-old father Kelly.

1966: Johan Cruyff (born Hendrik Johannes Cruijff) becomes the first Dutch player ever to be sent off in an international match as the Netherlands lose 2-1 in a friendly against Czechoslovakia. Such was his perceived importance to the Dutch national side that the Royal Dutch Football Association outrageously punished his red card by banning him from some domestic fixtures with Ajax rather than any international matches.

2000: Aung Kyaw Tun scores Myanmar's solitary goal in the 3-1 defeat against Thailand, at the age of 14 years and 93 days. This remains the only goal by a 14-year-old in a recognised international football fixture. (José Pérez scored for Uruguay in the 5-4 win against Argentina on 13 July 1913, but his date of birth was recorded as only '1898' – so he might have been 14 or 15.)

7 November

1896: The first-ever game of professional basketball is played at the Trenton Masonic, with Trenton YMCA hosting Brooklyn YMCA. The crowd were charged a nominal entrance fee, and each player was paid $15 to play ... except Fred Cooper who was given $16, making him the highest paid basketball player at the time. Trenton beat Brooklyn 15-1.

1933: Voters in Pennsylvania overturn the so-called blue law, which restricts activities on a Sunday, particularly competitive sports. The laws were brought in to promote keeping one day special for worship or rest, but the people decided they wanted their sport on a Sunday.

1943: The Detroit Lions and the New York Giants fight out a 0-0 draw. That was, at the time of writing, the last scoreless NFL game.

1986: Jean-Marc Boivin leads his team to a world record 117m depth in the lowest subglacial dive in history. They were diving under the Mer de Glace, the massive valley glacier on the northern slopes of the Mont Blanc massif in the French Alps.

1991: Legendary basketball player Magic Johnson, star of the Los Angeles Lakers, stuns the sports world when he goes public to announce that he is HIV positive, and that he will be retiring immediately. He was at pains to point out that neither his wife nor child were infected, and denied any homosexual activity, stating that he had no idea how he contracted it! He did later admit to a very promiscuous lifestyle during his playing days, and went public to warn everyone that heterosexuals can get HIV too. He was considered a hero for the stand he took.

1993: The Australian Grand Prix is the final Formula One race of the 1993 season. The race news was dominated by two of the biggest names ever in the sport. The race was won by Ayrton Senna in what would become his last ever Formula One victory. It was also the last ever Grand Prix for Alain Prost before retiring.

2010: Jimmy White wins his 30th career snooker title by beating Steve Davis 4-1 in Bradford to win the World Seniors Championship.

8 November

1917: Death of English cricketer Charlie Blythe, who took 2,506 wickets at an average of 16.81. He was one of only three players (along with Hedley Verity and Tom Goddard) to take 17 wickets on a single day's play. Blythe joined the British Army at the outbreak of the First World War and was killed in action during the Battle of Passchendaele.

1942: Birth of Puerto Rican jockey Angel Cordero who has won over 6,000 races in a long and successful career, including the Kentucky Oaks (twice), the Kentucky Derby (three times), the Jockey Club Gold Cup (three times) and the Preakness Stakes (twice).

1995: Death of Russian boxer Sergei Kobozev. Kobozev served in the Russian army as he began a career as an amateur boxer, including representing his country in the Seoul Olympics of 1988. As an amateur he won 22 of his 23 fights, and was in the process of turning professional. Then one day he simply disappeared and was never heard of again, with no known motive or clue as to what had happened. Fourteen years later his bones were discovered in the garden of one of the Russian mafia's head men. The recorded date of death is the date he went missing, as it was believed he was killed immediately.

2017: The U19 Championship group C qualifier between Qatar and Iraq ends in a 1-1 draw meaning the match goes to penalties. Qatar's young goalkeeper Shehab Mamdouh made what he believed was a match-winning penalty save and understandably got rather excited about it. However, the referee spotted an infringement and ordered the penalty to be retaken. He also booked Mamdouh for over-exuberant celebration. Sadly for him this was Mamdouh's second booking so the goalkeeper was sent off in the middle of a penalty shoot-out. Qatar's captain Nasser Abdulsalam took the responsibility himself to go in goal – and it was he who produced the match-winning save.

9 November

1918: Birth of American long-distance open water swimmer Florence Chadwick, the first woman to swim the English Channel in both directions – setting a record time for both journeys. She was also the first woman to swim the Catalina Channel in California, the Straits of Gibraltar, the Bosporus (aka the Strait of Istanbul) and the Dardanelles (aka the Hellespont).

1968: Death of Australian Test cricket wicketkeeper Wally Grout. Playing for his state he set a new world record when he caught eight batsmen in an innings. He died at the age of 41 of a heart attack, just three days after retiring from cricket.

1984: Larry Holmes makes the first defence of his IBF world heavyweight boxing title, beating James Smith by a technical knockout in the 12th round of a proposed 15. After the fight Holmes admitted: 'I was trying to make a lot of money real quick. And "Bonecrusher" popped in the picture. They gave me $3.5m to fight him. And I shouldn't have fought James "Bonecrusher" Smith because three weeks before that I had got a haemorrhoid operation. But for $3.5m to go out there and fight James "Bonecrusher" Smith? So I went out there and I fought him. I was bleeding after the fight, but I got $3.5m.'

2004: Emlyn Hughes, the most successful captain in the history of Liverpool Football Club, passes away from a brain tumour at the age of 57. Hughes also captained England on several occasions.

2011: Joseph Paterno (aka JoePa) is sacked as the head coach of the Penn State Nittany Lions football team after 45 years in charge. The most successful coach in the club's history, he was dismissed as part of the Penn State child sex abuse scandal. He died just 74 days after his dismissal. JoePa was not actually directly involved in the scandal, but was deemed guilty of covering up the actions of his defensive coach Jerry Sandusky.

2015: The World Anti-Doping Agency commission report recommends that the Russian Federation should be banned from all athletics competitions with immediate effect for running a 'state-supported' doping programme.

10 November

1919: At the age of 45 years and 73 days Welshman Billy Meredith becomes the oldest football international goalscorer of all time, when he scores in Wales's 2-1 victory against England. By an odd coincidence Meredith made his last appearance for Wales five months later … in a 2-1 win against England.

1961: Birth of the inspirational French Paralympic swimmer Béatrice Hess. Despite suffering from cerebral palsy, Hess competed in five Paralympic Games – every Games between 1984 and 2004, except for 1992 which she missed for health reasons. Her haul of 25 Paralympic medals (20 gold, five silver) makes her the second most successful athlete in the history of the Games.

1986: Death of Sir Gordon Richards, often considered the finest jockey of all time. Winner of the British flat-racing Champion Jockey 26 times, he remains the only flat jockey to have been knighted.

1990: Death of skier and mountaineer Steve McKinney at the age of just 37. McKinney had been the first skier to break the 200kmh barrier, clocking 200.22kmh (124.14mph). In 1986, while leading an expedition, he became the first man in history to hang-glide off Mount Everest.

2009: Death of German goalkeeper Robert Enke, who played for Benfica, Barcelona and Hannover 96, as well as eight times for the national side. Tragically Enke lost his daughter Lara in 2006 and never came to terms with the loss. Still grief-stricken, he took his own life by standing in front of an express train. He was 32 at the time.

2015: Death of Irish flat-racing jockey Pat Eddery, second in the all-time list of British flat race wins (behind Gordon Richards). He was named Champion Jockey 11 times, and counted among his successes winning the 1,000 Guineas, the 2,000 Guineas (three times), the Epsom Derby (three), the St Leger (four) and The Oaks (three).

11 November

1887: The foundation of Celtic football club in Glasgow, set up by a Catholic priest as a team to play exhibition matches for charity, raising money for the 'Poor Children's Dinner Table'.

1978: The New Zealand All Black team have been so dominant in rugby that it appears almost unbelievable that they would feel the need to cheat. Protecting a 100 per cent win record on their tour to the UK, the All Blacks visited Cardiff Arms Park. With moments to go they were trailing 12-10, but won a line-out deep in Welsh territory. As the line-out was taken giant lock Andy Haden (1.98m (6ft 6in), 113kg (250lbs)) fell away from the line-out as if he had been shoved and the referee awarded a penalty, which Brian McKechnie duly converted for a 13-12 victory. Television replays showed that Haden hadn't been touched. The incident became known as the 'Great dive to victory', and dogged Haden for the remainder of his 117-cap career.

1986: Ross Norman beats Jahangir Khan 9-5 9-7 7-9 9-1 to claim his first title in the World Open squash championship. The final marked Khan's first defeat in competition since losing to Geoff Hunt in 1981. His record of 555 victories is the longest winning streak for any individual athlete in any sport worldwide.

2009: The fastest goal of all time is scored in a Prince Faisal bin Fahad Cup match between Al Hilal and Al Shoalah. Al Hilal kicked off and a teammate tapped the ball to Nawaf Al Abed – who decided to try his luck from the halfway line. The goal was officially timed at two seconds.

2013: Harlem Globetrotter Thunder Law scores the longest successful basket from the very back corner of a slightly oversized court in Phoenix, Arizona. The shot was officially measured as 33.45m (109ft 9in).

12 November

1881: The first-ever meeting of the two teams which would now be recognised as the Manchester derby. The match was played at West Gorton, the home of St Mark's (who would soon become Ardwick City and later renamed Manchester City). Newton Heath LYR, now Manchester United, won the game 3-0 in what a reporter for a local newspaper described as a 'pleasant game'. With both teams small and insignificant the match did not carry the status it does today.

1892: Yale guard Pudge Heffelfinger is paid $500 by Allegheny American football club, and so becomes the first professional football player. Allegheny were playing Pittsburgh Athletic Club, and Pittsburgh had already offered Heffelfinger $250 to play for them, but he didn't feel the amount was worth losing his amateur status for. Allegheny won the game 4-0 with Heffelfinger scoring the only touchdown.

1939: The Protectorate of Bohemia and Moravia, based in occupied Czechoslovakia, play a so-called friendly fixture against Germany in the Hermann Göring Stadium, in Wroclaw, Nazi Germany. The final score was 4-4, largely thanks to a hat-trick by Moravian Josef Bican. Interestingly this was Bican's third international team – he had already played for both Austria and Czechoslovakia. Bican was also the world's most prolific goalscorer of all time with a record of 1,468 goals.

1961: Birth of Romanian gymnast Nadia Comăneci. During the 1976 Montreal Olympics Comăneci became the very first gymnast in history to score perfect 10.0 ... and then scored seven of them en route to three gold medals.

1986: Celtic, Liverpool and Scotland legend Kenny Dalglish wins his 102nd and final cap for Scotland against Luxembourg in a qualifying match for Euro 1988. Scotland won 3-0. Dalglish remains the only Scot to have won more than 100 caps.

13 November

1916: Death of Frederick Kelly, three times winner of the Diamond Sculls at Henley and gold medal rower at the 1908 Olympics, killed in action at Beaucourt-sur-Ancre in the Loire region of northern France. He had fought successfully in the Gallipoli conflict the previous year and won the Distinguished Service Cross for conspicuous gallantry.

1954: Great Britain beat France 16-12 to win the first-ever rugby league World Cup. In this inaugural contest only four teams took part – Great Britain, France, Australia and New Zealand. The vision for the World Cup came from Paul Barrière, the president of the French rugby league, who was keen to raise some funds for the sport after most of their assets were seized by the French rugby union after the Second World War.

1982: Ray Mancini, the lightweight boxing champion of the world, defeats Duk-koo Kim, by a knockout. At the beginning of the 14th round Mancini connected with his opponent, snapping his head back and sending him crashing to the canvas. Although he managed to get to his feet the referee intervened and awarded the contest to Mancini. Back in his corner Kim collapsed again and was rushed to hospital and diagnosed with having a blood clot on the brain. He lapsed into a coma and, despite surgery, died four days later. Even more tragically four months later Kim's mother took her own life by drinking poison. Four months later still the referee of the bout also took his own life. Mancini himself plunged into lengthy periods of depression, and was never the same man again.

2004: Arsenal win the North London derby, beating Tottenham 5-4 at White Hart Lane. Incredibly all nine goals were scored by different players.

2011: Death of South African international rugby player Solly Tyibilika, the first black player ever to score a try for the Springboks. He was shot in the entrance to a tavern while talking on the telephone. The perpetrators were never caught, so there was no confirmed cause of death nor confirmation of whether he was the intended target.

14 November

1749: Death of sumo wrestler Maruyama Gondazaemon at the age of just 35. He is officially recognised as the third yokozuna, although this position was not recognised until 150 years after his death. He was still active at the time of his death from dysentery.

1888: The opening of the first official golf club in the world – St Andrew's Golf Club in Yonkers, New York. At the beginning the course only had six holes, but over the years has developed into a popular and challenging par-71 course, most recently redesigned by Jack Nicklaus in 1983.

1893: Birth of Tommy Milton, the American race driver best remembered for back-to-back wins in the Indianapolis 500 – a feat made all the more remarkable from the fact he only had one functional eye. Despite his success, this disability would disqualify him from competing in modern motorsports.

1971: Birth of Australian cricket wicketkeeper Adam Gilchrist, aka Gilly, widely regarded as the finest wicketkeeper of all time.

2010: In winning the Abu Dhabi Grand Prix Sebastian Vettel becomes the youngest ever Formula One world champion – 166 days younger than Lewis Hamilton had been two years earlier when he first took the title. The 23-year-old German beat Spain's Fernando Alonso by four points in the title race.

15 November

1859: Way back in the unpleasant days of racial segregation black and coloured sportsmen invariably had to resort to forming their own teams to play, without the fame and fortune that was possible in the all-whites games. The first known record of a baseball game between two black teams was a local derby in New York City. The Henson Base Ball Club from Queens defeated the Unknowns of Brooklyn by a score of 54-43.

1903: Birth of New Zealand batsman Stewie Dempster. It is perhaps surprising that few have heard of him since of all those who have completed at least ten Test innings, Dempster's batting average is the second highest on record (65.72), behind only Don Bradman. Bizarrely as well as playing for the Kiwis Dempster also played representative matches for Scotland.

1947: An Australian XI closes the day's play at 342/4 against an Indian touring team, after Don Bradman has scored 172 in less than three hours. That was Bradman's 100th century, the first person to reach that landmark.

1964: Soccer legend Johan Cruyff, widely regarded as one of the finest soccer players of all time, makes his professional football debut, for Ajax against GVAV (which became FC Groningen in 1971). GVAV won the game 3-1, with the Ajax goal coming from Cruyff in the 87th minute.

1989: In the first Test match of the series between India and Pakistan, two future legends (one from each team) both make their debuts. For India Sachin Tendulkar plays his first match, scoring 15 runs in the first innings (and not batting in the second). He was out clean bowled by Pakistan debutant Waqar Younis.

16 November

1940: Cornell Big Red beat Dartmouth Big Green in a college American football game 3-0 in New Hampshire. However, after reviewing the game the referee publicly acknowledged that he had made a mistake in game play. Under the circumstances Cornell offered to forfeit the game and Dartmouth accepted, accepting a 7-3 victory – the only time the outcome of a college football game had been decided off the field of play.

1990: Day one of the inaugural Solheim Cup, a biennial golf tournament for female golfers between teams from America and Europe – the female equivalent of the Ryder Cup. This first event was held in Orlando, Florida, and was won by the US team by a score of 11½ to 4½.

1996: Death of Brazilian centre-forward Dondinho. His most successful period was playing for Bauru when he became a very prolific goalscorer, including once scoring five headed goals in one match. But he was better known as the father of Pelé. (Pelé once scored four headed goals in a game, but never five.)

2003: Lionel Messi (real name Lionel Andrés Messi Cuccittini) makes his debut for Barcelona at the age of just 16 years, four months and 23 days. Born and raised in Argentina, Messi was diagnosed with a growth hormone deficiency as a child. At 13 his family relocated to Barcelona after the football club offered to pay for his treatment. His debut was a friendly fixture against Porto of Portugal.

2014: During the world championships in Kazakhstan, Russian Tatiana Kashirina sets the new women's world record in weightlifting. For the snatch she lifts 155kg (24st 5lb), and then clears 193kg (30st 5lb) in the clean and jerk.

17 November

1905: The first playing of what is now known as the Australian Open sees 17 men compete for the singles title, as well as a men's doubles competition. There was no competition for women in the beginning. This first tournament was organised and overseen by the Lawn Tennis Association of Australia (now Tennis Australia), and was played at the Warehouseman's Cricket Ground in Melbourne. The tournament was not known as the Australian Open until 1969 – it was initially known as the Australasian Championship and was even played in New Zealand twice. In 1927 it became the Australian Championships, and finally the Australian Open. The first-ever game played in the inaugural Australasian Championship saw Australian Rodney Heath beating Timothy Fitchett 6-4 6-1 6-0 in what was the only first round tie. Since there were 17 entrants, this pair had to play a first-round match while the other 15 were given a bye to leave 16 players for round two. Heath beat compatriot Albert Curtis in the singles final in four sets.

1990: Birth of Hong Kong snooker star Ng On-Yee. In the 2018 Ladies' World Snooker Championship she became the first snooker world champion (male or female) to win the title without conceding a single frame in the tournament.

2006: Death of Hungarian footballer Ferenc Puskás, one of the most prolific goalscorers of all time. In the Spanish and Hungarian leagues he scored 514 goals in 529 appearances.

2013: In tenpin bowling a perfect game scores 300, achieved by scoring a strike on all ten throws and the two permitted additional throws gained from the final strike. In the Youth/Adult League in Florida Hannah Diem set a new world record by bowling a perfect game at the age of nine years, six months and 19 days.

18 November

1881: Birth of Canadian ice hockey goaltender Percy LeSueur, who played before the First World War before signing up and fighting in the Canadian army. After the war he returned to NHL as a referee, coach, manager and journalist. He invented the gauntlet-style gloves to protect the forearms, as well as designing a net for catching rising shots (the LeSueur net).

1985: The American football moment that fans vote the 'most shocking moment in history' when Joe Theismann of the Washington Redskins is tackled by Lawrence Taylor of the New York Giants live on television. The ferocity of Taylor's action snapped both the tibia and fibula, and was so strong that the *Washington Post*'s sports pages ran with the headline 'The hit that no one who saw it can ever forget'. Theismann never played again.

2015: Death of legendary All Black rugby union winger Jonah Lomu. He was just 19 when he became the youngest person ever to represent New Zealand and went on to play for them 63 times, scoring 37 tries. He was often considered the first truly global superstar of the sport. He was actually diagnosed with kidney problems while just 20 and tried to balance his health needs with his playing career. By 28 he was needing dialysis, and a year later he underwent a kidney transplant and did not play international rugby again. He was just 40 when he passed away of a heart attack triggered by ongoing renal issues.

19 November

1887: The first meeting of what would now be described as the North London derby. The Royal Arsenal visited Tottenham Marshes to play Tottenham. The game had to be abandoned with 15 minutes remaining due to poor light. Spurs were leading 2-1 at the time. The first completed match between the two was three months later at Arsenal's Plumstead ground with the Royal Arsenal winning 6-2, although Spurs only brought a team of nine players to the game.

1969: In the Brazilian league Santos are playing against CR Vasco at the Maracaná Stadium, in front of a crowd of 65,157. When Santos were awarded a penalty up stepped Pelé to fire home his 1,000th career goal in all competitions.

1976: Birth of Belgian duathlete Benny Vansteelant, without doubt the finest duathlete in history, winning more than 80 per cent of all the races he entered. Duathlons feature a run followed by a bike ride followed by a second run. Vansteelant won the world standard distance (10km–40km–5km) four times, and was world long-distance champion (10km–150km–30km) four times. Vansteelant was hit by a car while training, and was admitted to hospital with several severe injuries. Recovering in hospital he suddenly had a heart attack and died. He was just 30 years of age.

2004: The NBA game between Indiana Pacers and Detroit Pistons leads to a large fight which the Associated Press terms 'the most infamous brawl in NBA history'. Played at the Palace of Auburn Hills in Michigan, the match has since been dubbed the Malice at the Palace. With just 46 seconds left on the clock a fight broke out on the pitch in the highly charged atmosphere and this spread to the crowd. So severe was the fight that NBA subsequently suspended nine players for a total of 146 games between them (meaning a loss of salary of $11m). Five of the players were charged with criminal assault and given probation and community service. The Malice at the Palace saw increased security at future NBA games, as well as a big reduction in alcohol sales at all future fixtures.

2017: Death of Czech tennis player Jana Novotná of cancer, winner of Wimbledon 1998. She had her greatest success as a doubles player, winning 12 major women's titles with four different partners, winning each major at least twice. At the beginning of her career she also won four mixed doubles titles with American Jim Pugh.

20 November

1880: Newton Heath LYR Football Club lose their first-ever match 6-0 to Bolton Wanderers reserves. Newton Heath were a works team formed from workers of the Carriage and Wagon department of the Lancashire and Yorkshire Railway (LYR). By 1902 the club were facing a winding-up order with debts of £2,670, but were saved by four local businessmen who took over the club and changed its name … to Manchester United.

1902: The creation of the Tour de France. The race was the vision of Geo Lefevre and Henri Desgrange in an attempt to sell more copies of the French sport newspaper *L'Auto*. The original vision was a six-day race all across France.

1942: The NHL formally suspends all play within the regular season, announcing that there will be no more league matches until after the Second World War.

2015: Death of Namibian cricketer Raymond van Schoor. In a 50-over match against Free State he suddenly collapsed while batting. He was rushed into hospital where he died five days later. At the age of just 25 he had suffered a stroke at the crease.

2015: Russian Pavel Kulizhnikov sets a new speed skating record over 500m, with a time of 33.98 seconds during the World Cup. This equates to an average speed of 52.97kmh (32.91mph).

21 November

1874: Aston Villa Football Club is officially formed by members of the Villa Cross Wesleyan Chapel in Handsworth, Birmingham. Bizarrely their first match was against Aston Brook St Mary's rugby team – so they agreed to play the first half under rugby union rules and the second half under association football rules.

1885: Foundation of Southampton Football Club, originally known as St Mary's Young Men's Association FC. since the membership is formed from young men from St Mary's Anglican church.

1891: Aston Villa play Stoke in the game that was the deciding factor in 'time added on for stoppages', in rather bizarre circumstances. Aston Villa were leading 2-1 with just moments to go when the referee blew to award Stoke a penalty kick. Aware that time was running out, one of the Aston Villa players picked up the ball and booted it out of the ground. By the time the ball had been retrieved and returned the referee had already blown for full time and Aston Villa had won.

1902: Philadelphia Athletics defeat Kanaweola AC in New York in the first sporting night fixture, with the pitch lit artificially.

1992: Swedish swimmer Jan Karlsson swims a world record time of 23.80 seconds for the 50m butterfly. Just a couple of hours later his sister Louise swam a world record 31.19 seconds for the 50m freestyle.

22 November

1808: Norwegian-Dane Olaf Rye becomes the first person to clear more than 30 feet on a ski jump. The official distance jumped at Eidsberg church in Norway was 9.5m (31ft).

1917: The National Hockey League (NHL) is formed … with no teams! Four days later five clubs formally join, making it a viable competition.

1922: St Albans City are drawn away to Dulwich Hamlet in the fourth qualifying round of the FA Cup. St Albans set a new record, becoming the first (and as of 2019 only) team to score seven goals away from home and still lose. Dulwich won the tie 8-7.

1935: The first-ever professional cricket match to be played in what is now Pakistan. Sindh hosted Australia in Karachi 12 years before Pakistan even came into existence.

1943: Birth of Billie Jean Moffitt, who is far better known by her married name Billie Jean King. Her record in all forms of lawn tennis is phenomenal – 39 Grand Slam titles: 12 women's singles, 16 in women's doubles and 11 in mixed doubles. She also represented the US in both the Federation Cup (including seven wins) and the Wightman Cup (nine wins). An outspoken advocate for gender equality, King founded both the Women's Tennis Association and the Women's Sports Foundation.

1950: The lowest scoring game in NBA history sees the Fort Wayne Pistons beat the Minneapolis Lakers by a score of just 19-18. A combined score of just 37 was truly remarkable given that the next lowest combined total was 83 four years earlier.

1986: 'Iron' Mike Tyson becomes the youngest ever heavyweight boxing champion of the world at the age of 20 when he knocks out defending champion Trevor Berbick in the second round.

2014: Wales entertain the New Zealand All Blacks at the Principality Stadium. The All Blacks were captained by flanker Richie McCaw, who became the first person in the history of rugby to lead an international side for 100 games. Almost exactly a year later McCaw announced his international retirement after receiving a record 148 caps.

Billie Jean King

Born: 22 November 1943

Tennis legend who won 39 Grand Slam titles, gaining success in
singles, doubles and mixed doubles.

23 November

1904: The end of the third modern Olympic Games in St Louis, the first Games held in the United States. Given the location and the difficulties of transport and travel of the day the vast majority of competitors were American, so it was no surprise that the States finished top of the medal table with 78 gold medals – although the degree of domination was quite startling. Germany, Cuba and Canada won four gold medals each, and Hungary won two – the US won 81 per cent of all the gold medals available!

1990: Death of Bo Diaz, MLB catcher and the first Venezuelan to play in the major league. He died when he was crushed by a satellite dish he was adjusting on the roof of his home.

1996: The shortest officially recorded professional football career. When Southampton Football Club got a telephone call from someone claiming to be the ex-world footballer of the year George Weah, for some reason they believed him. The man claiming to be Weah further claimed he had a cousin who was just starting out but was going to be a star, so Southampton signed him. So Ali Dia found himself wearing the number 33 shirt on the bench that Saturday against Leeds United. After 32 minutes Southampton's England international Matthew Le Tissier was taken off injured, Ali Dia was brought on, and then taken off again in the 85th minute. Leeds won 2-0, and Dia never played for Southampton (or any other professional club) again. Le Tissier summed up his performance: 'He ran around the pitch like Bambi on ice; it was very embarrassing to watch.'

2007: Death of MLB pitcher Joe Kennedy. He was in Florida to be the best man at a friend's wedding. He awoke in the night and collapsed and was rushed into hospital but was dead on arrival. Just 28 years old, he left a wife and a one-year-old son. His wife was expecting their second child.

2013: Doncaster Knights winger Tyler Lewis breaks the world record for the fastest try in competitive rugby when he touches down in 7.24 seconds against the Old Albanians. The Doncaster fly-half kicked off and the bounce of the ball was misjudged by his opposition winger, bouncing over his head and straight into Lewis's hands who ran in uncontested.

2014: An Afghanistani suicide bomber kills 40 people at a volleyball tournament.

24 November

1887: The earliest known softball game takes place in Chicago as a celebration of Thanksgiving Day. Yale University and Harvard University had just competed in a college American football game. The celebrations afterwards quickly developed into a game which evolved into softball. Harvard beat Yale 41-40.

1894: Birth of Yorkshire and England batsman Herbert Sutcliffe. In the 21 seasons he played domestic cricket Yorkshire were the county champions 12 times. His 54 Tests resulted in a batting average of 60.73, making him statistically the best English batsman of all time.

1955: Birth of Ian Botham, widely regarded as one of the finest all-round cricketers of all time. He spent the majority of his career playing for Somerset and England, and in 1980 became only the second player in history to score the 'Test match double' of 100 runs and ten wickets in the same match (the first was Australian Alan Donaldson, and only Pakistan's Imran Khan has managed it since). As well as his cricket Botham also played professional football for three years, playing for Scunthorpe United. He has also done several events for charity, including walking from John O'Groats to Land's End.

1978: The conclusion of the inaugural Men's Hockey Champions Trophy, a field hockey tournament held in Pakistan. The eight-day competition saw five teams (Australia, Great Britain, New Zealand, Pakistan and Spain) play each other in a round-robin tournament, with Pakistan claiming the first Hockey Champions Trophy in winning all four matches.

2012: Death of Puerto Rican boxer Héctor Camacho. During his professional career he won at least one version of the world title at super-featherweight, lightweight, light-welterweight, welterweight, middleweight, light-middleweight and super-middleweight levels. He was also the man who sent Sugar Ray Leonard into permanent retirement. Camacho was shot and badly wounded while sitting in a car. His friend who had been driving was killed instantly, but Camacho survived for four days on life support before the machine was turned off.

25 November

1920: Death of American racing driver Gaston Chevrolet. Earlier in the year he had won the Indianapolis 500, breaking the European dominance of the sport at the time. He was the first driver to complete the 500-mile (800km) race without making a tyre change. He died in another race when he crashed his Frontenac, but had already gained sufficient points to be named 'Speed King of the Year' posthumously.

1938: Death of British racing driver Johnny Hindmarsh, winner of the 24 Hours of Le Mans in 1935 in a 4.5l Lagonda. As well as racing Hindmarsh also worked as a pilot and aviator. He was killed flight testing the new Hawker Hurricane for the armed forces. It is believed that the cockpit filled up with carbon monoxide and he passed out, so the plane dived almost vertically to the ground and exploded.

1953: The game dubbed the 'Match of the Century'. Hungary, aka the 'Golden Team', were ranked world number one, and were playing England at their Wembley fortress. The truth is that England were given a lesson in how to play exciting, expansive football. If anything the 6-3 scoreline flattered England, and the defeat led to a full review of English football both at international and club level.

1967: The second edition of the Games of the New Emerging Forces is held in Phnom Penh in Cambodia. Two thousand athletes entered from 17 nations – all from Asia (Cambodia, Ceylon, China PR, Indonesia, Iraq, Japan, North Korea, Laos, Lebanon, Mongolia, Nepal, Pakistan, Palestine, Syria, North Vietnam and Yemen). China PR won the event with 108 gold medals.

1996: Tony Drago of Malta compiles the fastest ever century break in the history of snooker, during a match in the UK Championship against John Higgins. Drago racked up a break of 103 in just three minutes and 31 seconds.

2005: Death of Manchester United and Northern Ireland legend George Best, often considered the greatest footballer who never played in a major tournament – mainly due to a combination of his own fitness and Northern Ireland's failings on the international stage. Of his attitude to life he confessed: 'I spent a lot of money on booze, birds and fast cars – the rest I just squandered.'

26 November

1913: The Chief of Police in San Francisco bans all women from entering any pavilion, arena or other venue when an official boxing match is taking place.

1914: On this date Heart of Midlothian from Edinburgh go from being the most successful team in Scotland to being a team existing in name only when every single member of the playing squad enlist together to join the British Army for the First World War. Seven members of the team would never again return to Scotland.

1917: Formation of the National Hockey League (NHL) in Montreal, with initially just four Canadian teams as members. The

Boston Bruins were the first American team to join the league, in 1924. The league has expanded over the years, and now has 31 teams – 24 from the US and seven from Canada. The League play-off champions each year are awarded the Stanley Cup, the oldest professional sports trophy in North America.

1986: At the UK Snooker Championship in Preston Alex Higgins once again lands himself in trouble. Locked at 7-7 in a first-to-nine battle with Mike Hallett for a place in the quarter-finals, Higgins asked for a comfort break which was granted. He returned a couple of minutes later and rattled off the final two frames with the best snooker he had played all tournament. Despite the fact everyone knew Higgins had the potential to play snooker of the highest quality, organisers were sceptical as to what he did on his comfort break since that appeared to be the turning point of the game. Therefore as soon as the match had finished Higgins was asked to give a urine sample to check for substances. Higgins was so unimpressed with this that he went up to the tournament director Paul Hatherell and head-butted him, and then kneed the head of security in his 'gentleman's area'. He was fined £200 for assault, £50 for criminal damage to a door and £12,000 by the World Snooker Body, along with a five-tournament ban.

2006: In the Portuguese football league Sporting Clube de Portugal play away to Associação Naval 1º de Maio, and secure a 1-0 win thanks to an 88th-minute free kick by their 20-year-old Brazilian left-back Ronny (full name Ronny Heberson Furtado de Araújo). That free kick was officially measured at a record 210.8kmh (131mph).

27 November

1878: Birth of American athlete Charles Dvorak, one of the pioneers of the pole vault. Hot favourite for the 1900 Olympics, he opted out of the event due to his personal faith on finding that the event was due to be staged on the Sunday. Three years later he set a new world record for the pole vault at 11ft 11in (3.63m), and finally won his Olympic gold the following year.

1979: Birth of American motocross racer Ricky Carmichael. He won the Motocross 450cc Championship seven times and the Supercross 450cc Championship five times. His performances earned him the nickname 'Goat' – an acronym standing for 'Greatest of all time'.

2011: Death of Welsh footballing legend Gary Speed, the most capped outfield player in Welsh history. He enjoyed a very successful career with Leeds United, Everton, Newcastle United, Bolton Wanderers and Sheffield United. After just a few months managing Sheffield United he was appointed as the manager of the Wales national team. In the 11 months he was the manager, he transformed the national side. At the age of 42 he tragically took his own life, hanging himself in his garage.

2014: Death of Australian Test and one-day cricketer Phil Hughes, who played for South Australia and Worcestershire as an opening batsman. In a Sheffield Shield match against New South Wales, Hughes, who had already scored 63, was hit in the neck by a bouncer from Sean Abbott. This split the vertebral artery causing severe bleeding on to the surface of the brain. After surgery he was put into an induced coma in Sydney hospital but never regained consciousness. He died two days after the initial injury, just three days before his 26th birthday.

2015: Play begins in the third and final Test match between Australia and New Zealand in Adelaide – the first-ever day-night Test match using the pink ball. Australia won the Test to take the series 2-0.

2016: Austrians Mario Langmann and Thomas Paulweber finish their world record badminton match after playing for 25 hours, 25 minutes and 44 seconds. This marked the longest match in badminton, although the match was designed as a world record attempt rather than in competitive play.

28 November

1951: Arsenal footballer Arthur Milton plays his one and only international match for England against Austria in a 2-2 draw. In 1958 and 1959 he played in six Test matches for England – becoming the 12th and last player to have represented England in both football and cricket.

1970: Chic Brodie is the highly experienced goalkeeper of Brentford when they play away to Colchester United. In the first half a dog ran on to the pitch from the crowd, charging at Brodie (because he had the ball). He hit Brodie hard, shattering his kneecap and damaging ligaments. While Brodie writhed in agony the dog headed off after the ball again. Brodie managed a couple of painful games later in the season, and hung up his boots at the end of the season at the age of just 33. Sadly that little dog had finished Brodie's professional career.

1993: Just a week before his 18th birthday Ronnie O'Sullivan becomes the youngest ever winner of a ranking tournament when he beats world number one Stephen Hendry 10-6 to win the UK Snooker Championship.

1999: In the Argentinean top league Vélez Sársfield beats Ferro Carril Oeste 6-1. Three of Vélez's goals were penalties, all successfully converted by José Luis Chilavert – the first (and only) known case of a goalkeeper scoring a hat-trick.

2016: Brazilian team Chapecoense are flying into Colombia for the final of the South American club competition when their aeroplane, LaMia Flight 2933, crashes, killing 71 of the 77 people on board. The plane was carrying 22 players and 23 officials of Chapecoense. Three players (Alan Ruschel, Follman and Neto) were among the survivors. Everyone else associated with the club perished. Goalkeeper Follman needed his leg amputated.

29 November

1896: Death of footballer Joe Powell. Powell was the captain of Woolwich Arsenal in their first season in the Football League. Unfortunately he broke his arm in a match against Kettering Town, and developed blood poisoning and tetanus as a result of which he died a couple of weeks later.

1899: Following an advertisement by Hans Gamper calling for local people interested in playing football, 11 men gather in the Gimnasio Solé, and Football Club Barcelona is born. In the early years the club was maintained through the passion and determination of Gamper: 'Barcelona cannot die and must not die. If there is nobody who is going to try, then I will assume the responsibility of running the club from now on.'

1971: The first-ever professional golf championship is played at Walt Disney World, played on the Palm and Magnolia courses of the Walt Disney World Resort. The inaugural event was officially called the Walt Disney World Open Invitational and was won by Jack Nicklaus by three strokes.

1975: Two-time Formula One world champion Graham Hill dies just four months after he retires from driving. Hill was piloting his private jet with four friends on board when he clipped some trees on a golf course in Hertfordshire in conditions of poor visibility. Hill remains the only driver to have achieved the Triple Crown of the Indianapolis 500, 24 Hours of Le Mans and the Formula One world championship.

1978: Nottingham Forest full-back Viv Anderson becomes the first black player to win a senior cap in international football for England in the home fixture against Czechoslovakia.

1998: Death of professional wrestler Giant Haystacks (born Martin Ruane). He was also very successful Stateside where he wrestled under the name Loch Ness Monster. He was renowned for his enormous size, standing 2.11m tall (6ft 11in), and tipping the scales at 311kg (48st 13lb).

2015: British boxer Tyson Fury beats Ukrainian Wladimir Klitschko to win the world boxing heavyweight championship in Düsseldorf. Klitshko had been world champion for nine years, but was out-thought by Fury who became only the fifth British world heavyweight champion (after Bob Fitzsimmons, Lennox Lewis, Frank Bruno and David Haye).

30 November

1857: Birth of Surrey and England opening batsman Robert Abel, aka 'The Guv'nor'. Despite standing just 5ft 4in (1.63m) he earned a reputation as a fearless and unorthodox batsman. He was the first England batsman to carry his bat through an innings in Test cricket.

1937: Birth of British cyclist Tom Simpson, the first Briton to wear the yellow jersey in the Tour de France in 1962. He dropped dead during the 13th stage of the Tour de France. He was just 29 years old. A post-mortem revealed a mixture of alcohol and amphetamines which, combined with the intense heat and the exertion of hill climbs, proved fatal.

1948: The year after Major League Baseball finally becomes an integrated sport, this date marked the official disbanding of the Negro National League. Teams who wished to remain segregated joined the Negro American League, which is still in existence.

1962: Birth of Bo Jackson. Jackson started in NFL having been drafted for the Tampa Bay Buccaneers, but refused to play for them – so entered the draft again the following year, joining the Los Angeles Raiders. A hip injury terminated his football career, and he moved over to baseball. As a baseball player he represented Kansas City Royals, Chicago White Sox and California Angels. Jackson is the only person in history to be officially named an All-Star in both baseball and football.

1980: Semi-finals and finals day in the inaugural women's world judo championship in New York City. Briton Jane Bridge took the gold in the lightest category, the U48kg. Ingrid Berghmans of Germany took gold in the open category.

1991: The final of the first-ever FIFA women's World Cup for association football is played in Guangzhou in China. The United States beat Norway 2-1.

2014: Paola Gianotti finishes her round-the-world cycle ride in Turin, Italy, in a new women's record time of 144 days. The record did carry some controversy, with many people claiming she had not taken the record because she did not abide by the official rules of the challenge. The rules stated that the travel must be continuous – any time spent stopped was added to the time. On 16 May Gianotti was involved in an accident on the road, which resulted in a fractured vertebra which took four months to heal. She did not restart her challenge until 18 September.

DECEMBER

1 December

1886: Arsenal Football Club are founded by a group of munitions workers in Woolwich, who are working on Dial Square at the very centre of the Royal Arsenal complex. When the club were first formed they were actually called Dial Square for about a month before becoming Royal Arsenal. It was as Royal Arsenal in 1891 that they became the first London soccer team to turn professional. In 1893 they became Woolwich Arsenal, a name that stuck for 20 years. In 1913 they became The Arsenal, and it was at this point they moved to the newly created stadium at Highbury. Finally they dropped the 'The' six years later when they finally settled on Arsenal – the fifth name of the club.

1939: Birth of American golfer Lee Trevino, one of the finest players of all time. With Mexican roots and an invariably cheerful demeanour, he was often referred to as 'The Merry Mex' by his fellow professionals.

1948: Birth of Pakistani Test cricketer Sarfraz Nawaz, the man usually credited for inventing reverse swing into a bowling action. Against Australia at Melbourne in 1979 he produced one of the most astonishing spells of bowling. His final spell saw him claim 7-4 off just six overs.

2006: Russell Baze rides his 9,531st winner on Butterfly Belle at Bay Meadows in California, to overtake Laffit Pincay and become the most successful jockey of all time. Baze retired in 2015 with a total of 12,844 wins, a record he still holds.

2 December

1907: The Association of Football Players' and Trainers' Union (aka the Players' Union) is formed, initially organised and overseen by Manchester United players Charlie Roberts and Billy Meredith.

The inaugural meeting was held in Manchester's Imperial Hotel. The agenda had just two items – increasing or cancelling the minimum wage, and removing restrictions on transfers.

1908: Death of athlete John Taylor. He was the first African American to win an Olympic gold medal, running the 400m leg of the medley relay in 49.8 seconds (the 200m legs were run by William Hamilton and Nathaniel Cartmell, and the 800m leg by Melvin Sheppard). Although he seemed fine, Taylor died shortly after his return to the US. The US management team announced that his death was 'much regretted by all who met him there'.

1974: Cowhide is used to make baseballs for the first time. Previously baseballs had to be made with horsehide.

1997: Death of iconic wrestler Big Daddy (real name Shirley Crabtree Jr), following a stroke. He began his wrestling career as a villain, frequently pairing up with Giant Haystacks in a tag team, but developed into a real fan favourite. He took his place in the *Guinness Book of Records* for having Britain's largest chest, measuring 64 inches.

1999: Day one of the Dubai Sevens – the first leg of the newly formed IRB sevens world series. During the first day the 16 teams were split into four pools of four, playing each other in a round-robin format with the top two of each pool entering the quarter-finals. New Zealand, who would go on to win the title, progressed from Pool A with Tonga, winning all their matches without conceding a single point.

3 December

1890: Death of Billy Midwinter, a man who holds a truly unique position in the history of cricket. Midwinter was born in England but his family emigrated to Australia when he was nine years old. He played in the first two Test matches in history, for Australia against England in 1877. He then returned to England, having been asked by W.G. Grace to play for Gloucestershire. There he joined up with the Australian touring team to play against England. He stayed on with Gloucestershire – and was then selected to tour with the England team to Australia! He played four Tests for England against Australia before deciding to emigrate back to Australia, and was promptly selected for their team – to play against England! Tragically in his 30s he lost his wife and two of his children and his business interests were failing. He became insane and was transferred to an asylum. He died later the same year at the age of 39.

1986: West Indies play the fifth match of the Champions Trophy against Sri Lanka at Sharjah. The West Indies posted 248/5 in their 50 overs. In reply Sri Lanka started poorly, and then capitulated, going from 50/4 to 55 all out. West Indies fast bowler Courtney Walsh took five of the last six wickets to register figures of 5-1 off 4.3 overs.

1999: The conclusion of the Dubai Sevens, which is the opening leg of the new world series for rugby sevens. New Zealand won this inaugural tournament, beating Fiji 38-14 in the final.

2014: The first Beer Mile World Championship takes place, and is won by Canadian Corey Gallagher in a time a fraction over five minutes. Elizabeth Herndon from the USA won the women's event. The Beer Mile is run on a standard athletics track over four laps, with each lap (even the first) started by drinking a standard 12 fl.oz. of beer (355ml) – meaning that by the time they start the fourth lap they have drunk 2.8 pints in the last five or so minutes.

2017: The second day of the third Test between India and Sri Lanka is interrupted by excessive pollution. The World Health Organisation recorded that conditions in Delhi showed pollution levels 15 times above acceptable standards. Players from both teams left the field to vomit, and many of the Sri Lankan players fielded wearing face masks and even used oxygen cylinders in the dressing rooms.

4 December

1909: The first Grey Cup Final is played, the main cup competition for Canadian football. The University of Toronto Varsity Blues team beat the Toronto Parkdale Canoe Club 26-6.

1931: Birth of Alex 'Fats' Delvecchio, Canadian ice hockey player, coach and manager. In a career spanning 24 seasons Delvecchio played 1,549 matches – all for the Detroit Red Wings, the most of any player playing for just one team. He gained 1,281 points, the second highest total in history.

1980: Death of Edmonton Eskimos running back Don 'Jeep' Warrington, a successful member of four winning Grey Cup championship teams. Shortly after the Eskimos had won their third consecutive Grey Cup, Warrington was involved a very serious car accident in Alberta. He died two days later of injuries sustained, at the age of just 32.

2011: Death of Brazil's attacking midfielder Sócrates (birth name Sócrates Brasileiro Sampaio de Souza Vieira de Oliveira). Widely regarded as one of the finest midfield players of all time, he played for Brazil in two World Cup finals tournaments and captained them in the 1982 finals. What marked Sócrates out as unique was that he continued to practise medicine even at the peak of his career. He died of septic shock after his health had declined for several years. Interestingly on the day he died his old club Corinthians drew 0-0 with Palmeiras to secure their first Brazilian title for six years. Many years earlier he had expressed a desire to 'die on a Sunday when Corinthians won a trophy'.

5 December

1921: The Football Association bans women's football teams from playing any official matches or from playing on FA-registered club grounds. This rapidly led to the formation of their own independent organisation – the English Ladies' Football Association, and they began to play their fixtures on rugby club grounds, who seemed to be far more accepting of their status.

1942: Southampton beat Arsenal 3-1 in a wartime exhibition football match. Tom Finney, a plumber by profession, had just signed professional terms for Preston North End when the Second World War broke out and he had not yet made his debut. After the war he became a key member of the England national team, and is regarded as the finest footballer ever to play for Preston. In this wartime match Finney made a guest appearance for Southampton.

1951: Death of American professional baseball legend 'Shoeless' Joe Jackson, so named because as an amateur he was suffering badly with blisters during one match, so took his shoes off to bat. The name just stuck. In 1911 Jackson secured the record season's batting average for a rookie, a record which remains unbeaten. He died of a heart attack, aged 64.

1963: Birth of British skier Eddie the Eagle (real name Michael Edwards). He found fame in 1988 by becoming Britain's first Olympic skier since 1928 – finishing last in both the 70m and the 90m ski jump. Eddie took the stunt world record by jumping over six buses.

1975: Birth of English snooker player Ronnie O'Sullivan, one of the finest players the snooker world has ever seen. O'Sullivan began playing at the age of seven, made his first competitive century break at the age of ten and became the British under-16 champion when only 13. He gained his first major professional success by winning the UK Championship at the age of 17 years.

2004: The Swiss league match between FC Schaffhausen and Servette FC appears to be heading to a tame goalless draw when Jean Beausejour taps in a potential winner for Servette. By way of celebration Paulo Diogo (who supplied the pass) leapt on the wire fence surrounding the pitch to receive the adulation of the crowd. Unfortunately his ring became hooked in the wires, and as he jumped down the fence claimed both his ring and the majority of his finger. While the match stewards hunted for the finger, the referee booked Diogo for excessive celebration! He was taken to hospital, but the doctors were unable to save the finger and had to amputate it to ensure a clean wound.

2017: Georgian Lasha Talakhadze sets a new world record for the snatch (weightlifting) during the World Championships when he lifts 220kg (34st 9lb).

6 December

1956: Hungary beat USSR 4-0 in the water polo semi-final fixture at the Melbourne Olympics. Tensions during the match were high for political reasons. In the last two minutes Hungarian player Ervin Zádor emerged from the water with blood pouring from an open wound above his eye. Zádor got out the water causing the crowd, already very volatile, to go into a frenzy. With just one minute to go and the result in no doubt the referee called off the match and awarded the match to the Hungarians. The match became known as the 'Blood in the water', although the quantity of blood was fairly minimal. The political situation in Hungary was such that Zádor and a few of his teammates never returned there, seeking asylum in western Europe.

1982: Birth of Spanish cyclist Alberto Contador, one of just two cyclists who have won each of the Grand Tours (Tour de France, Vuelta a España and the Giro d'Italia) at least twice.

1984: Martina Navratilova loses to Czechoslovak Helena Suková in the semi-finals at the Australian Open tennis championship. This was Navratilova's first defeat since losing the final of the Oakland tournament to another Czech Hana Mandlikova in February. The run saw her winning 74 consecutive matches, a record for the Open Era. In the ten-month run Navratilova won 13 tournaments, including the French Open, Wimbledon and the US Open.

2001: Death of New Zealand yachtsman Sir Peter Blake, who led New Zealand to successive victories in the America's Cup. He also won the Round-the-World Race, as well as holding the Jules Verne Trophy (for the fastest time around the world) for four years. In 2001 Blake was working in the Amazon delta studying global warming and pollution for the United Nations when a group of pirates boarded his vessel. Blake shot one of the pirates before being fatally wounded himself.

7 December

1734: Death of James Figg, the first English bare-knuckle boxing champion. Compared to the modern tendency of a boxer to fight maybe two or three bouts a year, Figg's career lasted for 12 years during which he fought an astonishing 270 fights, winning 269 of them! His one defeat was by Ned Sutton who took the title off him, and Figg immediately asked for a rematch.

1907: Tommy Burns knocks out Gunner Moir in the tenth round of a proposed 20. This was the first time that the gloved heavyweight championship of the world had been contested in Britain. It was also the first time a referee was seen in a boxing ring, with Eugene Corri officiating.

1963: The televised American football game between the US Army and the US Navy makes history when it becomes the first sporting fixture to show an instant replay of a passage of play to television audiences. The game commentator, Lindsey Nelson, announced to the audience: 'This is not live! Ladies and gentlemen, the Army did not score again!' Despite the clarification lots of viewers were confused and telephoned the CBS network to complain. Nevertheless, it wasn't long before this was a standard part of televised sport viewing.

1997: Death of Leeds United and Scotland footballing legend Billy Bremner. Bremner was captain of the great Leeds United team of the 1960s and 70s, leading them during the most successful period in the club's history. He died of a heart attack two days before his 55th birthday.

2006: Death of South Korean equestrian star Kim Hyung-chil. The Asian Games equestrian competition was made very challenging by heavy rain. Hyung-chil was riding Bundaberg Black when it struggled at the eighth jump on the cross-country course. First the horse threw him over, then the horse followed, slipped and landed directly on the rider, crushing his face and chest. He died shortly afterwards without regaining consciousness.

8 December

1863: Representatives from a dozen London and suburban football clubs meet at The Freemason's Tavern to agree (after several meetings dating back to 26 October) the first official rule book for playing football. There are understandably many significant differences between these first rules and the modern rules, which are constantly evolving. Back in 1863 there was no crossbar; goals could be scored at any height as long as it was deemed to have gone between the positions of the posts. Players could catch the ball, as long as they did so fairly and did not run with it or throw it. Any player ahead of the kicker was deemed to be offside. When the ball went out the first player to touch it could take the throw-in, but had to do so at right angles to the edge of the pitch. Teams changed ends every time a goal was scored. These initial rules made no reference to the duration of a match – it was limited to 90 minutes in 1877.

1880: Death of cricketer Edmund Hinkly. Hinkly was another one of those sports stars who was not as well known as perhaps he deserved. Playing for Kent County Cricket Club against an England XI at Lord's in 1848 he became the first cricketer to take all ten wickets in a first-class innings.

1886: The Amateur Hockey Association of Canada is formed – the world's first ice hockey league. The league was comprised of just six teams, including four from Montreal.

2015: The International Boxing Federation strips Tyson Fury of his IBF heavyweight world title due to his refusal to honour a contractual agreement. Having won the title just ten days earlier the IBF decision made Fury the shortest reigning world boxing champion in history.

9 December

1922: The 15th Australasian tennis championships is the first at which women are welcome, with an inaugural women's singles, women's doubles and mixed doubles. Fourteen women entered the singles competition, all from Australia. In the final on this date Mall Molesworth beat Esna Boyd 6-3 10-8.

1977: The day the NBA turned spectacularly ugly. In a game between Los Angeles Lakers and Houston Rockets, the Lakers's Kermit Washington hit Rudy Tomjanovich of the Rockets with such ferocity that he broke his nose and his jaw, fractured his skull and gave him a cerebral concussion. The hit was so vicious that the surgeon who subsequently worked on Tomjanovich likened his injuries to a 'cracked eggshell poorly fixed with Scotch tape'. Washington was fined $10,000 and given a 60-day suspension from the NBA. The ban was the longest in the history of the NBA, equating to 26 matches.

1978: Chicago Hustle play the Milwaukee Does in the first women's professional basketball fixture.

1993: Death of Northern Irish footballer and coach Danny Blanchflower, who captained Tottenham Hotspur to the domestic double in 1961. He famously said: 'The great fallacy is that the game is first and last about winning. It is nothing of the kind. The game is about glory, it is about doing things in style and with a flourish, about going out and beating the lot, not waiting for them to die of boredom.' He died of Alzheimer's disease and Parkinson's disease at the age of 67.

10 December

1659: Playing golf in the streets of the area which is now Albany, New York, is banned by legal declaration: 'The W. Commissary and Commissaries of Fort Orange and Village of Beverwyck, having heard divers complaints from the Burghers of this place, against playing at Golf along the streets, which causes great damage to the windows of the Houses, and exposes people to the danger of being wounded, and is contrary to the freedom of the Public Streets; Therefore their Worships, wishing to prevent the same, forbid all persons playing Golf in the Streets, on pain of forfeiting fl. 25 [Guilders] for each person who shall be found doing so.'

1889: The first official county championship for cricket is established at a meeting at Lord's. This would be contested in 1890 between Gloucestershire, Kent, Lancashire, Middlesex, Nottinghamshire, Surrey, Sussex and Yorkshire.

2011: After the final event of the season at Pipeline in Hawaii, Kelly Slater is crowned world surfing champion for the 11th and final time. At 39 he was also the oldest world champion, 19 years after he became the youngest.

2015: Death of Honduras defensive midfielder Arnold Sosa. He was in a shopping mall in his hometown when he was shot 18 times and died instantly. The motive for the attack has never been ascertained.

2017: Ted-Jan Bloemen sets a new world record time for speed skating over 5,000m during the World Cup meeting in Salt Lake City. Bloemen finished the 5km in a time of six minutes, 1.86 seconds at an average speed of 49.74kmh (30.91mph).

11 December

1866: The first-ever yacht race across the Atlantic Ocean takes place. One of the competitors was so eccentric that his name has become synonymous with news of the extraordinary – Gordon Bennett. Bennett was out drinking in October with fellow playboys Pierre Lorillar and George Osgood boasting about, among other things, how good their schooners were. The challenge was laid down – a race across the Atlantic – each yacht owner pays $30,000 with the winner taking the lot. Bennett hired Samuel Samuels to captain his team, one of the few people more eccentric than he was, who had once infamously amputated his own broken leg. With bad weather all three boats struggled. The three boats arrived at the Needles (the finishing line) within a short distance of each other, with Bennett's boat *Henrietta* winning. The winning time was 13 days and 22 hours for the 3,000-mile course. The sailors were personally congratulated by Queen Victoria. (One unrelated story just to demonstrate that $30,000 was not a ridiculous sum – these men were super-rich: Gordon Bennett once went to a restaurant and was so upset to see someone else sat at his favourite table that he immediately bought the restaurant just so that he could throw the man out!)

1892: Death of Swedish swimmer Nancy Edberg, a true pioneer in promoting women in sport. She started giving swimming lessons for women, but received criticism from society until Louise of the Netherlands (who was, at the time, Queen of Sweden) and her daughter Louise (who would later become Queen of Denmark) enrolled for lessons, when it started to become acceptable. Her other students included the Princess of Wales, Alexandra of Denmark and Empress Maria of Russia (aka Dagmar of Denmark). Edberg also taught women how to ice skate – which was considered even more improper for women, so much so that a large covered fence was erected around the rink to hide the women from public view!

1999: Death of champion show jumper Big Ben at the age of 23. He was the first horse to win two consecutive World Cup Finals. In his career Big Ben won more than $1.5m in prize money.

2008: UEFA announce that the women's European football tournament will be totally restructured and renamed the Champions League. For the inaugural competition UEFA invited the top two sides from the top eight leagues in Europe to join, although this has since evolved in line with the men's competition.

12 December

1933: One of the most vicious attacks in the history of ice hockey as Ace Bailey of the Toronto Maple Leafs is hit hard from behind by Eddie Shore of the Boston Bruins. When Bailey's head hit the ice he was knocked uncounscious and started to fit. Shore was suspended for 16 games, while Bailey never played again.

1959: Australian Jack Brabham wins the first of his three Formula One World Drivers' Championships by finishing fourth in the USA Grand Prix at Sebring. It was a long wait for the title – the penultimate race of the season was the Italian Grand Prix three months earlier.

1982: An NFL game between the Miami Dolphins and the New England Patriots is played in strong wind, heavy snow and freezing temperatures. With five minutes to go the Patriots were given a penalty kick 33 yards out. The conditions were so bad that a snow plough had to be brought on to the pitch to clear an area to enable the kick to take place. The kick was converted, and the Patriots won the game 3-0.

1997: The first FIFA Confederations Cup starts in Saudi Arabia. The event was restricted to eight nations, with representation from each of the FIFA confederations: Australia, Brazil, Czech Republic, Mexico, Saudi Arabia, South Africa, United Arab Emirates and Uruguay. Brazil beat Australia 6-0 in the final to win the inaugural competition. Brazil therefore set a new standard in holding both FIFA titles and their own confederation title simultaneously (World Cup, Confederations Cup and Copa America).

2001: Death of Josef Bican, the Czech-Austrian footballer who holds one of the most amazing world records in sport. Bican enjoyed a career lasting 25 years and played in 918 games – netting an incredible 1,468 times.

2016: Death of flat-racing jockey Walter Swinburn. In 1996 he had a fall and spent four days in a coma, after which he had epilepsy. Swinburn died when he fell from his bathroom window and dropped 12 feet on to a concrete courtyard. The coroner recorded an open verdict, unable to ascertain whether it was a simple accident, or whether he had suffered from an epileptic fit.

13 December

1875: Oxford and Cambridge play a varsity rugby match. Through an informal agreement between the two captains the sides are reduced to 15 a side from the traditional 20 – the first time a rugby match has officially been played as 15-a-side.

1899: Foundation of the Milan Cricket and Football Club. The Cricket Club made little significant contribution to world sport, but the football club fared much better. They won the 'King's medal' in 1900, followed by the Italian league in 1901. In 1908 Milan Football Club would split into AC Milan and Internazionale.

1941: Birth of Scottish footballer and football manager Sir Alex Ferguson. In his 26-year spell in charge of Manchester United he won an unprecedented 38 trophies, including 13 Premier League titles.

1983: While it is common for basketball teams to score more than 100 points in a game, the Denver Nuggets achieve a record that almost beggars belief – to score 184 points and still lose. In an NBA fixture in Colorado the Detroit Pistons beat the Nuggets 186-184.

2015: Irishman Conor McGregor knocks out Brazilian Jose Aldo in Las Vegas to win his first world featherweight title in mixed martial arts, organised by the Ultimate Fighting Championship. The two refused to touch gloves and went straight into the fight – which lasted precisely 13 seconds before McGregor's left hook rendered his opponent unconscious.

14 December

1901: The first official table tennis tournament is held in London, at the Royal Aquarium. Bizarrely there were two rival organisations established within a few days of each other, both claiming to be the official organisation – the Table Tennis Association and the Ping Pong Association. So to claim superiority both sought to organise an official competition, and the winners were the Table Tennis Association who managed to attract more than 250 entries. The first official tournament organised by the Ping Pong Association began on Boxing Day.

1903: England debutant Tip Foster comes out to bat on day two of the first Test against Australia in Sydney. He had been undefeated on 73 at the end of day one, and went on to score 287. That remains the highest score for a cricketer on their debut. Foster's other claim to fame was that he was the only man who captained England in both cricket and football.

1914: Formation of the Maserati motor company in Modena, Italy, by the Maserati brothers Alfeiro, Ernesto, Ettore and Bindo. The two older brothers also drove their cars in races, Ernesto winning the Italian drivers' championship twice.

1995: Death of double world champion skysurfer Rob Harris at the age of 28. He died when a stunt went wrong while being filmed skydiving for an advertisement for an energy drink.

2010: Death of Rushden & Diamonds and England C goalkeeper Dale Roberts. Tragically he took his own life at the age of just 24. Roberts had been struggling with an injury, but more significantly couldn't come to terms with the fact that his fiancée had had an affair with one of his own teammates. Rushden & Diamonds retired their number one jersey as a mark of respect.

15 December

1970: Birth of Italian jockey Frankie Dettori (real forename Lanfranco). Dettori left school at 13 to become a stable boy and apprentice jockey. The following year he transferred his apprenticeship to Newmarket and became the stable jockey after 12 months. In September 1996 he achieved the remarkable distinction of riding the winners in all seven races on the card at Ascot.

1973: Sandy Hawley becomes the first jockey in history to ride 500 race winners in a single season. By the time he retired in 1998, Hawley had ridden 6,449 winners with an estimated total purse of nearly $90m.

1979: During the first Test between Australia and England in Perth the home side finish the first day on 232/8 with Dennis Lillee unbeaten on 11. On day two Lillee came out to bat using an aluminium bat. The England captain Mike Brearley complained that the metal bat was damaging the ball. Lillee took a wooden bat reluctantly, hurling the aluminium one down to the ground. He lasted just a few more minutes before being caught.

1995: The date that revolutionised the face of modern football. In 1990 Jean-Marc Bosman had finished his contract with RFC Liège and wanted to move on, so wouldn't sign a new contract. He was offered a position with French team Dunkerque, but they refused to pay Liège's estimation and asking price, so Liège refused to release him and let him move. Bosman argued that since he

Frankie Dettori

Born: 15 December 1970

Italian-born jockey with more than 500 race victories, including
seven in one day at Ascot in 1996

didn't have a contract, he must be free to move wherever he wants and play for whoever he chose – so he took them to court. The European Court of Justice in Luxembourg found in his favour after five years, stating that the current system restricted free movement of workers, contravening the EC treaty. They decreed that Bosman and all other EU footballers had the right to a free transfer when their contract expired – a decision that has since become known as the Bosman ruling.

16 December

1871: Harrogate rugby club play their first-ever fixture, away against Leeds. Leeds managed to beat Harrogate by one goal and five touchdowns to one touchdown, despite only fielding 11 players to Harrogate's 16. This match would be Harrogate's only defeat in their first four seasons.

1905: The first time a national anthem is ever played at a sporting fixture. Wales were playing a home rugby game against the touring All Blacks team from New Zealand. The New Zealanders laid down a challenge before kick-off by performing their haka. Welsh winger Teddy Morgan responded to the haka by singing the Welsh national anthem *Hen Wlad Fy Nhadau* (tr. Old Land of my Fathers), and very soon the entire stadium were joining in the song. For the record Wales beat the All Blacks.

1952: Birth of West Indian pace bowler Joel 'Big Bird' Garner. The nickname came from Doctor Bird, the national bird of Jamaica distinguished by its long stilt-like legs (Garner was 6ft 8in (2.03m)). Indeed Garner was so tall some shorter batsmen complained that he was almost unplayable because he was delivering the ball from over the sight screen so it couldn't be read. Of all ODI bowlers who have taken more than 100 wickets Garner is the most successful of all time with an average of 18.84.

2013: England captain Alastair Cook plays his 100th Test match in Perth where Australia are hosting England. Sadly the momentous occasion was not marked by success when Cook got a golden duck in the second innings – his first golden duck in Test cricket.

17 December

1927: Having been selected to replace Archie Jackson in the New South Wales team, the 19-year-old Don Bradman makes his first-class cricket debut against Victoria. Bradman spent a little over three hours scoring 118 to announce his arrival on the big stage.

1946: Day five (of seven) of the second Test between Australia and England at Sydney and Australia mount a massive total of 659/8 declared. A very large chunk of that total was from the fifth wicket stand of 405 between Don Bradman and Sid Barnes. Bizarrely both batsmen were eventually out for 234. Australia won the Test by an innings and 33 runs.

1978: Birth of Filipino boxer Manny Pacquiao, consistently ranked one of the greatest pound-for-pound boxers of all time. At various stages of his career Pacquiao won versions of world titles at flyweight, super-bantamweight, featherweight, super-featherweight, lightweight, light-welterweight, welterweight and super-welterweight. Since retiring from boxing Pacquiao has become a politician, serving as a senator in the Philippines.

1991: The Cleveland Cavaliers beat Miami Heat 148-80 to register a record-breaking winning basketball margin of 68 points.

1992: Opening batsman Phil Simmons bowls for the West Indies against Pakistan. In the limited overs game it is rare to bowl a maiden over with batsmen looking for runs on every delivery. Simmons bowled the full allocation of ten overs – eight of which were maidens, taking four wickets for just three runs.

2014: Gus Andreone of Sarasota, Florida, records a hole-in-one at his local golf club at the Palm Aire Country Club. At 103 he is the oldest person ever to secure that achievement.

18 December

1898: Frenchman Gaston de Chasseloup-Laubat becomes the first person to drive at more than 60kmh when he is clocked at 63.15kmh (39.24mph).

1932: The Chicago Bears beat the Portsmouth Spartans in the first NFL Championship play-off game, a game arranged to decide on the league winner after the two teams finished level in the regular season. The Chicago Bears won 9-0 in what was one of the most bizarre games in history. Chicago was covered in snow and suffering freezing temperatures, so a decision was made to move the game indoors. However, no indoor venue locally was large enough to house a full-size pitch ... so organisers got creative with the rules. The largest available venue had been used the previous week for a circus, and one of the players was sick during the game having been overwhelmed by the enduring odour of elephant dung. To maximise the width the sidelines were butted up against the stands. The goalposts were moved from the endlines to the goal lines, and no drop kicks and field goals were allowed. The most inventive rule change was that every time a team crossed the ten-yard line the ball was moved back 20 yards so that the distance covered would be correct because the pitch length was too short.

1971: Death of American amateur golfer Bobby Jones Jr who, despite an incredibly successful career, opted to maintain his amateur status while continuing to work as a lawyer. In remaining amateur he was able to achieve a most unique 'Grand Slam' – winning the open and the amateur titles in both the US and the UK in 1930. He was also very influential off the greens – he founded and co-designed the Augusta National Golf Club, as well as co-founding the Masters Tournament.

1999: The Mountain View Golf Club in Hickory, North Carolina, is the site of the hole-in-one of Christian Carpenter ... at the age of four years and 195 days.

19 December

1904: Canadian ice hockey team the Dawson City Nuggets set off on their journey to play against Ottowa Hockey Club for the Stanley Cup. The match was not actually due to be played until 13 January, but the Nuggets needed to leave this early to make the trip. Their journey began from the frozen grounds in Yukon territory, with a nine-day walk accompanied by dog sleds to the port at Skagway to catch a boat to Seattle. From there they caught the train to Ottawa. Unsurprisingly given their exhaustion as well as their minor amateur status, the Nuggets lost both games.

1909: Formation of Bundesliga team Borussia Dortmund (full name: Ballspielverein Borussia 09 e.V. Dortmund). The club was formed as part of a larger sports club, by a group of disillusioned and disaffected youths who quit the club Trinity Youth because of the way it was run under the harsh and unbending Roman Catholic Church. ('Borussia', which a few football clubs have as a prefix, is Latin for Prussia, a German state and kingdom, 1524–1947.)

1930: Death of 48-year-old Johnny Douglas, a successful all-round England cricketer and an amateur boxer, who won Olympic gold in 1908. He drowned when the ship on which he and his father were travelling was wrecked after a collision in foggy weather when the two captains, who were brothers, were attempting to exchange Christmas greetings. Douglas drowned trying to save his father.

1983: The original FIFA World Cup trophy, the Jules Rimet Trophy, is stolen. After Brazil's third World Cup win they had been given the trophy, and it was housed in the headquarters of the Brazilian Football Confederation in Rio de Janeiro. The thieves were caught and arrested, but the trophy was never recovered.

1999: The NFL game between the Cleveland Browns and the Jacksonville Jaguars is one of the most unsavoury in NFL history. The Browns' offensive tackle Orlando Brown was hit directly in the eye by a flag accidently launched by referee Jeff Triplette. When the referee went to apologise Brown went mad and hit Triplette to the floor. Brown was immediately thrown out of the game and suspended by the NFL. The suspension was, however, lifted when the authorities learned the extent of Brown's eye injury – he missed the next three seasons with partial blindness.

20 December

1881: Birth of Branch Rickey, the man who signed black player Jackie Robinson, thereby breaking MLB's colour barriers. He also drafted Roberto Clemente, the first Hispanic superstar.

1886: Birth of American tennis star Hazel Wightman, founder of the Wightman Cup as an annual competition between American and British ladies. For three consecutive years, 1909–1911, Wightman won the hat-trick of singles, women's doubles and mixed doubles at the US Open. She also won Olympic gold for both the doubles and the mixed doubles in the 1924 Paris Olympics.

1917: Death of French racing cyclist Lucien Breton. Breton won a bike in a lottery when he was 16 and got seriously into racing. His real name was Lucien Mazan, but he adopted the name Breton so that his father wouldn't know he was racing – his father wanted him to do a 'proper job'. Breton became the first man in history to win the Tour de France twice. He was actually a very early victim of drink driving when a drunk cart driver ploughed his horse and cart into Breton.

1998: Birth of French centre-forward Kylian Mbappé, who starts his professional career as a 16-year-old with Monaco. At the age of just 19 he became the second most expensive player in the world when he transferred to Paris Saint-Germain for €180 million. He became only the second teenager after Pelé to score in a World Cup Final in 2018, as France beat Croatia 4-2.

21 December

1849: The first skating club is formed in Philadelphia, Pennsylvania.

1891: The first-ever game of basketball. Dr James Naismith was teaching physical education in Springfield in Massachusetts. He was asked to come up with a new game that the students could play indoors in winter that would help keep them in shape and yet would be safe to play. The goal of Dr Naismith's game would be to throw a football into a peach basket, which would be nailed up high on the wall. The original peach baskets did not have their bottoms knocked out, so whenever someone scored, the game would be temporarily halted while someone went up a ladder to get the ball. No dribbling was allowed, only passing and the person with the ball had to stay in place. This inaugural game among his students was played with nine players on each team with 30 minutes' play (two 15-minute halves).

1957: People often say that football is a game of two halves. Charlton Athletic's home tie against Huddersfield Town in the first division was a game of three half-hour periods. During the first half hour, not a lot happened. After 27 minutes Charlton's captain Derek Ulton was taken to hospital. In the days before substitutes this left Charlton down to ten men for an hour and Huddersfield took control, leading 5-1 after an hour. Somehow Charlton rallied despite still being a man down, such that the final score was Charlton 7 Huddersfield 6.

2015: Two of the heavyweights of world soccer, Sepp Blatter and Michel Platini, are banned from any involvement in football for a period of eight years having been found guilty of ethics violations. One of the accusations was that Blatter made a 'disloyal payment' of $2m to Platini (whatever a disloyal payment is).

22 December

1862: Birth of Connie Mack, the baseball catcher, manager and team owner. Incredibly Mack managed Philadelphia Athletic from their formation in 1901 until his retirement at the age of 87 after the 1950 season.

1894: The foundation of the United States Golf Association (initially called simply the Amateur Golf Association) in New York City. The association would serve several purposes including overseeing the development of the rules and running national championships.

1909: Death of Pittsburgh Pirates baseball star James Sebring. In 1903 he became the first person in history to hit a home run in any World Series. He died at the age of 27 of Bright's disease.

1962: The 1,000,000th point is scored in NBA history. With basketball littered with timeouts it is impossible to confirm exactly who scored this historic point. Three matches were taking place simultaneously: Detroit Pistons vs. Chicago Bulls, New York Knicks vs. Boston Celtics and Syracuse Nationals (now Philadelphia 76ers) vs. San Fransisco Warriors (now Golden State Warriors). So it was a player from one of those six teams who scored point number one million, but nobody knows who.

1980: Day one of the third Test between Pakistan and the West Indies in Karachi. In their first innings Pakistan were dismissed for 128, including a world record six ducks. The bowlers were remarkably consistent – Sylvester Clarke took 4-27, Colin Croft took 3-27 and Joel Garner took 2-27.

23 December

1924: Birth of Bob Kurland, one of the most successful basketball players of all time. Standing seven foot tall, he was best known as the captain and centre for Oklahoma A&M Aggies (now called Oklahoma State Cowboys), leading them to three national titles. He also led the US to Olympic gold in two consecutive Games.

1956: Birth of Italian racing driver Michele Alboreto, one of the most successful drivers in history. He won the European Formula Three Championship crown, the 24 Hours of Le Mans and the 12 Hours of Sebring. He also raced in Formula One for 14 seasons, finishing as runner-up to Alain Prost in the 1985 championship.

2005: Death of Lajos Baróti, Hungarian footballer who is widely regarded as one of the finest coaches of all time. He managed the Hungarian national team, leading them to Olympic gold in 1964, and then managed Újpesti Dózsa for the next three years, leading them to three league championships and two domestic cup wins. He only left there when he was given the opportunity to coach on the national stage again, taking charge of Peru.

2012: Death of Brazilian kickboxer and mixed martial artist Morpheus Maiorino. In his career he held a host of titles including state champion in jiujitsu, world heavyweight karate champion and world kickboxing champion in the heavyweight division. Maiorino was prajioud silver in Muay Thai, third degree black belt in kickboxing, black belt in karate and purple belt in jiujitsu. He died at the age of just 33 of a heart attack.

24 December

1889: A revolution in the world of cycling as Daniel Stover and William Hance patent their new invention – a bicycle with a brake operated by pedalling backwards.

1932: Birth of Kent and England cricketer Colin Cowdrey, who is actually born in India. Cowdrey was the first man to reach the milestone of 100 Test matches, celebrating his 100th Test by scoring a century against Australia in 1968. Overall he played 114 Test matches, scoring 7,624 runs. He scored 22 Test centuries, and became the first batsman to score centuries against six other nations (Australia, New Zealand, India, Pakistan, West Indies and South Africa) – scoring centuries against all of these teams both home and away.

1969: Curt Flood writes to the baseball commissioner asking to be a free agent. He may have lost his case but this paved the way for major changes in the sport. Flood's team, the St Louis Cardinals, had sold him to the Philadelphia Phillies, but he didn't want to go – so he didn't! Instead he wrote to the commissioner. The commissioner initially found in favour of the Cardinals but the case dragged on and Flood still refused to move. He didn't play at all in 1970, but the Cardinals relented in 1971 and sold him to the Washington Senators. Eventually the authorities introduced the 10/5 rule (aka the Curt Flood rule) which stated that any player who had played for ten years in professional baseball, including at least five years with their current team, could choose if and when they moved – the first major step towards players being free agents and not possessions of their teams.

1998: Death of polymath Syl Apps. A successful Canadian footballer at McMaster University, he was best known for 13 seasons spent as an ice hockey professional with the Toronto Maple Leafs. Apps was also an Olympic pole vaulter, and took gold medal at the 1934 British Empire Games in London. Upon sporting retirement, he became a Conservative Member of Provincial Parliament in Ontario.

2000: Tunisian football team Espérance concede a goal in their fixture against US Monastir – the first goal they have conceded all season, having begun the year with ten consecutive clean sheets.

25 December

1872: Twenty players representing England and another 20 representing Scotland play a competitive match of rugby union in Calcutta in West Bengal in India – the foundation of the Calcutta

Cup match. Six years later 270 silver rupees were melted down to make the actual trophy. To emphasise the Indian origins of the competition the three handles are king cobras, while an indian elephant sits on top. The first official Calcutta Cup game was contested in Edinburgh in 1879 and ended in a draw. On 28 February 1880 England became the first winners of the cup in Manchester, scoring two goals and three tries to Scotland's one goal.

1875: Death of Scottish golfer known as Young Tom Morris, one of the pioneers of the sport. He remains the only person to have won the Open in four consecutive years. Playing a team match (his partner was his father, Old Tom) in Berwick in September, he received word that his wife had entered a difficult labour. The Morrises finished the match before returning to St Andrews – and by the time they arrived both the wife and the baby were dead. Tom was devastated, and died nearly four months later at the age of just 24.

1914: The soldiers of the British Army and the German Army famously arrange a football match between themselves to celebrate Christmas. The game took place near Wulverghem in Belgium, although nobody kept the score.

1940: Everton play Liverpool in a Merseyside derby on Christmas morning, with their attack led by England's Tommy Lawton. With FA rules and regulations relaxed during wartime, Lawton then turned out for Tranmere away to Crewe in the afternoon.

1965: Sherman Poppen, living in snowy Muskegon in Michigan, invents the world's first snowboard. He was simply looking for ways to keep his children entertained in the long winter months. The design was fairly straightforward – he simply reshaped an old waterski and added some bindings to keep the boots secure. It would be a few years before they were called snowboards – Poppen's wife Nancy christened the new bit of equipment a snurfer (an amalgamation of the words snow and surfer).

2007: Korean boxing champion Choi Yo-sam successfully defends his WBO intercontinental flyweight title against Heri Amol from

Indonesia. He was knocked down with just five seconds of the fight remaining, and so beat the count and retained the title. However, after the bell he collapsed and was rushed into hospital, where he died nine days later of brain injuries. (What sort of organisation plans a boxing match, where two men are just trying to hurt each other, on Christmas Day?)

26 December

1297: The first reference of a 'golf-type' game taking place. In Loenen aan de Vecht in Holland players hit a leather ball with a stick, the winner being the one who could reach a target with the fewest number of hits.

1908: Jack Johnson becomes the first black world heavyweight boxing champion. Johnson had been keen to have a tilt at the world title but had sadly found his efforts to do so were met with resistance due to his colour. Champions like James J. Jeffries refused to face him. Johnson eventually got his chance, and beat reigning champion Tommy Burns from Canada. The fight took place in Sydney, Australia. The sporting world now cried out for a 'great white hope' to come and reclaim the title. Even the *New York Times* wrote: 'If the black man wins, thousands and thousands of his ignorant brothers will misinterpret his victory as justifying claims to much more than mere physical equality with their white neighbours.' One of the 'great white hope' candidates was world middleweight champion Stanley Ketchel, who was knocked out in the 12th with incredible ferocity. Film strip still exists of Ketchel looking stunned and dazed on the canvas … and in the background Johnson can be seen picking Ketchel's teeth out of his glove.

1919: The New York Yankees buy Babe Ruth from the Boston Red Sox for the unprecedented sum of $100,000. The sale was necessary due to financial difficulties for the owner of the Red Sox. As part of the sale he also negotiated a $350,000 loan from the Yankees' owner.

1942: Arsenal lose 5-1 at home to Chelsea in the Football League South. Bizarrely this was their second meeting in 24 hours … Chelsea had beaten Arsenal 5-2 at Stamford Bridge on Christmas Day. Despite these two results, Arsenal would go on to win the league.

1998: The beginning of the annual 'blue water classic', the Sydney to Hobart Yacht Race – a distance of 630 nautical miles (1,170km). One hundred and fifteen yachts lined up to start the race – but only 44 would finish it due to some of the worst weather conditions the race had ever witnessed. Five boats were destroyed, while six sailors lost their lives.

27 December

1890: The British Barbarians play their first-ever rugby match, beating Hartlepool Rovers 9-4. The club had only been formed in April, the vision of WP Carpmael who wanted a cosmopolitan club with high calibre players of exemplary reputation both on and off the field – there would be no discrimination in terms of race, colour, creed or club. The only stipulation was that the team must contain at least one uncapped player.

1892: The first-ever all black college football game sees Biddle College (later the Johnson C. Smith University) beat Livingston College 4-0, in the snows of North Carolina. Due to the lack of funding the team uniforms were actually made by the young ladies of the colleges.

1910: Birth of Neville Crump, one of the finest National Hunt trainers of all time. Among many other successes were three Grand National winners. Everyone in high level sport will have stories about when they were cheated out of victory by an umpire, referee or some other official. Crump was once asked whether he thought some elderly member of the aristocracy would make a good racecourse steward and he replied 'Oh, he'd be perfect. He's deaf, he's blind and he knows f**k all about racing.'

1937: German immigration officials refuse to allow Argentinean Juan Carlos Zabala entry into the country. Zabala was the Olympic champion for the marathon from the 1932 Games. The officials never offered any explanation as to why he was barred.

1957: Keff, Night Owl and Wimpy finish in a dead heat at the Westport Trotting Club in New Zealand. This was the first triple dead heat in any horse race which was determined by the use of photography at the finish line.

2009: The New York Jets win 29-15 against Indianapolis Colts in the National Football League. The match finishes the Colts' run of 23 consecutive victories dating back more than a year, the longest run in American football.

28 December

1842: The first record of any formal game of cricket being played in New Zealand, despite the fact only one club is involved! A local paper reported on a game at Wellington Club where a 'Red team' from the club played a 'Blue team'.

1926: Victoria close their first innings against New South Wales with a record innings total of 1,107. There was still enough time to allow their bowlers to dismiss the opposition for a second time, so that Victoria won the game by an innings and 656 runs.

1958: The Baltimore Colts beat the New York Giants 23-17 in the first-ever sudden-death overtime game in NFL history. Despite Baltimore's domination throughout most of the game, the game finished at 17-17. Being a final the players stood around genuinely perplexed – nobody had informed them what would happen in the event of a draw. Referee Ron Gibbs called the captains over to explain that they would play a maximum of 30 minutes of extra time, and the next score – any score – would win, and the game would stop immediately. With just six minutes of the possible 30 remaining Baltimore scored a touchdown to take the title.

1975: The so-called 'Hail Mary' play is born with just 32 seconds remaining in the NFC divisional play-off game. With the Minnesota Vikings leading 14-11, Dallas Cowboys quarterback Roger Staubach threw a 50-yard pass for the winning touchdown from Drew Pearson. Staubach later reflected, 'I just threw it and prayed.'

2008: The Detroit Lions finish their NFL season with a 31-21 loss to the Green Bay Packers. This marked the first time in NFL history that any team had gone an entire season winless. The Lions' record was played 16, lost 16.

29 December

1862: The first officially recognised football match takes place between Sheffield FC and Hallam FC at Bramall Lane. The game was staged to raise money for the Lancashire Distress Fund, and ended goalless.

1909: Death of Scottish footballer James Main. Playing for Hibernian against Partick Thistle on a frozen pitch on Christmas Day, Main received a hard kick in the stomach from Frank Branscombe. He was taken to hospital where it was determined he had a ruptured bowel, and he died of his injuries four days later. Players of both sides were quick to exonerate Branscombe, who had apparently slipped on the icy surface.

1962: The latest date at which any Formula One season has finished when the South African Grand Prix is run.

1976: Death of Belgian middle-distance runner Ivo Van Damme at the age of just 22. As a schoolboy he was a soccer player but switched to athletics when he was 15, the 800m being his forté. After breaking the Belgian record for this distance he then took the European indoor 800m title. He travelled to the south of France, preparing to marry his fiancée in the new year, but tragically died in a car accident.

1988: Death of British motor racing driver Mike Beuttler, a true trailblazer being the first (and to date only) racing driver in

Formula One who is openly gay. After retiring he moved to Los Angeles, where he died of an AIDS-related illness.

2013: Formula One legend Michael Schumacher suffers a serious injury while he is skiing with his 14-year-old son Mick. He was coming down the Combe de Saulire in the French Alps. While crossing an unsecured region off-piste he slipped over and cracked his head on a rock, despite wearing a ski helmet. He was airlifted to hospital where he was put in a medically induced coma. After nine months he was taken home for further rehabilitation, although sadly progress has been very slow.

2017: Sebastian Abreu signs for Audax Italiano in Chile. In a 22-year career Abreu has signed permanent deals 19 times, in addition to 12 loan agreements. Audax Italiano was Abreu's 26th different club – a world record (27th if one includes the 70 caps he earned with Uruguay).

30 December

1970: Estimated date of death of world heavyweight boxing champion Sonny Liston. He was actually found by his wife on 5 January in a state of decomposition; police estimated the date of death from the number of milk bottles and from newspapers near the front door of his home. Liston fought for 17 years, winning the world heavyweight title. He was due to defend his title against Canadian George Chuvalo – but Chuvalo didn't agree to the fight until the new year. He later reflected: 'When I signed to fight him he'd been dead for a week. I sent a telegram to the promoter, agreeing terms to the fight at the Montreal Forum. A day or so later a news report flashes up saying former heavyweight champion of the world Sonny Liston found dead at his Las Vegas home. I'd actually signed a contract to face a dead man.'

1975: Birth of Tiger Woods (birth name Eldrick Tont Woods), widely regarded as one of the finest golfers of all time. He turned professional when he was just 20 and within a year had won three PGA Tour events and his first major, the 1997 Masters.

1986: A bus carrying the Swift Current Broncos ice hockey team crashes, resulting in the deaths of four of the team. The team from Lethbridge in Alberta, Canada, were travelling to an away fixture against the Regina Pats from neighbouring Saskatchewan. The bus hit black ice, became airborne and landed on its side, skidding to a stop against an embankment.

1999: Death of Australian long-distance swimmer Des Renford, best known for swimming the English Channel 19 times, earning the unofficial title 'King of the Channel'. He also broke the record for swimming around Alcatraz Island, taking 23 minutes off the previous best. Renford died when he had a heart attack (his fourth) while swimming. He was taken to hospital but died later the same evening.

2015: Death of American boxer Howard Davis, who took up the sport having been inspired by a film about Muhammad Ali. In 1976 Davis won Olympic gold in Montreal for winning the lightweight boxing title, just a week after his mother had died. He was awarded the Val Barker Trophy, the trophy for the boxer deemed the most outstanding at the Olympics, beating the likes of Leon Spinks, Michael Spinks and Sugar Ray Leonard.

31 December

1826: Death of John Small, widely regarded as the finest cricketer of the 18th century, as well as one of the innovators of the game. He was the man who introduced the middle stump into the game, as well as being influential in determining the maximum width of the bat. Records show that he started playing when he was 19, and finally retired from the game at 61.

1898: Opening of the Montreal Arena (aka the Westmount Arena), an indoor arena in Quebec, Canada. It held 10,000 people, 4,300 of whom were seated. It was the first ice hockey arena designed with semi-circular ends, allowing players to 'rim round', an idea rapidly adopted by other venues. Sadly the arena only stood for 20 years until a fire in the ice-making plant burned the building down.

1967: The Green Bay Packers host the Dallas Cowboys in what is the coldest ever NFL game at the Lambeau Field. The match was played in temperatures of $-13°F$ ($-25°C$), with a wind chill of $-48°F$ ($-44°C$). Lambeau Field's under-soil heating broke down before the game, leaving the ground rock solid. Officials had to scream out decisions since the referee's whistle froze against his lips, rendering it unusable. For the record the Packers won 21-17.

1972: Australian Margaret Court beats compatriot Evonne Goolagong 6-4 7-5 to win a record 11th Australian Open singles title. It was her 22nd major title out of the 24 she completed. She also won 19 women's doubles and 21 mixed doubles titles in her career, giving her a record 64 major titles in total. Her record is quite staggering, a couple of years standing out as particular highlights. In 1965 she won all four mixed doubles majors, and three of the four majors in the singles, being the runner-up in the other. In 1969, of the 12 major titles she entered (four singles, four women's doubles and four mixed doubles), Court won eight titles, was runner-up twice, and losing semi-finalist in the other two.

1972: Death of Roberto Walker, the Puerto Rican baseball player who spent his entire career of 18 seasons with the Pittsburgh Pirates. Walker used to spend time during every off season working with aid relief. At the end of 1972 he was on an overladen plane which was due to deliver aid to earthquake victims in Nicaragua when the plane crashed. There were no survivors.

1980: Birth of New Zealand All Black rugby player Richie McCaw. With 148 caps, McCaw was the most capped rugby player of all time. He captained the All Blacks for 110 of his 148 caps.

2006: The final rugby game is played at Dublin's Lansdowne Road Stadium, with Leinster beating Ulster 20-12 in a match in the Celtic League.

2017: Crystal Palace manage to hold Premier League leaders Manchester City to a goalless draw at Selhurst Park, ending a PL run of 18 consecutive victories by City. It was also the first time all season that City had failed to score in the league.

Also available at all good book stores

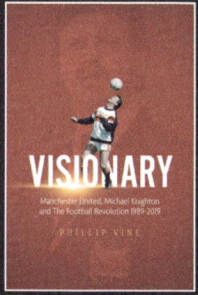

9781785315770

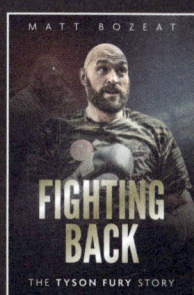

9781785315527

9781785315510

9781785315220

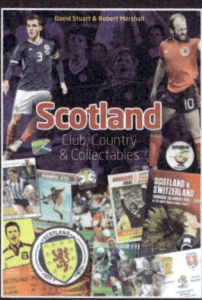

9781785315459

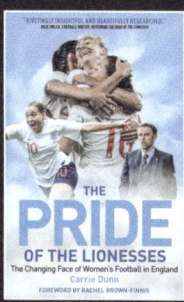

9781785315411

9781785316142

9781785314896

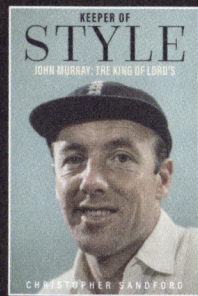

9781785314872

9781785315671

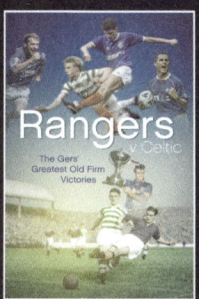

9781785315688

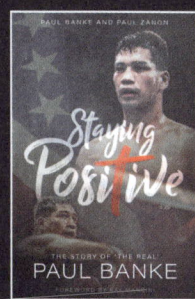

9781785315404